Elements of Literature®

Fourth Course

The Holt Reader

HOLT, RINEHART AND WINSTON
A Harcourt Education Company

Orlando • Austin • New York • San Diego • London

ISBN 978-0-03-099629-0

ISBN 0-03-099629-5

1 2 3 4 5 179 11 10 09 08

Contents

To the Student

A Book for You

Teachers open the door, but you must enter by yourself.
—Chinese Proverb

The more you put into reading, the more you get out of it. This book is designed to do just that—help you interact with the selections you read by marking them up, asking your own questions, taking notes, recording your own ideas, and responding to the questions of others.

A Book Designed for Your Success

The Holt Reader goes hand in hand with *Elements of Literature*. It is designed to help you interact with the selections and master important language arts skills.

The Holt Reader has three types of selections: literature, informational texts, and documents that you may encounter in your various activities. All the selections include the same basic preparation, support, and review materials. Vocabulary previews, skill descriptions, graphic organizers, review questions, and other tools help you understand and enjoy the selections. Moreover, tips and questions in the side margins ensure that you can apply and practice the skills you are learning as you read.

A Book for Your Own Thoughts and Feelings

Reading is about *you*. It is about connecting your thoughts and feelings to the thoughts and feelings of the writer. Make this book your own. The more you give of yourself to your reading, the more you will get out of it. We encourage you to write in this book. Jot down how you feel about the selection. Write down questions you have about the text. Note details you think need to be cleared up or topics that you would like to investigate further.

A Walk Through the Book

The Holt Reader is arranged in collections, just like *Elements of Literature,* the book on which this one is based. Each collection has a theme or basic idea. The stories, poems, articles, or documents within the collection follow that theme. Let's look at how the arrangement of *The Holt Reader* helps you enjoy a collection as a whole and the individual selections within the collection.

Before Reading the Collection

Literary and Academic Vocabulary
Literary and academic vocabulary refers to the specialized language that is used to talk about books, tests, and formal writing. Each collection begins with the literary and academic terms that you need to know to master the skills for that collection.

Before Reading the Selection

Preparing to Read
From experience, you know that you understand something better if you have some idea of what's going to happen. So that you can get the most from the reading, this page previews the skills and vocabulary that you will see in the reading.

Literary Focus
For fiction selections—stories, poems, and plays—this feature introduces the literary skill that is the focus for the selection. Examples and graphic elements help explain the literary skill.

Reading Focus
Also in fiction selections, this feature highlights a reading skill you can apply to the story, poem, or play. The feature points out why this skill is important and how it can help you become a better reader.

Informational Text Focus
For informational, or nonfiction, selections, this feature introduces you to the format and characteristics of nonfiction texts. Those texts may be essays, newspaper articles, Web sites, employment regulations, application forms, or other similar documents.

Selection Vocabulary
This feature introduces you to selection vocabulary that may be unfamiliar. Each entry gives the pronunciation and definition of the word as well as a sentence in which the word is used correctly.

Word Study
Various activities reinforce what you have learned about the selection's vocabulary.

While Reading the Selection

Background gives you basic information on the selection, its author, or the time period in which the story, essay, poem, or article was written.

Side-Column Notes
Each selection has notes in the side column that guide your reading. Many notes ask you to underline or circle in the text itself. Others provide lines on which you can write your responses to questions.

Types of Notes

Several different types of notes throughout the selection provide practice for the skills introduced on the Preparing to Read pages. The notes help you with various strategies for understanding the text. The types of side-column notes are

- **Quick Check** notes ask you to pause at certain points so that you can think about basic ideas before proceeding further. Your teacher may use these notes for class discussions.
- **Literary Focus** notes practice the skill taught in the Literary Focus feature on the Preparing to Read page. Key words related to the specific skill are highlighted.
- **Reading Focus** notes practice the reading skill from the Preparing to Read page.
- **Literary Analysis** notes take basic comprehension one step further and ask you to think more deeply about what you have read.
- **Language Coach** notes reinforce the language skill found in the Preparing to Read pages of *Elements of Literature*.
- **Vocabulary** notes examine selection vocabulary, academic vocabulary, and topics related to how words are used.

After Reading the Selection

Skills Practice

For some selections, graphic organizers reinforce the skills you have practiced throughout the selection.

Applying Your Skills

This feature helps you review the selection. It provides additional practice with selection vocabulary and literary, reading, and informational text focus skills.

After Reading the Collection

Skills Review

On the first page of the Skills Review, you can practice using the collection's academic vocabulary and selection vocabulary.

Language Coach

The second Skills Review page draws on the Language Coach skills in the *Elements of Literature* Preparing to Read pages. This feature asks you to apply those skills to texts from throughout the collection.

Writing Activity

You may have found that you need more practice writing. These short writing activities challenge you to apply what you have learned to your own ideas and experiences.

Oral Language Activity

Writing Activities alternate with Oral Language Activities. These features are designed to help you express your thoughts clearly aloud. The features are particularly helpful if you are learning English or if you need practice with Standard English.

Plot and Setting

© Images.com/Corbis

Literary and Academic Vocabulary for Collection 1

aspects (AS PEHKTS) *adj.:* parts or features of a subject; facets.
There are many aspects of Jack's top-secret military career that he can't tell to anyone.

credible (KREH DUH BUHL) *a.:* believable; trustworthy.
Samantha's story of her trip to another planet was not very credible.

tension (TEHN SHUHN) *n.:* strained condition.
There was a great deal of tension between Daniel and his professor because of their difference of opinion.

evaluation (EE VAL YOO AY SHUHN) *n.:* judgment; assessment.
I'm hoping to get a good evaluation on my book report.

plot (PLAHT) *n.:* the series of related events in a story.
The actors in the movie were great, but the plot was difficult to follow.

climax (KLY MAKS) *n.:* the most exciting part of a story.
We don't get to know what the bad guy looks like until the story's climax.

resolution (REH ZUH LOO SHUHN) *n.:* how a story closes, or ends.
I hope she finds true love so that the story can have a happy resolution.

flashback (FLASH BAK) *n.:* a scene that occurs out of sequence and recalls something that happened in the past.
The action of the movie paused, and the main character had a flashback that showed viewers what he did 10 years ago.

foreshadowing (FAWR SHA DOH WIHNG) *n.:* a clue or clues in a story that tell what will happen later.
The foreshadowing in the opening paragraph made it obvious that Jonas would find out that he was adopted.

internal conflict (IHN TUR NUHL KAHN FLIKT) *n.:* a struggle that occurs within a character's mind or heart.
Janet's internal conflict is that she wants to be nice but she has to act tough.

external conflict (EHK STEHR NUHL KAHN FLIKT) *n.:* a struggle against outside forces, such as nature and other people.
The external conflict took place between the captain and the dangerous sea.

Contents of the Dead Man's Pocket

by Jack Finney

LITERARY FOCUS: PLOT—TIME AND SEQUENCE

The series of related events in a story is called the **plot**. These events are often told in **chronological order**, the order in which they actually occur. Most short stories can be read in one sitting, usually in less than an hour. The events in a short story, however, may span hours, weeks, months, or years. "Contents of the Dead Man's Pocket" is striking because its events take place in "real time." In other words, the time it takes you to read the story roughly equals the time frame of the story itself.

READING FOCUS: UNDERSTANDING CAUSE AND EFFECT

A **cause** is what makes something happen. An **effect** is the result, or what happens. Imagine, for example, that a hurricane blows through a seaside town. The fierce winds overturn boats and destroy houses. The winds are the cause, and the effect is the damage.

In many stories, the events that make up the plot are closely related: One event causes another event, which leads to another event, and so on. To find a cause, ask yourself, "Why did this event happen?" To identify an effect, ask yourself, "What happened as a result of this event? Keep in mind that an effect or result can stem from several causes, and that one cause can lead to several effects.

To help you track cause-and-effect relationships as you read, keep a chart like the one below. In the left column, list the cause; in the right column, list the effect. List the causes and effects in chronological order so you can see how each event leads to the next.

SKILLS FOCUS

Literary Skills
Understand plot and chronological order.

Reading Skills
Understand cause and effect.

Cause	Effect
The apartment door is opened.	A sheet of yellow paper is blown out the window.

Vocabulary Development

Contents of the Dead Man's Pocket

SELECTION VOCABULARY

projection (PRUH JEHK SHUHN) *n.* something that juts out from a surface.

Tom's paper was trapped between the ledge and the decorative projection sticking out from the wall.

exhalation (EHKS HUH LAY SHUHN) *n.:* something breathed out; breath.

After holding his breath, Tom felt an exhalation of air as he breathed again.

imperceptibly (IHM PUHR SEHP TUH BLEE) *adv.:* in such a slight way as to be almost unnoticeable.

Tom moved along the edge imperceptibly, taking tiny, cautious steps.

rebounded (RIH BOWND IHD) *v.:* bounced back.

After he broke the window, Tom's arm rebounded, bouncing backward from the force of the blow.

irrelevantly (IH REHL UH VUHNT LEE) *adv.:* in a way not relating to the point or situation.

Tom thought irrelevantly about the apartment furnishings, as if the cozy rooms could stop him from falling to his death.

WORD STUDY

DIRECTIONS: What do the words *imperceptibly* and *irrelevantly* have in common? Each begins with a version of the same prefix. A prefix is a word part that is attached to the front of a word to change its meaning. Both *im-* and *ir-* are prefixes meaning "not." So, imperceptibly means "not perceptibly" or "not noticeably" and irrelevantly means "not relevantly" or "not relatedly." Look in the dictionary for some other examples of words that begin with the prefixes *im-*, *ir-*, or *in-*. Write them and their meanings below.

_____

_____

CONTENTS OF THE DEAD MAN'S POCKET

by Jack Finney

At the little living-room desk Tom Benecke rolled two sheets of flimsy[1] and a heavier top sheet, carbon paper sandwiched between them, into his portable. **A** *Interoffice Memo,* the top sheet was headed, and he typed tomorrow's date just below this; then he glanced at a creased yellow sheet, covered with his own handwriting, beside the typewriter. "Hot in here," he muttered to himself. Then, from the short hallway at his back, he heard the muffled clang of wire coat hangers in the bedroom closet, and at this reminder of what his wife was doing he thought: hot guilty
10 conscience.

He got up, shoving his hands into the back pockets of his gray wash slacks, stepped to the living-room window beside the desk and stood breathing on the glass, watching the expanding circlet of mist, staring down through the autumn night at Lexington Avenue,[2] eleven stories below. He was a tall, lean, dark-haired young man in a pullover sweater, who looked as though he had played not football, probably, but basketball in college. Now he placed the heels of his hands against the top edge of the lower window frame and shoved upward. But as usual the
20 window didn't budge, and he had to lower his hands and then shoot them hard upward to jolt the window open a few inches. He dusted his hands, muttering.

But still he didn't begin his work. He crossed the room to the hallway entrance and, leaning against the doorjamb, hands shoved into his back pockets again, he called, "Clare?" When his wife answered, he said, "Sure you don't mind going alone?" **B**

1. **flimsy** *n.:* thin paper used for typing carbon copies. Before computers and copying machines, copies of business communications were made with carbon paper.
2. **Lexington Avenue:** one of the main streets in New York City.

"No." Her voice was muffled, and he knew her head and shoulders were in the bedroom closet. Then the tap of her high heels sounded on the wood floor, and she appeared at the end

30   of the little hallway, wearing a slip, both hands raised to one ear, clipping on an earring. She smiled at him—a slender, very pretty girl with light brown, almost blond, hair—her prettiness emphasized by the pleasant nature that showed in her face. "It's just that I hate you to miss this movie; you wanted to see it, too."

"Yeah, I know." He ran his fingers through his hair. "Got to get this done, though." **C**

She nodded, accepting this. Then, glancing at the desk across the living room, she said, "You work too much, though, Tom—and too hard."

40   He smiled. "You won't mind, though, will you, when the money comes rolling in and I'm known as the Boy Wizard of Wholesale Groceries?"

"I guess not." She smiled and turned back toward the bedroom.

At his desk again, Tom lighted a cigarette; then a few moments later, as Clare appeared, dressed and ready to leave, he set it on the rim of the ashtray. "Just after seven," she said. "I can make the beginning of the first feature."

He walked to the front-door closet to help her on with her

50   coat. He kissed her then and, for an instant, holding her close, smelling the perfume she had used, he was tempted to go with

Copyright © by Holt, Rinehart and Winston. All rights reserved.

C QUICK CHECK

Why is Tom staying home, even though he wanted to see the movie?

_____

_____

_____

_____

_____

Contents of the Dead Man's Pocket   **5**

A LITERARY FOCUS

Based on what you have read so far, what do you think the **plot** of this story will be? State the general idea of the plot in two or three sentences.

_____

_____

_____

_____

_____

_____

_____

_____

_____

B READING FOCUS

What is the **effect** of wind rushing through the apartment?

_____

_____

_____

_____

_____

_____

her; it was not actually true that he had to work tonight, though he very much wanted to. This was his own project, unannounced as yet in his office, and it could be postponed. But then they won't see it till Monday, he thought once again, and if I give it to the boss tomorrow he might read it over the weekend . . . **A** "Have a good time," he said aloud. He gave his wife a little swat and opened the door for her, feeling the air from the building hallway, smelling faintly of floor wax, stream gently past his face.

60   He watched her walk down the hall, flicked a hand in response as she waved, and then he started to close the door, but it resisted for a moment. As the door opening narrowed, the current of warm air from the hallway, channeled through this smaller opening now, suddenly rushed past him with accelerated force. Behind him he heard the slap of the window curtains against the wall and the sound of paper fluttering from his desk, and he had to push to close the door.

     Turning, he saw a sheet of white paper drifting to the floor in a series of arcs, and another sheet, yellow, moving toward the

70 window, caught in the dying current flowing through the narrow opening. As he watched, the paper struck the bottom edge of the window and hung there for an instant, plastered against the glass and wood. Then as the moving air stilled completely, the curtains swinging back from the wall to hang free again, he saw the yellow sheet drop to the window ledge and slide over out of sight. **B**

     He ran across the room, grasped the bottom of the window and tugged, staring through the glass. He saw the yellow sheet, dimly now in the darkness outside, lying on the ornamental ledge a yard below the window. Even as he watched, it was

80 moving, scraping slowly along the ledge, pushed by the breeze that pressed steadily against the building wall. He heaved on the window with all his strength, and it shot open with a bang, the window weight rattling in the casing. But the paper was past his reach and, leaning out into the night, he watched it scud[3] steadily along the ledge to the south, half plastered against the building wall. Above the muffled sound of the street traffic far below,

3. **scud** _v.:_ glide or move swiftly.

he could hear the dry scrape of its movement, like a leaf on the pavement.

90 The living room of the next apartment to the south projected a yard or more further out toward the street than this one; because of this the Beneckes paid seven and a half dollars less rent than their neighbors. And now the yellow sheet, sliding along the stone ledge, nearly invisible in the night, was stopped by the projecting blank wall of the next apartment. **C** It lay motionless, then, in the corner formed by the two walls—a good five yards away, pressed firmly against the ornate corner ornament of the ledge by the breeze that moved past Tom Benecke's face.

He knelt at the window and stared at the yellow paper for a full minute or more, waiting for it to move, to slide off the ledge 100 and fall, hoping he could follow its course to the street, and then hurry down in the elevator and retrieve it. But it didn't move, and then he saw that the paper was caught firmly between a projection of the convoluted[4] corner ornament and the ledge. **D** He thought about the poker from the fireplace, then the broom, then the mop—discarding each thought as it occurred to him. There was nothing in the apartment long enough to reach that paper.

It was hard for him to understand that he actually had to abandon it—it was ridiculous—and he began to curse. Of 110 all the papers on his desk, why did it have to be this one in particular! On four long Saturday afternoons he had stood in supermarkets, counting the people who passed certain displays, and the results were scribbled on that yellow sheet. From stacks of trade publications, gone over page by page in snatched half hours at work and during evenings at home, he had copied facts, quotations, and figures onto that sheet. And he had carried it with him to the Public Library on Fifth Avenue, where he'd spent a dozen lunch hours and early evenings adding more. All were needed to support and lend authority to his idea for a 120 new grocery-store display method; without them his idea was

---

4. **convoluted** (KHAN VUH LOOT IHD) *adj.:* intricate; coiled.

Circle the **prefix** in the word *invisible*. What does the prefix mean? What does *invisible* mean?

_____

_____

_____

D VOCABULARY

Selection Vocabulary

The word *projection* means "something that juts out from a surface." The paper has been blown against a piece of the corner ornament that sticks out from the building. What might have happened to the paper if there were no projection there?

_____

_____

_____

_____

A (QUICK CHECK)

Why is the yellow paper so important to Tom? Underline the details in this paragraph that tell you why.

B (LITERARY FOCUS)

Now what do you think the **plot** of this story will be? If your answer is different than before, what made you change your mind?

_____

_____

_____

_____

_____

_____

_____

C (LITERARY ANALYSIS)

What do Tom's thoughts tell you about him and his long-term ambitions?

_____

_____

_____

_____

_____

_____

_____

a mere opinion. And there they all lay, in his own improvised shorthand—countless hours of work—out there on the ledge. **A**

For many seconds he believed he was going to abandon the yellow sheet, that there was nothing else to do. The work could be duplicated. But it would take two months, and the time to present this idea was *now,* for use in the spring displays. He struck his fist on the window ledge. Then he shrugged. Even though his plan was adopted, he told himself, it wouldn't bring him a raise in pay—not immediately, anyway, or as a direct result.

130 It won't bring me a promotion either, he argued—not of itself. **B**

But just the same—and he couldn't escape the thought—this and other independent projects, some already done and others planned for the future, would gradually mark him out from the score of other young men in his company. They were the way to change from a name on the payroll to a name in the minds of the company officials. They were the beginning of the long, long climb to where he was determined to be—at the very top. And he knew he was going out there in the darkness, after the yellow sheet fifteen feet beyond his reach. **C**

140 By a kind of instinct, he instantly began making his intention acceptable to himself by laughing at it. The mental picture of himself sidling along the ledge outside was absurd—it was actually comical—and he smiled. He imagined himself describing it; it would make a good story at the office and, it occurred to him, would add a special interest and importance to his memorandum, which would do it no harm at all.

To simply go out and get his paper was an easy task—he could be back here with it in less than two minutes—and he knew he wasn't deceiving himself. The ledge, he saw, measuring it

150 with his eye, was about as wide as the length of his shoe, and perfectly flat. And every fifth row of brick in the face of the building, he remembered—leaning out, he verified this—was indented half an inch, enough for the tips of his fingers, enough to maintain balance easily. It occurred to him that if this ledge and wall were only a yard aboveground—as he knelt at the window staring

out, this thought was the final confirmation of his intention—he could move along the ledge indefinitely.

On a sudden impulse, he got to his feet, walked to the front closet, and took out an old tweed jacket; it would be cold out-
160 side. He put it on and buttoned it as he crossed the room rapidly toward the open window. In the back of his mind he knew he'd better hurry and get this over with before he thought too much, and at the window he didn't allow himself to hesitate.

He swung a leg over the sill, then felt for and found the ledge a yard below the window with his foot. Gripping the bottom of the window frame very tightly and carefully, he slowly ducked his head under it, feeling on his face the sudden change from the warm air of the room to the chill outside. With infinite care he brought out his other leg, his mind concentrating on
170 what he was doing. Then he slowly stood erect. Most of the putty, dried out and brittle, had dropped off the bottom edging of the window frame, he found, and the flat wooden edging provided a good gripping surface, a half inch or more deep, for the tips of his fingers. **D**

Now, balanced easily and firmly, he stood on the ledge outside in the slight, chill breeze, eleven stories above the street, staring into his own lighted apartment, odd and different-seeming now.

First his right hand, then his left, he carefully shifted his
180 fingertip grip from the puttyless window edging to an indented row of bricks directly to his right. It was hard to take the first shuffling sideways step then—to make himself move—and the fear stirred in his stomach, but he did it, again by not allowing himself time to think. And now—with his chest, stomach, and the left side of his face pressed against the rough cold brick—his lighted apartment was suddenly gone, and it was much darker out here than he had thought. **E**

Without pause he continued—right foot, left foot, right foot, left—his shoe soles shuffling and scraping along the rough stone,
190 never lifting from it, fingers sliding along the exposed edging of brick. He moved on the balls of his feet, heels lifted slightly; the

D QUICK CHECK

Consider what has happened so far. In your own words, explain why Tom decides to go out on the ledge.

_____

_____

_____

_____

_____

_____

E VOCABULARY

Academic Vocabulary

How do the descriptions in this section increase *tension*, or strained condition?

_____

_____

_____

_____

_____

A READING FOCUS

What might be an **effect** of looking down that Tom is trying to avoid?

_____

_____

_____

_____

_____

© Pictor International/Image State/Alamy.

ledge was not quite as wide as he'd expected. But leaning slightly inward toward the face of the building and pressed against it, he could feel his balance firm and secure, and moving along the ledge was quite as easy as he had thought it would be. He could hear the buttons of his jacket scraping steadily along the rough bricks and feel them catch momentarily, tugging a little, at each mortared crack. He simply did not permit himself to look down, though the compulsion[5] to do so never left him; nor did he allow

200 himself actually to think. **A** Mechanically—right foot, left foot, over and again—he shuffled along crabwise, watching the projecting wall ahead loom steadily closer. . . .

Then he reached it, and at the corner—he'd decided how he was going to pick up the paper—he lifted his right foot and placed it carefully on the ledge that ran along the projecting wall at a right angle to the ledge on which his other foot rested. And now, facing the building, he stood in the corner formed by the two walls, one foot on the ledging of each, a hand on the shoulder-high indentation of each wall. His forehead was pressed

210 directly into the corner against the cold bricks, and now he

5. **compulsion** *n.:* driving force.

carefully lowered first one hand, then the other, perhaps a foot farther down, to the next indentation in the rows of bricks. **B**

Very slowly, sliding his forehead down the trough of the brick corner and bending his knees, he lowered his body toward the paper lying between his outstretched feet. Again he lowered his fingerholds another foot and bent his knees still more, thigh muscles taut, his forehead sliding and bumping down the brick V. Half squatting now, he dropped his left hand to the next indentation and then slowly reached with his right hand toward
220 the paper between his feet.

He couldn't quite touch it, and his knees now were pressed against the wall; he could bend them no farther. But by ducking his head another inch lower, the top of his head now pressed against the bricks, he lowered his right shoulder and his fingers had the paper by a corner, pulling it loose. At the same instant he saw, between his legs and far below, Lexington Avenue stretched out for miles ahead.

He saw, in that instant, the Loew's theater sign, blocks ahead past Fiftieth Street; the miles of traffic signals, all green now;
230 the lights of cars and street lamps; countless neon signs; and the moving black dots of people. And a violent, instantaneous explosion of absolute terror roared through him. For a motionless instant he saw himself externally—bent practically double, balanced on this narrow ledge, nearly half his body projecting out above the street far below—and he began to tremble violently, panic flaring through his mind and muscles, and he felt the blood rush from the surface of his skin. **C**

In the fractional moment before horror paralyzed him, as he stared between his legs at that terrible length of street far
240 beneath him, a fragment of his mind raised his body in a spasmodic jerk to an upright position again, but so violently that his head scraped hard against the wall, bouncing off it, and his body swayed outward to the knife-edge of balance, and he very nearly plunged backward and fell. **D** Then he was leaning far into the corner again, squeezing and pushing into it, not only his face but

B LITERARY FOCUS

List in **chronological order** the actions Tom takes in this paragraph. Why does the author give us all this information?

_____

_____

_____

_____

_____

_____

_____

_____

_____

_____

_____

_____

C QUICK CHECK

Underline the words in this paragraph that tell why Tom's fear suddenly increases.

D READING FOCUS

What is the **cause** of Tom almost falling?

_____

_____

_____

_____

his chest and stomach, his back arching; and his fingertips clung with all the pressure of his pulling arms to the shoulder-high half-inch indentation in the bricks.

250   He was more than trembling now; his whole body was racked with a violent shuddering beyond control, his eyes squeezed so tightly shut it was painful, though he was past awareness of that. His teeth were exposed in a frozen grimace, the strength draining like water from his knees and calves. It was extremely likely, he knew, that he would faint, slump down along the wall, his face scraping, and then drop backward, a limp weight, out into nothing. And to save his life he concentrated on holding on to consciousness, drawing deliberate deep breaths of cold air into his lungs, fighting to keep his senses aware.

Then he knew that he would not faint, but he could not 260   stop shaking nor open his eyes. He stood where he was, breathing deeply, trying to hold back the terror of the glimpse he had had of what lay below him; and he knew he had made a mistake in not making himself stare down at the street, getting used to it and accepting it, when he had first stepped out onto the ledge.

It was impossible to walk back. **A** He simply could not do it. He couldn't bring himself to make the slightest movement. The strength was gone from his legs; his shivering hands—numb, cold, and desperately rigid—had lost all deftness;[6] his easy ability to move and balance was gone. Within a step or two, if he tried 270   to move, he knew that he would stumble clumsily and fall.

Seconds passed, with the chill faint wind pressing the side of his face, and he could hear the toned-down volume of the street traffic far beneath him. Again and again it slowed and then stopped, almost to silence; then presently, even this high, he would hear the click of the traffic signals and the subdued roar of the cars starting up again. During a lull in the street sounds, he called out. Then he was shouting *"Help!"* so loudly it rasped his throat. But he felt the steady pressure of the wind, moving between his face and the blank wall, snatch up his cries as he 280   uttered them, and he knew they must sound directionless and

---

6.   **deftness** *n.:* skillfulness; coordination.

distant. And he remembered how habitually, here in New York, he himself heard and ignored shouts in the night. If anyone heard him, there was no sign of it, and presently Tom Benecke knew he had to try moving; there was nothing else he could do.

Eyes squeezed shut, he watched scenes in his mind like scraps of motion-picture film—he could not stop them. He saw himself stumbling suddenly sideways as he crept along the ledge and saw his upper body arc outward, arms flailing. He saw a dangling shoestring caught between the ledge and the sole of his
290 other shoe, saw a foot start to move, to be stopped with a jerk, and felt his balance leaving him. He saw himself falling with a terrible speed as his body revolved in the air, knees clutched tight to his chest, eyes squeezed shut, moaning softly.

Out of utter necessity, knowing that any of these thoughts might be reality in the very next seconds, he was slowly able to shut his mind against every thought but what he now began to do. With fear-soaked slowness, he slid his left foot an inch or two toward his own impossibly distant window. Then he slid the fingers of his shivering left hand a corresponding distance.
300 For a moment he could not bring himself to lift his right foot from one ledge to the other; then he did it, and became aware of the harsh exhalation of air from his throat and realized that he was panting. **B** As his right hand, then, began to slide along the brick edging, he was astonished to feel the yellow paper pressed to the bricks underneath his stiff fingers, and he uttered a terrible, abrupt bark that might have been a laugh or a moan. He opened his mouth and took the paper in his teeth, pulling it out from under his fingers.

By a kind of trick—by concentrating his entire mind on first
310 his left foot, then his left hand, then the other foot, then the other hand—he was able to move, almost imperceptibly, trembling steadily, very nearly without thought. But he could feel the terrible strength of the pent-up horror on just the other side of the flimsy barrier he had erected in his mind; and he knew that if it broke through he would lose this thin, artificial control of his body. **C**

B VOCABULARY

Selection Vocabulary
Underline the words in this sentence that help you determine the meaning of *exhalation*.

C LITERARY FOCUS

How does what Tom is feeling here connect to the **plot** of this story?

_____

_____

_____

_____

_____

_____

_____

_____

_____

_____

_____

_____

_____

_____

_____

_____

_____

_____

A LITERARY ANALYSIS

If keeping his eyes closed made him feel safer, why does Tom now keep his eyes open and directed away from the windows across the street?

_____

_____

_____

_____

_____

_____

_____

B READING FOCUS

What is the **cause** of the "barrier" breaking?

_____

_____

_____

_____

_____

_____

_____

During one slow step he tried keeping his eyes closed; it made him feel safer, shutting him off a little from the fearful reality of where he was. Then a sudden rush of giddiness swept 320 over him and he had to open his eyes wide, staring sideways at the cold rough brick and angled lines of mortar, his cheek tight against the building. He kept his eyes open then, knowing that if he once let them flick outward, to stare for an instant at the lighted windows across the street, he would be past help. **A**

He didn't know how many dozens of tiny sidling steps he had taken, his chest, belly, and face pressed to the wall; but he knew the slender hold he was keeping on his mind and body was going to break. He had a sudden mental picture of his apartment on just the other side of this wall—warm, cheerful, 330 incredibly spacious. And he saw himself striding through it, lying down on the floor on his back, arms spread wide, reveling[7] in its unbelievable security. The impossible remoteness of this utter safety, the contrast between it and where he now stood, was more than he could bear. And the barrier broke then, and the fear of the awful height he stood on coursed through his nerves and muscles. **B**

A fraction of his mind knew he was going to fall, and he began taking rapid blind steps with no feeling of what he was doing, sidling with a clumsy desperate swiftness, fingers scrab-340 bling along the brick, almost hopelessly resigned to the sudden backward pull and swift motion outward and down. Then his moving left hand slid onto not brick but sheer emptiness, an impossible gap in the face of the wall, and he stumbled.

His right foot smashed into his left anklebone; he staggered sideways, began falling, and the claw of his hand cracked against glass and wood, slid down it, and his fingertips were pressed hard on the puttyless edging of his window. His right hand smacked gropingly beside it as he fell to his knees; and, under the full weight and direct downward pull of his sagging body, 350 the open window dropped shudderingly in its frame till it closed and his wrists struck the sill and were jarred off.

---

7. **reveling** (REH vuh lihng) _v._: taking great pleasure or delight.

For a single moment he knelt, knee bones against stone on the very edge of the ledge, body swaying and touching nowhere else, fighting for balance. Then he lost it, his shoulders plunging backward, and he flung his arms forward, his hands smashing against the window casing on either side; and—his body moving backward—his fingers clutched the narrow wood stripping of the upper pane.  ·

360 For an instant he hung suspended between balance and falling, his fingertips pressed onto the quarter-inch wood strips. Then, with utmost delicacy, with a focused concentration of all his senses, he increased even further the strain on his fingertips hooked to these slim edgings of wood. Elbows slowly bending, he began to draw the full weight of his upper body forward, knowing that the instant his fingers slipped off these quarter-inch strips he'd plunge backward and be falling. Elbows imperceptibly bending, body shaking with the strain, the sweat starting from his forehead in great sudden drops, he pulled, his

© Alan Schein Photography/Corbis.

List in **chronological order** the most important events that have happened so far in the story.

_____
_____
_____
_____
_____
_____
_____
_____
_____
_____
_____
_____
_____

B **VOCABULARY**

Selection Vocabulary

Tom's arm _rebounded_ from the window. Name three other things that might rebound, or bounce back, when they hit something with a lot of force.

_____
_____
_____
_____

370 entire being and thought concentrated in his fingertips. Then, suddenly, the strain slackened and ended, his chest touching the windowsill, and he was kneeling on the ledge, his forehead pressed to the glass of the closed window.

Dropping his palms to the sill, he stared into his living room—at the red-brown davenport[8] across the room, and a magazine he had left there; at the pictures on the walls and the gray rug; the entrance to the hallway; and at his papers, typewriter, and desk, not two feet from his nose. A movement from his desk caught his eye and he saw that it was a thin curl of blue smoke; his cigarette, the ash long, was still burning in the

380 ashtray where he'd left it—this was past all belief—only a few minutes before.

His head moved, and in faint reflection from the glass before him, he saw the yellow paper clenched in his front teeth. Lifting a hand from the sill he took it from his mouth; the moistened corner parted from the paper, and he spat it out. **A**

For a moment, in the light from the living room, he stared wonderingly at the yellow sheet in his hand and then crushed it into the side pocket of his jacket.

He couldn't open the window. It had been pulled not

390 completely closed, but its lower edge was below the level of the outside sill; there was no room to get his fingers underneath it. Between the upper sash and the lower was a gap not wide enough—reaching up, he tried—to get his fingers into; he couldn't push it open. The upper window panel, he knew from long experience, was impossible to move, frozen tight with dried paint.

Very carefully observing his balance, the fingertips of his left hand again hooked to the narrow stripping of the window casing, he drew back his right hand, palm facing the glass, and then

400 struck the glass with the heel of his hand.

His arm rebounded from the pane, his body tottering, and he knew he didn't dare strike a harder blow. **B**

---

8. **davenport** (DA VUHN PAWRT) _n._: large sofa or couch.

But in the security and relief of his new position, he simply smiled; with only a sheet of glass between him and the room just before him, it was not possible that there wasn't a way past it. Eyes narrowing, he thought for a few moments about what to do. Then his eyes widened, for nothing occurred to him. But still he felt calm; the trembling, he realized, had stopped. At the back of his mind there still lay the thought that once he was again in his home, he could give release to his feelings. He actually *would* lie on the floor, rolling, clenching tufts of the rug in his hands. He would literally run across the room, free to move as he liked, jumping on the floor, testing and reveling in its absolute security, letting the relief flood through him, draining the fear from his mind and body. His yearning for this was astonishingly intense, and somehow he understood that he had better keep this feeling at bay. **C**

He took a half dollar from his pocket and struck it against the pane, but without any hope that the glass would break and with very little disappointment when it did not. After a few moments of thought he drew his leg up onto the ledge and picked loose the knot of his shoelace. He slipped off the shoe and, holding it across the instep, drew back his arm as far as he dared and struck the leather heel against the glass. The pane rattled, but he knew he'd been a long way from breaking it. His foot was cold and he slipped the shoe back on. He shouted again, experimentally, and then once more, but there was no answer.

The realization suddenly struck him that he might have to wait here till Clare came home, and for a moment the thought was funny. He could see Clare opening the front door, withdrawing her key from the lock, closing the door behind her, and then glancing up to see him crouched on the other side of the window. He could see her rush across the room, face astounded and frightened, and hear himself shouting instructions: "Never mind how I got here! Just open the wind—" She couldn't open it, he remembered, she'd never been able to; she'd always had to call him. She'd have to get the building superintendent or a neighbor,

C **LITERARY ANALYSIS**

Why might Tom have to keep his desire for security and relief "at bay," or under control?

_____

_____

_____

_____

_____

_____

_____

and he pictured himself smiling and answering their questions as he climbed in. "I just wanted to get a breath of fresh air, so—"

440   He couldn't possibly wait here till Clare came home. It was the second feature she'd wanted to see, and she'd left in time to see the first. She'd be another three hours or— He glanced at his watch; Clare had been gone eight minutes. It wasn't possible, but only eight minutes ago he had kissed his wife goodbye. She wasn't even at the theater yet!

    It would be four hours before she could possibly be home, and he tried to picture himself kneeling out here, fingertips hooked to these narrow strippings, while first one movie, preceded by a slow listing of credits, began, developed, reached

450 its climax, and then finally ended. There'd be a newsreel next, maybe, and then an animated cartoon, and then interminable scenes from coming pictures. And then, once more, the beginning of a full-length picture—while all the time he hung out here in the night. **A**

    He might possibly get to his feet, but he was afraid to try. Already his legs were cramped, his thigh muscles tired; his knees hurt, his feet felt numb, and his hands were stiff. He couldn't possibly stay out here for four hours or anywhere near it. Long before that his legs and arms would give out; he would be forced

460 to try changing his position often—stiffly, clumsily, his coordination and strength gone—and he would fall. Quite realistically, he knew that he would fall; no one could stay out here on this ledge for four hours.

    A dozen windows in the apartment building across the street were lighted. Looking over his shoulder, he could see the top of a man's head behind the newspaper he was reading; in another window he saw the blue-gray flicker of a television screen. No more than twenty-odd yards from his back were scores of people, and if just one of them would walk idly to his

470 window and glance out. . . . For some moments he stared over his shoulder at the lighted rectangles, waiting. But no one appeared. The man reading his paper turned a page and then continued his

reading. A figure passed another of the windows and was immediately gone.

In the inside pocket of his jacket he found a little sheaf of papers, and he pulled one out and looked at it in the light from the living room. It was an old letter, an advertisement of some sort; his name and address, in purple ink, were on a label pasted to the envelope. Gripping one end of the envelope in his teeth,
480   he twisted it into a tight curl. From his shirt pocket he brought out a book of matches. He didn't dare let go the casing with both hands but, with the twist of paper in his teeth, he opened the matchbook with his free hand; then he bent one of the matches in two without tearing it from the folder, its red-tipped end now touching the striking surface. With his thumb, he rubbed the red tip across the striking area.

He did it again, then again, and still again, pressing harder each time, and the match suddenly flared, burning his thumb. But he kept it alight, cupping the matchbook in his hand and
490   shielding it with his body. He held the flame to the paper in his mouth till it caught. Then he snuffed out the match flame with his thumb and forefinger, careless of the burn, and replaced the book in his pocket. Taking the paper twist in his hand, he held it flame down, watching the flame crawl up the paper, till it flared bright. Then he held it behind him over the street, moving it from side to side, watching it over his shoulder, the flame flickering and guttering in the wind.

There were three letters in his pocket and he lighted each of them, holding each till the flame touched his hand and then
500   dropping it to the street below. At one point, watching over his shoulder while the last of the letters burned, he saw the man across the street put down his paper and stand—even seeming, to Tom, to glance toward his window. But when he moved, it was only to walk across the room and disappear from sight.

There were a dozen coins in Tom Benecke's pocket and he dropped them, three or four at a time. But if they struck anyone, or if anyone noticed their falling, no one connected them with their source, and no one glanced upward. **B**

B **QUICK CHECK**

Why is Tom burning the letters and dropping coins?

_____

_____

_____

_____

_____

_____

_____

510 His arms had begun to tremble from the steady strain of clinging to this narrow perch, and he did not know what to do now and was terribly frightened. Clinging to the window stripping with one hand, he again searched his pockets. But now—he had left his wallet on his dresser when he'd changed clothes— there was nothing left but the yellow sheet. It occurred to him irrelevantly that his death on the sidewalk below would be an eternal mystery; the window closed—why, how, and from where could he have fallen? **A** No one would be able to identify his body for a time, either—the thought was somehow unbearable and increased his fear. All they'd find in his pockets would be the

520 yellow sheet. *Contents of the dead man's pockets,* he thought, *one sheet of paper bearing penciled notations—incomprehensible.*

He understood fully that he might actually be going to die; his arms, maintaining his balance on the ledge, were trembling steadily now. And it occurred to him then with all the force of a revelation that, if he fell, all he was ever going to have out of life he would then, abruptly, have had. Nothing, then, could ever be changed; and nothing more—no least experience or pleasure— could ever be added to his life. He wished, then, that he had not allowed his wife to go off by herself tonight—and on similar

530 nights. He thought of all the evenings he had spent away from her, working; and he regretted them. He thought wonderingly of his fierce ambition and of the direction his life had taken; he thought of the hours he'd spent by himself, filling the yellow sheet that had brought him out here. *Contents of the dead man's pockets,* he thought with sudden fierce anger, *a wasted life.*

He was simply not going to cling here till he slipped and fell; he told himself that now. There was one last thing he could try; he had been aware of it for some moments, refusing to think about it, but now he faced it. Kneeling here on the ledge, the

540 fingertips of one hand pressed to the narrow strip of wood, he could, he knew, draw his other hand back a yard perhaps, fist clenched tight, doing it very slowly till he sensed the outer limit of balance, then, as hard as he was able from the distance, he could drive his fist forward against the glass. If it broke, his fist

smashing through, he was safe; he might cut himself badly, and probably would, but with his arm inside the room, he would be secure. But if the glass did not break, the rebound, flinging his arm back, would topple him off the ledge. He was certain of that. **B**

550   He tested his plan. The fingers of his left hand clawlike on the little stripping, he drew back his other fist until his body began teetering backward. But he had no leverage now—he could feel that there would be no force to his swing—and he moved his fist slowly forward till he rocked forward on his knees again and could sense that his swing would carry its greatest force. Glancing down, however, measuring the distance from his fist to the glass, he saw that it was less than two feet.

It occurred to him that he could raise his arm over his head, to bring it down against the glass. But, experimentally in slow
560   motion, he knew it would be an awkward blow without the force of a driving punch, and not nearly enough to break the glass.

Facing the window, he had to drive a blow from the shoulder, he knew now, at a distance of less than two feet; and he did not know whether it would break through the heavy glass. It might; he could picture it happening, he could feel it in the nerves of his arm. And it might not; he could feel that too—feel his fist striking this glass and being instantaneously flung back by the unbreaking pane, feel the fingers of his other hand breaking loose, nails scraping along the casing as he fell. **C**

570   He waited, arm drawn back, fist balled, but in no hurry to strike; this pause, he knew, might be an extension of his life. And to live even a few seconds longer, he felt, even out here on this ledge in the night, was infinitely better than to die a moment earlier than he had to. His arm grew tired, and he brought it down and rested it.

Then he knew that it was time to make the attempt. He could not kneel here hesitating indefinitely till he lost all courage to act, waiting till he slipped off the ledge. Again he drew back his arm, knowing this time that he would not bring it down

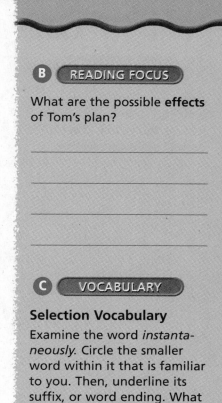

B READING FOCUS

What are the possible **effects** of Tom's plan?

_____

_____

_____

_____

C VOCABULARY

Selection Vocabulary

Examine the word _instantaneously._ Circle the smaller word within it that is familiar to you. Then, underline its suffix, or word ending. What does _instantaneously_ mean?

_____

_____

_____

A **LITERARY ANALYSIS**

At the end of the story, why does Tom laugh when he sees the yellow sheet of paper fly out the window?

_____

_____

_____

_____

_____

_____

_____

_____

_____

_____

_____

_____

_____

580 till he struck. His elbow protruding over Lexington Avenue far below, the fingers of his other hand pressed down bloodlessly tight against the narrow stripping, he waited, feeling the sick tenseness and terrible excitement building. It grew and swelled toward the moment of action, his nerves tautening. He thought of Clare—just a wordless, yearning thought—and then drew his arm back just a bit more, fist so tight his fingers pained him, and knowing he was going to do it. Then with full power, with every last scrap of strength he could bring to bear, he shot his arm forward toward the glass, and he said "Clare!"

590 He heard the sound, felt the blow, felt himself falling forward, and his hand closed on the living-room curtains, the shards and fragments of glass showering onto the floor. And then, kneeling there on the ledge, an arm thrust into the room up to the shoulder, he began picking away the protruding slivers and great wedges of glass from the window frame, tossing them in onto the rug. And, as he grasped the edges of the empty window frame and climbed into his home, he was grinning in triumph.

He did not lie down on the floor or run through the apartment, as he had promised himself; even in the first few

600 moments it seemed to him natural and normal that he should be where he was. He simply turned to his desk, pulled the crumpled yellow sheet from his pocket, and laid it down where it had been, smoothing it out; then he absently laid a pencil across it to weight it down. He shook his head wonderingly, and turned to walk toward the closet.

There he got out his topcoat and hat and, without waiting to put them on, opened the front door and stepped out, to go find his wife. He turned to pull the door closed and warm air from the hall rushed through the narrow opening again. As he saw the

610 yellow paper, the pencil flying, scooped off the desk and, unimpeded by the glassless window, sail out into the night and out of his life, Tom Benecke burst into laughter and then closed the door behind him. **A**

Applying Your Skills

Contents of the Dead Man's Pocket

VOCABULARY DEVELOPMENT

DIRECTIONS: Complete the sentences with vocabulary words from the Word Box. One word will not be used.

Word Box

projection
exhalation
imperceptibly
rebounded
irrelevantly

1. Tom's feet moved slowly and almost _____ along the ledge.

2. The yellow sheet of paper was caught on a _____ of the building wall.

3. Tom thought _____ about what questions people might ask if he fell from the ledge.

4. His arm _____ from the window pane when he tried unsuccessfully to strike through the glass.

LITERARY FOCUS: PLOT—TIME AND SEQUENCE

Choose a section of the story that is at least 30 lines long. On a separate sheet of paper, create a time line showing the **plot** of that section in **chronological order**.

READING FOCUS: UNDERSTANDING CAUSE AND EFFECT

Complete the chart by writing either a **cause** or **effect** in the chart below.

Cause	Effect
Tom wanted to make himself stand out from the other workers in the company.	1.
2.	Under the downward pull of his body, the window slammed shut.
Tom thought of Clare and called out her name as he tried again to break the glass.	3.

SKILLS FOCUS

Literary Skills
Understand plot and chronological order.

Reading Skills
Understand cause and effect.

The Trip

by Laila Lalami

LITERARY FOCUS: SETTING AND MOOD

Can you imagine any of the *Star Wars* movies not taking place "a long time ago in a galaxy far, far away"? It's impossible! *Star Wars* is a good example of how important setting is to a story. **Setting** is the time and place in which a story takes place. As you read a story, ask yourself when the story happens—the past, present, or future? Then, find out where the story happens. In outer space? On a farm? In someone's apartment?

The setting has a lot to do with the **mood** of the story. The mood is the atmosphere, or the feeling, of the world in which the story takes place. For example, a horror story set in a cemetery might have a spooky mood. Writers use adjectives to describe the people, places, and events of a story; this sets up the mood.

READING FOCUS: VISUALIZING

To get the most out of what you read, it helps to visualize as you go along. **Visualizing** is imagining a story as though you were a part of it. Try to picture exactly what the writer describes. Focus on the rich details the writer uses to describe the setting. Visualizing helps you imagine not only a setting, but a character's thoughts and feelings as well.

As you read "The Trip," write down words that help you imagine the setting in a chart like the one below. Remember that the setting may change as the story unfolds.

Setting	Descriptive Language
Strait of Gibraltar at night	The waves are inky black, except for hints of foam here and there, glistening white under the moon, like tombstones in a dark cemetery.

SKILLS FOCUS

Literary Skills
Understand the relationship between setting and mood.

Reading Skills
Visualize what the writer is describing.

Vocabulary Development

The Trip

SELECTION VOCABULARY

pondered (PAHN DUHRD) *v.:* thought over; considered carefully.
   Jerome pondered his vote for class president.

destinies (DEHS TUH NEEZ) *n.:* what becomes of people or things in the end.
   The destinies of the lost suitcases were difficult to determine.

exudes (EHG ZOODZ) *v.:* seems to radiate; oozes.
   Stephanie exudes happiness and joy every time she wins a tennis match.

putrid (PYOO TRIHD) *adj.:* foul; decaying or rotten.
   The smell of the air near the garbage dump was putrid.

prospects (PRAHS PEHKTS) *n.:* things expected or looked forward to; outlook for the future.
   After graduating from college with honors, Melinda's job prospects looked very bright.

WORD STUDY

DIRECTIONS: Take a blank piece of paper and fold it in half both vertically and horizontally. Then unfold the paper. It should have four sections, like this:

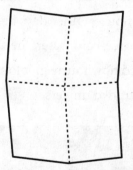

In the upper left section, write one of the Selection Vocabulary words. In the upper right section, write the definition (try to remember the definition without looking above first!). In the lower left section, write a sentence using the word. In the last section, after reading the story, write a sentence from the story in which word appears. Repeat these steps until you have a completed sheet of paper for each of the vocabulary words. Or, write all the words, definitions, and sentences on the same sheet.

THE TRIP

by Laila Lalami

BACKGROUND

The main character in "The Trip" is Murad. He is an educated young man from Morocco, located in northern Africa. He attempts to travel across the Strait of Gibraltar in a small boat with several other people. The strait is a narrow waterway in the Mediterranean Sea that separates Morocco from Spain. It is a journey that is both dangerous and illegal, but Murad makes this trip to find work and to build a better life.

A **VOCABULARY**

Selection Vocabulary

The word *pondered* means "thought over, considered carefully." Circle other words or phrases in the first paragraph that have a similar meaning.

Fourteen kilometers. Murad has pondered that number hundreds of times in the last year, trying to decide whether the risk was worth it. Some days he told himself that the distance was nothing, a brief inconvenience, that the crossing would take as little as thirty minutes if the weather was good. He spent hours thinking about what he would do once he was on the other side, imagining the job, the car, the house. Other days he could think only about the coast guards, the ice-cold water, the money he'd have to borrow, and he wondered how fourteen kilometers could separate not just

10 two countries but two universes. **A**

From "The Trip" from *Hope and Other Dangerous Pursuits* by Laila Lalami. Copyright 2005 © by Laila Lalami. Reproduced by permission of **Algonquin Books of Chapel Hill, a Division of Workman Publishing.**

© Fernando Garcia/Cover/Corbis

Tonight the sea appears calm, with only a slight wind now and then. The captain has ordered all the lights turned off, but with the moon up and the sky clear, Murad can still see around him. The six-meter Zodiac inflatable[1] is meant to accommodate eight people. Thirty huddle in it now, men, women, and children, all with the anxious look of those whose destinies are in the hands of others—the captain, the coast guards, God. **B** Murad has three layers on: undershirt, turtleneck, and jacket; below, a pair of thermal underwear, jeans, and sneakers. With only three

20 hours' notice, he didn't have time to get waterproof pants. He touches a button on his watch, a Rolex knockoff he bought from a street vendor in Tangier,[2] and the display lights up: 3:15 A.M. He scratches at the residue the metal bracelet leaves on his wrist, then pulls his sleeve down to cover the timepiece. Looking around him, he can't help but wonder how much Captain Rahal and his gang stand to make. If the other passengers paid as much as Murad did, the take is almost 600,000 dirhams, enough for an apartment or small house in a Moroccan beach town like Asilah or Cabo Negro. **C**

30 He looks at the Spanish coastline, closer with every breath. The waves are inky black, except for hints of foam here and there, glistening white under the moon, like tombstones in a dark cemetery. Murad can make out the town where they're headed. Tarifa. The mainland point of the Moorish invasion in 711.[3] Murad used to regale tourists with anecdotes about how Tariq Ibn Ziyad had led a powerful Moor army across the Straits and, upon landing in Gibraltar, ordered all the boats burned. He'd told his soldiers that they could march forth and defeat the enemy or turn back and die a coward's death. **D**

40 The men had followed their general, toppled the Visigoths, and established an empire that ruled over Spain for more than seven hundred years. Little did they know that we'd be back,

---

1. **Zodiac inflatable**: a small inflatable boat that has a motor.
2. **Tangier** (TAN JEER): a city in northern Morocco, on the Strait of Gibraltar.
3. **Moorish** (MUR IHSH): relating to the Moors, a population of Muslim people from northwestern Africa.

B LITERARY FOCUS

Underline the word in this paragraph that helps describe the **mood** of the beginning of the story.

C VOCABULARY

Selection Vocabulary

Circle one word in this sentence that helps you understand what a *dirham* is. Looking at the context, what do you think the word means?

_____

_____

_____

D LITERARY FOCUS

Can you guess the story's **setting**? Write your guess on the lines below.

_____

_____

_____

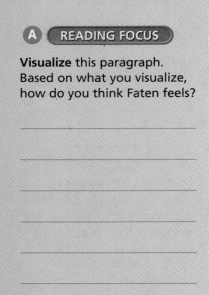

Visualize this paragraph. Based on what you visualize, how do you think Faten feels?

_____

_____

_____

_____

_____

_____

Murad thinks. Only instead of a fleet, here we are in an inflatable boat—not just Moors, but a motley mix of people from the ex-colonies, without guns or armor; without a charismatic leader.

It's worth it, though, Murad tells himself. Some time on this flimsy boat and then a job. It will be hard at first. He'll work in the fields like everyone else, but he'll look for something better. He isn't like the others—he has a plan. He doesn't want to break

50   his back for the *spagnol*, spend the rest of his life picking their oranges and tomatoes. He'll find a real job, where he can use his training. He has a degree in English and, in addition, he speaks Spanish fluently, unlike some of the harraga.[4]

His leg goes numb. He moves his ankle around. To his left, the girl (he thinks her name is Faten) shifts slightly, so that her thigh no longer presses against his. She looks eighteen, nineteen maybe. "My leg was asleep," he whispers. Faten nods to acknowledge him but doesn't look at him. She pulls her black cardigan tight around her chest and stares down at her shoes. He

60   doesn't understand why she's wearing a hijab scarf on her hair for a trip like this. Does she imagine she can walk down the street in Tarifa in a headscarf without attracting attention? She'll get caught, he thinks.

Back on the beach, while they all were waiting for Rahal to get ready, Faten sat alone, away from everyone else, as though she were sulking. She was the last one to climb into the boat, and Murad had to move to make room for her. He couldn't understand her reluctance. It didn't seem possible to him that she would have paid so much money and not been eager to leave

70   when the moment came. **A**

Across from Murad is Aziz. He's tall and lanky and he sits hunched over to fit in the narrow space allotted to him. This is his second attempt at crossing the Strait of Gibraltar. He told Murad that he'd haggled with Rahal over the price of the trip, argued that, as a repeat customer, he should get a deal. Murad tried to bargain, too, but in the end he still had to borrow almost

---

4. **harraga**: Moroccan slang term for people fleeing to Spain.

20,000 dirhams from one of his uncles, and the loan is on his mind again. He'll pay his uncle back as soon as he can get a job.

Aziz asks for a sip of water. Murad hands over his bottle of
80 Sidi Harazem and watches him take a swig. When he gets the bottle back, he offers the last bit to Faten, but she shakes her head. Murad was told he should keep his body hydrated, so he's been drinking water all day. He feels a sudden urge to urinate and leans forward to contain it.

Next to Aziz is a middle-aged man with greasy hair and a large scar across his cheek, like Al Pacino in *Scarface*. **B** He wears jeans and a short-sleeved shirt. Murad heard him tell someone that he was a tennis instructor. His arms are muscular, his biceps bulging, but the energy he exudes is rough, like that of
90 a man used to trouble with the law. Murad notices that Scarface has been staring at the little girl sitting next to him. She seems to be about ten years old, but the expression on her face is that of an older child. Her eyes, shiny under the moonlight, take up most of her face. Scarface asks her name. "Mouna," she says. He reaches into his pocket and offers her chewing gum, but the girl quickly shakes her head.

Her mother, Halima, asked Murad the time before they got on the boat, as though she had a schedule to keep. She gives Scarface a dark, forbidding look, wraps one arm around her
100 daughter and the other around her two boys, seated to her right. Halima's gaze is direct, not shifty like Faten's. She has an aura of quiet determination about her, and it stirs feelings of respect in Murad, even though he thinks her irresponsible, or at the very least foolish, for risking her children's lives on a trip like this.

On Aziz's right is a slender African woman, her corn-rows tied in a loose ponytail. While they were waiting on the beach to depart, she peeled an orange and offered Murad half. She said she was Guinean. She cradles her body with her arms and rocks gently back and forth. Rahal barks at her to stop. She looks up,
110 tries to stay immobile, and then throws up on Faten's boots. Faten cries out at the sight of her sullied shoes.

B QUICK CHECK

Scarface is a 1983 movie about a Cuban man who comes to the United States and becomes a violent gangster. Al Pacino is the name of the actor who plays the main character. Why does Murad compare the man in the boat to Al Pacino?

_____

_____

_____

_____

_____

"Shut up," Rahal snaps.

The Guinean woman whispers an apology in French. Faten waves her hand, says that it's okay, says she understands. Soon the little boat reeks of vomit. Murad tucks his nose inside his turtleneck. It smells of soap and mint and it keeps out the stench, but within minutes the putrid smell penetrates the shield anyway. Now Halima sits up and exhales loudly, her children still huddling next to her. Rahal glares at her, tells her to hunch down to keep the boat balanced.

"Leave her alone," Murad says.

Halima turns to him and smiles for the first time. He wonders what her plans are, whether she's meeting a husband or a brother there or if she'll end up cleaning houses or working in the fields. He thinks about some of the illegals who, instead of going on a boat, try to sneak in on vegetable trucks headed from Morocco to Spain. Last year the Guardia Civil[5] intercepted a tomato truck in Algeciras and found the bodies of three illegals, dead from asphyxiation[6], lying on the crates. **A** At least on a boat there is no chance of that happening. He tries to think of something else, something to chase away the memory of the picture he saw in the paper.

The outboard motor idles. In the sudden silence, everyone turns to look at Rahal, collectively holding their breath. He pulls the starter cable a few times, but nothing happens.

"What's wrong?" Faten asks, her voice laden with anxiety.

Rahal doesn't answer.

"Try again," Halima says.

Rahal yanks at the cable.

"This trip is cursed," Faten whispers. Everyone hears her.

Rahal bangs the motor with his hand. Faten recites a verse from the second sura of the Qur'an: "'God, there is no God but Him, the Alive, the Eternal. **B** Neither slumber nor sleep overtaketh Him—'"

---

5. **Guardia Civil**: Spanish police force with both military and civilian functions.
6. **asphyxiation** (AS FIHK SEE AY SHUHN): lack of air.

"Quiet," Scarface yells. "We need some quiet to think." Looking at the captain, he asks, "Is it the spark plug?"

"I don't know. I don't think so," says Rahal.

Faten continues to pray, this time more quietly, her lips moving fast. "'Unto Him belongeth all that is in the heavens and the earth . . .'"

Rahal yanks at the cable again.

Aziz calls out, "Wait, let me see." He gets on all fours, over the vomit, and moves slowly to keep the boat stable.

Faten starts crying, a long and drawn-out whine. All eyes are on her. Her hysteria is contagious, and Murad can hear someone sniffling at the other end of the boat.

"What are you crying for?" Scarface asks, leaning forward to look at her face.

"I'm afraid," she whimpers.

"Baraka!" he orders.

"Leave her be," Halima says, still holding her children close.

"Why did she come if she can't handle it?" he yells, pointing at Faten.

Murad pulls his shirt down from his face. "Who the hell do you think you are?" He's the first to be surprised by his anger. He is tense and ready for an argument.

"And who are you?" Scarface says. "Her protector?"

A cargo ship blows its horn, startling everyone. It glides in the distance, lights blinking.

"Stop it," Rahal yells. "Someone will hear us!" **C**

Aziz examines the motor, pulls at the hose that connects it to the tank. "There's a gap here," he tells Rahal, and he points

150

160

170

C (**VOCABULARY**)

Academic Vocabulary

An *external conflict* occurs when a character opposes nature, another person, or a group. Describe one external conflict that occurs on this page.

_____

_____

_____

_____

_____

_____

_____

to the connector. "Do you have some tape?" Rahal opens his supplies box and takes out a roll of duct tape. Aziz quickly wraps some around the hose. The captain pulls the cable once, twice. Finally the motor wheezes painfully and the boat starts moving.

"Praise be to God," Faten says, ignoring Scarface's glares.

The crying stops and a grim peace falls on the boat.

180   Tarifa is about 250 meters away now. It'll only take another few minutes. The Guinean woman throws a piece of paper overboard. Murad figures it's her ID. She'll probably pretend she's from Sierra Leone so she can get political asylum. He shakes his head. No such luck for him.

The water is still calm, but Murad knows better than to trust the Mediterranean. He's known the sea all his life and he knows how hard it can pull. Once, when he was ten years old, he went mussel picking with his father at the beach in Al Hoceima. As they were working away, Murad saw a dark, beautiful bed of mussels hanging from their beards inside a hollow rock. He low-
190   ered himself in and was busy pulling at them when a wave filled the grotto and flushed him out. His father grabbed Murad, still holding the bucket, out of the water. Later, Murad's father would tell his friends at the café an adorned version of this story, which would be added to his repertoire of family tales that he narrated on demand. A

"Everyone out of the boat now!" Rahal shouts. You have to swim the rest of the way."

Aziz immediately rolls out into the water and starts swimming.

200   Like the other passengers, Murad looks on, stunned. They expected to be taken all the way to the shore, where they could easily disperse and then hide. The idea of having to swim the rest of the way is intolerable, especially for those who are not natives of Tangier and accustomed to its waters.

Halima raises a hand at Rahal. "You thief! We paid you to take us to the coast."

Rahal says, "You want to get us all arrested as harraga? Get out of the boat if you want to get there. It's not that far. I'm turning back."

210   Someone makes an abrupt movement to reason with Rahal, to force him to go all the way to the shore, but the Zodiac loses balance and then it's too late. Murad is in the water now. His clothes are instantly wet, and the shock of the cold water all over his body makes his heart go still for a moment. He bobs, gasps for air, realizes that there's nothing left to do but swim. So he wills his limbs, heavy with the weight of his clothes, to move.

    Around him, people are slowly scattering, led by the cross-currents. **B** Rahal struggles to right his boat and someone, Murad can't quite tell who, is hanging on to the side. He hears
220 howls and screams, sees a few people swimming in earnest. Aziz, who was first to get out of the boat, is already far ahead of the others, going west. Murad starts swimming toward the coast, afraid he might be pulled away by the water. From behind, he hears someone call out. He turns and holds his hand out to Faten. She grabs it and the next second she is holding both his shoulders. He tries to pull away, but her grip tightens.

    "Use one hand to move," he yells.

    Her eyes open wider but her hands do not move. He forces one of her hands off him and manages to make a few strokes. Her
230 body is heavy against his. Each time they bob in the water, she holds on tighter. There is water in his ears now and her cries are not as loud. He tries to loosen her grip but she won't let go. He yells out. Still she holds on. The next time they bob, water enters his nose and it makes him cough. They'll never make it if she doesn't loosen her grip and help him. He pushes her away. Free at last, he moves quickly out of her reach. "Beat the water with your arms," he yells. She thrashes wildly. "Slower," he tells her, but he can see that it is hopeless, she can't swim. A sob forms in his throat. If only he had a stick or a buoy that he could hand her so
240 that he could pull her without risking that they both drown. He's already drifting away from her, but he keeps calling out, telling

B (LANGUAGE COACH)

A **synonym** is a word or phrase with the same or almost the same meaning as another word. Name one synonym for *scattering*.

_____

A **VOCABULARY**

Academic Vocabulary

Describe Murad's *internal conflict*, or the conflict that occurs within his own mind, in this paragraph. What are the opposing forces in his mind?

_____

_____

_____

_____

_____

_____

_____

_____

B **LITERARY FOCUS**

The **mood** of the story has changed. What words tell you what the new mood is?

_____

_____

_____

_____

_____

_____

her to calm down and start swimming. His fingers and toes have gone numb, and he has to start swimming or he'll freeze to death. He faces the coast. He closes his eyes, but the image of Faten is waiting for him behind the lids. **A** Eyes open again, he tries to focus on the motion of his limbs.

There is a strange quietness in the air. He swims until he feels the sand against his feet. He tries to control his breathing, the beating of his heart in his ears. He lies on the beach, the
250 water licking his shoes. The sun is rising, painting the sand and the buildings far ahead a golden shade of orange. With a sigh, Murad relieves his bladder. The sand around him warms up but cools again in seconds. He rests there for a little while, then pushes himself to his knees. **B**

He stands, legs shaking. He turns around and scans the dark waters, looking for Faten. He can see a few forms swimming, struggling, but it's hard to tell who is who. Aziz is nowhere to be seen, but the Guinean woman is getting out of the water a few meters away.

260 In the distance, a dog barks.

Murad knows he doesn't have much time before the Guardia Civil come after them. He takes a few steps and drops to his knees on the sand, which feels warmer than the water.

With a trembling hand, he opens a side pocket of his cargos and extracts a plastic bag. In it is a mobile phone, with a Spanish SIM card.[7] He calls Rubio, the Spaniard who will drive him north to Catalonia.

"Soy Murad. El amigo de Rahal."

"Espéreme por la caña de azucar."

270 "Bien."[8]

He takes a few steps forward, but he doesn't see the sugar cane Rubio mentioned. He continues walking anyway. A hotel appears on the horizon. Another dog barks, and the sound soon turns into a howl. He walks toward it and spots the sugar cane. A small path appears on the left side and he sits at its end. He takes

---

7. **SIM Card:** a device used in cellular phones.
8. **"Soy Murad . . . Bien":** "I am Murad. Rahal's friend." "Wait for me by the sugar cane." "Okay."

his shoes off, curls his frigid toes in the wet socks and massages them. Replacing his shoes, he lies back and takes a deep breath of relief. He can't believe his luck. He made it.

It will be all right now. He comforts himself with the familiar fantasy that sustained him back home, all those nights when he couldn't fall asleep, worrying about how he would pay rent or feed his mother and brothers. He imagines the office where he'll be working; he can see his fingers moving quickly and precisely over his keyboard; he can hear his phone ringing. He pictures himself going home to a modern, well-furnished apartment, his wife greeting him, the TV in the background. **C**

A light shines on him. Rubio is fast. No wonder it cost so much to hire him. Murad sits up. The light is away from his eyes only a moment, but it is long enough to see the dog, a German shepherd, and the infinitely more menacing form holding the leash.

The officer from the Guardia Civil wears fatigues, and a black beret cocked over his shaved head. His name tag reads Martinez. He sits inside the van with Murad and the other illegals, the dog at his feet. **D** Murad looks at himself: his wet shoes, his dirty pants stuck against his legs, the bluish skin under his nails. He keeps his teeth clenched to stop himself from shivering beneath the blanket the officer gave him. It's only fourteen kilometers, he thinks. If they hadn't been forced into the water, if he'd swum faster, if he'd gone west instead of east, he would have made it.

When he climbs down from the van, Murad notices a wooded area up the hill just a few meters away, and beyond it, a road. The guards are busy helping a woman who seems to have collapsed from the cold. Murad takes off, running as fast as he can. Behind him, he hears a whistle and the sound of boots, but he continues running, through the trees, his feet barely touching the crackled ground. When he gets closer to the road, he sees it is a four-lane highway, with cars whizzing by. It makes him pause. Martinez grabs him by the shirt. **E**

280

290

300

310

C QUICK CHECK

What does Murad hope his new life will be like in Spain?

_____

_____

_____

_____

D QUICK CHECK

At first, what does Murad think the light is? What does the light turn out to be?

_____

_____

_____

_____

_____

E VOCABULARY

Academic Vocabulary

The _climax_ is the most exciting part of the story. The _resolution_ is the closing of the story. Is this the climax or the resolution of the story? How do you know?

_____

_____

_____

_____

A VOCABULARY

Selection Vocabulary

Destiny means "what becomes of people in the end." What does Murad think Aziz's destiny is?

_____

_____

_____

_____

_____

B LITERARY FOCUS

When the **setting** of the story changes to the Guardia Civil post, how does the **mood** of the story change as well?

_____

_____

_____

_____

_____

_____

_____

The clock on the wall at the Guardia Civil post shows six in the morning. Murad sits on a metal chair, handcuffed. There are men and women, all wrapped in blankets like him, huddled close together to stay warm. He doesn't recognize many of them; most came on other boats. Scarface sits alone, smoking a cigarette, one leg resting on the other, one shoe missing. There is no sign of Aziz. He must have made it. Just to be sure, he asks the Guinean woman a few seats down from him. "I haven't seen him," she says.

Lucky Aziz. **A** Murad curses his own luck. If he'd landed
320 just a hundred meters west, away from the houses and the hotel, he might have been able to escape. His stomach growls. He swallows hard. How will he be able to show his face again in Tangier? **B** He stands up and hobbles to the dusty window. He sees Faten outside, her head bare, in a line with some of the other boatmates, waiting for the doctors, who wear surgical masks on their faces, to examine them. A wave of relief washes over him, and he gesticulates as best as he can with his handcuffs, calling her name. She can't hear him, but eventually she looks up, sees him, then looks away.

330 A woman in a dark business suit arrives, her high heels clicking on the tiled floor "*Soy sus abogada*,"[9] she says, standing before them. She tells them they are here illegally and that they must sign the paper that the Guardia Civil are going to give them. While everyone takes turns at signing, the woman leans against the counter to talk to one of the officers. She raises one of her legs behind her as she talks, like a little girl. The officer says something in a flirtatious tone, and she throws her head back and laughs.

Murad puts in a false name even though it won't matter. He
340 is taken to the holding station, the sand from the beach still stuck on his pants. On his way there, he sees a body bag on the ground. A sour taste invades his mouth. He swallows but can't contain it. He doubles over and the officer lets go of him. Murad stumbles to the side of the building and vomits. It could have been him

---

9. **"Soy sus abogada"**: "I am your lawyer."

in that body bag; it could have been Faten. Maybe it was Aziz or Halima.

     The guard takes him to a moldy cell already occupied by two other prisoners, one of whom is asleep on the mattress. Murad sits on the floor and looks up through the window at the

350   patch of blue sky. Seagulls flutter from the side of the building and fly away in formation, and for a moment he envies them their freedom. But tomorrow the police will send him back to Tangier. His future there stands before him, unalterable, despite his efforts, despite the risk he took and the price he paid. He will have to return to the same old apartment, to live off his mother and sister, without any prospects or opportunity. He thinks of Aziz, probably already on a truck headed to Catalonia, and he wonders—if Aziz can make it, why not him? At least now he knows what to expect. It will be hard to convince his mother,

360   but in the end he knows he will prevail on her to sell her gold bracelets. If she sells all seven of them, it will pay for another trip. And next time, he'll make it. **C**

C **VOCABULARY**

Academic Vocabulary
The *resolution* is how the story closes, or ends. What is the resolution of the story?

_____

_____

_____

_____

_____

_____

_____

_____

The Trip

USE A CONCEPT WEB

DIRECTIONS: In the concept web below, write the name of a different character from "The Trip" in each bubble. Then, write 1–3 words or sentences from the text that help you **visualize** each character.

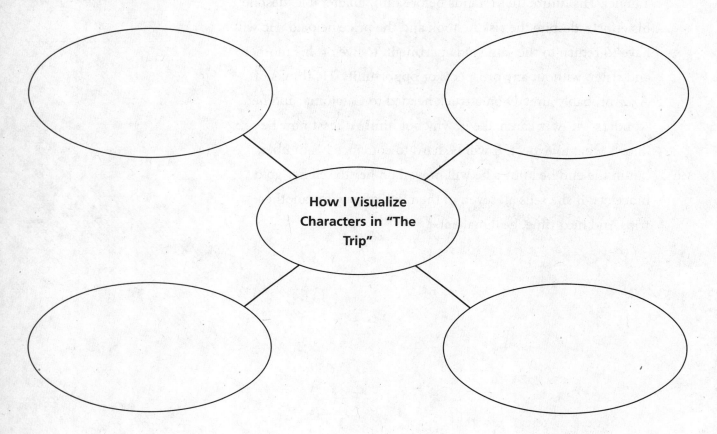

How I Visualize Characters in "The Trip"

Applying Your Skills

The Trip

VOCABULARY DEVELOPMENT

DIRECTIONS: Complete the paragraph with vocabulary words from the Word Box. One word will not be used.

Word Box

- pondered
- destinies
- exudes
- putrid
- prospects

At the beginning of the story, Murad (1) _____ a feeling of anxiety and fear. He had (2) _____ his decision to travel from Morocco to Spain. Murad hopes that his (3) _____ in Spain will be good, and that he will be able to find work. The (4) _____ of Murad and Aziz are different. Murad is caught by the Guardia Civil, and he believes that Aziz made it to Spain safely.

LITERARY FOCUS: SETTING AND MOOD

DIRECTIONS: Use the chart below to analyze the **mood** of the story. In the left column, list two settings from the story. In the middle column, describe the mood of each setting. In the right column, write language from the **text** that describes the mood.

Setting	Mood	Language that describes mood

READING FOCUS: VISUALIZING

DIRECTIONS: Use the chart below to help you **visualize**. List two of the settings from the story in the left column. In the right column, use descriptive language from the story to describe each setting.

Setting	Descriptive Language

Literary Skills
Understand the relationship between setting and mood.

Reading Skills
Visualize what the writer is describing.

from In the Shadow of Man

by Jane Goodall

INFORMATIONAL TEXT FOCUS: MAIN IDEA AND SUPPORTING DETAILS

The **main idea** is the central idea, or the most important information, of a piece of writing. Entire articles, books, and even the paragraphs within them can all have a main idea. In a paragraph, a single topic sentence may state the main idea clearly and simply. However, sometimes you have to look at the **supporting details**—facts, examples, quotes, anecdotes—and decide what the main idea is.

Tips for Finding the Main Idea of an Article

- Read the article's title; it will often suggest the main idea.
- Skim the article's introduction to see if it states the main idea.
- Read the last paragraph of the article to see if the writer has summarized the main idea there.

SELECTION VOCABULARY

devoid (DIH VOYD) *adj.:* completely missing; lacking.
One chimpanzee was devoid of shoulder hair.

belligerent (BUH LIHJ UHR UHNT) *adj.:* warlike; fond of fighting.
One of the chimpanzees was belligerent and often threatened Goodall.

WORD STUDY

DIRECTIONS: Use a thesaurus to find synonyms for the vocabulary words above. When you come to a vocabulary word in the story, see which synonyms could replace the word. On the lines below, rewrite the sentence in which the word appears using one of the synonyms you found.

_____

_____

_____

_____

_____

SKILLS FOCUS

Informational Text Skills
Find the main idea and supporting details in an article.

from IN THE SHADOW OF MAN

by Jane Goodall

> **BACKGROUND**
> Jane Goodall is known for her detailed observations of chimpanzees in their natural environment. Between 1960 and 1975, Goodall observed chimpanzee behavior in the Gombe Stream Game Reserve in Tanzania. Her research corrected several misunderstandings about chimpanzees. As this selection opens, Goodall has established a camp and is about to observe the chimpanzees in their natural habitat.

As the weeks went by the chimpanzees became less and less afraid. Quite often when I was on one of my food-collecting expeditions I came across chimpanzees unexpectedly, and after a time I found that some of them would tolerate my presence provided they were in fairly thick forest and I sat still and did not try to move closer than sixty to eighty yards. And so, during my second month of watching from the Peak, when I saw a group settle down to feed, I sometimes moved closer and was thus able to make more detailed observations. **A**

A **READING FOCUS**

Underline the sentence that contains the **main idea** of the first paragraph.

© Michael Nichols/National Geographic Society

From "First Observations" from *In the Shadow of Man* by Jane Goodall. Copyright © 1971 by Hugo and Jane van Lawick-Goodall. All rights reserved. Reproduced by permission of **Houghton Mifflin Company** and electronic format by permission of **Soko Publications c/o G. T. E. Parsons, Esquire.**

A (QUICK CHECK)

Why does Goodall name the animals rather than number them?

_____

_____

_____

_____

_____

_____

B (VOCABULARY)

Selection Vocabulary

Underline the words that give clues to the meaning of the word *devoid*. Then write two words or phrases that mean the opposite of *devoid of*.

_____

_____

_____

_____

C (LANGUAGE COACH)

Belligerent is a **derivation** of the Latin word *belliger*, meaning "waging war." How does this relate to Mr. McGregor's behavior?

_____

_____

_____

_____

10   It was at this time that I began to recognize a number of different individuals. As soon as I was sure of knowing a chimpanzee if I saw it again, I named it. Some scientists feel that animals should be labeled by numbers—that to name them is anthropomorphic[1]—but I have always been interested in the *differences* between individuals, and a name is not only more individual than a number but also far easier to remember. **A** Most names were simply those which, for some reason or other, seemed to suit the individuals to whom I attached them. A few chimps were named because some facial expression or mannerism reminded 20   me of human acquaintances.

The easiest individual to recognize was Mr. McGregor. The crown of his head, his neck, and his shoulders were almost entirely devoid of hair, but a slight frill remained around his head rather like a monk's tonsure.[2] **B** He was an old male—perhaps between thirty and forty years of age (chimpanzees in captivity can live more than fifty years). During the early months of my acquaintance with him, Mr. McGregor was somewhat belligerent. If I accidentally came across him at close quarters he would threaten me with an upward and backward jerk of his head 30   and a shaking of branches before climbing down and vanishing from my sight. **C** He reminded me, for some reason, of Beatrix Potter's old gardener in *The Tale of Peter Rabbit*.

Ancient Flo with her deformed, bulbous nose and ragged ears was equally easy to recognize. Her youngest offspring at that time were two-year-old Fifi, who still rode everywhere on her mother's back, and her juvenile son, Figan, who was always to be seen wandering around with his mother and little sister. He was then about seven years old; it was approximately a year before he would attain puberty. Flo often traveled with another old mother, 40   Olly. Olly's long face was also distinctive; the fluff of hair on the back of her head—though no other feature—reminded me of my aunt, Olwen. Olly, like Flo, was accompanied by two children, a

---

1. **anthropomorphic** (AN THRUH PUH MAWR FIHK): giving human qualities to non-human things.
2. **tonsure** (TAWN SHUHR): top of a man's head left bare by shaving. Certain orders of monks have a tonsure.

daughter younger than Fifi, and an adolescent son about a year older than Figan.

Then there was William, who, I am certain, must have been Olly's blood brother. I never saw any special signs of friendship between them, but their faces were amazingly alike. They both had long upper lips that wobbled when they suddenly turned their heads. William had the added distinctions of several thin,

50 deeply etched scar marks running down his upper lip from his nose. **D**

Two of the other chimpanzees I knew well by sight at that time were David Graybeard and Goliath. Like David and Goliath in the Bible, these two individuals were closely associated in my mind because they were very often together. Goliath, even in those days of his prime, was not a giant, but he had a splendid physique and the springy movements of an athlete. **E** He probably weighed about one hundred pounds. David Graybeard was less afraid of me from the start than were any

60 of the other chimps. I was always pleased when I picked out his handsome face and well-marked silvery beard in a chimpanzee group, for with David to calm the others, I had a better chance of approaching to observe them more closely.

Before the end of my trial period in the field I made two really exciting discoveries—discoveries that made the previous months of frustration well worth while. And for both of them I had David Graybeard to thank.

One day I arrived on the Peak and found a small group of chimps just below me in the upper branches of a thick tree. As

70 I watched I saw that one of them was holding a pink-looking object from which he was, from time to time, pulling pieces with his teeth. There was a female and a youngster and they were both reaching out toward the male, their hands actually touching his mouth. Presently the female picked up a piece of the pink thing and put it to her mouth: it was at this moment that I realized the chimps were eating meat. **F**

After each bite of meat the male picked off some leaves with his lips and chewed them with the flesh. Often, when he

---

D **READING FOCUS**

Which sentence best supports the **main idea** that William and Olly must be blood brothers? Underline it in the text.

E **VOCABULARY**

Word Study

Look up the word *prime* in the dictionary. Which of its meanings is used in this sentence?

_____

_____

_____

F **READING FOCUS**

What is the **main idea** of this paragraph? What **supporting details** show you this?

_____

_____

_____

_____

_____

_____

_____

from **In the Shadow of Man**   **43**

80 had chewed for several minutes on this leafy wad, he spat out the remains into the waiting hands of the female. Suddenly he dropped a small piece of meat, and in a flash the youngster swung after it to the ground. Even as he reached to pick it up the undergrowth exploded and a little bushpig charged toward him. Screaming, the juvenile leaped back into the tree. The pig remained in the open, snorting and moving backward and forward. Soon I made out the shapes of three small striped piglets. Obviously the chimps were eating a baby pig. The size was right and later, when I realized that the male was David Graybeard, I moved closer and saw that he was indeed eating piglet.

90   For three hours I watched the chimps feeding. David occasionally let the female bite pieces from the carcass and once he actually detached a small piece of flesh and placed it in her outstretched hand. When he finally climbed down there was still meat left on the carcass; he carried it away in one hand, followed by the others.

    Of course I was not sure, then, that David Graybeard had caught the pig for himself, but even so, it was tremendously exciting to know that these chimpanzees actually ate meat. Previously scientists had believed that although these apes might occasion-

100 ally supplement their diet with a few insects or small rodents and the like they were primarily vegetarians and fruit eaters. No one had suspected that they might hunt larger mammals. A

    It was within two weeks of this observation that I saw something that excited me even more. By then it was October and the short rains had begun. The blackened slopes were softened by feathery new grass shoots and in some places the ground was carpeted by a variety of flowers. The Chimpanzees' Spring, I called it. I had had a frustrating morning, tramping up and down three valleys with never a sign or sound of a chimpanzee.

110 Hauling myself up the steep slope of Mlinda Valley I headed for the Peak, not only weary but soaking wet from crawling through dense undergrowth. Suddenly I stopped, for I saw a slight movement in the long grass about sixty yards away. Quickly focusing my binoculars I saw that it was a single chimpanzee,

and just then he turned in my direction. I recognized David Graybeard.

Cautiously I moved around so that I could see what he was doing. He was squatting beside the red earth mound of a termite nest, and as I watched I saw him carefully push a long grass stem down into a hole in the mound. After a moment he withdrew it and picked something from the end with his mouth. I was too far away to make out what he was eating, but it was obvious that he was actually using a grass stem as a tool.

I knew that on two occasions casual observers in West Africa had seen chimpanzees using objects as tools: one had broken open palm-nut kernels by using a rock as a hammer and a group of chimps had been observed pushing sticks into an underground bee's nest and licking off the honey. **B** Somehow I had never dreamed of seeing anything so exciting myself.

120

© Karl Ammann/Corbis

B READING FOCUS

Underline the **supporting details** in this paragraph for the main idea that others had previously observed chimpanzees using tools.

A **VOCABULARY**

Word Study

Underline the clues in this sentence that hint at the definition of the word *frond*. Then write the definition of the word on the lines below.

_____

_____

_____

_____

_____

130 For an hour David feasted at the termite mound and then he wandered slowly away. When I was sure he had gone I went over to examine the mound. I found a few crushed insects strewn about, and a swarm of worker termites sealing the entrances of the nest passages into which David had obviously been poking his stems. I picked up one of his discarded tools and carefully pushed it into a hole myself. Immediately I felt the pull of several termites as they seized the grass, and when I pulled it out there were a number of worker termites and a few soldiers, with big red heads, clinging on with their mandibles.[3] There they remained, sticking
140 out at right angles to the stem with their legs waving in the air.

Before I left I trampled down some of the tall dry grass and constructed a rough hide—just a few palm fronds leaned up against the low branch of a tree and tied together at the top. Ⓐ I planned to wait there the next day. But it was another week before I was able to watch a chimpanzee "fishing" for termites again. Twice chimps arrived, but each time they saw me and moved off immediately. Once a swarm of fertile winged termites—the princes and princesses, as they are called—flew off on their nuptial flight, their huge white wings fluttering frantically
150 as they carried the insects higher and higher. Later I realized that it is at this time of year, during the short rains, when the worker termites extend the passages of the nest to the surface preparing for these emigrations. Several such swarms emerge between October and January. It is principally during these months that the chimpanzees feed on termites.

On the eighth day of my watch David Graybeard arrived again, together with Goliath, and the pair worked there for two hours. I could see much better: I observed how they scratched open the sealed-over passage entrances with a thumb or forefin-
160 ger. I watched how they bit ends off their tools when they became bent, or used the other end, or discarded them in favor of new ones. Goliath once moved at least fifteen yards from the heap to select a firm-looking piece of vine, and both males often picked

---

3. **mandibles** (MAN DUH BUHLS): parts of the mouth that bite or hold food.

three or four stems while they were collecting tools, and put the spares beside them on the ground until they wanted them.

Most exciting of all, on several occasions they picked small leafy twigs and prepared them for use by stripping off the leaves. This was the first recorded example of a wild animal not merely *using* an object as a tool, but actually modifying an object and thus showing the crude beginnings of tool*making*.

Previously man had been regarded as the only tool-making animal. Indeed, one of the clauses commonly accepted in the definition of man was that he was a creature who "made tools to a regular and set pattern." The chimpanzees, obviously, had not made tools to any set pattern. Nevertheless, my early observations of their primitive toolmaking abilities convinced a number of scientists that it was necessary to redefine man in a more complex manner than before. Or else, as Louis Leakey put it, we should by definition have to accept the chimpanzee as Man. **B**

I sent telegrams to Louis about both of my new observations—the meat-eating and the toolmaking—and he was of course wildly enthusiastic. In fact, I believe that the news was helpful to him in his efforts to find further financial support for my work. It was not long afterward when he wrote to tell me that the National Geographic Society in the United States had agreed to grant funds for another year's research. **C**

170

180

B **READING FOCUS**

What do you think is the **main idea** of the entire selection? Does the title support your main idea? Why or why not?

_____

_____

_____

_____

_____

_____

_____

_____

_____

C **READING FOCUS**

Does the final paragraph of the text summarize the **main idea** of the selection? Explain your answer.

_____

_____

_____

_____

_____

_____

_____

Skills Practice

from In the Shadow of Man

USE A CONCEPT MAP

A concept map can help you find the supporting details and main idea of a paragraph, an article, or a book. Choose a long paragraph from *In the Shadow of Man*. In the outside ovals, write down supporting details from the paragraph and the line numbers for the sentences with those details. Then, decide on the main idea of the paragraph from these details and write it in the center oval.

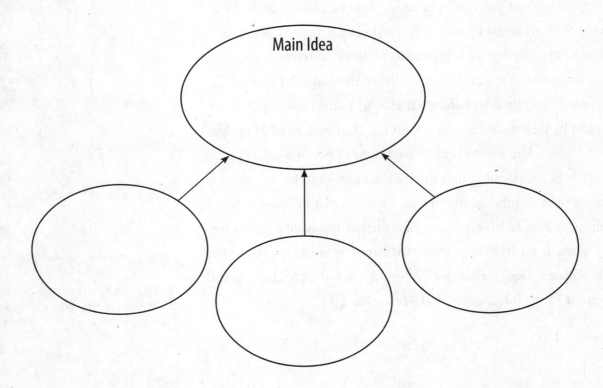

Applying Your Skills

from In the Shadow of Man

VOCABULARY DEVELOPMENT

Use the correct word from the Word Box to fill in the blanks in the following sentences.

Word Box

devoid

belligerent

1. The lion was very _____; it ran at the trainer and attempted to tackle him.

2. The grouchy man was totally _____ of any sense of humor.

INFORMATIONAL TEXT FOCUS: MAIN IDEA AND SUPPORTING DETAILS

Fill in the blank boxes in the chart with **main ideas** and **supporting details** you found in the story.

Main Idea	Supporting Detail
Chimpanzees are much more like humans than previously thought.	
	The chimpanzees pulled at the pink flesh of the pig and put it in each others' mouths.
Chimpanzees use and make their own tools.	
	The National Geographic Society granted Goodall funds for another year of research.

Skills Review

Collection 1

VOCABULARY REVIEW

DIRECTIONS: Complete the story below by filling in the blanks with the vocabulary words from the Word Box. Each word may only be used once. Not all the words will be used.

Word Box

aspects
belligerent
credible
destinies
devoid
evaluation
exhalation
exudes
imperceptibly
irrelevantly
pondered
projection
prospects
putrid
rebounded
tension

I frowned and pushed away the _____ glass of milk in front of me. It had gone sour. I was happy that my sister had been kind enough to make breakfast for me, but somehow everything had just gone wrong. After thinking about it, my _____ of the situation was that my sister was completely _____ of any ability to make a good breakfast. She was a bad cook. I _____ for a long time how a person could burn eggs so badly. I thought her cooking skills might have _____ when she handed me a stack of beautiful chocolate chip pancakes, but I soon found out that a few raisins and a dead fly had _____ made their way into the pancakes.

The _____ of sausage and bacon in the near future made me afraid of what else might happen, so I shouted at my sister, "Stop! No more!"

My sister had worked hard on breakfast, so this caused a lot of _____ between us. She couldn't figure out why I was being _____ towards her. I explained about the milk, eggs, and pancakes, and I told her that she had made a terrible breakfast.

"I'm sorry," she said. "But, I'll make it up to you by cooking dinner!"

Collection 1

LANGUAGE COACH

DIRECTIONS: Remember that a **prefix** is a letter or group of letters added to the beginning of a word that changes the word's meaning. Some of the words below have prefixes, while others do not. Circle any prefixes found in the words below. To help you decide if a word contains a prefix, think about what each word would look like without a prefix. The word *under*, for example, appears to have the prefix *un–*, but if we take away *un–* we are left with *der*, which is not a real English word. Use a dictionary to check your answers.

immature	unchanged	illogical
illegal	immense	preview
realistic	pressure	atypical
unwanted	retell	agile

WRITING LANGUAGE SKILLS

DIRECTIONS: The goal of a summary is to give readers an accurate but brief view of a piece of writing they may not have read. On a separate sheet of paper, write a one- or two-paragraph summary of either "Contents of the Dead Man's Pocket," "The Trip," or the selection from "In the Shadow of Man." Identify the main idea of the selection and state that idea in a sentence. Add additional sentences to cover the major points that the writer uses to support his or her idea.

Character

Quilting Time (1986) by Romare Bearden (1914–1988).
Collection of the Detroit Institute of the Arts.
Mosaic on Plywood/Bridgeman Art Library

Literary and Academic Vocabulary for Collection 2

acquire (UH KWYR) *v.:* get or gain.
> The main character will acquire a new knowledge of himself by the end of the story.

attitude (AT UH TOOD) *n.:* a state of mind of feeling about something.
> She had a positive attitude towards work.

reveal (RIH VEEL) *v.:* make known, show
> The way a person acts in a crisis may reveal a lot about his or her character.

tradition (TRUH DIHSH UHN) *n.:* handing down of beliefs, opinions, customs, and stories.
> The tradition of passing down quilts from mother to daughter resulted in a beautiful family collection.

traits (TRAYTS) *n.:* special qualities.
> Having a thick beard and having a loud voice are traits my father and I share.

characterization (KAR UHK TUHR UH ZAY SHUHN) *n.:* the way a writer reveals character.
> The characterization of Bilbo is very realistic.

motivations (MOH TIH VAY SHUHNZ) *n.:* the reasons for a character's behavior.
> Lucca's motivation for working is that she needs money to buy a piano.

protagonist (PROH TAG UH NIHST) *n.:* the character who drives the action.
> The main character of a story is the protagonist.

antagonist (AN TAG UH NIHST) *n.:* the character who prevents the protagonist from getting what he or she wants.
> The antagonist tried to prevent her from reaching her goal.

Everyday Use
For Your Grandmama

by Alice Walker

LITERARY FOCUS: CHARACTER TRAITS

Character **traits** are the special qualities unique to a person. Character traits include a person's features, beliefs, habits, and personality quirks. In literature, you learn of characters' traits by paying attention to the details given by the story's narrator and other characters. Another way to learn of a character's traits is through his or her actions. A character's traits make him or her act in ways that affect the development of a story. In "Everyday Use," look for details that help you determine the character traits of a mother and her two daughters.

READING FOCUS: MAKING INFERENCES ABOUT CHARACTERS

In literature, as in real life, we are not always told directly about the people we meet. Instead, we observe their actions and their appearance. We listen to what they say and to what others say about them. From these details we make **inferences**—intelligent guesses—about the personalities, thoughts, and backgrounds of the people we meet in real life and about the characters we meet in stories.

Use the skill As you read "Everyday Use," take note of what the characters say and do. Use a chart like this one to keep track of the details:

Character	Story Detail

SKILLS FOCUS

Literary Skills
Understand character traits.

Reading Skills
Make inferences about characters.

Vocabulary Development

Everyday Use
For Your Grandmama

SELECTION VOCABULARY

sidle (SY DUHL) *v.:* move in a slow, sideways manner.
> *Maggie will sidle through the doorway as though she doesn't want to be seen.*

furtive (FUR TIHV) *adj.:* secretive; trying not to be seen.
> *Dee likes to make a big entrance, but Maggie is furtive and shy.*

cowering (KOW UHR IHNG) *v.* used as *adj.:* crouching or hiding in shame or fear.
> *Maggie was cowering, barely visible, behind her mother.*

oppress (UH PREHS) *v.:* hold down unjustly; burden.
> *Dee believed society wanted to oppress her and her heritage.*

WORD STUDY

DIRECTIONS: Below are words or phrases that have meanings similar to each of the selection vocabulary words listed above. Write the correct vocabulary word next to the word or phrase that best matches its meaning. Some words will be used more than once.

1. hiding fearfully _____

2. discriminate against _____

3. shift to one side _____

4. trying not to be noticed _____

5. cautious _____

6. treat unfairly _____

EVERYDAY USE

For Your Grandmama

by Alice Walker

I will wait for her in the yard that Maggie and I made so clean and wavy yesterday afternoon. A yard like this is more comfortable than most people know. It is not just a yard. It is like an extended living room. When the hard clay is swept clean as a floor and the fine sand around the edges lined with tiny, irregular grooves, anyone can come and sit and look up into the elm tree and wait for the breezes that never come inside the house.

Maggie will be nervous until after her sister goes: She will stand hopelessly in corners, homely and ashamed of the burn
10 scars down her arms and legs, eyeing her sister with a mixture of envy and awe. She thinks her sister has held life always in the palm of one hand, that "no" is a word the world never learned to say to her. **A** You've no doubt seen those TV shows where the child who has "made it" is confronted, as a surprise, by her own mother and father, tottering in weakly from backstage. (A pleasant surprise, of course: What would they do if parent and child came on the show only to curse out and insult each other?) On TV mother and child embrace and smile into each other's faces. Sometimes the mother and father weep; the child
20 wraps them in her arms and leans across the table to tell how she would not have made it without their help. **B** I have seen these programs.

Sometimes I dream a dream in which Dee and I are suddenly brought together on a TV program of this sort. Out of a dark and soft-seated limousine I am ushered into a bright room filled with many people. There I meet a smiling, gray, sporty man like Johnny Carson who shakes my hand and tells me what a fine

"Everyday Use" from *In Love & Trouble: Stories of Black Women* by Alice Walker. Copyright © 1973 by Alice Walker. Reprinted by permission of **Harcourt, Inc. and electronic format by permission of Wendy Weil Agency, Inc.**

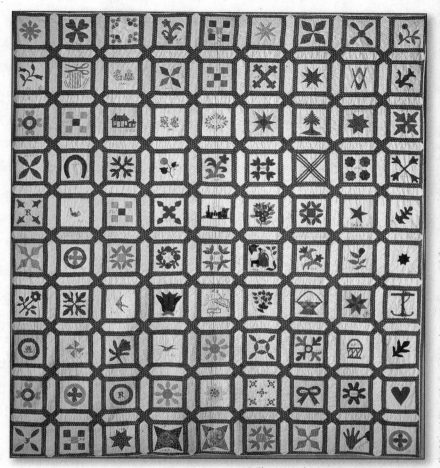

© The Newark Museum/Art Resource, NY

C **READING FOCUS**

In this paragraph, Mama tells about a dream in which Dee embraces her on TV. What **inference** can you make about what Mama might really want from Dee?

_____

_____

_____

_____

_____

_____

D **LITERARY FOCUS**

In this paragraph, there are many details that give you hints about Mama's **character traits.** Circle Mama's description of her appearance. Then, underline the details showing how Dee would like her mother to be.

girl I have. Then we are on the stage, and Dee is embracing me with tears in her eyes. She pins on my dress a large orchid, even

30 though she had told me once that she thinks orchids are tacky flowers. **C**

In real life I am a large, big-boned woman with rough, man-working hands. In the winter I wear flannel nightgowns to bed and overalls during the day. I can kill and clean a hog as mercilessly as a man. My fat keeps me hot in zero weather. I can work outside all day, breaking ice to get water for washing; I can eat pork liver cooked over the open fire minutes after it comes steaming from the hog. One winter I knocked a bull calf straight in the brain between the eyes with a sledgehammer and had the

40 meat hung up to chill before nightfall. But of course all this does not show on television. I am the way my daughter would want me to be: a hundred pounds lighter, my skin like an uncooked barley pancake. My hair glistens in the hot bright lights. Johnny Carson has much to do to keep up with my quick and witty tongue. **D**

But that is a mistake. I know even before I wake up. Who ever knew a Johnson with a quick tongue? Who can even imagine me looking a strange white man in the eye? It seems to me I have talked to them always with one foot raised in flight, with my head turned in whichever way is farthest from them.

50 Dee, though. She would always look anyone in the eye. Hesitation was no part of her nature. A

"How do I look, Mama?" Maggie says, showing just enough of her thin body enveloped in pink skirt and red blouse for me to know she's there, almost hidden by the door.

"Come out into the yard," I say.

Have you ever seen a lame animal, perhaps a dog run over by some careless person rich enough to own a car, sidle up to someone who is ignorant enough to be kind to him? That is the way my Maggie walks. She has been like this, chin on chest, eyes

60 on ground, feet in shuffle, ever since the fire that burned the other house to the ground. B

Dee is lighter than Maggie, with nicer hair and a fuller figure. She's a woman now, though sometimes I forget. How long ago was it that the other house burned? Ten, twelve years? Sometimes I can still hear the flames and feel Maggie's arms sticking to me, her hair smoking and her dress falling off her in little black papery flakes. Her eyes seemed stretched open, blazed open by the flames reflected in them. And Dee. I see her standing off under the sweet gum tree she used to dig gum out of, a look

70 of concentration on her face as she watched the last dingy gray board of the house fall in toward the red-hot brick chimney. C Why don't you do a dance around the ashes? I'd wanted to ask her. She had hated the house that much.

I used to think she hated Maggie, too. But that was before we raised the money, the church and me, to send her to Augusta[1] to school. She used to read to us without pity, forcing words, lies, other folks' habits, whole lives upon us two, sitting trapped and ignorant underneath her voice. She washed us in a river of make-believe, burned us with a lot of knowledge we didn't necessarily

---

1. **Augusta:** city in Georgia.

80　need to know. Pressed us to her with the serious ways she read, to shove us away at just the moment, like dimwits, we seemed about to understand. **D**

Dee wanted nice things. A yellow organdy dress to wear to her graduation from high school; black pumps to match a green suit she'd made from an old suit somebody gave me. She was determined to stare down any disaster in her efforts. Her eyelids would not flicker for minutes at a time. Often I fought off the temptation to shake her. At sixteen she had a style of her own: and knew what style was.

90　I never had an education myself. After second grade the school closed down. Don't ask me why: In 1927 colored asked fewer questions than they do now. Sometimes Maggie reads to me. She stumbles along good-naturedly but can't see well. She knows she is not bright. Like good looks and money, quickness passed her by. She will marry John Thomas (who has mossy teeth in an earnest face), and then I'll be free to sit here and I guess just sing church songs to myself. **E** Although I never was a good singer. Never could carry a tune. I was always better at a man's job. I used to love to milk till I was hooked in the side in '49.
100　Cows are soothing and slow and don't bother you, unless you try to milk them the wrong way.

I have deliberately turned my back on the house. It is three rooms, just like the one that burned, except the roof is tin; they don't make shingle roofs anymore. There are no real windows, just some holes cut in the sides, like the portholes in a ship, but not round and not square, with rawhide holding the shutters up on the outside. This house is in a pasture, too, like the other one. No doubt when Dee sees it she will want to tear it down. She wrote me once that no matter where we "choose" to live, she
110　will manage to come see us. But she will never bring her friends. Maggie and I thought about this and Maggie asked me, "Mama, when did Dee ever *have* any friends?"

She had a few. Furtive boys in pink shirts hanging about on washday after school. Nervous girls who never laughed. Impressed with her, they worshiped the well-turned phrase, the

D READING FOCUS

From Mama's description of Dee's behavior, what **inference** can you make about her feelings toward Dee?

_____

_____

_____

_____

E VOCABULARY

Academic Vocabulary
What does this sentence *reveal*, or make known, about Mama's feelings toward Maggie?

_____

_____

_____

_____

_____

What does this paragraph say about Dee's **character traits**?

_____

_____

_____

How do Dee and her boyfriend contrast with Mama and Maggie?

_____

_____

_____

_____

_____

_____

_____

cute shape, the scalding[2] humor that erupted like bubbles in lye. She read to them. **A**

When she was courting Jimmy T, she didn't have much time to pay to us but turned all her faultfinding power on him. He *flew* to marry a cheap city girl from a family of ignorant, flashy people. She hardly had time to recompose herself.

When she comes, I will meet—but there they are!

Maggie attempts to make a dash for the house, in her shuffling way, but I stay her with my hand. "Come back here," I say. And she stops and tries to dig a well in the sand with her toe.

It is hard to see them clearly through the strong sun. But even the first glimpse of leg out of the car tells me it is Dee. Her feet were always neat looking, as if God himself shaped them with a certain style. From the other side of the car comes a short, stocky man. Hair is all over his head a foot long and hanging from his chin like a kinky mule tail. I hear Maggie suck in her breath. "Uhnnnh" is what it sounds like. Like when you see the wriggling end of a snake just in front of your foot on the road. "Uhnnnh." **B**

Dee next. A dress down to the ground, in this hot weather. A dress so loud it hurts my eyes. There are yellows and oranges enough to throw back the light of the sun. I feel my whole face warming from the heat waves it throws out. Earrings gold, too, and hanging down to her shoulders. Bracelets dangling and making noises when she moves her arm up to shake the folds of the dress out of her armpits. The dress is loose and flows, and as she walks closer, I like it. I hear Maggie go "Uhnnnh" again. It is her sister's hair. It stands straight up like the wool on a sheep. It is black as night and around the edges are two long pigtails that rope about like small lizards disappearing behind her ears.

"Wa-su-zo-Tean-o!"[3] she says, coming on in that gliding way the dress makes her move. The short, stocky fellow with the

---

2. **scalding** (SKAHLD IHNG) *v.* used as *adj.:* burning hot; here, biting or stinging.
3. **Wa-su-zo-Tean-o**: a greeting used by the Buganda people of Uganda that means "good morning."

150　hair to his navel is all grinning, and he follows up with "Asalam-alakim,[4] my mother and sister!" **C** He moves to hug Maggie but she falls back, right up against the back of my chair. I feel her trembling there, and when I look up I see the perspiration falling off her chin.

　　"Don't get up," says Dee. Since I am stout, it takes something of a push. You can see me trying to move a second or two before I make it. She turns, showing white heels through her sandals, and goes back to the car. Out she peeks next with a Polaroid. She stoops down quickly and lines up picture after picture of me sitting there in front of the house with Maggie cowering behind
160　me. **D** She never takes a shot without making sure the house is included. When a cow comes nibbling around in the edge of the yard, she snaps it and me and Maggie *and* the house. Then she puts the Polaroid in the back seat of the car and comes up and kisses me on the forehead.

　　Meanwhile, Asalamalakim is going through motions with Maggie's hand. Maggie's hand is as limp as a fish, and probably as cold, despite the sweat, and she keeps trying to pull it back. It looks like Asalamalakim wants to shake hands but wants to do it fancy. Or maybe he don't know how people shake hands.
170　Anyhow, he soon gives up on Maggie. **E**

　　"Well," I say. "Dee."

　　"No, Mama," she says. "Not 'Dee,' Wangero Leewanika Kemanjo!"

　　"What happened to 'Dee'?" I wanted to know.

　　"She's dead," Wangero said. "I couldn't bear it any longer, being named after the people who oppress me."

　　"You know as well as me you was named after your aunt Dicie," I said. Dicie is my sister. She named Dee. We called her "Big Dee" after Dee was born.
180　　"But who was *she* named after?" asked Wangero.

　　"I guess after Grandma Dee," I said.

　　"And who was *she* named after?" asked Wangero.

4.　**Asalamalakim:** (AH SUH LAHM AH LAY KOOM), an Arabic greeting meaning "peace to you."

C 〔READING FOCUS〕

What **inferences** can you make about Dee and the man with her from what they say here?

_____

_____

_____

_____

_____

D 〔VOCABULARY〕

Selection Vocabulary

Cowering means "hiding in shame or fear." How does this relate to Maggie's personality?

_____

_____

_____

_____

_____

E 〔LITERARY ANALYSIS〕

Mama refers to Dee's friend as *Asalamalakim*, the Arabic greeting he had used. Why does she use this word instead of asking what his name is?

_____

_____

_____

_____

_____

The Model A was a car produced in the late 1920s. Knowing this, what **inference** can you make from the actions of Dee (Wangero) and her friend about their attitudes toward Mama?

_____

_____

_____

_____

_____

_____

"Her mother," I said, and saw Wangero was getting tired. "That's about as far back as I can trace it," I said. Though, in fact, I probably could have carried it back beyond the Civil War through the branches.

"Well," said Asalamalakim, "there you are."

"Uhnnnh," I heard Maggie say.

"There I was not," I said, "before 'Dicie' cropped up in our
190   family, so why should I try to trace it that far back?"

He just stood there grinning, looking down on me like somebody inspecting a Model A car. Ⓐ Every once in a while he and Wangero sent eye signals over my head.

"How do you pronounce this name?" I asked.

"You don't have to call me by it if you don't want to," said Wangero.

"Why shouldn't I?" I asked. "If that's what you want us to call you, we'll call you."

"I know it might sound awkward at first," said Wangero.

200   "I'll get used to it," I said. "Ream it out again."

Well, soon we got the name out of the way. Asalamalakim had a name twice as long and three times as hard. After I tripped over it two or three times, he told me to just call him Hakim-a-barber. I wanted to ask him was he a barber, but I didn't really think he was, so I didn't ask.

"You must belong to those beef-cattle peoples down the road," I said. They said "Asalamalakim" when they met you, too, but they didn't shake hands. Always too busy: feeding the cattle, fixing the fences, putting up salt-lick shelters, throwing down
210   hay. When the white folks poisoned some of the herd, the men stayed up all night with rifles in their hands. I walked a mile and a half just to see the sight.

Hakim-a-barber said, "I accept some of their doctrines, but farming and raising cattle is not my style." (They didn't tell me, and I didn't ask, whether Wangero—Dee—had really gone and married him.)

We sat down to eat and right away he said he didn't eat collards, and pork was unclean. Wangero, though, went on

through the chitlins and corn bread, the greens, and everything
else. She talked a blue streak over the sweet potatoes. Everything
delighted her. **B** Even the fact that we still used the benches her
daddy made for the table when we couldn't afford to buy chairs.

"Oh, Mama!" she cried. Then turned to Hakim-a-barber.
"I never knew how lovely these benches are. You can feel the
rump prints," she said, running her hands underneath her and
along the bench. Then she gave a sigh, and her hand closed over
Grandma Dee's butter dish. "That's it!" she said. "I knew there
was something I wanted to ask you if I could have." She jumped
up from the table and went over in the corner where the churn
stood, the milk in it clabber[5] by now. She looked at the churn and
looked at it. **C**

"This churn top is what I need," she said. "Didn't Uncle
Buddy whittle it out of a tree you all used to have?"

"Yes," I said.

"Uh huh," she said happily. "And I want the dasher,[6] too."

"Uncle Buddy whittle that, too?" asked the barber.

Dee (Wangero) looked up at me.

"Aunt Dee's first husband whittled the dash," said Maggie so
low you almost couldn't hear her. "His name was Henry, but they
called him Stash." **D**

"Maggie's brain is like an elephant's," Wangero said,
laughing. "I can use the churn top as a centerpiece for the alcove
table," she said, sliding a plate over the churn, "and I'll think of
something artistic to do with the dasher."

When she finished wrapping the dasher, the handle stuck
out. I took it for a moment in my hands. You didn't even have
to look close to see where hands pushing the dasher up and
down to make butter had left a kind of sink in the wood. In fact,
there were a lot of small sinks; you could see where thumbs and
fingers had sunk into the wood. It was beautiful light-yellow
wood, from a tree that grew in the yard where Big Dee and Stash
had lived.

220

230

240

250

---

5. **clabber** (KLAB ur) *n:* thickened or curdled sour milk.
6. **dasher:** *n.:* pole that stirs the milk in a churn.

B LITERARY ANALYSIS

Some people don't eat
certain types of food because
of their religious beliefs.
What does this scene show
about Hakim-a-barber and
Dee (Wangero)?

_____

_____

_____

_____

_____

C QUICK CHECK

According to Mama, Dee
never liked her home before.
How has Dee's attitude
changed?

_____

_____

_____

_____

_____

D LITERARY FOCUS

What do Maggie's words
reveal about her **character
traits**?

_____

_____

_____

_____

_____

After dinner Dee (Wangero) went to the trunk at the foot of my bed and started rifling through it. Maggie hung back in the kitchen over the dishpan. Out came Wangero with two quilts. They had been pieced by Grandma Dee, and then Big Dee and me had hung them on the quilt frames on the front porch and quilted them. One was in the Lone Star pattern. The other was Walk Around the Mountain. In both of them were
260 scraps of dresses Grandma Dee had worn fifty and more years ago. Bits and pieces of Grandpa Jarrell's paisley shirts. And one teeny faded blue piece, about the size of a penny matchbox, that was from Great Grandpa Ezra's uniform that he wore in the Civil War.

"Mama," Wangero said sweet as a bird. "Can I have these old quilts?"

I heard something fall in the kitchen, and a minute later the kitchen door slammed.

"Why don't you take one or two of the others?" I asked.
270 "These old things was just done by me and Big Dee from some tops your grandma pieced before she died." **A**

"No," said Wangero. "I don't want those. They are stitched around the borders by machine."

"That'll make them last better," I said.

"That's not the point," said Wangero. "These are all pieces of dresses Grandma used to wear. She did all this stitching by hand. Imagine!" She held the quilts securely in her arms, stroking them.

"Some of the pieces, like those lavender ones, come from old clothes her mother handed down to her," I said, moving up to
280 touch the quilts. Dee (Wangero) moved back just enough so that I couldn't reach the quilts. They already belonged to her.

"Imagine!" she breathed again, clutching them closely to her bosom.

"The truth is," I said, "I promised to give them quilts to Maggie, for when she marries John Thomas." **B**

She gasped like a bee had stung her.

"Maggie can't appreciate these quilts!" she said. "She'd probably be backward enough to put them to everyday use." **C**

"I reckon she would," I said. "God knows I been saving 'em for long enough with nobody using 'em. I hope she will!" I didn't want to bring up how I had offered Dee (Wangero) a quilt when she went away to college. Then she had told me they were old-fashioned, out of style.

"But they're *priceless!*" she was saying now, furiously; for she has a temper. "Maggie would put them on the bed and in five years they'd be in rags. Less than that!"

"She can always make some more," I said. "Maggie knows how to quilt."

Dee (Wangero) looked at me with hatred. "You just will not understand. The point is *these* quilts, these quilts!"

"Well," I said, stumped. "What would *you* do with them?"

"Hang them," she said. As if that was the only thing you *could* do with quilts.

Maggie by now was standing in the door. I could almost hear the sound her feet made as they scraped over each other.

"She can have them, Mama," she said, like somebody used to never winning anything or having anything reserved for her. "I can 'member Grandma Dee without the quilts." **D**

I looked at her hard. She had filled her bottom lip with checkerberry snuff, and it gave her face a kind of dopey, hangdog look. It was Grandma Dee and Big Dee who taught her how to quilt herself. She stood there with her scarred hands hidden in the folds of her skirt. She looked at her sister with something like fear, but she wasn't mad at her. This was Maggie's portion. This was the way she knew God to work.

When I looked at her like that, something hit me in the top of my head and ran down to the soles of my feet. Just like when I'm in church and the spirit of God touches me and I get happy and shout. I did something I never had done before: hugged Maggie to me, then dragged her on into the room, snatched the quilts out of Miss Wangero's hands, and dumped them into

C LITERARY FOCUS

What does Dee's response tell you about her **character traits** and what she thinks of Maggie's character traits?

_____
_____
_____
_____
_____
_____

D QUICK CHECK

What is so important about these quilts?

_____
_____
_____
_____
_____
_____

Quilts on the Line (1990) by Anna Belle Lee Washington/Superstock

Maggie's lap. Maggie just sat there on my bed with her mouth open. **A**

"Take one or two of the others," I said to Dee.

But she turned without a word and went out to Hakim-a-barber.

"You just don't understand," she said, as Maggie and I came out to the car.

"What don't I understand?" I wanted to know.

330 "Your heritage," she said. **B** And then she turned to Maggie, kissed her, and said, "You ought to try to make something of yourself, too, Maggie. It's really a new day for us. But from the way you and Mama still live, you'd never know it."

She put on some sunglasses that hid everything above the tip of her nose and her chin.

Maggie smiled, maybe at the sunglasses. But a real smile, not scared. After we watched the car dust settle, I asked Maggie to bring me a dip of snuff. And then the two of us sat there just enjoying, until it was time to go in the house and go to bed. **C**

Applying Your Skills

Everyday Use
For Your Grandmama

VOCABULARY DEVELOPMENT

DIRECTIONS: Complete the passage by filling in the blanks with the correct words from the Word Box. One word will not be used.

Word Box

sidle

furtive

cowering

oppress

I saw my brother sneaking out of my room, his (1) _____ movements were slow and silent. When he saw me, the poor kid was flinching, practically (2) _____ under my gaze. "I was just looking at your CDs," he told me. At least he admitted it. Although I was annoyed, I decided not to (3) _____ him with any "big-brother" lecture.

LITERARY FOCUS: CHARACTER TRAITS

DIRECTIONS: Choose a section of dialogue from the story. On a separate sheet of paper, write a short paragraph explaining what the conversation reveals about the **traits** of the characters involved.

READING FOCUS: MAKING INFERENCES ABOUT CHARACTERS

DIRECTIONS: Complete the chart by making **inferences** about each character based on the details provided.

Character	Detail	Inference
Mama	"I never had an education myself." (line 90)	1.
Maggie	"Maggie attempts to make a dash for the house, in her shuffling way. . . ." (lines 123–124)	2.
Dee	"Maggie can't appreciate these quilts." (line 287)	3.

SKILLS FOCUS

Literary Skills
Understand character traits.

Reading Skills
Make inferences about characters.

Two Kinds

by Amy Tan

LITERARY FOCUS: CHARACTER INTERACTIONS AND MOTIVATION

The characters in a story may take many different kinds of actions, from taking a trip to asking someone else for help. The reason why characters do what they do is called their **motivation**. Characters are motivated to act because they want something. When a character is prevented from getting what he or she wants, conflicts arise. Sometimes one character prevents another one from getting what he or she wants. As you read, look for **character interactions** in which characters are motivated to influence each other.

Record Conflicts   As you read the following excerpt from the book *The Joy Luck Club,* keep a list of the conflicts that arise throughout the story.

READING FOCUS: MAKING INFERENCES ABOUT MOTIVATION

Authors don't always explain a character's motivation directly. Instead, they plant clues. A reader has to **make inferences**, or reasonable guesses, about what the clues mean. To infer, or make inferences about, a character's motivation, pay attention to what the character thinks, says, and does. Then make a guess based on those clues and what you already know about the story, the character, and human nature.

Use the Skill   As you read, make a chart like the one below. For each character, record possible clues to his or her motivations. Once you have found some of these clues, make a guess as to what that character's motivation might be.

**SKILLS
FOCUS**

Literary Skills
Understand character interactions; understand character motivation.

Reading Skills
Make inferences about motivation.

Character	Clue	Motivation
Jing-mei	daydreams about becoming a prodigy	wants to be extraordinary, perfect; wants her parents to love her
Jing-mei's mother		

Vocabulary Development

Two Kinds

SELECTION VOCABULARY

prodigy (PRAHD UH JEE) *n.:* child having extraordinary talent.
    Her mother knows Jing-mei could be a prodigy.

listlessly (LIHST LIHS LEE) *adv.:* without energy or interest.
    Jing-mei reacts listlessly to her mother's tests.

mesmerizing (MEHS MUH RYZ IHNG) *v.* used as *adj.:* spellbinding; fascinating.
    Jing-mei's mother finds the piano piece mesmerizing.

discordant (DIHS KAWR DUHNT) *adj.:* clashing; not harmonious.
    Jing-mei's lack of practice shows in her discordant performance.

fiasco (FEE AS KOH) *n.:* total failure.
    For Jingmei, the talent show is a fiasco.

nonchalantly (NAHN SHUH LUHNT LEE, NAHN SHUH LAHNT LEE) *adv.:* without interest or concern; indifferently.
    Jing-mei refuses her mother nonchalantly at first.

WORD STUDY

DIRECTIONS: In the sentences below, the boldfaced vocabulary word is used incorrectly. Explain how each boldfaced word is used incorrectly.

1. The play was a **fiasco**—everyone knew their lines and the actors played their parts perfectly.

_____

_____

2. George **nonchalantly** double-checked every one of his answers before turning his test in to the teacher.

_____

_____

3. The audience was so **mesmerized** by the movie that they began to talk to each other and ignore the film.

_____

_____

TWO KINDS

by Amy Tan

BACKGROUND

The protagonist of "Two Kinds," Jing-mei, is an American girl born to Chinese parents. Like other children of immigrants, Chinese American children often have one foot in the world their parents left behind and one foot in the United States. The differences between the two cultures can cause a conflict between second-generation American children and their parents. Parents' unrealistic expectations can cause further conflict.

A **VOCABULARY**

Selection Vocabulary

Underline the sentence in this paragraph that gives a clue to the meaning of *prodigy*.

My mother believed you could be anything you wanted to be in America. You could open a restaurant. You could work for the government and get good retirement. You could buy a house with almost no money down. You could become rich. You could become instantly famous.

"Of course you can be prodigy, too," my mother told me when I was nine. "You can be best anything. What does Auntie Lindo know? Her daughter, she is only best tricky." **A**

America was where all my mother's hopes lay. She had come
10   here in 1949 after losing everything in China: her mother and father, her family home, her first husband, and two daughters,

© Contemplation (2006) by Hao Shiming (b. 1977, He Ze, Shandon Province, China). Chinese ink on silk (90 x 71 cm) Courtesy of the Artist.

twin baby girls. But she never looked back with regret. There were so many ways for things to get better. **B**

We didn't immediately pick the right kind of prodigy. At first my mother thought I could be a Chinese Shirley Temple.[1] We'd watch Shirley's old movies on TV as though they were training films. My mother would poke my arm and say, "*Ni kan*"—You watch. And I would see Shirley tapping her feet, or singing a sailor song, or pursing her lips into a very round O while saying, "Oh my goodness."

"*Ni kan*," said my mother as Shirley's eyes flooded with tears. "You already know how. Don't need talent for crying!"

Soon after my mother got this idea about Shirley Temple, she took me to a beauty training school in the Mission district and put me in the hands of a student who could barely hold the scissors without shaking. Instead of getting big fat curls, I emerged with an uneven mass of crinkly black fuzz. My mother dragged me off to the bathroom and tried to wet down my hair.

"You look like Negro Chinese," she lamented, as if I had done this on purpose.

The instructor of the beauty training school had to lop off these soggy clumps to make my hair even again. "Peter Pan is very popular these days," the instructor assured my mother. I now had hair the length of a boy's, with straight-across bangs that hung at a slant two inches above my eyebrows. I liked the haircut and it made me actually look forward to my future fame.

In fact, in the beginning, I was just as excited as my mother, maybe even more so. I pictured this prodigy part of me as many different images, trying each one on for size. I was a dainty ballerina girl standing by the curtains, waiting to hear the right music that would send me floating on my tiptoes. I was like the Christ child lifted out of the straw manger, crying with holy indignity. I was Cinderella stepping from her pumpkin carriage with sparkly cartoon music filling the air. **C**

---

1. **Shirley Temple** (1928–): child movie star who was popular during the 1930s. Mothers all across the United States tried to set their daughters' hair to look like Shirley Temple's sausage curls.

B READING FOCUS

Make an **inference** about what motivates Jing-mei's mother to want her daughter to be the best.

_____

_____

_____

_____

C VOCABULARY

Academic Vocabulary

What is Jing-mei's *attitude*, or feeling, so far about becoming a prodigy?

_____

_____

_____

_____

A **LITERARY FOCUS**

What is Jing-mei's **motivation** for becoming a prodigy?

_____
_____
_____
_____
_____

B **LITERARY ANALYSIS**

Why does Jing-mei's mother ask her all these questions?

_____
_____
_____
_____
_____
_____

C **QUICK CHECK**

Do you think these tests will help Jing-mei to become a prodigy? Why or why not?

_____
_____
_____
_____
_____
_____
_____

In all of my imaginings, I was filled with a sense that I would soon become *perfect*. My mother and father would adore me. I would be beyond reproach. I would never feel the need to sulk for anything. **A**

But sometimes the prodigy in me became impatient. "If

50 you don't hurry up and get me out of here, I'm disappearing for good," it warned. "And then you'll always be nothing."

Every night after dinner, my mother and I would sit at the Formica kitchen table. She would present new tests, taking her examples from stories of amazing children she had read in *Ripley's Believe It or Not,* or *Good Housekeeping, Reader's Digest,* and a dozen other magazines she kept in a pile in our bathroom. My mother got these magazines from people whose houses she cleaned. And since she cleaned many houses each week, we had a great assortment. She would look through them all, searching for

60 stories about remarkable children.

The first night she brought out a story about a three-year-old boy who knew the capitals of all the states and even most of the European countries. A teacher was quoted as saying the little boy could also pronounce the names of the foreign cities correctly.

"What's the capital of Finland?" my mother asked me, looking at the magazine story. **B**

All I knew was the capital of California, because Sacramento was the name of the street we lived on in Chinatown. "Nairobi!"[2]

70 I guessed, saying the most foreign word I could think of. She checked to see if that was possibly one way to pronounce "Helsinki" before showing me the answer.

The tests got harder—multiplying numbers in my head, finding the queen of hearts in a deck of cards, trying to stand on my head without using my hands, predicting the daily temperatures in Los Angeles, New York, and London. **C**

One night I had to look at a page from the Bible for three minutes and then report everything I could remember. "Now

---

2. **Nairobi** (NY ROH BEE): capital of Kenya, a nation in Africa.

Jehoshaphat had riches and honor in abundance and . . . that's all

80　I remember, Ma," I said.

And after seeing my mother's disappointed face once again, something inside of me began to die. I hated the tests, the raised hopes and failed expectations. Before going to bed that night, I looked in the mirror above the bathroom sink and when I saw only my face staring back—and that it would always be this ordinary face—I began to cry. Such a sad, ugly girl! I made high-pitched noises like a crazed animal, trying to scratch out the face in the mirror.

And then I saw what seemed to be the prodigy side of

90　me—because I had never seen that face before. I looked at my reflection, blinking so I could see more clearly. The girl staring back at me was angry, powerful. This girl and I were the same. I had new thoughts, willful thoughts, or rather thoughts filled with lots of won'ts. I won't let her change me, I promised myself. I won't be what I'm not. **D**

So now, on nights when my mother presented her tests, I performed listlessly, my head propped on one arm. I pretended to be bored. **E** And I was. I got so bored I started counting the bellows of the foghorns out on the bay while my mother drilled

100　me in other areas. The sound was comforting and reminded me of the cow jumping over the moon. And the next day, I played a game with myself, seeing if my mother would give up on me before eight bellows. After a while I usually counted only one, maybe two bellows at most. At last she was beginning to give up hope. **F**

Two or three months had gone by without any mention of my being a prodigy again. And then one day my mother was watching *The Ed Sullivan Show* on TV. The TV was old and the sound kept shorting out. Every time my mother got halfway up

110　from the sofa to adjust the set, the sound would go back on and Ed would be talking. As soon as she sat down, Ed would go silent again. She got up, the TV broke into loud piano music. She sat down. Silence. Up and down, back and forth, quiet and loud. It

D LITERARY FOCUS

After this decision from Jing-mei, what kind of **character interaction** do you think might take place between her and her mother in the future?

_____

_____

_____

_____

_____

E VOCABULARY

Selection Vocabulary

Underline the phrase in this sentence that helps you understand the meaning of the word *listlessly*. What does *listlessly* mean?

_____

_____

_____

_____

F QUICK CHECK

How is Jing-mei's plan going?

_____

_____

A **LANGUAGE COACH**

Remember that **synonyms** are words with similar meanings. Underline the word in this paragraph that is a synonym of the word *mesmerizing*.

B **LITERARY FOCUS**

What does this **character interaction** show about Jing-mei and her mother?

_____

_____

_____

_____

_____

_____

_____

was like a stiff embraceless dance between her and the TV set. Finally she stood by the set with her hand on the sound dial.

She seemed entranced by the music, a little frenzied piano piece with this mesmerizing quality, sort of quick passages and then teasing, lilting ones before it returned to the quick, playful parts. **A**

120 "*Ni kan,*" my mother said, calling me over with hurried hand gestures. "Look here."

I could see why my mother was fascinated by the music. It was being pounded out by a little Chinese girl, about nine years old, with a Peter Pan haircut. The girl had the sauciness of a Shirley Temple. She was proudly modest like a proper Chinese child. And she also did this fancy sweep of a curtsy, so that the fluffy skirt of her white dress cascaded slowly to the floor like the petals of a large carnation.

In spite of these warning signs, I wasn't worried. Our family

130 had no piano and we couldn't afford to buy one, let alone reams of sheet music and piano lessons. So I could be generous in my comments when my mother bad-mouthed the little girl on TV.

"Play note right, but doesn't sound good! No singing sound," complained my mother.

"What are you picking on her for?" I said carelessly. "She's pretty good. Maybe she's not the best, but she's trying hard." I knew almost immediately I would be sorry I said that.

"Just like you," she said. "Not the best. Because you not trying." She gave a little huff as she let go of the sound dial and

140 sat down on the sofa. **B**

The little Chinese girl sat down also to play an encore of "Anitra's Dance" by Grieg.[3] I remember the song, because later on I had to learn how to play it.

Three days after watching *The Ed Sullivan Show*, my mother told me what my schedule would be for piano lessons and piano practice. She had talked to Mr. Chong, who lived on the first floor of our apartment building. Mr. Chong was a retired piano

---

3. **Grieg** (GREEG): Edvard Grieg (1843–1907), Norwegian composer. "Anitra's Dance" is from his *Peer Gynt Suite*.

teacher, and my mother had traded housecleaning services for weekly lessons and a piano for me to practice on every day, two hours a day, from four until six.

When my mother told me this, I felt as though I had been sent to hell. I whined and then kicked my foot a little when I couldn't stand it anymore.

"Why don't you like me the way I am? I'm *not* a genius! I can't play the piano. And even if I could, I wouldn't go on TV if you paid me a million dollars!" I cried.

My mother slapped me. "Who ask you be genius?" she shouted. "Only ask you be your best. For you sake. You think I want you be genius? Hnnh! What for! Who ask you!"

"So ungrateful," I heard her mutter in Chinese. "If she had as much talent as she has temper, she would be famous now." **C**

Mr. Chong, whom I secretly nicknamed Old Chong, was very strange, always tapping his fingers to the silent music of an invisible orchestra. He looked ancient in my eyes. He had lost most of the hair on top of his head and he wore thick glasses and had eyes that always looked tired and sleepy. But he must have been younger than I thought, since he lived with his mother and was not yet married.

I met Old Lady Chong once and that was enough. She had this peculiar smell like a baby that had done something in its pants. And her fingers felt like a dead person's, like an old peach I once found in the back of the refrigerator; the skin just slid off the meat when I picked it up. **D**

I soon found out why Old Chong had retired from teaching piano. He was deaf. "Like Beethoven!" he shouted to me. "We're both listening only in our head!" And he would start to conduct his frantic silent sonatas.[4]

Our lessons went like this. He would open the book and point to different things, explaining their purpose: "Key! Treble!

---

4. **sonatas** (SUH NAHT UHZ): musical compositions, usually for one or two instruments.

C **READING FOCUS**

What can you **infer** about the motivation of Jing-mei's mother for saying all this?

_____

_____

_____

_____

D **QUICK CHECK**

In your own words, describe Mr. Chong and his mother.

_____

_____

_____

_____

_____

_____

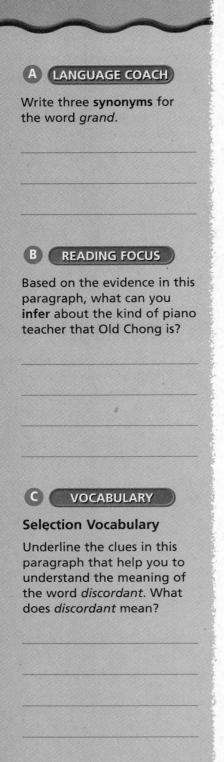

A **LANGUAGE COACH**

Write three **synonyms** for the word *grand*.

_____

_____

_____

B **READING FOCUS**

Based on the evidence in this paragraph, what can you **infer** about the kind of piano teacher that Old Chong is?

_____

_____

_____

C **VOCABULARY**

Selection Vocabulary

Underline the clues in this paragraph that help you to understand the meaning of the word *discordant*. What does *discordant* mean?

_____

_____

_____

180   Bass! No sharps or flats! So this is C major! Listen now and play after me!"

And then he would play the C scale a few times, a simple chord, and then, as if inspired by an old, unreachable itch, he gradually added more notes and running trills and a pounding bass until the music was really something quite grand. **A**

I would play after him, the simple scale, the simple chord, and then I just played some nonsense that sounded like a cat running up and down on top of garbage cans. Old Chong smiled and applauded and then said, "Very good! But now you must

190   learn to keep time!"

So that's how I discovered that Old Chong's eyes were too slow to keep up with the wrong notes I was playing. He went through the motions in half-time. To help me keep rhythm, he stood behind me, pushing down on my right shoulder for every beat. He balanced pennies on top of my wrists so I would keep them still as I slowly played scales and arpeggios.[5] He had me curve my hand around an apple and keep that shape when playing chords. He marched stiffly to show me how to make each finger dance up and down, staccato,[6] like an obedient little soldier.

200   He taught me all these things, and that was how I also learned I could be lazy and get away with mistakes, lots of mistakes. If I hit the wrong notes because I hadn't practiced enough, I never corrected myself. I just kept playing in rhythm. And Old Chong kept conducting his own private reverie.[7] **B**

So maybe I never really gave myself a fair chance. I did pick up the basics pretty quickly, and I might have become a good pianist at that young age. But I was so determined not to try, not to be anybody different, that I learned to play only the most earsplitting preludes, the most discordant hymns. **C**

210   Over the next year, I practiced like this, dutifully in my own way. And then one day I heard my mother and her friend Lindo

---

5.   **arpeggios** (AHR PEH JEE OHS): chords whose notes are played quickly, one after another, rather than at the same time.
6.   **stacatto** (STUH KAHT OH): with clear-cut breaks between notes.
7.   **reverie** (REHV UH REE): daydream.

© Photodisc/Superstock

Jong both talking in a loud bragging tone of voice so others could hear. It was after church, and I was leaning against the brick wall, wearing a dress with stiff white petticoats. Auntie Lindo's daughter, Waverly, who was about my age, was standing farther down the wall, about five feet away. We had grown up together and shared all the closeness of two sisters squabbling over crayons and dolls. In other words, for the most part, we hated each other. I thought she was snotty. **D** Waverly Jong had gained

220 a certain amount of fame as "Chinatown's Littlest Chinese Chess Champion."

"She bring home too many trophy," lamented Auntie Lindo that Sunday. "All day she play chess. All day I have no time do nothing but dust off her winnings." She threw a scolding look at Waverly, who pretended not to see her.

"You lucky you don't have this problem," said Auntie Lindo with a sigh to my mother.

And my mother squared her shoulders and bragged: "Our problem worser than yours. If we ask Jing-mei wash dish, she

230 hear nothing but music. It's like you can't stop this natural talent."

And right then, I was determined to put a stop to her foolish pride. **E**

D QUICK CHECK

What kind of relationship does Jing-mei have with Waverly?

_____

_____

_____

_____

E LITERARY ANALYSIS

Based on what you have read so far, what do you think Jing-mei is going to do?

_____

_____

_____

_____

_____

_____

_____

What **motivates** Jing-mei to not take her playing seriously?

_____

_____

_____

_____

_____

_____

A few weeks later, Old Chong and my mother conspired to have me play in a talent show which would be held in the church hall. By then, my parents had saved up enough to buy me a secondhand piano, a black Wurlitzer spinet with a scarred bench. It was the showpiece of our living room.

For the talent show, I was to play a piece called "Pleading Child" from Schumann's[8] _Scenes from Childhood_. It was a simple,

240   moody piece that sounded more difficult than it was. I was supposed to memorize the whole thing, playing the repeat parts twice to make the piece sound longer. But I dawdled over it, playing a few bars and then cheating, looking up to see what notes followed. I never really listened to what I was playing. I daydreamed about being somewhere else, about being someone else. **A**

The part I liked to practice best was the fancy curtsy: right foot out, touch the rose on the carpet with a pointed foot, sweep to the side, left leg bends, look up and smile.

250   My parents invited all the couples from the Joy Luck Club[9] to witness my debut. Auntie Lindo and Uncle Tin were there. Waverly and her two older brothers had also come. The first two rows were filled with children both younger and older than I was. The littlest ones got to go first. They recited simple nursery rhymes, squawked out tunes on miniature violins, twirled Hula-Hoops, pranced in pink ballet tutus, and when they bowed or curtsied, the audience would sigh in unison, "Awww," and then clap enthusiastically.

When my turn came, I was very confident. I remember my

260   childish excitement. It was as if I knew, without a doubt, that the prodigy side of me really did exist. I had no fear whatsoever, no nervousness. I remember thinking to myself, This is it! This is it! I looked out over the audience, at my mother's blank face, my father's yawn, Auntie Lindo's stiff-lipped smile, Waverly's sulky

---

8. **Schumann's** (SHOO MAHNZ): Robert Schumann (1810–1856), German composer.
9. **Joy Luck Club:** social club to which Jing-mei's mother and three other Chinese mothers belong.

expression. I had on a white dress layered with sheets of lace, and a pink bow in my Peter Pan haircut. As I sat down I envisioned people jumping to their feet and Ed Sullivan rushing up to introduce me to everyone on TV.

270 And I started to play. It was so beautiful. I was so caught up in how lovely I looked that at first I didn't worry how I would sound. So it was a surprise to me when I hit the first wrong note and I realized something didn't sound quite right. And then I hit another, and another followed that. A chill started at the top of my head and began to trickle down. Yet I couldn't stop playing, as though my hands were bewitched. **B** I kept thinking my fingers would adjust themselves back, like a train switching to the right track. I played this strange jumble through two repeats, the sour notes staying with me all the way to the end.

When I stood up, I discovered my legs were shaking. Maybe
280 I had just been nervous and the audience, like Old Chong, had seen me go through the right motions and had not heard anything wrong at all. I swept my right foot out, went down on my knee, looked up and smiled. The room was quiet, except for Old Chong, who was beaming and shouting, "Bravo! Bravo! Well done!" But then I saw my mother's face, her stricken face. The audience clapped weakly, and as I walked back to my chair, with my whole face quivering as I tried not to cry, I heard a little boy whisper loudly to his mother, "That was awful," and the mother whispered back, "Well, she certainly tried."

290 And now I realized how many people were in the audience, the whole world it seemed. I was aware of eyes burning into my back. I felt the shame of my mother and father as they sat stiffly throughout the rest of the show.

We could have escaped during intermission. Pride and some strange sense of honor must have anchored my parents to their chairs. **C** And so we watched it all: the eighteen-year-old boy with a fake mustache who did a magic show and juggled flaming hoops while riding a unicycle. The breasted girl with white makeup who sang from *Madama Butterfly*[10] and got honorable

---

10. *Madama Butterfly*: opera by the Italian composer Giacomo Puccini (1858–1924).

B VOCABULARY

Word Study

Notice how the word *bewitched* has the word *witch* in it. Considering this, what do you think *bewitched* means? Check your answer in a dictionary.

_____

_____

_____

C READING FOCUS

What **inference** does Jing-mei make about her parents' motivation for staying?

_____

_____

_____

_____

_____

Two Kinds **79**

A VOCABULARY

Selection Vocabulary

Knowing what happened at the talent show, infer what the word *fiasco* means and write its definition on the lines below.

_____

_____

_____

B READING FOCUS

What can you **infer** about Jing-mei's attitude toward China, and therefore, America?

_____

_____

_____

_____

_____

_____

_____

300 mention. And the eleven-year-old boy who won first prize playing a tricky violin song that sounded like a busy bee.

After the show, the Hsus, the Jongs, and the St. Clairs from the Joy Luck Club came up to my mother and father.

"Lots of talented kids," Auntie Lindo said vaguely, smiling broadly.

"That was somethin' else," said my father, and I wondered if he was referring to me in a humorous way, or whether he even remembered what I had done.

310 Waverly looked at me and shrugged her shoulders. "You aren't a genius like me," she said matter-of-factly. And if I hadn't felt so bad, I would have pulled her braids and punched her stomach.

But my mother's expression was what devastated me: a quiet, blank look that said she had lost everything. I felt the same way, and it seemed as if everybody were now coming up, like gawkers at the scene of an accident, to see what parts were actually missing. When we got on the bus to go home, my father was humming the busy-bee tune and my mother was silent. I kept thinking she wanted to wait until we got home before shouting at

320 me. But when my father unlocked the door to our apartment, my mother walked in and then went to the back, into the bedroom. No accusations. No blame. And in a way, I felt disappointed. I had been waiting for her to start shouting, so I could shout back and cry and blame her for all my misery.

I assumed my talent-show fiasco meant I never had to play the piano again. **A** But two days later, after school, my mother came out of the kitchen and saw me watching TV.

"Four clock," she reminded me as if it were any other day. I was stunned, as though she were asking me to go through the

330 talent-show torture again. I wedged myself more tightly in front of the TV.

"Turn off TV," she called from the kitchen five minutes later.

I didn't budge. And then I decided. I didn't have to do what my mother said anymore. I wasn't her slave. This wasn't China. **B**

I had listened to her before and look what happened. She was the stupid one.

She came out from the kitchen and stood in the arched entryway of the living room. "Four clock," she said once again, louder.

"I'm not going to play anymore," I said nonchalantly. "Why should I? I'm not a genius."

She walked over and stood in front of the TV. I saw her chest was heaving up and down in an angry way.

"No!" I said, and I now felt stronger, as if my true self had finally emerged. So this was what had been inside me all along.

"No! I won't!" I screamed.

She yanked me by the arm, pulled me off the floor, snapped off the TV. She was frighteningly strong, half pulling, half carrying me toward the piano as I kicked the throw rugs under my feet. She lifted me up and onto the hard bench. I was sobbing by now, looking at her bitterly. Her chest was heaving even more and her mouth was open, smiling crazily, as if she were pleased I was crying. **C**

"You want me to be someone that I'm not!" I sobbed. "I'll never be the kind of daughter you want me to be!"

"Only two kinds of daughters," she shouted in Chinese. "Those who are obedient and those who follow their own mind! Only one kind of daughter can live in this house. Obedient daughter!"

"Then I wish I wasn't your daughter. I wish you weren't my mother," I shouted. As I said these things, I got scared. It felt like worms and toads and slimy things crawling out of my chest, but it also felt good, as if this awful side of me had surfaced, at last.

"Too late change this," said my mother shrilly.

And I could sense her anger rising to its breaking point. I wanted to see it spill over. And that's when I remembered the babies she had lost in China, the ones we never talked about.

"Then I wish I'd never been born!" I shouted. "I wish I were dead! Like them." **D**

It was as if I had said the magic words. Alakazam!—and her face went blank, her mouth closed, her arms went slack, and she

---

C **LITERARY ANALYSIS**

How do you think Jing-mei's mother is feeling? How can you tell?

_____

_____

_____

_____

D **LITERARY FOCUS**

The **character interaction** taking place in this conversation is a result of the main conflict in the story. What is the main conflict?

_____

_____

_____

_____

_____

_____

Two Kinds **81**

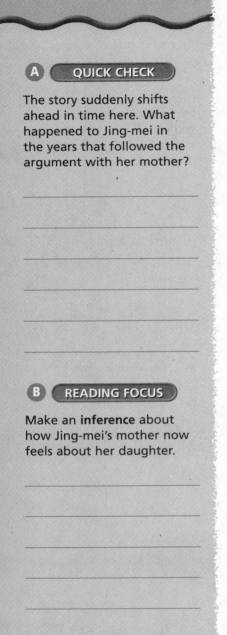

backed out of the room, stunned, as if she were blowing away like a small brown leaf, thin, brittle, lifeless.

It was not the only disappointment my mother felt in me. In the years that followed, I failed her so many times, each time asserting my own will, my right to fall short of expectations. I didn't get straight A's. I didn't become class president. I didn't get into Stanford.[11] I dropped out of college. **A**

For unlike my mother, I did not believe I could be anything I wanted to be. I could only be me.

And for all those years, we never talked about the disaster at the recital or my terrible accusations afterward at the piano bench. All that remained unchecked, like a betrayal that was now unspeakable. So I never found a way to ask her why she had hoped for something so large that failure was inevitable.

And even worse, I never asked her what frightened me the most: Why had she given up hope?

For after our struggle at the piano, she never mentioned my playing again. The lessons stopped. The lid to the piano was closed, shutting out the dust, my misery, and her dreams.

So she surprised me. A few years ago, she offered to give me the piano, for my thirtieth birthday. I had not played in all those years. I saw the offer as a sign of forgiveness, a tremendous burden removed.

"Are you sure?" I asked shyly. "I mean, won't you and Dad miss it?"

"No, this your piano," she said firmly. "Always your piano. You only one can play."

"Well, I probably can't play anymore," I said. "It's been years."

"You pick up fast," said my mother, as if she knew this was certain. "You have natural talent. You could been genius if you want to."

"No, I couldn't."

"You just not trying," said my mother. And she was neither angry nor sad. She said it as if to announce a fact that could never be disproved. "Take it," she said. **B**

---

11. **Stanford:** high-ranking university in Stanford, California.

But I didn't at first. It was enough that she had offered it to me. And after that, every time I saw it in my parents' living room, standing in front of the bay windows, it made me feel proud, as if it were a shiny trophy I had won back.

410   Last week I sent a tuner over to my parents' apartment and had the piano reconditioned, for purely sentimental reasons. My mother had died a few months before, and I had been getting things in order for my father, a little bit at a time. **C** I put the jewelry in special silk pouches. The sweaters she had knitted in yellow, pink, bright orange—all the colors I hated—I put those in mothproof boxes. I found some old Chinese silk dresses, the kind with little slits up the sides. I rubbed the old silk against my skin, then wrapped them in tissue and decided to take them home with me.

420   After I had the piano tuned, I opened the lid and touched the keys. It sounded even richer than I remembered. Really, it was a very good piano. Inside the bench were the same exercise notes with handwritten scales, the same secondhand music books with their covers held together with yellow tape.

I opened up the Schumann book to the dark little piece I had played at the recital. It was on the left-hand side of the page, "Pleading Child." It looked more difficult than I remembered. I played a few bars, surprised at how easily the notes came back to me.

430   And for the first time, or so it seemed, I noticed the piece on the right-hand side. It was called "Perfectly Contented." I tried to play this one as well. It had a lighter melody but the same flowing rhythm and turned out to be quite easy. "Pleading Child" was shorter but slower; "Perfectly Contented" was longer but faster. And after I played them both a few times, I realized they were two halves of the same song. **D**

C **LITERARY FOCUS**

What might be some of the "sentimental reasons" that give Jing-mei **motivation** to have the piano tuned?

_____

_____

_____

_____

D **LITERARY ANALYSIS**

What do you think Jing-mei is trying to tell us in this last paragraph?

_____

_____

_____

_____

_____

Skills Practice

Two Kinds

USE A CONCEPT MAP

Now that you have read "Two Kinds," think about the different kinds of **character interactions** that took place in the story. What sorts of conversations did the characters have? Did they have any arguments? Did they agree about anything? Remember that each character had a **motivation**, or reason, for saying and behaving the way he or she did.

DIRECTIONS: Fill in the concept map below with an example of a major character interaction from the story. In the first bubble on the left, name one character and her or his motivation. In the second bubble, name the other character who is involved in the interaction, along with his or her motivation. In the bubble on the right, name and describe the interaction that occurred (an argument, a conversation, etc.) because of their motivations.

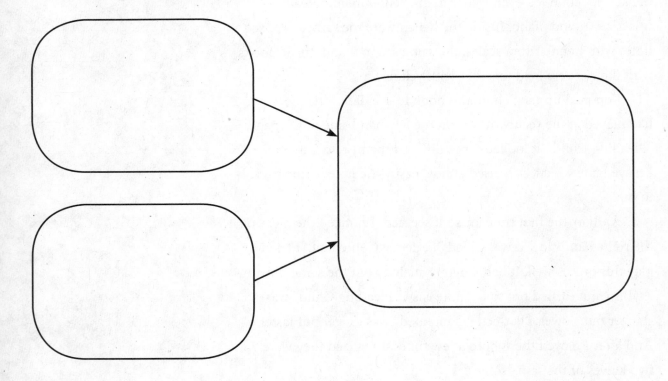

Applying Your Skills

Two Kinds

VOCABULARY DEVELOPMENT

DIRECTIONS: Create sentences using each vocabulary word from the Word Box on the lines below.

Word Box

- prodigy
- listlessly
- mesmerizing
- discordant
- fiasco
- nonchalantly

1. _____

2. _____

3. _____

4. _____

5. _____

6. _____

LITERARY FOCUS: CHARACTER INTERACTIONS AND MOTIVATION

DIRECTIONS: When characters interacting in a story have different needs and desires, this causes a conflict.

Provide two examples of **character interactions** in which opposing wants or desires cause a conflict.

1. _____

2. _____

READING FOCUS: MAKING INFERENCES ABOUT MOTIVATION

DIRECTIONS: As you read, you must often use clues from the story to **make inferences** about what is **motivating** a character to do something. Without looking at the story, write two clues that hinted at the character motivations that are listed in the right column.

Clues	Motivations
1.	Jing-mei's mother wants Jing-mei to be a prodigy.
2.	
3.	Jing-mei wants to be an individual and not do everything her mother wants her to do.
4.	

SKILLS FOCUS

Literary Skills
Understand character interactions; understand character motivation.

Reading Skills
Make inferences about motivation.

MLK's Legacy: An Interview with Congressman John Lewis *and* A Young Boy's Stand

INFORMATIONAL TEXT FOCUS: SYNTHESIZING SOURCES— DRAWING CONCLUSIONS

When you do research, you need to look at different sources to get a balanced view. One kind of source is a **primary source**, which is a first-hand account that has not been interpreted or edited. Putting together and evaluating information from different sources is called **synthesizing** information. Synthesizing will help you to **draw conclusions**, or make judgments, about what you read. To synthesize the information from these sources, first find the main idea and supporting details of each source. Determine if the source is credible. Does the writer provide enough information to support the main ideas? If so, what conclusion can you draw about the subject?

SELECTION VOCABULARY

from **MLK's Legacy**

compassionate (KUHM PASH UH NIHT) *adj.:* sympathetic; willing to help others.
> *Congressman Lewis offered examples of Dr. King's compassionate nature.*

discrimination (DIHS KRIHM UH NAY SHUHN) *n.:* prejudiced treatment.
> *The Civil Right Movement helped people who faced discrimination.*

undisputed (UHN DIHS PYOO TIHD) *adj.:* without doubt.
> *The importance of Dr. King's leadership is undisputed.*

from **A Young Boy's Stand**

hostile (HAHS TUHL) *adj.:* very unfriendly.
> *The hostile dog attacked the mailman.*

WORD STUDY

DIRECTIONS: Write a synonym (a word with a similar meaning) and an antonym (a word with the opposite meaning) for the selection vocabulary words below.

1. compassionate _____

2. hostile _____

SKILLS FOCUS

Informational Text Skills
Synthesize sources and draw conclusions from one or more sources.

MLK's Legacy: An Interview with Congressman John Lewis

from NPR.org

> **BACKGROUND**
>
> Until the late 1950s, schools, restaurants, and other public facilities in many Southern states were segregated. Dr. Martin Luther King Jr., a Baptist minister from Montgomery, Alabama, organized a series of non-violent protests throughout the country to combat segregation. In the following interview that took place online, the host (and others) ask Congressman John Lewis to comment on the legacy of MLK.

January 14, 1999

npr_host: At this point we'd like to welcome Congressman Lewis.

Congressman_John_Lewis: Good evening. It's great to be here.

npr_host: Can you tell us a bit about your firsthand experience with the Civil Rights Movement? **A**

Congressman_John_Lewis: I was born in Alabama, 50 miles from Montgomery, in southeast Alabama, in a little town of about 13,000 people just outside of Troy. When I would visit the cities of Montgomery or Birmingham, I saw the signs that said white men and white women, I saw the signs that said colored
10   lady, colored men. In 1950 when I was 10 years old I tried to check a book out of the local library, I tried to get a library card and I was told that the library was only for white people and not people of color. It had an unbelievable impact on me. I couldn't understand it. But in 1955 when I was fifteen years

A QUICK CHECK

Based on this first question, what do you think will be the main idea, or central point, of the interview?

_____

_____

_____

A READING FOCUS

Draw a conclusion about the credibility of Congressman Lewis as a source for information on the Civil Rights Movement and Dr. King. Explain your answer.

_____

_____

_____

B VOCABULARY

Selection Vocabulary

Circle words in lines 18–20 that offer clues to the meaning of *compassionate*. What does *compassionate* mean?

_____

_____

© Flip Schulke/Corbis

old I heard about Martin Luther King Jr. and Rosa Parks.[1] And, three years later I met MLK and a year later I got involved in the Civil Rights Movement. **A**

Congressman_John_Lewis: Dr. King was one of the most inspiring human beings I ever met. He was such a warm,

20   compassionate and loving human being. **B**

npr_host: How was Dr. King inspiring on a personal level, as much as in public?

Congressman_John_Lewis: MLK Jr. taught me how to say no to segregation and I can hear him saying now . . . when you

---

1.   **Rosa Parks:** On December 1, 1955, Rosa Parks, an African American woman, was arrested for refusing to give up her seat on a bus to a white person in Montgomery, Alabama. The bus boycott staged in protest of Parks's arrest grew into a massive organized effort that was the first of many protests in the Civil Rights Movement.

straighten up your back—no man can ride you. He said stand up straight and say no to racial discrimination.

npr_host: You took very quick action. Tell us more, please.

Congressman_John_Lewis: As a young student I got involved in that, studying the philosophy and the discipline of nonvio-

30 lence. **C** And as students—young people, black and white, we would go downtown in Nashville, Atlanta, Birmingham and other cities in the South . . . and we would sit down—we did what we called sit-ins at lunch counters. These places refused to serve black students. And we'd have white students and black students sitting together. And some of the places were like Woolworth stores, where you could go in and buy things, but you couldn't order a hamburger. And while [we were] sitting, sometimes people would come in and beat us, light cigarettes out in our hair, down our backs, throw us off the lunch counter

40 stools, and sometimes kick us and leave us lying down on the floor. We got arrested. When I was growing up I was told over and over again—don't get into trouble. So as students we were getting into trouble—but it was good trouble. **D**

krockett_2065101 asks: What is the one thing that you remember most about MLK?

Congressman_John_Lewis: Dr. King had a great sense of humor and he loved a good meal. From time to time when we were traveling in the South he would see some restaurant or a hole-in-the wall place to eat and he would say, we should stop—

50 we should get something to eat, it may be our last chance, we should go on a full stomach.

Congressman_John_Lewis: But on one occasion, on—March 1965 we were walking along, marching, and it started to rain. I didn't have anything on my head. He had a little brown cap he was wearing. He took the cap off his head and gave it to me and he said, "John, you should put this on—you've been hurt." A few days earlier I had been beaten by a group of state troopers and I had a concussion. So he thought it was important that my head

C VOCABULARY

Word Study

Nonviolence is "the policy of rejecting violence and using peaceful means to achieve political goals." The word is an antonym of *violence*. An antonym is a word that has the opposite meaning of another word. List some other words that you can turn into their opposites by adding *non-*.

_____

_____

_____

_____

D QUICK CHECK

What is a sit-in? What are the dangers of participating in a sit-in?

_____

_____

_____

_____

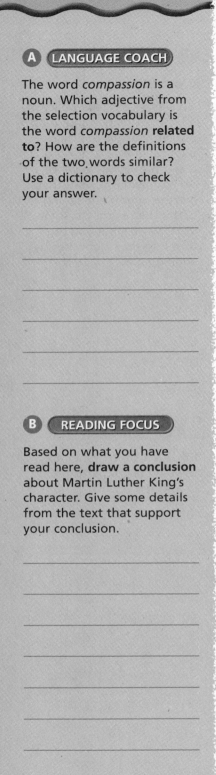

be protected. I'll never forget it; it was such an act of compassion and concern. **A**

Musicman_21 asks: Was it intimidating meeting MLK?

Congressman_John_Lewis: Well, the first time I met him, I was only eighteen years old in 1958, and he had emerged for me as someone bigger than life. Two miles from where I grew up in Alabama, there was a white college—Troy State College—and I had applied to go there. I never heard anything from the school so I wrote MLK a letter and told him about my desire to go to the school. He wrote me back and sent me a round trip Greyhound bus ticket and invited me to come to Montgomery to meet with him. One Saturday, my father drove me to the Greyhound bus station, I traveled the 50 miles from my home. A young black lawyer met me at the bus station in Montgomery and drove me to the First Baptist Church—that was Rev. Abernathy . . . a friend of Dr. King and a leader in the local movement with Dr. King. We entered the office of the church and MLK stood up from behind a desk and he said something like, "Are you the boy from Troy? Are you John Lewis?"

Congressman_John_Lewis: I was scared, I was nervous, I didn't know what I was going to say. And I said—Dr. King, I am John Robert Lewis. I gave my whole name, I didn't want there to be any mistake.

Congressman_John_Lewis: That was the beginning of our relationship. We became friends. We became brothers in a struggle. He was my leader. He was my hero. **B**

DC_Vyf asks: Why did you decide to run for congress?

Congressman_John_Lewis: When I would make trips to D.C. during the height of the Civil Rights Movement . . . I had a chance to meet many members of Congress and I had been involved in getting people to register (to vote) and I thought somehow and someway I could make a contribution by being involved in politics.

DC_Vyf asks: How does one keep struggling for social change in this environment? How does one keep [one's] spirits up?

Congressman_John_Lewis: You must never, ever give up. Let me give you an example. I just finished a book called *Walking with the Wind: A Memoir of the Movement*; it's published by Simon and Schuster.  In the prologue of the book, I tell a story about when I was growing up and I was only about seven or eight years old, but I remember like it was yesterday.

100   **Congressman_John_Lewis:** One Saturday afternoon a group of my sisters and brothers, along with some of my first cousins, about twelve or fifteen of us—young children were outside playing in the yard, and a storm came up . . . an unbelievable storm occurred and the only adult around was my aunt who lived in this old house. A shotgun house—a house with a tin roof, small . . . The wind started blowing, the lightening started flashing and we were all in the house. My aunt was terrified, she

---

C   **VOCABULARY**

Academic Vocabulary

Based on what you know of Congressman John Lewis, what might one *acquire*, or gain, by reading a book he wrote about his past?

_____

_____

_____

_____

_____

_____

_____

A LITERARY ANALYSIS

What do you think is the lesson of the story that Congressman Lewis is telling? How can that lesson be applied to the Civil Rights Movement?

_____

_____

_____

_____

_____

_____

B QUICK CHECK

What does Congressman Lewis think Dr. King's role, or function, would be in America today?

_____

_____

_____

_____

C READING FOCUS

Now that you have read the entire interview, **draw conclusions** about Dr. King's impact on our country.

_____

_____

_____

_____

_____

thought the house would blow away. So she suggested we should hold hands and we were crying, all of us.

110   **Congressman_John_Lewis:** So when one side of the house appeared to be lifted from its foundation we'd try and hold it down with our little bodies . . . and when the other corner of the house appeared to be lifting up we'd walk over there . . . trying to hold it down. Thunder may roll, lightning may flash . . . but we may never leave the house. **A**

Karq asks: How do you think MLK would fare in today's political arena?

Congressman_John_Lewis: Today, MLK would be the undisputed moral leader in America. If he were here today . . . he'd
120   say we're majoring in minor things. He'd be very disappointed that we're wasting so much of our time, so much of our energy and resources on investigation rather than dealing with the basic needs of people. **B**

Lovely_Ca_97 asks: If there is any advice you could give to our generation, what would it be?

Congressman_John_Lewis: This generation should study contemporary history: read the books, listen to the tapes, watch the video, study the early days of the Civil Rights Movement and be inspired. They too can act. **C**

A Young Boy's Stand on a New Orleans Streetcar

from StoryCorps, December 1, 2006

It was 56 years ago that Jerome Smith, then ten years old, removed the screen that acted as a barrier between white and black passengers on a New Orleans streetcar. "The streetcar became very hostile," Smith recalls. **A**

The event took place five years before Rosa Parks energized the Civil Rights Movement on December 1, 1955, when she refused to give up her bus seat to a white passenger in Montgomery, Alabama.

Smith says that as he sat in the white section of the street
10 car in Louisiana, an older black woman from the rear of the car descended on him, hitting him so hard that "it felt like there was a bell ringing in my head."

The woman loudly said she'd teach the boy a lesson, telling him, "You should never do that, disrespect white people. You have no business trying to sit with them."

She forced Smith off the streetcar, and around the back of an auto store. But once they were behind the building, the woman's tone changed.

"Never, ever stop," the woman told Smith as she began to
20 cry. "I'm proud of you," she said. "Don't you ever quit."

Smith, who went on to help found the New Orleans chapter of CORE, The Congress of Racial Equality, says it was that moment that made him who he is today.

"Even though I didn't know the words 'civil rights' then," Smith says, "that opened up the door."

Smith currently directs the Tambourine and Fan, a New Orleans organization that teaches young people about civil rights, leadership and political engagement. **B C**

A VOCABULARY

Selection Vocabulary

Hostile means "very unfriendly." Why do you think the streetcar became *hostile*?

_____

_____

_____

_____

_____

B READING FOCUS

What information in this selection is characteristic of a **primary source**?

_____

_____

_____

_____

C LITERARY ANALYSIS

How do you think Smith's experiences as a child influenced his choice of career?

_____

_____

_____

_____

_____

MLK's Legacy: An Interview with Congressman John Lewis *and* A Young Boy's Stand

USE A VENN DIAGRAM

DIRECTIONS: Complete the Venn diagram below. List similarities between the two articles where the ovals overlap, and list differences between them in the proper ovals.

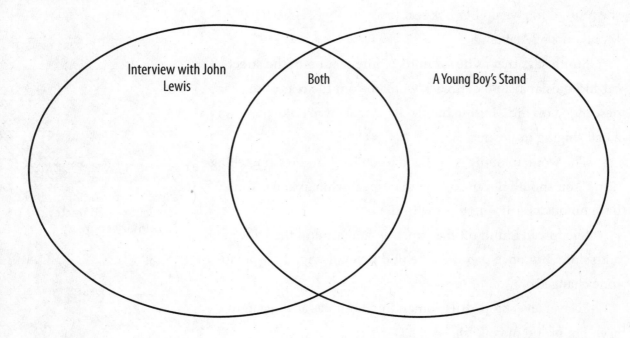

Interview with John Lewis

Both

A Young Boy's Stand

Applying Your Skills

MLK's Legacy: An Interview with Congressman John Lewis *and* A Young Boy's Stand

VOCABULARY DEVELOPMENT

DIRECTIONS: Write a few sentences summarizing one of these two selections using two or more words from the Word Box.

Word Box

compassionate

discrimination

undisputed

hostile

_____

_____

_____

_____

INFORMATIONAL TEXT FOCUS: SYNTHESIZING SOURCES—DRAWING CONCLUSIONS

DIRECTIONS: Synthesize the information from the two sources listed in the chart below, and fill in the main idea and supporting details from each.

	"An Interview with Congressman John Lewis"	"A Young Boy's Stand"
Main Idea	1.	3.
Supporting Details	2.	4.

SKILLS FOCUS

Informational Text Skills
Synthesize sources and draw conclusions from one or more sources.

Skills Review

Collection 2

VOCABULARY REVIEW

DIRECTIONS: Review the selection and academic vocabulary by filling in the blanks with words from the Word Box. Each word may only be used once. Note that not all the words will be used.

Word Box

acquire
attitude
compassionate
cowering
discordant
discrimination
fiasco
furtive
hostile
listlessly
mesmerizing
nonchalantly
oppress
prodigy
reveal
sidle
tradition
undisputed

1. The very _____ woman next door wrote a nice card to my mother when she was in the hospital.

2. My younger brother is only 6 years old and he plays chess better than anyone I know; he is a _____.

3. Because we had no interest in being there, we walked through the woods _____.

4. Tracey always looks at life with a smile; she has a good _____.

5. Not allowing a person to work at a company because the person is different is an example of _____.

6. All the big signs and flashing lights in Times Square caught our attention and were _____.

7. Allowing the orchestra members to start playing whenever they felt like it was a complete _____.

8. The detective will _____ to us who committed the crime once he has studied all of the evidence.

9. When Jeff gets in a bad mood, he can be very _____ toward others.

10. During the whole time Paula was carelessly swinging the frying pan back and forth in the kitchen, I was _____ in the corner, hoping not to get hurt.

Skills Review

Collection 2

LANGUAGE COACH

DIRECTIONS: Synonyms are words that have similar meanings. Antonyms are words that have opposite meanings. Complete the chart by filling in a synonym and an antonym for each vocabulary word.

Vocabulary word	Synonym	Antonym
1. furtive		
2. acquire		
3. oppress		
4. undisputed		
5. nonchalantly		

ORAL LANGUAGE ACTIVITY

DIRECTIONS: Work with a partner to perform an interview. Decide who is going to be the interviewer and who is going to be the subject of the interview. You may pick any topic you like, but base it on your partner's areas of interest and knowledge. For example, you might interview your partner about a family tradition that is different from your own. You might ask his or her opinion about an issue in your school or community. You could also ask your partner about special interests such as music or sports. Be sure to ask at least four questions. Record the interview or jot down the questions and answers on a separate sheet of paper. When you are finished, report your findings to the rest of the class.

Collection

3

Narrator and Voice

© Dream Child (1990) by Graham Arnold

Literary and Academic Vocabulary for Collection 3

complex (KUHM PLEHKS) *adj.:* made up of many parts; complicated.

Although the story sounds simple, the plot is rather complex.

correspond (KAWR UH SPAHND) *v.:* to agree or be in harmony; to be similar.

Often a character's voice corresponds to his or her actions.

perceive (PUHR SEEV) *v.:* to be aware of, to sense; to observe.

They did not perceive any danger in the still, clear waters.

incorporate (IHN KOHR PUH RAYT) *v.:* make something a part of something else; include.

Writers often incorporate details from their own background in their writing.

omniscient (OHM NIH SHEHNT) *adj.:* all-knowing.

An omniscient narrator in a story can tell us what each character thinks and feels.

voice (VOYS) *n.:* distinctive use of language.

No two writers have the same voice.

diction (DIHK SHUHN) *n.:* choice of words.

The narrator's diction reveals a large vocabulary.

The Storyteller

by Saki

LITERARY FOCUS: OMNISCIENT NARRATOR

An **omniscient narrator** knows the thoughts, feelings, and motives of all the characters in a story. A writer sometimes uses an all-knowing narrator to express his or her own point of view and purpose for writing a story.

Keep a List of Descriptive Words and Phrases While you read "The Storyteller," pay attention to Saki's use of the omniscient narrator. How does he describe the various characters? What adjectives and adverbs does he use to describe their actions and words? These are ways in which you may become aware of the author's point of view. Keep a list of descriptive words and phrases that tell you how the narrator feels about the characters.

READING FOCUS: IDENTIFYING WRITER'S PURPOSE

Think about a story you might like to write. Ask yourself *why* you chose that topic. Why that particular setting? Why that character? Asking these same questions will help you determine the writer's **purpose**, or reason, for writing. One good way to detect a writer's purpose is to note his or her attitude toward the characters. How does the writer describe what the characters do and say?

Use the Skill As you read "The Storyteller" and notice the ways in which the writer describes the characters through the narrator, consider the writer's purpose. Is the writer criticizing someone or something? What does he seem to approve of or praise? Keep a chart like the one below to help you find clues that reveal the writer's attitude.

Writer approves of . . .	Writer is critical of . . .
the children's response to the aunt's story, which includes asking "exactly the question the bachelor wanted to ask"	the way the aunt and the children remind the narrator of a "housefly that refused to be discouraged"

SKILLS FOCUS

Literary Skills
Understand omniscient narrator.

Reading Skills
Determine the writer's purpose.

Vocabulary Development

The Storyteller

SELECTION VOCABULARY

sultry (SUHL TREE) *adj.:* hot and humid; sweltering
The passengers were uncomfortable in the sultry train car.

persistent (PUHR SIHS TUHNT) *adj.:* continuing; stubborn.
The children were persistent with their many questions.

resolute (REHZ UH LOOT) *adj.:* determined.
The young girl's resolute willpower was admirable.

petulant (PEHCH UH LUHNT) *adj.:* impatient; irritable; peevish.
The children grew petulant as their questions went unanswered.

conviction (KUHN VIHK SHUHN) *n.:* strong belief; certainty.
All of the children agreed with conviction that their aunt's story was horrible.

WORD STUDY

DIRECTIONS: Fill in the blanks in the following sentences with the correct selection vocabulary word from the list above.

1. He was _____ in his belief that he could finish the exam on time; he was determined.

2. A summer day in Alabama is probably going to be very _____!

3. Her words demonstrated her strong _____ that she was the best candidate.

4. That _____ salesman has been to my door three times today.

5. My daughter hasn't had her nap yet today, and so now she's being _____.

THE STORYTELLER

by Saki

BACKGROUND
Saki, whose real name was Hector Hugh Munro, was a British writer born in 1870. He became known for his short stories that satirized, or made fun of, life. Like other satires, this story makes fun of someone or something both for entertainment and to make a point.

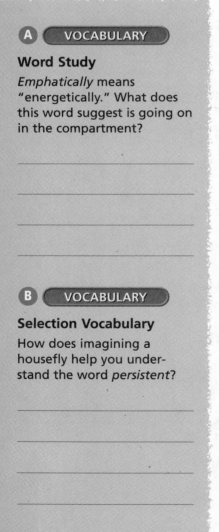

A **VOCABULARY**

Word Study
Emphatically means "energetically." What does this word suggest is going on in the compartment?

_____

_____

_____

_____

B **VOCABULARY**

Selection Vocabulary
How does imagining a housefly help you understand the word *persistent*?

_____

_____

_____

_____

It was a hot afternoon, and the railway carriage was correspondingly sultry, and the next stop was at Templecombe, nearly an hour ahead. The occupants of the carriage were a small girl, and a smaller girl, and a small boy. An aunt belonging to the children occupied one corner seat, and the further corner seat on the opposite side was occupied by a bachelor who was a stranger to their party, but the small girls and the small boy emphatically occupied the compartment. **A** Both the aunt and the children were conversational in a limited, persistent way,

10 reminding one of the attentions of a housefly that refused to be discouraged. **B** Most of the aunt's remarks seemed to begin with "Don't," and nearly all the children's remarks began with "Why?" The bachelor said nothing out loud.

"Don't, Cyril, don't," exclaimed the aunt, as the small boy began smacking the cushions of the seat, producing a cloud of dust at each blow.

"Come and look out of the window," she added.

The child moved reluctantly to the window. "Why are those sheep being driven out of that field?" he asked.

20 "I expect they are being driven to another field where there is more grass," said the aunt weakly.

"But there is lots of grass in that field," protested the boy; "there's nothing else but grass there. Aunt, there's lots of grass in that field."

"Perhaps the grass in the other field is better," suggested the aunt fatuously.[1]

"Why is it better?" came the swift, inevitable question.

"Oh, look at those cows!" exclaimed the aunt. Nearly every field along the line had contained cows or bullocks, but she spoke
30   as though she were drawing attention to a rarity. **C**

"Why is the grass in the other field better?" persisted Cyril.

The frown on the bachelor's face was deepening to a scowl. He was a hard, unsympathetic man, the aunt decided in her mind. She was utterly unable to come to any satisfactory decision about the grass in the other field. **D**

The smaller girl created a diversion by beginning to recite "On the Road to Mandalay."[2] She only knew the first line, but she put her limited knowledge to the fullest possible use. She repeated the line over and over again in a dreamy but resolute
40   and very audible voice; it seemed to the bachelor as though someone had had a bet with her that she could not repeat the line aloud two thousand times without stopping. **E** Whoever it was who had made the wager was likely to lose his bet.

"Come over here and listen to a story," said the aunt, when the bachelor had looked twice at her and once at the communication cord.[3]

The children moved listlessly toward the aunt's end of the carriage. Evidently her reputation as a storyteller did not rank high in their estimation.
50   In a low, confidential voice, interrupted at frequent intervals by loud, petulant questions from her listeners, she began an unenterprising and deplorably uninteresting story about a little

---

1. **fatuously** (FACH oo uhs lee): foolishly.
2. **"On the Road to Mandalay"**: long poem by the English writer Rudyard Kipling (1865–1936). The first line is "By the old Moulmein Pagoda, lookin' eastward to the sea."
3. **communication cord**: on a train, a cord that can be pulled to call the conductor.

C READING FOCUS

Examining dialogue can help you to understand a writer's **purpose**. What can you tell about the children and their aunt from this dialogue?

_____

_____

_____

_____

_____

_____

D LITERARY FOCUS

As an **omniscient narrator**, the writer can tell us what is going on in the aunt's mind. Underline the words that that tell you the aunt's private thoughts.

E VOCABULARY

Selection Vocabulary

Resolute means "determined." Underline the words in this sentence that show how the smaller girl is *resolute*.

The word *line* has **multiple meanings**. Which meaning is being used here?

_____

_____

_____

B **LITERARY FOCUS**

Because the story is told by an **omniscient narrator**, you get a good idea of all the characters' feelings and thoughts. Look at this conversation. Write what you think are each character's feelings and thoughts at this point in the story.

_____

_____

_____

_____

_____

_____

_____

_____

_____

_____

_____

girl who was good, and made friends with everyone on account of her goodness, and was finally saved from a mad bull by a number of rescuers who admired her moral character.

"Wouldn't they have saved her if she hadn't been good?" demanded the bigger of the small girls. It was exactly the question that the bachelor had wanted to ask.

"Well, yes," admitted the aunt lamely, "but I don't think they
60 would have run quite so fast to her help if they had not liked her so much."

"It's the stupidest story I've ever heard," said the bigger of the small girls, with immense conviction.

"I didn't listen after the first bit, it was so stupid," said Cyril.

The smaller girl made no actual comment on the story, but she had long ago recommenced a murmured repetition of her favorite line. **A**

"You don't seem to be a success as a storyteller," said the bachelor suddenly from his corner.

70 The aunt bristled in instant defense at this unexpected attack.

"It's a very difficult thing to tell stories that children can both understand and appreciate," she said stiffly.

"I don't agree with you," said the bachelor. **B**

"Perhaps you would like to tell them a story," was the aunt's retort.

"Tell us a story," demanded the bigger of the small girls.

"Once upon a time," began the bachelor, "there was a little girl called Bertha, who was extraordinarily good."

80 The children's momentarily aroused interest began at once to flicker; all stories seemed dreadfully alike, no matter who told them.

"She did all that she was told, she was always truthful, she kept her clothes clean, ate milk puddings as if they were jam tarts, learned her lessons perfectly, and was polite in her manners."

"Was she pretty?" asked the bigger of the small girls.

"Not as pretty as any of you," said the bachelor, "but she was horribly good."

There was a wave of reaction in favor of the story; the word horrible in connection with goodness was a novelty that commended itself. It seemed to introduce a ring of truth that was absent from the aunt's tales of infant life.

"She was so good," continued the bachelor, "that she won several medals for goodness, which she always wore, pinned onto her dress. There was a medal for obedience, another medal for punctuality, and a third for good behavior. **C** They were large metal medals and they clicked against one another as she walked. No other child in the town where she lived had as many as three medals, so everybody knew that she must be an extra good child."

"Horribly good," quoted Cyril.

"Everybody talked about her goodness, and the Prince of the country got to hear about it, and he said that as she was so very good she might be allowed once a week to walk in his park, which was just outside the town. It was a beautiful park, and no children were ever allowed in it, so it was a great honor for Bertha to be allowed to go there."

"Were there any sheep in the park?" demanded Cyril.

"No," said the bachelor, "there were no sheep."

"Why weren't there any sheep?" came the inevitable question arising out of that answer.

The aunt permitted herself a smile, which might almost have been described as a grin. **D**

"There were no sheep in the park," said the bachelor, "because the Prince's mother had once had a dream that her son would either be killed by a sheep or else by a clock falling on him. For that reason the Prince never kept a sheep in his park or a clock in his palace."

The aunt suppressed a gasp of admiration. **E**

"Was the Prince killed by a sheep or by a clock?" asked Cyril.

"He is still alive, so we can't tell whether the dream will come true," said the bachelor unconcernedly; "anyway, there were

90

100

110

120

C QUICK CHECK

What are the the three medals that Bertha gets?

_____

_____

_____

D LITERARY ANALYSIS

Why do you think the aunt "permitted herself a smile" at this point of the story?

_____

_____

_____

_____

_____

E READING FOCUS

The aunt is clearly impressed with the bachelor. What, exactly, do you think she is impressed with, and how might this relate to the writer's **purpose**?

_____

_____

_____

_____

_____

_____

_____

A QUICK CHECK

How does the bachelor handle the children's questions differently from the way the aunt does at the beginning of the story?

_____

_____

_____

_____

_____

_____

no sheep in the park, but there were lots of little pigs running all over the place."

"What color were they?"

"Black with white faces, white with black spots, black all over, gray with white patches, and some were white all over."

The storyteller paused to let a full idea of the park's treasures sink into the children's imaginations; then he resumed:

130 "Bertha was rather sorry to find that there were no flowers in the park. She had promised her aunts, with tears in her eyes, that she would not pick any of the kind Prince's flowers, and she had meant to keep her promise, so of course it made her feel silly to find that there were no flowers to pick."

"Why weren't there any flowers?"

"Because the pigs had eaten them all," said the bachelor promptly. "The gardeners had told the Prince that you couldn't have pigs and flowers, so he decided to have pigs and no flowers." **A**

140 There was a murmur of approval at the excellence of the Prince's decision; so many people would have decided the other way.

"There were lots of other delightful things in the park. There were ponds with gold and blue and green fish in them, and trees with beautiful parrots that said clever things at a moment's notice, and hummingbirds that hummed all the popular tunes of the day. Bertha walked up and down and enjoyed herself immensely, and thought to herself: 'If I were not so extraordinarily good I should not have been allowed to come into this 150 beautiful park and enjoy all that there is to be seen in it,' and her three medals clinked against one another as she walked and helped to remind her how very good she really was. Just then an enormous wolf came prowling into the park to see if it could catch a fat little pig for its supper."

"What color was it?" asked the children, amid an immediate quickening of interest.

"Mud-color all over, with a black tongue and pale gray eyes that gleamed with unspeakable ferocity. The first thing

that it saw in the park was Bertha; her pinafore[4] was so
spotlessly white and clean that it could be seen from a great
distance. Bertha saw the wolf and saw that it was stealing
toward her, and she began to wish that she had never been
allowed to come into the park. **B** She ran as hard as she could,
and the wolf came after her with huge leaps and bounds. She
managed to reach a shrubbery of myrtle bushes and she hid
herself in one of the thickest of the bushes. The wolf came
sniffing among the branches, its black tongue lolling out of its
mouth and its pale gray eyes glaring with rage. Bertha was
terribly frightened and thought to herself: 'If I had not been so
extraordinarily good I should have been safe in the town at this
moment.' **C** However, the scent of the myrtle was so strong
that the wolf could not sniff out where Bertha was hiding, and
the bushes were so thick that he might have hunted about in
them for a long time without catching sight of her, so he thought
he might as well go off and catch a little pig instead. Bertha was
trembling very much at having the wolf prowling and sniffing
so near her, and as she trembled the medal for obedience
clinked against the medals for good conduct and punctuality.
The wolf was just moving away when he heard the sound of the
medals clinking and stopped to listen; they clinked again in a
bush quite near him. He dashed into the bush, his pale gray eyes

160

170

180

---

4. **pinafore** (PIHN UH FOHR): apronlike garment that young girls used to
   wear over their dresses.

© R Sula Neziere/Mary Evans Picture Library

B LANGUAGE COACH

Many words have **multiple meanings**, and sometimes the meanings are very different. Look at the word *stealing* here. What is its meaning? Use a dictionary if you need to. What is another, more familiar, meaning of *stealing*?

_____

_____

_____

C VOCABULARY

Academic Vocabulary

Think back to the aunt's earlier story about a "good girl." Compare and contrast it with the bachelor's "good girl" story. Which story has a more *complex*, or complicated, message and plot? Explain.

_____

_____

_____

Fairy Child Crying, (1968–1969) by Peter Blake, watercolor.

A **LITERARY ANALYSIS**

Why do you think the children liked the story so much?

_____

_____

_____

_____

_____

B **READING FOCUS**

Considering the bachelor's reply to the aunt, it is clear he does not like the aunt and thinks his story was better. What about the aunt do you think the bachelor objects to? What does this tell you about the writer's **purpose**?

_____

_____

_____

_____

_____

_____

_____

_____

_____

_____

_____

_____

gleaming with ferocity and triumph, and dragged Bertha out and devoured her to the last morsel. All that was left of her were her shoes, bits of clothing, and the three medals for goodness."

"Were any of the little pigs killed?"

"No, they all escaped."

"The story began badly," said the smaller of the small girls, "but it had a beautiful ending."

190   "It is the most beautiful story that I ever heard," said the bigger of the small girls, with immense decision.

"It is the only beautiful story I have ever heard," said Cyril. **A**

A dissentient[5] opinion came from the aunt.

"A most improper story to tell young children! You have undermined the effect of years of careful teaching."

"At any rate," said the bachelor, collecting his belongings preparatory to leaving the carriage, "I kept them quiet for ten minutes, which was more than you were able to do."

"Unhappy woman!" he observed to himself as he walked

200   down the platform of Templecombe station; "for the next six months or so those children will assail her in public with demands for an improper story!" **B**

---

5.   **dissentient** (DIHS SEHN SHUHNT): dissenting; disagreeing.

The Storyteller

VOCABULARY DEVELOPMENT

DIRECTIONS: A choice of three words is given for each selection vocabulary word. Select the one that is closest in meaning to the original word.

1. sultry	angry	nasty	hot
2. petulant	empty	moody	weird
3. resolute	determined	worldly	large
4. persistent	enthusiastic	stubborn	tired

LITERARY FOCUS: OMNISCIENT NARRATOR

DIRECTIONS: List three instances from "The Storyteller" in which the **omniscient narrator** provides information that would not have been given if one of the characters were narrating instead.

1. _____

2. _____

3. _____

READING FOCUS: WRITER'S PURPOSE

DIRECTIONS: Explain how each of the clues listed below might illustrate one of Saki's **purposes** for writing this story. The first one has been done for you.

Clue	Writer's Purpose
The aunt's story is "deploringly uninteresting."	Adults often have trouble entertaining and relating to children.
The aunt keeps saying "don't" and the children keep asking "why?"	1.
The children think the bachelor's story is beautiful, but the aunt thinks it is improper.	2.

SKILLS FOCUS

Literary Skills
Understand omniscient narrator.

Reading Skills
Determine the writer's purpose.

Evacuation Order No. 19

by Julie Otsuka

LITERARY FOCUS: THIRD-PERSON LIMITED NARRATOR

A **third-person limited narrator**, who is not a character in a story, zooms in on the thoughts, actions, and feelings of only one character. You can only infer, or make an educated guess, about what the other characters in the story are thinking and feeling.

As you read "Evacuation Order No. 19," keep in mind that it is told by a third-person limited narrator. Would you like to know more than just what Mrs. Hayashi sees and does? What kinds of things are you curious about?

READING FOCUS: DRAWING CONCLUSIONS

In "Evacuation Order No. 19," you may find that you have questions about the plot soon after you begin reading. Though you might find this frustrating, the writer actually does this on purpose in order to keep you interested and allow you to dig for the hidden truths in the story on your own. As you read, think about what the narrator is *not* telling you, and **draw conclusions** about what those actions mean. You should base your conclusions on evidence from the story and your knowledge of history.

Use the Skill   Use a chart like the one below to note details in the story that hint at what is happening. In the first column, list these details as you read. In the next column, list your conclusions about the meaning of the details.

SKILLS FOCUS

Literary Skills
Understand third-person limited narrator.

Reading Skills
Learn how to draw conclusions based on characters' actions.

Story Detail	My Conclusion
Mrs. Hayashi begins packing.	The sign must say she has to evacuate.

Vocabulary Development

Evacuation Order No. 19

SELECTION VOCABULARY

severed (SEHV UHRD) *v.*: cut; broke off.

    Mrs. Hayashi severed the string with a knife.

rationing (RASH UHN IHNG) *v.*: distributing in small amounts.

    During the war, the government was rationing a variety of supplies.

censored (SEHN SUHRD) *v.*: examined for the purpose of removing anything objectionable.

    Government employees censored letters from foreigners during the war.

drenched (DREHNCHT) *v.*: used as *adj.*: soaked.

    After the rain, the soil in the Hayashis' garden was drenched.

WORD STUDY

DIRECTIONS: Write a sentence for each of the vocabulary words listed above. In each sentence, give clues to the meaning of the vocabulary word by defining or explaining it, or by giving examples.

1. _____

   _____

2. _____

   _____

3. _____

   _____

4. _____

   _____

EVACUATION ORDER NO. 19

by Julie Otsuka

> **BACKGROUND**
> After Japanese planes bombed Pearl Harbor in Hawaii on December 7, 1941, the United States declared war on Japan. Some Americans feared that people of Japanese descent living in the United States might be enemies of the nation, so President Franklin D. Roosevelt signed an order that sent them to special prison camps for the duration of the war. In all, about 120,000 people had to move to the camps.

A READING FOCUS

At this point, the writer has not told us what the sign says. What **conclusion** can you **draw** about what the sign says?

_____

_____

_____

_____

"Evacuation Order No. 19" from *When the Emperor Was Divine: A Novel* by Julie Otsuka. Copyright © 2002 by Julie Otsuka, Inc. Reproduced by permission of **Alfred A. Knopf, Inc.**, a division of **Random House, Inc.**

Overnight the sign had appeared. **A** On billboards and trees and all of the bus stop benches. It hung in the window of Woolworth's. It hung by the entrance to the YMCA. It was nailed to the door of the municipal court and stapled, at eye level, to every other telephone pole along University Avenue. Mrs. Hayashi was returning a book to the library when she saw the sign in a post office window. It was a sunny day in Berkeley[1] in the spring of 1942 and she was wearing new glasses and could see everything clearly for the first time in weeks. She no longer had to squint but she squinted out of habit anyway. She read the sign from top to bottom and then, still squinting, she took out a pen and read the sign from top to bottom again. The print was small and dark. Some of it was tiny. She wrote down a few words on the back of a bank receipt, then turned around and went home and began to pack.

When the overdue notice from the library arrived in the mail nine days later she still had not finished packing. The children had just left for school and boxes and suitcases were scattered across the floor of the house. She tossed the envelope into the nearest suitcase and walked out the door.

---

1. **Berkeley:** city in California along the shore of San Francisco Bay.

American Diary: April 21, 1942 (1997) by Roger Shimomura. Acrylic. 11 × 4 inches. Collection of Esther Weissman. Courtesy of the Artist.

Outside the sun was warm and the palm fronds were clacking idly against the side of the house. She pulled on her white silk gloves and began to walk east on Ashby. She crossed California Street and bought several bars of Lux soap and a large jar of face cream at the Rumford Pharmacy. She passed the thrift shop and the boarded-up grocery but saw no one she knew on the sidewalk. At the newsstand on the corner of Grove she bought a copy of the *Berkeley Gazette*. She scanned the headlines quickly. The Burma Road had been severed and one of the

30   Dionne quintuplets—Yvonne—was still recovering from an ear operation. Sugar rationing would begin on Tuesday.[2] She folded the paper in half but was careful not to let the ink darken her gloves.

At Lundy's Hardware she stopped and looked at the display of victory garden shovels in the window. They were well-made shovels with sturdy metal handles and she thought, for a moment, of buying one—the price was right and she did not like to pass up a bargain. Then she remembered that she already had a shovel at home in the shed. In fact, she had two. She did

40   not need a third. She smoothed down her dress and went into the store. **B**

"Nice glasses," Joe Lundy said the moment she walked through the door.

---

2. **Burma Road . . . Dionne quintuplets** The Burma Road, about 700 miles long, was completed in 1938 by the Chinese and was used to transport supplies during China's war with Japan. The Dionne quintuplets, born in 1934 in Canada, were the first quintuplets known to have survived infancy.

B **LANGUAGE COACH**

Several words in this paragraph end in -*ed*, a suffix in which the *e* is silent. What do the pronunciations of these words have in common? What letter is silent in all these words?

_____

_____

_____

_____

This story uses a **third-person limited narrator**. If it were written with an omniscient, or all-knowing, narrator, what more might we know about Joe Lundy?

_____

_____

_____

_____

B **LITERARY ANALYSIS**

Why do you think Mrs. Hayashi wishes she had used Joe's first name before? Think about what the writer might want you to feel at this point in the story.

_____

_____

_____

_____

"You think?" she asked. "I'm still not used to them yet." She picked up a hammer and gripped the handle firmly. "Do you have anything bigger?" she asked. Joe Lundy said that what she had in her hand was the biggest hammer he had. She put the hammer back on the rack.

"How's your roof holding out?" he asked.

50   "I think the shingles are rotting. It just sprung another leak."

"It's been a wet year."

Mrs. Hayashi nodded. "But we've had some nice days." She walked past the venetian blinds and the blackout shades[3] to the back of the store. She picked out two rolls of tape and a ball of twine and brought them back to the register. "Every time it rains I have to set out the bucket," she said. She put down two quarters on the counter.

"Nothing wrong with a bucket," said Joe Lundy. He pushed the quarters back toward her across the counter but he did not

60   look at her. "You can pay me later," he said. Then he began to wipe the side of the register with a rag. There was a dark stain there that would not go away.

"I can pay you now," she said.

"Don't worry about it." He reached into his shirt pocket and gave her two caramel candies wrapped in gold foil. "For the children," he said. She slipped the caramels into her purse but left the money. She thanked him for the candy and walked out of the store. **A**

"That's a nice red dress," he called out after her.

70   She turned around and squinted at him over the top of her glasses. "Thank you," she said. "Thank you, Joe." Then the door slammed behind her and she was alone on the sidewalk again and she realized that in all the years she had been going to Joe Lundy's store she had never once called him by his name until now. Joe. It sounded strange to her. Wrong, almost. But she had said it. She had said it out loud. She wished she had said it earlier. **B**

---

3. **blackout shades:** black shades drawn to hide house lights that might be used by enemy airplanes during night air raids.

She wiped her forehead with her handkerchief. The sun was bright and Mrs. Hayashi was not a woman who liked to sweat

80 in public. She took off her glasses and crossed to the shady side of the street. At the corner of Shattuck she took the streetcar downtown. She got off in front of J. F. Hink's department store and rode the escalator to the third floor and asked the salesman if they had any duffel bags but they did not, they were all sold out. He had sold the last one a half hour ago. He suggested she try JCPenney but they were sold out of duffel bags there too. They were sold out of duffel bags all over town. **C**

When she got home she took off her red dress and put on her faded blue one—her housedress. She twisted her hair up into

90 a bun and put on an old pair of comfortable shoes. She had to finish packing. She rolled up the Oriental rug in the living room. She took down the mirrors. She took down the curtains and shades. She carried the tiny bonsai tree out to the yard and set it down on the grass beneath the eaves where it would not get too much shade or too much sun but just the right amount of each. She brought the wind-up Victrola and the Westminster chime clock downstairs to the basement.

Upstairs, in the boy's room, she unpinned the One World One War map of the world from the wall and folded it neatly

100 along the crease lines. She wrapped up his stamp collection, and the painted wooden Indian with the long headdress he had won at the Sacramento State Fair. She pulled out his Joe Palooka comic books from under the bed. She emptied the drawers. Some of his clothes—the clothes he would need—she left out for him to put into his suitcase later. She placed his baseball glove on his pillow. The rest of his things she put into boxes and carried into the sunroom. **D**

The door to the girl's room was closed. Above the doorknob was a note that had not been there the day before. It said, "Do

110 Not Disturb." Mrs. Hayashi did not open the door. She went down the stairs and removed the pictures from the walls. There were only three: the painting of Princess Elizabeth that hung

C **READING FOCUS**

Draw a conclusion about why all the duffel bags are sold out.

_____

_____

D **QUICK CHECK**

What is Mrs. Hayashi doing?

_____

_____

_____

_____

A READING FOCUS

Draw a conclusion about Mrs. Hayashi's feelings toward what's happening in *The Gleaners*.

_____

_____

in the dining room, the picture of Jesus in the foyer, and, in the kitchen, a framed reproduction of Millet's *The Gleaners*.[4] She placed Jesus and the little princess together facedown in a box. She made sure to put Jesus on top. She took The *Gleaners* out of its frame and looked at the picture one last time. She wondered why she had let it hang in the kitchen for so long. It bothered her, the way those peasants were forever bent over above that endless

120 field of wheat. "Look up!" she wanted to say to them. "Look up, look up!" *The Gleaners*, she decided, would have to go. She set the picture outside with the garbage. **A**

In the living room she emptied all the books from the shelves except Audubon's *Birds of America*. In the kitchen she emptied the cupboards. She set aside a few things for later that evening. Everything else—the china, the silver, the set of ivory chopsticks her mother had sent to her fifteen years ago from Hawaii on her wedding day—she put into boxes. She taped the boxes shut with the tape she had bought from Lundy's

130 Hardware Store and carried them one by one up the stairs to the sunroom. When she was done she locked the door with two padlocks and sat down on the landing with her dress pushed up above her knees and lit a cigarette. Tomorrow she and the children would be leaving. She did not know where they were going or how long they would be gone or who would look after the house while they were away. She knew only that tomorrow they had to go.

There were things they could take with them: bedding and linen, forks, spoons, plates, bowls, cups, clothes. These were the

140 words she had written down on the back of the bank receipt. Pets were not allowed. That was what the sign had said.

It was late April. It was the fourth week of the fifth month of the war and Mrs. Hayashi, who did not always follow the rules, followed the rules. She gave the cat to the Greers next door. She caught the chicken that had been running wild in the yard since

---

4. ***The Gleaners:*** famous painting by the French artist Jean Millet (1814–1875) showing three peasants bending over to gather kernels of wheat.

the fall and snapped its neck beneath the handle of a broomstick. She plucked out the feathers and set the carcass into a pan of cold water in the sink.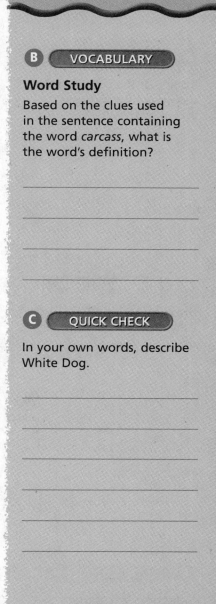

By early afternoon Mrs. Hayashi's handkerchief was soaked.
150 She was breathing hard and her nose was itching from the dust. Her back ached. She slipped off her shoes and massaged the bunions on her feet, then went into the kitchen and turned on the radio. Enrico Caruso was singing "La donna è mobile" again. His voice was full and sweet. She opened the refrigerator and took out a plate of rice balls stuffed with pickled plums. She ate them slowly as she listened to the tenor sing. The plums were dark and sour. They were just the way she liked them.

When the aria was over she turned off the radio and put two rice balls into a blue bowl. She cracked an egg over the bowl
160 and added some salmon she had cooked the night before. She brought the bowl outside to the back porch and set it down on the steps. Her back was throbbing but she stood up straight and clapped her hands three times. A small white dog came limping out of the trees.

"Eat up, White Dog," she said. White Dog was old and ailing but he knew how to eat. His head bobbed up and down above the bowl. She sat down beside him and watched. When the bowl was empty he looked up at her. One of his eyes was clouded over. She rubbed his stomach and his tail thumped against the wooden
170 steps. ⓒ

"Good dog," she said.

She stood up and walked across the yard and White Dog followed her. The tomato garden had gone to seed and the plum tree was heavy with rotting fruit. Weeds were everywhere. She had not mowed the grass for months. Junior usually did that. Junior was her husband. Junior's father was Isamu Hayashi, Senior, but Junior was just Junior. Once in a while he was Sam. Last December Junior had been arrested and sent to Missoula, Montana, on a train. In March he had been sent to Fort Sam
180 Houston, Texas. Now he was living just north of the Mexican border in Lordsburg, New Mexico. Every few days he sent her

Ⓑ VOCABULARY

Word Study
Based on the clues used in the sentence containing the word *carcass*, what is the word's definition?

_____
_____
_____
_____

Ⓒ QUICK CHECK

In your own words, describe White Dog.

_____
_____
_____
_____
_____
_____

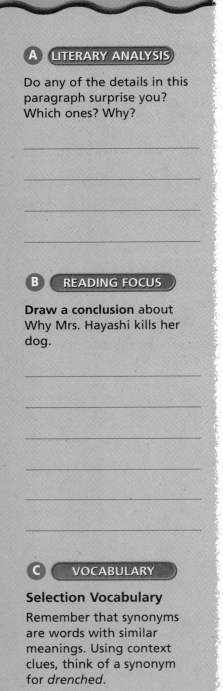

A — LITERARY ANALYSIS

Do any of the details in this paragraph surprise you? Which ones? Why?

_____

_____

_____

_____

B — READING FOCUS

Draw a conclusion about Why Mrs. Hayashi kills her dog.

_____

_____

_____

_____

_____

_____

C — VOCABULARY

Selection Vocabulary

Remember that synonyms are words with similar meanings. Using context clues, think of a synonym for *drenched*.

_____

a letter. Usually he told her about the weather. The weather in Lordsburg was fine. On the back of every envelope was stamped "Alien Enemy Mail, Censored." **A**

Mrs. Hayashi sat down on a rock beneath the persimmon tree. White Dog lay at her feet and closed his eyes. "White Dog," she said, "look at me." White Dog raised his head. She was his mistress and he did whatever she asked. She put on her white silk gloves and took out a roll of twine. "Now just keep looking at me," she said. She tied White Dog to the tree. "You've been a good dog," she said. "You've been a good white dog."

Somewhere in the distance a telephone rang. White Dog barked. "Hush," she said. White Dog grew quiet. "Now roll over," she said. White Dog rolled over and looked up at her with his good eye. "Play dead," she said. White Dog turned his head to the side and closed his eyes. His paws went limp. Mrs. Hayashi picked up the large shovel that was leaning against the trunk of the tree. She lifted it high in the air with both hands and brought the blade down swiftly on his head. White Dog's body shuddered twice and his hind legs kicked out into the air, as though he were trying to run. Then he grew still. A trickle of blood seeped out from the corner of his mouth. She untied him from the tree and let out a deep breath. The shovel had been the right choice. Better, she thought, than a hammer. **B**

Beneath the tree she began to dig a hole. The soil was hard on top but soft and loamy beneath the surface. It gave way easily. She plunged the shovel into the earth again and again until the hole was deep. She picked up White Dog and dropped him into the hole. His body was not heavy. It hit the earth with a quiet thud. She pulled off her gloves and looked at them. They were no longer white. She dropped them into the hole and picked up the shovel again. She filled up the hole. The sun was hot and the only place there was any shade was beneath the trees. Mrs. Hayashi was standing beneath the trees. She was forty-one and tired. The back of her dress was drenched with sweat. **C** She brushed

190

200

210

her hair out of her eyes and leaned against the tree. Everything looked the same as before except the earth was a little darker where the hole had been. Darker and wetter. She plucked two persimmons from a low hanging branch and went back inside
220 the house.

When the children came home from school she reminded them that early the next morning they would be leaving. Tomorrow they were going on a trip. They could only bring with them what they could carry.

"I already know that," said the girl. She knew how to read signs on trees. She tossed her books onto the sofa and told Mrs. Hayashi that her teacher Mr. Rutherford had talked for an entire hour about prime numbers and coniferous trees.

"Do you know what a coniferous tree is?" the girl asked.
230 Mrs. Hayashi had to admit that she did not. "Tell me," she said, but the girl just shook her head no.

"I'll tell you later," she said. She was ten years old and she knew what she liked. Boys and black licorice and Dorothy Lamour.[5] Her favorite song on the radio was "Don't Fence Me In." She adored her pet macaw.[6] She went to the bookshelf and took down *Birds of America*. She balanced the book on her head and walked slowly, her spine held erect, up the stairs to her room. **D**

A few seconds later there was a loud thump and the book
240 came tumbling back down the stairs. The boy looked up at his mother. He was seven and a small, black fedora was tilted to one side of his head. **E** "She has to stand up straighter," he said softly. He went to the foot of the stairs and stared at the book. It had landed face open to a picture of a small brown bird. A marsh wren. "You have to stand up straighter," he shouted.

"It's not that," came the girl's reply. "It's my head."

"What's wrong with your head?" shouted the boy.

---

5. **Dorothy Lamour** (1914–1996): popular movie star of the late 1930s and 1940s. During World War II she helped sell government bonds.
6. **macaw** (MUH KAW): exotic-looking parrot from South and Central America.

D **LITERARY FOCUS**

Even though the writer tells us what the girl likes, we don't know how she feels about having to leave the next morning. Knowing what you do about the **third-person limited narrator,** why do you think this is so?

_____

_____

_____

_____

E **VOCABULARY**

Word Study
Based on the way it is used in the sentence, what do you think a *fedora* is? Check your answer with a dictionary.

_____

_____

_____

A READING FOCUS

Draw a conclusion about why Mrs. Hayashi doesn't say anything to her son about White Dog.

_____

_____

_____

_____

B LITERARY ANALYSIS

Why do you think the boy not only refuses to take the hat off, but wears it each day?

_____

_____

_____

_____

"Too round. Too round on *top*."

He closed the book and turned to his mother. "Where's 250 White Dog?" he asked.

He went out to the porch and clapped his hands three times.

"White Dog!" he yelled. He clapped his hands again. "White Dog!" He called out several more times, then went back inside and stood beside Mrs. Hayashi in the kitchen. She was slicing persimmons. Her fingers were long and white and they knew how to hold a knife. "That dog just gets deafer every day," he said. **A**

He sat down and turned the radio on and off, on and off, while Mrs. Hayashi arranged the persimmons on a plate. 260 The Radio City Symphony was performing Tchaikovsky's *1812 Overture*. Cymbals were crashing. Cannons boomed. Mrs. Hayashi set the plate down in front of the boy. "Eat," she said. He reached for a persimmon just as the audience burst into applause. "Bravo," they shouted, "bravo, bravo!" The boy turned the dial to see if he could find *Speaking of Sports* but all he could find was the news and a Sammy Kaye serenade. He turned off the radio and took another persimmon from the plate.

"It's so hot in here," he said.

"Take off your hat then," said Mrs. Hayashi, but the boy 270 refused. The hat was a present from Junior. It was big on him but he wore it every day. **B** She poured him a glass of cold barley water and he drank it all in one gulp.

The girl came into the kitchen and went to the macaw's cage by the stove. She leaned over and put her face close to the bars. "Tell me something," she said.

The bird fluffed his wings and danced from side to side on his perch. "Baaaak," he said.

"That's not what I wanted to hear," said the girl.

"Take off your hat," said the bird.

280 The girl sat down and Mrs. Hayashi gave her a glass of cold barley water and a long silver spoon. The girl licked the spoon

and stared at her reflection. Her head was upside down. She dipped the spoon into the sugar bowl.

"Is there anything wrong with my face?" she asked.

"Why?" said Mrs. Hayashi.

"People were staring."

"Come over here."

The girl stood up and walked over to her mother.

"Let me look at you," said Mrs. Hayashi.

290 "You took down the mirrors," the girl said.

"I had to. I had to put them away."

"Tell me how I look."

Mrs. Hayashi ran her hands across the girl's face.

"You look fine," she said. "You have a fine nose."

"What else?" asked the girl.

"You have a fine set of teeth."

"Teeth don't count."

"Teeth are essential."

Mrs. Hayashi rubbed the girl's shoulders. The girl leaned

300 back against her mother's knees and closed her eyes.

Mrs. Hayashi pressed her fingers deep into the girl's neck until she felt her begin to relax. "If there was something wrong with my face," the girl asked, "would you tell me?"

"Turn around."

The girl turned around.

"Now look at me."

She looked at her mother.

"You have the most beautiful face I have ever seen."

"You're just saying that."

310 "No, I mean it." **C**

The boy turned on the radio. The weatherman was giving the forecast for the next day. He was predicting rain and cooler temperatures. "Sit down and drink your water," the boy said to his sister. "Don't forget to take your umbrella tomorrow," said the weatherman.

The girl sat down. She drank her barley water and began to tell Mrs. Hayashi all about coniferous trees. Most of them were

C READING FOCUS

Draw a conclusion as to what motivates the girl to ask her mother about her face. Does this help you draw a larger conclusion about the entire story? Explain.

_____

_____

_____

_____

_____

_____

_____

_____

A LITERARY ANALYSIS

Why do you think the girl wants her mother to tell her to practice? Why can't her mother do so?

_____

_____

_____

_____

_____

_____

evergreens but some were just shrubs. Not all of them had cones. Some of them, like the yew, only had seedpods.

320   "That's good to know," said Mrs. Hayashi. Then she stood up and told the girl it was time to practice the piano for Thursday's lesson.

"Do I have to?"

Mrs. Hayashi thought for a moment. "No," she said, "only if you want to."

"Tell me I have to."

"I can't." **A**

The girl went out to the living room and sat down on the piano bench. "The metronome's[7] gone," she called out.

330   "Just count to yourself then," said Mrs. Hayashi.

". . . three, five, seven . . ." The girl put down her knife and paused. They were eating supper at the table. Outside it was dusk. The sky was dark purple and a breeze was blowing in off the bay. Hundreds of jays were twittering madly in the Greers' magnolia tree next door. A drop of rain fell on the ledge above the kitchen sink and Mrs. Hayashi stood up and closed the window.

"Eleven, thirteen," said the girl. She was practicing her prime numbers for Monday's test.

"Sixteen?" said the boy.

340   "No," said the girl. "Sixteen's got a square root."

"I forgot," said the boy. He picked up a drumstick and began to eat.

"You never knew," said the girl.

"Forty-one," said the boy. "Eighty-six." He wiped his mouth with a napkin. "Twelve," he added.

The girl looked at him. Then she turned to her mother.

"There's something wrong with this chicken," she said. "It's too tough." She put down her fork. "I can't swallow another bite."

"Don't, then," said Mrs. Hayashi.

---

7.   **metronome** (MEHT RUH NOHM): clockwork device that beats time, used to help the player keep tempo on the piano.

350　　　"I'll eat it," said the boy. He plucked a wing from his sister's plate and put it into his mouth. He ate the whole thing. Then he spit out the bones and asked Mrs. Hayashi where they were going the next day.

　　　"I don't know," she said.

　　　The girl stood up and left the table. She sat down at the piano and began to play a piece by Debussy from memory. "Golliwogg's Cakewalk." The melody was slow and simple. She had played it at a recital the summer before and her father had sat in the audience and clapped and clapped. She played the

360　piece all the way through without missing a note. **B** When she began to play it a second time the boy got up and went to his room and began to pack.

　　　The first thing he put inside of his suitcase was his baseball glove. He slipped it into the large pocket with the red satin lining. The pocket bulged. He threw in his clothes and tried to close the lid but the suitcase was very full. He sat on top of it and the lid sank down slowly as the air hissed out. Suddenly he stood up again. The lid sprang open. There was something he had forgotten. He went to the closet in the hall and brought back his

370　polka-dotted umbrella. He held it out at arm's length and shook his head sadly. The umbrella was too long. There was no way it would fit inside the suitcase.

　　　Mrs. Hayashi stood in the kitchen, washing her hands. The children had gone to bed and the house was quiet. The pipes were still hot from the day and the water from the faucet was warm. She could hear thunder in the distance—thunder and, from somewhere deep beneath the house, crickets. The crickets had come out early that year and she liked to fall asleep to their chirping. She looked out the window above the sink. The sky was

380　still clear and she could see a full moon through the branches of the maple tree. The maple was a sapling with delicate leaves that turned bright red in the fall. Junior had planted it for her four summers ago. She turned off the tap and looked around for

B LITERARY FOCUS

As you know by now, the **third-person limited narrator** does not allow us to learn about the girl's feelings. Infer how she feels about this piece, and explain your inference. Compare and contrast her feelings to how the boy feels about his hat.

_____

_____

_____

_____

_____

_____

_____

A LITERARY ANALYSIS

How do the words the bird repeats help us better understand Mrs. Hayashi's feelings?

_____

_____

_____

_____

the dish towel but it was not there. She had already packed the towels. They were in the suitcase by the door in the hall.

She dried her hands on the front of her dress and went to the bird cage. She lifted off the green cloth and undid the wire clasp on the door. "Come on out," she said. The bird stepped cautiously onto her finger and looked at her. "It's only me,"

390 she said. He blinked. His eyes were black and bulbous. They had no center.

"Get over here," he said, "get over here now." He sounded just like Junior. If she closed her eyes she could easily imagine that Junior was right there in the room with her.

Mrs. Hayashi did not close her eyes. She knew exactly where Junior was. He was sleeping on a cot—a cot or maybe a bunk bed—somewhere in a tent in Lordsburg where the weather was always fine. She pictured him lying there with one arm flung across his eyes and she kissed the top of the bird's head. **A**

400 "I am right here," she said. "I am right here, right now."

She gave him a sunflower seed and he cracked the shell open in his beak. "Get over here," he said again.

She opened the window and set the bird out on the ledge.

"You're all right," the bird said.

She stroked the underside of his chin and he closed his eyes. "Silly bird," she whispered. She closed the window and locked it. Now the bird was outside on the other side of the glass. He

tapped the pane three times with his claw and said something but
she did not know what it was. She could not hear him anymore.

410   She rapped back.

"Go," she said. The bird flapped his wings and flew up into
the maple tree. She grabbed the broom from behind the stove
and went outside and shook the branches of the tree. A spray of
water fell from the leaves. "Go," she shouted. "Get on out of here."

The bird spread his wings and flew off into the night.

She went back inside the kitchen and took out a bottle of
plum wine from beneath the sink. Without the bird in the cage,
the house felt empty. She sat down on the floor and put the
bottle to her lips. She swallowed once and looked at the place

420   on the wall where *The Gleaners* had hung. The white rectangle
was glowing in the moonlight. She stood up and traced around
its edges with her finger and began to laugh—quietly at first, but
soon her shoulders were heaving and she was doubled over and
gasping for breath. She put down the bottle and waited for the
laughter to stop but it would not, it kept on coming until finally
the tears were running down her cheeks. She picked up the bottle
again and drank. The wine was dark and sweet. She had made
it herself last fall. She took out her handkerchief and wiped her
mouth. Her lips left a dark stain on the cloth. She put the cork

430   back into the bottle and pushed it in as far as it would go. "La
donna è mobile," she sang to herself as she went down the stairs
to the basement. She hid the bottle behind the old rusted furnace
where no one would ever find it. **B**

In the middle of the night the boy crawled into her bed and
asked her, over and over again, "What is that funny noise? What
is that funny *noise*?"

Mrs. Hayashi smoothed down his black hair. "Rain," she
whispered.

The boy understood. He fell asleep at once. Except for

440   the sound of the rain the house was quiet. The crickets were
no longer chirping and the thunder had come and gone.
Mrs. Hayashi lay awake worrying about the leaky roof. Junior

B READING FOCUS

Draw conclusions about
Mrs. Hayashi's character from
her actions in this paragraph.
Why do you think she does
all these things?

_____

_____

_____

_____

_____

_____

_____

_____

_____

Academic Vocabulary

How does the information in this paragraph *correspond* (be similar) to, everything that has happened up to this point?

had meant to fix it but he never had. She got up and placed a tin bucket on the floor to catch the water. She felt better after she did that. She climbed back into bed beside the boy and pulled the blanket up around his shoulders. He was chewing in his sleep and she wondered if he was hungry. Then she remembered the candy in her purse. The caramels. She had forgotten about the caramels. What would Joe Lundy say? He would tell her she was

450 wearing a nice red dress. He would tell her not to worry about it. She knew that. She closed her eyes. She would give the caramels to the children in the morning. That was what she would do. She whispered a silent prayer to herself and drifted off to sleep as the water dripped steadily into the bucket. The boy shrugged off the blanket and rolled up against the wall where it was cool.

In a few hours he and the girl and Mrs. Hayashi would report to the Civil Control Station at the First Congregational Church on Channing Way. They would pin their identification numbers to their collars and grab their suitcases and climb onto the bus. The

460 bus would drive south on Shattuck and then turn west onto Ashby Avenue. Through the dusty pane of the window Mrs. Hayashi would see the newsstand on the corner of Grove. She would see the boarded-up grocery and the sign in front of it—a new sign, a sign she had not seen before—that said, "Thank you for your patronage. God be with you until we meet again." A She would see the thrift shop and the Rumford Pharmacy. She would see her house with its gravel walkway and its small but reliable rosebush

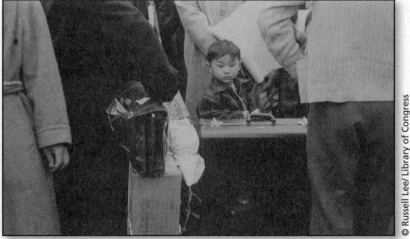

that had blossomed every May for the last ten years in a row. She would see Mrs. Greer next door watering her lawn but she would
470 not wave to her. The bus would speed through a yellow light and turn left onto Route 80, then cross the Bay Bridge and take them away. **B**

Three years and four months later they would return. It would be early autumn and the war would be over. The furniture in the house would be gone but the house would still be theirs. The sunroom would be empty. The stovepipe would be missing from the stove and there would be no motor inside the washing machine. In the mailbox there would be an overdue notice. Mrs. Hayashi would owe the library $61.25 in fines and
480 her borrowing privileges would be temporarily suspended. The bonsai tree would be dead but the maple would be thriving. So would the persimmon tree. Six months later Junior would come home from New Mexico a tired and sick old man. Mrs. Hayashi would not recognize him at first but the girl would know who her father was the moment he stepped off the train. The following summer Junior would have a stroke and Mrs. Hayashi would go to work for the first time in her life. For five and sometimes six days a week she would clean other people's houses much better than she ever had her own. Her back would
490 grow strong and the years would go by quickly. Junior would have two more strokes and then die. The children would grow up. The boy would become a lieutenant colonel in the army and the girl would become my mother. She would tell me many things but she would never speak of the war. The bottle of plum wine would continue to sit, unnoticed, gathering dust behind the furnace in the basement. It would grow darker and sweeter with every passing year. The leak in the roof has still, to this day, not been properly fixed. **C**

B **LITERARY FOCUS**

The **third-person limited narrator** lets us know what happens to Mrs. Hayashi. Consider all the things she sees in this paragraph and draw a conclusion as to what she is probably feeling.

_____

_____

_____

_____

C **LITERARY ANALYSIS**

What happens to the point of view of the narrator in this paragraph? What does this change tell you about the identity of the narrator?

_____

_____

_____

_____

_____

Skills Practice

Evacuation Order No. 19

USE A CONCEPT MAP

Mrs. Hayashi is not only the main character in the story, but she is the only character that we truly learn about from the **third-person limited narrator.** In other words, we are limited in our knowledge of the other characters, but Mrs. Hayashi's thoughts, feelings, and actions are shared with us.

DIRECTIONS: Fill in the outer ovals with examples of Mrs. Hayashi's thoughts, feelings, and actions from the story. Do not record any thoughts, feelings, or actions of other characters.

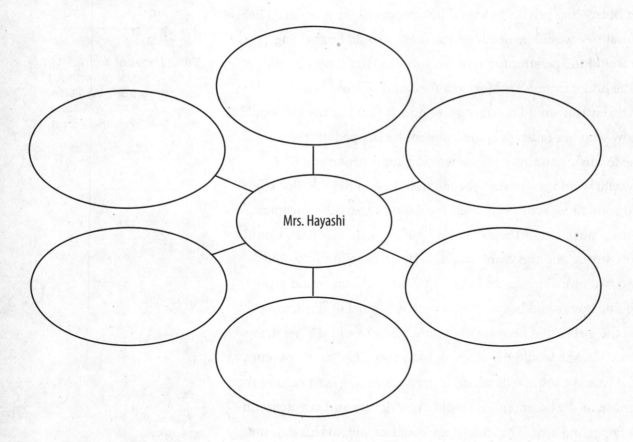

Applying Your Skills

Evacuation Order No. 19

VOCABULARY DEVELOPMENT

DIRECTIONS: Fill in the blanks in the following sentences with the correct words from the Word Box.

Word Box

severed

rationing

censored

drenched

1. I accidentally left the windows of my car open during the rainstorm, and now the seats are _____.

2. My neighbor _____ his connection to the United States and moved to Norway.

3. Movies are always _____ before they are shown on airplanes because people of all ages will be watching them.

4. There were shortages of many materials during the war, so the government was forced to begin _____ the most needed items.

LITERARY FOCUS: THIRD-PERSON LIMITED NARRATOR

When a story is told from the point of view of a **third-person limited narrator**, you know only the thoughts, feelings, and actions of one character.

DIRECTIONS: Choose a character other than Mrs. Hayashi from the story. Then, write a short paragraph on a separate sheet of paper describing what you believe the character is thinking and feeling during the story. Support your ideas with details from the text.

READING FOCUS: DRAWING CONCLUSIONS

DIRECTIONS: Remember that a writer may not clearly state a character's reasons for acting a certain way. When this happens, you have to **draw conclusions** about what their actions might mean. Read each action and the reason for it. If the reason given is incorrect, re-write the conclusion on a separate sheet of paper to make it correct.

Action	Reason
Mrs. Hayashi packs her bags.	The government is forcing her to move.
She kills and buries her dog.	She does not like the dog.
The girl asks her mother if there's anything wrong with her face.	The girl has been made fun of for being Japanese.
Mrs. Hayashi goes to work for the first time.	Mrs. Hayashi always wanted to get a job of her own.

SKILLS FOCUS

Literary Skills
Understand third-person limited narrator.

Reading Skills
Learn how to draw conclusions based on characters' actions.

Islam in America

by Patricia Smith

We Are Each Other's Business

by Eboo Patel

INFORMATIONAL TEXT FOCUS: ANALYZING AUDIENCE AND PURPOSE

Every author begins with a **purpose**, or a reason for writing. It might be to tell a story, provide information, argue for change, or express personal feelings. Before writing, authors also need to know their **audience**—the readers—so they can choose the right attitude, or **tone**, in which to communicate their message.

SELECTION VOCABULARY

affiliations (UH FIHL EE AY SHUHNZ) *n.:* connections, relationships.
   People form affiliations with religious, social, and cultural groups.

integration (IHN TUH GRAY SHUHN) *n.:* the process of combining or including.
   The integration of diverse groups into one society can be a difficult process.

misperceptions (MIHS PUHR SEHP SHUHNZ) *n.:* incorrect ideas or understandings.
   Many people have misperceptions of Muslim beliefs and practices.

prohibits (PROH HIHB IHTS) *v.:* forbids; prevents.
   Some people believe that Islamic teaching prohibits dating.

piety (PY UH TEE) *n.:* religious devotion.
   Patel believes that expressions of piety are not enough; belief must be demonstrated by a person's actions.

bigotry (BIHG UH TREE) *n.:* intolerance or prejudice.
   The student showed bigotry when he shouted anti-Semitic slurs in school.

complicity (KUHM PLIHS UH TEE) *n.:* being an accomplice or partner in wrongdoing.
   His complicity in vandalizing the car made him feel guilty.

SKILLS FOCUS

Informational Text Skills
Determine a writer's audience; understand author's purpose.

WORD STUDY

DIRECTIONS: Use a dictionary to help you find the verb form of the nouns below. Write the meaning of the verb next to each word.

1. noun: *affiliation*; verb: _____
2. noun: *integration*; verb: _____
3. noun: *prohibition*; verb: _____

ISLAM IN AMERICA

by Patricia Smith

BACKGROUND
There are more than one billion Muslims living in the world
today. Muslims are people devoted to the religion of Islam,
which teaches that there is only one God, named Allah. Muslims
believe that Allah communicated the words of the Quran
(sometimes spelled *Koran*), the sacred text of the Islamic faith,
to a prophet named Muhammad. Since 1965, many Muslims
from Middle Eastern countries have immigrated to America.

Like most American teenagers, 17-year-old Sana Haq enjoys
hanging out with her friends and going to the movies. She
just got her driver's license, and she's stressing over college
applications. But Sana, a high school senior from Norwood, N.J.,
is an observant Muslim, and that makes her different from most
of her friends.

She prays five times a day, as Islam requires. She wears
only modest clothing—no shorts, no bathing suits, nothing too
snug. Going to the mall for a pair of jeans can turn into a week-
10 long quest because most are too tight or low-cut to meet her
definition of "decent." **A**

Islam, she says, affects every aspect of her life. "If you ask
me to describe myself in one word, that word would be Muslim,"
says Sana, who was born in the U.S. to Pakistani immigrants.
"Not American, not Pakistani, not a teenager. Muslim. It's the
most important thing to me."

Largely because of immigrant families like Sana's, Islam is
one of the fastest growing religions in the U.S. Since the Census
doesn't track religious affiliations, the number of American
20 Muslims is hard to pin down, but estimates range from
1.5 million to 9 million. **B**

A READING FOCUS

How much do you think the
writer assumes the **audience**
knows about the religion
of Islam?

_____

_____

_____

B VOCABULARY

Selection Vocabulary
Affiliations are connections
or relationships. What other
kinds of affiliations might a
person have?

_____

_____

_____

_____

"Islam in America" by Patricia Smith from *The New York Times: Upfront*, vol. 138, no. 8,
January 9, 2006. Copyright © 2006 by **Scholastic Inc.** Reproduced by permission of the publisher.

Copyright © by Holt, Rinehart and Winston. All rights reserved.

A **READING FOCUS**

At this point, what do you think is the writer's **purpose** for writing this article?

_____

_____

_____

Whatever its size, the Muslim community in the U.S. is very diverse. According to a 2004 poll by Georgetown University and Zogby polling, South Asians (Indians, Pakistanis, Bangladeshis, etc.) are the largest group, followed by Arabs and African-Americans. (Starting in the 1960s, a significant number of blacks in the U.S. converted to Islam.) Thirty-six percent of American Muslims were born in the U.S; the other 64 percent come from 80 different countries. . . .

30 Trying to carve an American Muslim identity out of this diversity is one of the challenges facing young Muslims. They are creating traditions and a culture that is particular to them and not imported from another majority-Muslim country," says Tayyibah Taylor, editor of *Azzizah*, a Muslim women's magazine published in Atlanta. "Something that blends their American way of thinking and their American way of living with Islamic guidelines." A

Contrast with Europe

As a group, American Muslims have a higher median income than Americans as a whole, and they vote in higher numbers. In
40 addition, they are increasingly contributing to American culture, forming Muslim comedy groups, rap groups, Scout troops, magazines, and other media.

Their integration into American society and culture stands in contrast to Europe's Muslim communities, which have

remained largely on the economic and political fringes. **B**
In November 2005 Muslims rioted in many French cities.

In parts of the U.S. with large Muslim populations, Islam
mingles with American traditions. At Dearborn High School
in Dearborn, Mich., about one third of the students—and the
50 football team—are Muslims. Because Ramadan (the Muslim
holy month that requires dawn-to-dusk fasting) coincided with
football season this year, Muslim players had to wake up at 4:30
for a predawn breakfast; go through their classes without eating
or drinking; and start most Friday night games before darkness
allowed them to break their fasts.

"When you start your day off fasting and you get to football
at the end of the day, that's the challenge," says Hassan Cheaib,
a 17-year-old senior. "You know you've worked hard. You know
you've been faithful. . . After fasting all day, you feel like a
60 warrior." **C**

Because some of Islam's social tenets—modesty and chastity,
for example—are so different from American norms, they can
present a challenge for young Muslims. For Sana, adherence to
Islam means she doesn't date. "Dating means going out with
someone and spending intimate time with them, and for me,
that's not allowed," she explains. "But it's not that I don't talk to
guys. I have guy friends."

Impact of 9/11

The terrorist attacks of Sept. 11, 2001, were a transformative
moment for Muslims in America. On the one hand, there has
70 been an increase in anti-Muslim feeling, discrimination, and
hate crimes. On the other hand, many Muslims have responded
by taking more interest in their religion and reaching out to
more non-Muslims.

"September 11 exposed American Muslims for the first
time to a large degree of hostility," says Ishan Bagby, a professor
of Islamic Studies at the University of Kentucky. "So Muslims
have come to the conclusion that isolation is a danger, because

B **LANGUAGE COACH**

Look at the word
integration. The **suffix** *-tion*
is added to the end of a
word to change its meaning.
What is the root word of
integration? What does it
mean? How does the suffix
change its meaning? Use the
dictionary if you need help.

_____

_____

_____

_____

C **QUICK CHECK**

Why did Hassan have to fast?

_____

_____

_____

_____

A **READING FOCUS**

What does this fact tell you about the writer's **purpose** for writing?

_____

_____

_____

_____

B **VOCABULARY**

Academic Vocabulary

How do some people mistakenly *perceive*, or view, Islam?

_____

_____

_____

_____

_____

C **VOCABULARY**

Word Study

What do you think a *mosque* is? Use the clues in the sentence to help you. Use a dictionary to check your answer.

_____

_____

_____

_____

if people don't know you it's easy for them to accept the worst stereotypes."

80   According to one 2003 poll, 63 percent of Americans say they do not have a good understanding of Islam as a religion. **A** Indeed, many young Muslims spend a lot of time correcting common misperceptions about Islam: that it condones terrorism (it doesn't); and that it denies women equal rights (it doesn't, though many majority-Muslim cultures and countries do). **B**

When Ibrahim Elshamy, 18, was growing up in Manchester, N.H., Islam was a regular part of his life. Every Friday he left school at lunch to attend services at a mosque. **C** Now a freshman at Dartmouth College in Hanover, N.H., his religion
90   remains important. Two days after his arrival on campus, he contacted the Muslim student group. And five times a day, he returns to his dorm room to say his prayers.

In college, Ibrahim has found for the first time a Muslim community in which he feels at home. The mosque he and his Egyptian father attended in Manchester attracted many Arab, Asian, and African immigrants. The problem with that, he says, was that people melded their cultural traditions with their practice of Islam. As an American-born Muslim, he found that frustrating.

100   "Here at Dartmouth, it was extremely refreshing," he says, "because I was finally around Muslims who were exactly like me in that respect."

Professor Bagby says many young Muslims want to distinguish between Islam's teachings and the cultural traditions
110   often associated with Islam, particularly the role of women. Stressing that nothing in the Koran

itself prohibits women's full participation (in religion or in life), American women are increasingly demanding not only equal participation but leadership roles in the mosque. "It's definitely rocking some boats," says Tayyibah Taylor of *Azzizah*.

'More American'

Samiyyah Ali, 17, grew up in Atlanta and describes herself as a practicing Muslim, rather than an observant one. She uses the principles of Islam to guide her but doesn't worry about following every last tenet. Like 20 percent of American Muslims, she is African-American. Her parents converted to Islam before she was born.

Other than her name, there's not much about Samiyyah that would tell a stranger she is Muslim. She's a senior at Westminster Academy, a coed private school where she's a cheerleader, on the varsity track and field team, in the dance club, and on the school newspaper staff. And she does date.

She views the Koran as something that should not be followed literally, much like other historical documents that should be understood in context. "A lot of stuff is still applicable—honor and respect is always applicable," says Samiyyah. "But other things that are cultural—even ideas about sex—need to be taken in context. Back then people got married when they were fourteen. Maybe because my family is a convert family, we're just not so orthodox." **D**

The Muslim community in America is currently undergoing a generational shift. Most American mosques were formed by first-generation immigrants, and as their American-born children take over, the norms are changing.

"Islam in America will feel a lot different in the next 40 years," Professor Bagby says. "It'll feel more American, that's for sure." **E**

D LITERARY ANALYSIS

Compare and contrast Samiyyah Ali's religious practice with that of Sana Haq's from the beginning of the article.

_____

_____

_____

_____

_____

_____

_____

E READING FOCUS

Describe the writer's **tone** in this article.

_____

_____

_____

_____

_____

_____

_____

_____

WE ARE EACH OTHER'S BUSINESS

by Eboo Patel

> **BACKGROUND**
>
> Pluralism has been defined as "a condition in which ethnic or other minority groups are able to maintain their identities in a society." In a pluralistic society, individuals or groups retain their individual, cultural, or religious identities and still consider themselves a part of the larger society—without being in conflict with it. In some ways, pluralism is a contrast to the "melting pot" idea of the United States, in which people from diverse cultures leave behind their cultural norms and adopt new ones in order to become American.

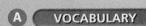

A **VOCABULARY**

Selection Vocabulary
Using context clues, what do you think *piety* means?

_____

_____

_____

B **READING FOCUS**

At this point in the article, what do you think the writer's **purpose** for writing might be?

_____

_____

"We Are Each Other's Business" by Eboo Patel from *This I Believe: The Personal Philosophies of Remarkable Men and Women*, edited by Jay Allison and Dan Gediman with John Gregory and Viki Merrick. Copyright © 2006 by This I Believe, Inc. Reproduced by permission of **Henry Holt and Company, LLC.**

I am an American Muslim. I believe in Pluralism. In the Holy Quran,[1] God tells us, "I created you into diverse nations and tribes that you may come to know one another." I believe America is humanity's best opportunity to make God's wish that we come to know one another a reality.

In my office hangs Norman Rockwell's illustration *Freedom of Worship*. A Muslim holding a Quran in his hands stands near a Catholic woman fingering her rosary. Other figures have their hands folded in prayer and their eyes filled with piety. **A** They

10   stand shoulder-to-shoulder facing the same direction, comfortable with the presence of one another and yet apart. It is a vivid depiction of a group living in peace with its diversity, yet not exploring it.

We live in a world where the forces that seek to divide us are strong. To overcome them, we must do more than simply stand next to one another in silence. **B**

I attended high school in the western suburbs of Chicago. The group I ate lunch with included a Jew, a Mormon, a Hindu, a Catholic and a Lutheran. We were all devout to a degree, but we almost never talked about religion. Someone at the table would

---

1. **Holy Quran:** the main religious text of Islam (sometimes spelled *Koran*).

20 announce that they couldn't eat a certain kind of food, or any
food at all, for a period of time. We all knew religion hovered
behind this, but nobody ever offered any explanation deeper than
"my mom said," and nobody ever asked for one. **C**

A few years after we graduated, my Jewish friend from the
lunchroom reminded me of an experience we both wish had
never happened. A group of thugs in our high school had taken
to scrawling anti-Semitic slurs on classroom desks and shouting
them in the hallway. **D**

I did not confront them. I did not comfort my Jewish friend.
30 Instead I averted my eyes from their bigotry, and I avoided the
eyes of my friend because I couldn't stand to face him.

My friend told me he feared coming to school those days,
and he felt abandoned as he watched his close friends do nothing.
Hearing him tell me of his suffering—and my complicity—is the
single most humiliating experience of my life. **E**

My friend needed more than my silent presence at the lunch
table. I realize now that to believe in pluralism means I need the
courage to act on it. Action is what separates a belief from an
opinion. Beliefs are imprinted through actions.

40 In the words of the American poet Gwendolyn Brooks: "We
are each other's business; we are each other's harvest; we are each
other's magnitude and bond."

I cannot go back in time and take away the suffering of
my Jewish friend, but through action I can prevent it from
happening to others. **F**

C **READING FOCUS**

What kind of **audience**
do you think this article is
written for?

_____

_____

_____

D **VOCABULARY**

Word Study

What do you think *anti-Semitic* means? Re-read the
entire paragraph to help you
figure out the meaning.

_____

_____

_____

E **QUICK CHECK**

Underline the text that
shows why the Jewish friend
felt abandoned.

_____

_____

_____

F **LITERARY ANALYSIS**

How are we "each other's
business"?

_____

_____

_____

_____

Islam in America *and*
We Are Each Other's Business

USE CHARTS

DIRECTIONS: Complete the charts below to help you determine the intended audience of each article.

Islam in America	
What does the author assume about readers' knowledge?	1.
What is the author's attitude toward the subject?	2.
What is the author's attitude toward readers?	3.
Who would be interested in this topic?	4.

Intended Audience: _____

We Are Each Other's Business	
What does the author assume about readers' knowledge?	5.
What is the author's attitude toward the subject?	6.
What is the author's attitude toward readers?	7.
Who would be interested in this topic?	8.

Intended Audience: _____

Applying Your Skills

Islam in America *and* We Are Each Other's Business

VOCABULARY DEVELOPMENT

DIRECTIONS: Write a short paragraph using at least four of the words in the Word Box. Your paragraph should be about something you read in either of the two selections.

Word Box

affiliations

integration

misperceptions

prohibits

piety

bigotry

complicity

_____

_____

_____

_____

_____

_____

_____

_____

INFORMATIONAL TEXT FOCUS: ANALYZING AUDIENCE AND PURPOSE

DIRECTIONS: Use the chart below to summarize and review the two selections you just read. Then, identify the **purpose**, **tone**, and **audience** for each story.

	"Islam in America"	"We Are Each Other's Business"
Purpose		
Tone		
Audience		

SKILLS FOCUS

Informational Text Skills
Determine a writer's audience; understand auther's purpose.

Collection 3

VOCABULARY REVIEW

DIRECTIONS: Review the selection and academic vocabulary by filling in the blanks with words from the Word Box. Not all the words will be used.

Word Box

affiliations
bigotry
censored
complex
complicity
conviction
correspond
drenched
incorporate
integration
misperceptions
perceive
persistent
petulant
piety
prohibits
rationing
resolute
severed
sultry

1. The law _____ robbing a bank and punishes those who do.

2. The soldiers never gave up; they were very _____.

3. When the tree fell down, it _____ the telephone lines, preventing us from making calls all day.

4. I tried to reach the level of _____ my brother had by praying more often.

5. I saw a _____ child whining to her mother in the toy store.

6. People often have _____, or incorrect ideas, about things they don't understand.

7. Barbara felt passionately about animal rights, so she gave her speech with _____.

8. The school newspaper _____ the opinion page because one student wrote very inappropriate things.

9. Everyone was hungry because the cafeteria began _____ food as a result of the shortage.

10. It was so hot that our clothes were _____ with sweat.

Skills Review

Collection 3

LANGUAGE COACH

DIRECTIONS: Remember that a **suffix** is a word part added to the end of another word. Often (but not always) the addition will change the original word's meaning. Look at the chart below. Each row has a word followed by its part of speech, a suffix, a new word, and the new word's part of speech. Fill in the empty boxes with the correct information. The first row is done for you as an example.

Word	Part of Speech	Suffix Added	New Word	New Part of Speech
partial	adjective	-ly	partially	adverb
			manhood	
narrate		-or		noun
			criticism	
secret		-ive		
			nauseous	
equal		-ity		

WRITING ACTIVITY

DIRECTIONS: Write a few sentences explaining the difference between an omniscient narrator and a third-person limited narrator. Then, write a paragraph or two explaining how "The Storyteller" and "Evacuation Order No. 19" would be different if they had been written using a different kind of narrator.

Collection
4

Symbolism and Irony

© Mark Karrass/Corbis

Literary and Academic Vocabulary for Collection 4

derive (DIH RYV) *v.:* obtain from a source or origin.

Symbolism helps you derive meaning from a story.

function (FUHNGK SHUHN) *v.:* act in a specific manner; work.

Your television will only function if it is plugged in.

interact (IHN TUHR AKT) *v.:* act upon each other.

We can tell a lot about characters by the way they interact with each other.

significant (SIHG NIHF UH KUHNT) *adj.:* full of meaning; important.

The sister's knitting is a significant symbol in the story.

irony (Y RUH NEE) *n.:* when something surprising occurs that is the opposite of what was expected.

Did you notice the irony that the man spent $100 on lottery tickets and then won $100 with his last ticket?

symbol (SIHM BUHL) *n.:* an object, event, setting, animal, or person that has deeper connections and associations beyond itself; something that represents something else.

Adam's bike was a symbol of freedom, independence, and adventure.

Through the Tunnel

by Doris Lessing

LITERARY FOCUS: SYMBOLISM

A **symbol** is a person, a place, an object, or an event that stands both for itself and for something beyond itself. For example, cars are a means of transportation, but in a story a car may also symbolize independence, freedom, maturity, responsibility—or even death. "Through the Tunnel" contains several symbols. As you read, decide which people, places, or things could be symbols for something else. When you have finished reading, think about why those symbols were chosen to be part of the story and what meanings those symbols create.

READING FOCUS: MONITORING YOUR READING

When you **monitor your reading**, you pay close attention to what happens while you read. For example, you may notice important details or think of questions raised by a story. It will be helpful to re-read, even several times, to understand the deeper meanings of the story.

Monitor your reading as you read "Through the Tunnel." Fill in the chart below to note details that raise questions about the story's meaning. Then re-read, looking for answers to your questions.

Details	Questions
Jerry keeps diving to search for the hidden tunnel.	Why is he so determined to find the tunnel?

SKILLS FOCUS

Literary Skills
Understand symbols.

Reading Skills
Monitor your reading by asking questions.

Vocabulary Development

Through the Tunnel

SELECTION VOCABULARY

contrition (KUHN TRIHSH UHN) *n.*: regret or sense of guilt at having done wrong.
> *Jerry felt contrition when he thought of his mother alone on the beach.*

defiant (DIH FY UHNT) *adj.*: challenging authority.
> *Jerry was defiant when he asked for the goggles.*

inquisitive (IHN KWIHZ UH TIHV) *adj.*: questioning or curious.
> *His interest in the tunnel was more than inquisitive; it was almost an obsession.*

minute (MY NOOT) *adj.*: very small; tiny.
> *With the goggles in place, Jerry was able to see many minute fish drifting through the water.*

incredulous (IHN KREHJ UH LUHS) *adj.*: disbelieving; skeptical.
> *Jerry felt incredulous when he realized he could hold his breath for two minutes.*

WORD STUDY

DIRECTIONS: The word *minute* is a homograph—its meaning depends on the way it is pronounced. Pronounced "MIH NIHT", it means "a unit of time." Pronounced "MY NOOT", it means "small, or tiny." Find the two meanings and pronunciations for each of the following homographs:

1. bow _____

_____

2. lead _____

_____

3. bass _____

_____

4. close _____

_____

5. dove _____

_____

THROUGH THE TUNNEL

by Doris Lessing

"Through the Tunnel" from *The Habit of Loving* by Doris Lessing. Copyright © 1955 by Doris Lessing. Reproduced by permission of **HarperCollins Publishers, Inc.** and electronic format by permission of **Jonathan Clowes, Ltd., London,** on behalf of **Doris Lessing.**

Courtesy of the Mary Robertson/George Krevsky Gallery

Going to the shore on the first morning of the vacation, the young English boy stopped at a turning of the path and looked down at a wild and rocky bay and then over to the crowded beach he knew so well from other years. His mother walked on in front of him, carrying a bright striped bag in one hand. Her other arm, swinging loose, was very white in the sun. The boy watched that white naked arm and turned his eyes, which had a frown behind them, toward the bay and back again to his mother. When she felt he was not with her, she swung around. **A** "Oh, there you are, Jerry!" she said. She looked impatient, then smiled. "Why, darling, would you rather not come with me? Would you rather—" She frowned, conscientiously worrying over what amusements he might secretly be longing for, which she had been too busy or too careless to imagine. **B** He was very familiar with that anxious, apologetic smile. Contrition sent him running after her. And yet, as he ran, he looked back over his shoulder at

10

the wild bay; and all morning, as he played on the safe beach, he was thinking of it.

Next morning, when it was time for the routine of swimming and sunbathing, his mother said, "Are you tired of the usual beach, Jerry? Would you like to go somewhere else?"

"Oh, no!" he said quickly, smiling at her out of that unfailing impulse of contrition—a sort of chivalry.[1] **C** Yet, walking down the path with her, he blurted out, "I'd like to go and have a look at those rocks down there."

She gave the idea her attention. It was a wild-looking place, and there was no one there, but she said, "Of course, Jerry. When you've had enough, come to the big beach. Or just go straight back to the villa, if you like." She walked away, that bare arm, now slightly reddened from yesterday's sun, swinging. And he almost ran after her again, feeling it unbearable that she should go by herself, but he did not.

She was thinking, Of course he's old enough to be safe without me. Have I been keeping him too close? He mustn't feel he ought to be with me. I must be careful.

He was an only child, eleven years old. She was a widow. She was determined to be neither possessive nor lacking in devotion. She went worrying off to her beach. **D**

As for Jerry, once he saw that his mother had gained her beach, he began the steep descent to the bay. From where he was, high up among red-brown rocks, it was a scoop of moving bluish green fringed with white. As he went lower, he saw that it spread among small promontories and inlets of rough, sharp rock, and the crisping, lapping surface showed stains of purple and darker blue. Finally, as he ran sliding and scraping down the last few yards, he saw an edge of white surf and the shallow, luminous movement of water over white sand and, beyond that, a solid, heavy blue.

He ran straight into the water and began swimming. He was a good swimmer. He went out fast over the gleaming sand, over

---

1. **chivalry** (SHIH VUHL REE) : here, an act of gentlemanly politeness.

C VOCABULARY

Selection Vocabulary

Since *contrition* is described here as "a sort of chivalry," you can conclude that Jerry's contrition is a feeling of regret or guilt at having done something to offend his mother. Why does Jerry feel guilt?

_____

_____

_____

_____

_____

_____

_____

D LITERARY ANALYSIS

What kind of relationship do you think Jerry and his mother have, and why?

_____

_____

_____

_____

_____

_____

_____

_____

A **READING FOCUS**

As you **monitor your reading**, underline details in this paragraph that hint at possible danger for Jerry.

B **LITERARY FOCUS**

Why do you think Jerry wants to be with the other boys so badly? What are the boys a **symbol** of in this story?

C **LITERARY ANALYSIS**

Why does Jerry feel proud of himself?

_____

_____

_____

_____

_____

a middle region where rocks lay like discolored monsters under the surface, and then he was in the real sea—a warm sea where irregular cold currents from the deep water shocked his limbs. **A**

When he was so far out that he could look back not only on the little bay but past the promontory that was between it and the big beach, he floated on the buoyant surface and looked for his mother. There she was, a speck of yellow under an umbrella that looked like a slice of orange peel. He swam back to shore, relieved at being sure she was there, but all at once very lonely.

60 On the edge of a small cape that marked the side of the bay away from the promontory was a loose scatter of rocks. Above them, some boys were stripping off their clothes. They came running, naked, down to the rocks. The English boy swam toward them but kept his distance at a stone's throw. They were of that coast; all of them were burned smooth dark brown and speaking a language he did not understand. To be with them, of them, was a craving that filled his whole body. **B** He swam a little closer; they turned and watched him with narrowed, alert dark eyes. Then one smiled and waved. It was enough. In

70 a minute, he had swum in and was on the rocks beside them, smiling with a desperate, nervous supplication. They shouted cheerful greetings at him; and then, as he preserved his nervous, uncomprehending smile, they understood that he was a foreigner strayed from his own beach, and they proceeded to forget him. But he was happy. He was with them.

They began diving again and again from a high point into a well of blue sea between rough, pointed rocks. After they had dived and come up, they swam around, hauled themselves up, and waited their turn to dive again. They were big boys—men,

80 to Jerry. He dived, and they watched him; and when he swam around to take his place, they made way for him. He felt he was accepted and he dived again, carefully, proud of himself. **C**

Soon the biggest of the boys poised himself, shot down into the water, and did not come up. The others stood about, watching. Jerry, after waiting for the sleek brown head to appear, let out a yell of warning; they looked at him idly and turned their eyes back toward the water. After a long time, the boy came up on the other side of a big dark rock, letting the air out of his lungs in a sputtering gasp and a shout of triumph. Immediately the rest of them dived in. One moment, the morning seemed full of chattering boys; the next, the air and the surface of the water were empty. But through the heavy blue, dark shapes could be seen moving and groping.

Jerry dived, shot past the school of underwater swimmers, saw a black wall of rock looming at him, touched it, and bobbed up at once to the surface, where the wall was a low barrier he could see across. There was no one visible; under him, in the water, the dim shapes of the swimmers had disappeared. Then one and then another of the boys came up on the far side of the barrier of rock, and he understood that they had swum through some gap or hole in it. He plunged down again. He could see nothing through the stinging salt water but the blank rock. When he came up, the boys were all on the diving rock, preparing to attempt the feat again. **D** And now, in a panic of failure, he yelled up, in English, "Look at me! Look!" and he began splashing and kicking in the water like a foolish dog.

They looked down gravely, frowning. He knew the frown. At moments of failure, when he clowned to claim his mother's attention, it was with just this grave, embarrassed inspection that she rewarded him. Through his hot shame, feeling the pleading grin on his face like a scar that he could never remove, he looked up at the group of big brown boys on the rock and shouted, *"Bonjour! Merci! Au revoir! Monsieur, monsieur!"*[2] while he hooked his fingers round his ears and waggled them. **E**

Water surged into his mouth; he choked, sank, came up. The rock, lately weighted with boys, seemed to rear up out of the water as their weight was removed. They were flying down past him now, into the water; the air was full of falling bodies.

---

2. *Bonjour! Merci! Au revoir! Monsieur, monsieur!:* French for "Hello! Thank you! Goodbye! Mister, mister!"—probably the only French words Jerry knows.

D QUICK CHECK

Underline details that explain what the big boys are doing.

E VOCABULARY

Academic Vocabulary

To explore how the big boys *interact* with, or act upon, Jerry, compare and contrast Jerry's efforts to gain the attention of the big boys with his behavior when he first meets them. What does this say about Jerry and the boys?

_____

_____

_____

_____

_____

_____

_____

_____

_____

_____

_____

_____

_____

_____

_____

_____

© Ali Kabas/Alamy

Then the rock was empty in the hot sunlight. He counted one,

120 two, three . . .

At fifty, he was terrified. They must all be drowning beneath him, in the watery caves of the rock! At a hundred, he stared around him at the empty hillside, wondering if he should yell for help. He counted faster, faster, to hurry them up, to bring them to the surface quickly, to drown them quickly—anything rather than the terror of counting on and on into the blue emptiness of the morning. And then, at a hundred and sixty, the water beyond the rock was full of boys blowing like brown whales. They swam back to the shore without a look at him. **A**

130 He climbed back to the diving rock and sat down, feeling the hot roughness of it under his thighs. The boys were gathering up their bits of clothing and running off along the shore to another promontory. They were leaving to get away from him. He cried openly, fists in his eyes. There was no one to see him, and he cried himself out. **B**

It seemed to him that a long time had passed, and he swam out to where he could see his mother. Yes, she was still there, a yellow spot under an orange umbrella. He swam back to the big rock, climbed up, and dived into the blue pool among the fanged

140 and angry boulders. Down he went, until he touched the wall of

rock again. But the salt was so painful in his eyes that he could not see.

He came to the surface, swam to shore, and went back to the villa to wait for his mother. Soon she walked slowly up the path, swinging her striped bag, the flushed, naked arm dangling beside her. "I want some swimming goggles," he panted, defiant and beseeching. **C** **D**

She gave him a patient, inquisitive look as she said casually, "Well, of course, darling." **E**

150 But now, now, now! He must have them this minute, and no other time. He nagged and pestered until she went with him to a shop. As soon as she had bought the goggles, he grabbed them from her hand as if she were going to claim them for herself, and was off, running down the steep path to the bay.

Jerry swam out to the big barrier rock, adjusted the goggles, and dived. The impact of the water broke the rubber-enclosed vacuum, and the goggles came loose. He understood that he must swim down to the base of the rock from the surface of the water. He fixed the goggles tight and firm, filled his lungs, and

160 floated, face down, on the water. Now he could see. It was as if he had eyes of a different kind—fish eyes that showed everything clear and delicate and wavering in the bright water.

Under him, six or seven feet down, was a floor of perfectly clean, shining white sand, rippled firm and hard by the tides. Two grayish shapes steered there, like long, rounded pieces of wood or slate. They were fish. He saw them nose toward each other, poise motionless, make a dart forward, swerve off, and come around again. It was like a water dance. A few inches above them the water sparkled as if sequins were dropping through it.

170 Fish again—myriads of minute fish, the length of his fingernail—were drifting through the water, and in a moment he could feel the innumerable tiny touches of them against his limbs. It was like swimming in flaked silver. The great rock the big boys had swum through rose sheer out of the white sand—black, tufted lightly with greenish weed. He could see no gap in it. He swam down to its base.

C READING FOCUS

To help you **monitor your reading,** underline the detail that explains why Jerry wants his mother to buy him goggles.

D VOCABULARY

Selection Vocabulary

Defiant means "challenging authority." Why does Jerry act defiantly?

_____

_____

_____

_____

_____

E LANGUAGE COACH

Inquisitive comes from the Latin word *quaerere,* meaning "to seek." However, *inquisitive* means "curious." How are *inquisitive* and *quaerere* alike?

_____

_____

_____

_____

_____

_____

_____

C LITERARY ANALYSIS

Why do you think Jerry doesn't reveal his plans to his mother?

_____

_____

_____

_____

_____

_____

_____

_____

_____

180

Again and again he rose, took a big chestful of air, and went down. Again and again he groped over the surface of the rock, feeling it, almost hugging it in the desperate need to find the entrance. And then, once, while he was clinging to the black wall, his knees came up and he shot his feet out forward and they met no obstacle. He had found the hole.

He gained the surface, clambered about the stones that littered the barrier rock until he found a big one, and with this in his arms, let himself down over the side of the rock. He dropped, with the weight, straight to the sandy floor. Clinging tight to the anchor of stone, he lay on his side and looked in under the dark shelf at the place where his feet had gone. He could see the hole. It was an irregular, dark gap; but he could not see deep into it. He

190

let go of his anchor, clung with his hands to the edges of the hole, and tried to push himself in. **A**

He got his head in, found his shoulders jammed, moved them in sidewise, and was inside as far as his wrist. He could see nothing ahead. Something soft and clammy touched his mouth; he saw a dark frond[3] moving against the grayish rock, and panic filled him. He thought of octopuses, of clinging weed. He pushed himself out backward and caught a glimpse, as he retreated, of a harmless tentacle of seaweed drifting in the mouth of the tunnel. But it was enough. He reached the sunlight, swam to shore, and

200

lay on the diving rock. He looked down into the blue well of water. He knew he must find his way through that cave, or hole, or tunnel, and out the other side. **B**

First, he thought, he must learn to control his breathing. He let himself down into the water with another big stone in his arms, so that he could lie effortlessly on the bottom of the sea. He counted. One, two, three. He counted steadily. He could hear the movement of blood in his chest. Fifty-one, fifty-two. . . . His chest was hurting. He let go of the rock and went up into the air. He saw that the sun was low. He rushed to the villa and found his

210

mother at her supper. She said only, "Did you enjoy yourself?" and he said, "Yes." **C**

---

3. **frond** (FRAHND): large leaf or leaflike part of seaweed.

All night the boy dreamed of the water-filled cave in the rock, and as soon as breakfast was over, he went to the bay.

That night, his nose bled badly. For hours he had been underwater, learning to hold his breath, and now he felt weak and dizzy. His mother said, "I shouldn't overdo things, darling, if I were you."

That day and the next, Jerry exercised his lungs as if everything, the whole of his life, all that he would become,
220   depended upon it. Again his nose bled at night, and his mother insisted on his coming with her the next day. It was a torment to him to waste a day of his careful self-training, but he stayed with her on that other beach, which now seemed a place for small children, a place where his mother might lie safe in the sun. It was not his beach. **D**

He did not ask for permission, on the following day, to go to his beach. He went, before his mother could consider the complicated rights and wrongs of the matter. A day's rest, he discovered, had improved his count by ten. The big boys had
230   made the passage while he counted a hundred and sixty. He had been counting fast, in his fright. Probably now, if he tried, he could get through that long tunnel, but he was not going to try yet. A curious, most unchildlike persistence, a controlled impatience, made him wait. In the meantime, he lay underwater on the white sand, littered now by stones he had brought down from the upper air, and studied the entrance to the tunnel. He knew every jut and corner of it, as far as it was possible to see. It was as if he already felt its sharpness about his shoulders.

He sat by the clock in the villa, when his mother was
240   not near, and checked his time. He was incredulous and then proud to find he could hold his breath without strain for two minutes. **E** The words "two minutes," authorized by the clock, brought close the adventure that was so necessary to him. **F**

In another four days, his mother said casually one morning, they must go home. On the day before they left, he would do it. He would do it if it killed him, he said defiantly to himself. But

D LITERARY ANALYSIS

How has Jerry's view about the other beach changed?

_____

_____

_____

_____

E VOCABULARY

Selection Vocabulary
Incredulous means "disbelieving, skeptical." Why might Jerry be incredulous?

_____

_____

_____

F LITERARY FOCUS

Why is the tunnel such an important **symbol** in this story? What does it represent to Jerry?

_____

_____

_____

_____

_____

_____

_____

A LITERARY ANALYSIS

What poses a challenge to
Jerry now?

_____

_____

_____

_____

_____

_____

_____

two days before they were to leave—a day of triumph when he
increased his count by fifteen—his nose bled so badly that he
turned dizzy and had to lie limply over the big rock like a bit of
250 seaweed, watching the thick red blood flow onto the rock and
trickle slowly down to the sea. He was frightened. Supposing he
turned dizzy in the tunnel? Supposing he died there, trapped?
Supposing—his head went around, in the hot sun, and he almost
gave up. He thought he would return to the house and lie down,
and next summer, perhaps, when he had another year's growth in
him—then he would go through the hole.

But even after he had made the decision, or thought he had,
he found himself sitting up on the rock and looking down into
the water; and he knew that now, this moment, when his nose
260 had only just stopped bleeding, when his head was still sore and
throbbing—this was the moment when he would try. If he did
not do it now, he never would. He was trembling with fear that
he would not go; and he was trembling with horror at the long,
long tunnel under the rock, under the sea. Even in the open
sunlight, the barrier rock seemed very wide and very heavy; tons
of rock pressed down on where he would go. If he died there, he
would lie until one day—perhaps not before next year—those big
boys would swim into it and find it blocked.

He put on his goggles, fitted them tight, tested the
270 vacuum. **A** His hands were shaking. Then he chose the biggest
stone he could carry and slipped over the edge of the rock until
half of him was in the cool enclosing water and half in the hot
sun. He looked up once at the empty sky, filled his lungs once,
twice, and then sank fast to the bottom with the stone. He let it
go and began to count. He took the edges of the hole in his hands
and drew himself into it, wriggling his shoulders in sidewise as
he remembered he must, kicking himself along with his feet.

Soon he was clear inside. He was in a small rock-bound
hole filled with yellowish-gray water. The water was pushing him
280 up against the roof. The roof was sharp and pained his back. He
pulled himself along with his hands—fast, fast—and used his

legs as levers. His head knocked against something; a sharp pain dizzied him. Fifty, fifty-one, fifty-two . . . He was without light, and the water seemed to press upon him with the weight of rock. Seventy-one, seventy-two . . . There was no strain on his lungs. He felt like an inflated balloon, his lungs were so light and easy, but his head was pulsing. **B**

He was being continually pressed against the sharp roof, which felt slimy as well as sharp. Again he thought of octopuses, and wondered if the tunnel might be filled with weed that could tangle him. He gave himself a panicky, convulsive kick forward, ducked his head, and swam. His feet and hands moved freely, as if in open water. The hole must have widened out. He thought he must be swimming fast, and he was frightened of banging his head if the tunnel narrowed.

A hundred, a hundred and one . . . The water paled. Victory filled him. His lungs were beginning to hurt. A few more strokes and he would be out. He was counting wildly; he said a hundred and fifteen and then, a long time later, a hundred and fifteen again. The water was a clear jewel-green all around him. Then he saw, above his head, a crack running up through the rock. Sunlight was falling through it, showing the clean, dark rock of the tunnel, a single mussel[4] shell, and darkness ahead.

He was at the end of what he could do. He looked up at the crack as if it were filled with air and not water, as if he could put his mouth to it to draw in air. A hundred and fifteen, he heard himself say inside his head—but he had said that long ago. **C** He must go on into the blackness ahead, or he would drown. His head was swelling, his lungs cracking. A hundred and fifteen, a hundred and fifteen, pounded through his head, and he feebly clutched at rocks in the dark, pulling himself forward, leaving the brief space of sunlit water behind. He felt he was dying. He was no longer quite conscious. He struggled on in the darkness between lapses into unconsciousness. An immense, swelling pain filled his head, and then the darkness cracked with an explosion

---

4. **mussel:** shellfish, similar to a clam or an oyster, that attaches itself to rocks.

B QUICK CHECK

How does Jerry feel now?

_____

_____

_____

_____

_____

C LITERARY ANALYSIS

Why is Jerry stuck at counting one hundred and fiften?

_____

_____

_____

_____

_____

_____

of green light. His hands, groping forward, met nothing; and his feet, kicking back, propelled him out into the open sea.

He drifted to the surface, his face turned up to the air. He was gasping like a fish. He felt he would sink now and drown; 320 he could not swim the few feet back to the rock. Then he was clutching it and pulling himself up onto it. He lay face down, gasping. He could see nothing but a red-veined, clotted dark. His eyes must have burst, he thought; they were full of blood. He tore off his goggles and a gout[5] of blood went into the sea. His nose was bleeding, and the blood had filled the goggles. **A**

He scooped up handfuls of water from the cool, salty sea, to splash on his face, and did not know whether it was blood or salt water he tasted. After a time, his heart quieted, his eyes cleared, and he sat up. He could see the local boys diving and playing half 330 a mile away. He did not want them. He wanted nothing but to get back home and lie down. **B**

In a short while, Jerry swam to shore and climbed slowly up the path to the villa. He flung himself on his bed and slept, waking at the sound of feet on the path outside. His mother was coming back. He rushed to the bathroom, thinking she must not see his face with bloodstains, or tearstains, on it. He came out of the bathroom and met her as she walked into the villa, smiling, her eyes lighting up.

"Have a nice morning?" she asked, laying her hand on his 340 warm brown shoulder a moment.

"Oh, yes, thank you," he said.

"You look a bit pale." And then, sharp and anxious, "How did you bang your head?"

"Oh, just banged it," he told her.

She looked at him closely. He was strained; his eyes were glazed-looking. She was worried. And then she said to herself, Oh, don't fuss! Nothing can happen. He can swim like a fish.

They sat down to lunch together.

---

5. **gout** (GOUT) *n.:* large glob.

350 "Mummy," he said, "I can stay underwater for two minutes—three minutes, at least." It came bursting out of him.

"Can you, darling?" she said. "Well, I shouldn't overdo it. I don't think you ought to swim anymore today."

She was ready for a battle of wills, but he gave in at once. It was no longer of the least importance to go to the bay. **C**

C LITERARY ANALYSIS

In your own words, explain why Jerry no longer wants to go to the bay.

_____

_____

_____

_____

_____

_____

_____

_____

Through the Tunnel

USE A SYMBOL CHART

"Through the Tunnel" contains a number of **symbols**—people, places, and things that stand for both themselves and something else. The chart below lists some passages from the story. In the right column, identify the symbol in each, and write what you think it means.

Passage from story	Symbol/Meaning
"It was a torment to him to waste a day of his careful self-training, but he stayed with her on that other beach, which now seemed a place for small children, a place where his mother might lie safe in the sun." (lines 221–224)	1.
"And yet, as he ran, he looked back over his shoulder at the wild bay; and all morning, as he played on the safe beach, he was thinking of it." (lines 16–18)	2.
"After they had dived and come up, they swam around, hauled themselves up, and waited their turn to dive again. They were big boys— men, to Jerry." (lines 77–80)	3.
"He could see the hole. It was an irregular, dark gap; but he could not see deep into it. . . . He knew he must find his way through that cave, or hole, or tunnel, and out the other side." (lines 188–202)	4.

Applying Your Skills

Through the Tunnel

VOCABULARY DEVELOPMENT

DIRECTIONS: Complete the passage by filling in each blank with the correct vocabulary word from the Word Box.

Word Box

contrition

defiant

inquisitive

minute

incredulous

Despite weeks of begging, Li couldn't get permission to drive the car alone. But he was feeling (1) _____, so he got the keys and drove off anyway. Jesse was (2) _____ and wanted to see what was in the lake. There, he watched what seemed like millions of tiny, (3) _____ fish. Suddenly, he found himself in the water. He was (4) _____, filled with disbelief that he had actually fallen into the water. When he returned home, he had to explain why he was wet. After that, Jesse felt (5) _____ for disobeying them.

LITERARY FOCUS: SYMBOLISM

DIRECTIONS: Choose one **symbol** from the story. On the lines below, explain that symbol's meaning and significance.

_____

_____

READING FOCUS: MONITORING YOUR READING

DIRECTIONS: Re-read "Through the Tunnel" to find answers to the questions you wrote in your chart. Add a third column to the chart to record the answers to your questions, as shown below.

Details	Questions	Answers
Jerry keeps diving to search for the hidden tunnel.	Why is he so determined to find the tunnel?	Maybe it represents growing up and becoming independent from his mother.

A Very Old Man with Enormous Wings

by Gabriel García Márquez

LITERARY FOCUS: MAGIC REALISM AND IRONY

Writers create **magic realism** by inserting a few fantastic, or far-fetched, details into otherwise realistic tales. For example, in this story, a regular man (real) surprisingly has a pair of wings (fantasy). Magic realists often use **irony** to help readers see the fantasy elements in real life and the real-life elements in fantasy. Irony is the difference between what is expected and what actually happens.

READING FOCUS: ANALYZING DETAILS

One way a writer can get you involved in a story is by using descriptive **details.** A writer will describe how things look, sound, feel, smell, and taste so that you feel like you're in the middle of the story.

Use the Skill While you read "A Very Old Man with Enormous Wings," record descriptive details the writer uses to help you picture the setting and the old man. Record the details in the table below.

Details about setting	Details about old man
The beach "became a stew of mud and rotten shellfish."	"He was dressed like a ragpicker."

SKILLS FOCUS

Literary Skills
Understand magical realism and irony.

Reading Skills
Analyze details.

Vocabulary Development

A Very Old Man with Enormous Wings

SELECTION VOCABULARY

stench (STEHNCH) *n.:* very bad smell.

The dead fish gave off an unbearable stench.

impeded (IHM PEED IHD) *v.:* obstructed; blocked, as by some obstacle.

The old man's movements were impeded by his enormous wings.

frivolous (FRIHV UH LUHS) *adj.:* not properly serious; silly.

Onlookers who came in the morning were less frivolous than those earlier visitors, who treated the angel as if it were a circus animal.

prudence (PROO DUHNS) *n.:* good judgment; cautiousness.

The priest showed prudence in warning people that the devil often used carnival tricks to confuse them.

meager (MEE GUHR) *adj.:* small amount; not full or rich.

The letters from Rome were meager and showed no sense of urgency.

WORD STUDY

DIRECTIONS: Fill in the blanks with the correct word from the selection vocabulary list above.

1. A _____ lawsuit has been brought against me—someone is claiming I ruined their shoes by sneezing near them!

2. The foul _____ of the rotten meat drifted through the kitchen and into the living room.

3. I thought the President's _____ about the decision was appropriate, considering it was a risky law to pass.

4. The thick branches _____ me as I hiked through the dense woods.

5. I only had a _____ amount of money in my wallet, so I could not afford to buy you a gift.

A VERY OLD MAN WITH ENORMOUS WINGS

by Gabriel García Márquez

A **READING FOCUS**

Underline the descriptive **details** the author uses to describe the beach.

B **VOCABULARY**

Selection Vocabulary

Use context clues to determine what *impeded* means and write the definition below. Circle the clues that help you figure out the definition.

_____

_____

_____

On the third day of rain they had killed so many crabs inside the house that Pelayo had to cross his drenched courtyard and throw them into the sea, because the newborn child had a temperature all night and they thought it was due to the stench. The world had been sad since Tuesday. Sea and sky were a single ash-gray thing, and the sands of the beach, which on March nights glimmered like powdered light, had become a stew of mud and rotten shellfish. **A** The light was so weak at noon that when Pelayo was coming back to the house after throwing away the crabs, it was hard for him to see what it was that was moving and groaning in the rear of the courtyard. He had to go very close to see that it was an old man, a very old man, lying face down in the mud, who, in spite of his tremendous efforts, couldn't get up, impeded by his enormous wings. **B**

Frightened by that nightmare, Pelayo ran to get Elisenda, his wife, who was putting compresses on the sick child, and he took her to the rear of the courtyard. They both looked at the fallen body with mute stupor.[1] He was dressed like a ragpicker. There were only a few faded hairs left on his bald skull and very

Courtesy of the artist, Clifford Goodenough

---

1. **stupor** (STOO PUHR): dullness of the mind and senses.

"A Very Old Man with Enormous Wings" from *Leaf Storm and Other Stories* by Gabriel García Márquez, translated by Gregory Rabassa. Copyright © 1971 by Gabriel García Márquez. Reproduced by permission of **HarperCollins Publishers, Inc.** and electronic format by permission of **Agencia Literaria Carmen Balcells, S.A. [NO WEB]**

few teeth in his mouth, and his pitiful condition of a drenched great grandfather had taken away any sense of grandeur he might have had. His huge buzzard wings, dirty and half plucked, were forever entangled in the mud. They looked at him so long and so closely that Pelayo and Elisenda very soon overcame their surprise and in the end found him familiar. Then they dared speak to him, and he answered in an incomprehensible dialect with a strong sailor's voice. That was how they skipped over the inconvenience of the wings and quite intelligently concluded that he was a lonely castaway from some foreign ship wrecked by the storm. **C** And yet, they called in a neighbor woman who knew everything about life and death to see him, and all she needed was one look to show them their mistake.

"He's an angel," she told them. "He must have been coming for the child, but the poor fellow is so old that the rain knocked him down." **D**

On the following day everyone knew that a flesh-and-blood angel was held captive in Pelayo's house. Against the judgment of the wise neighbor woman, for whom angels in those times were the fugitive survivors of a celestial conspiracy,[2] they did not have the heart to club him to death. Pelayo watched over him all afternoon from the kitchen, armed with his bailiff's[3] club, and before going to bed, he dragged him out of the mud and locked him up with the hens in the wire chicken coop. In the middle of the night, when the rain stopped, Pelayo and Elisenda were still killing crabs. A short time afterward the child woke up without a fever and with a desire to eat. Then they felt magnanimous[4] and decided to put the angel on a raft with fresh water and provisions for three days and leave him to his fate on the high seas. But when they went out into the courtyard with the first light of dawn, they found the whole neighborhood in front of the chicken coop having fun with the

---

2. **celestial conspiracy:** According to the Book of Revelation in the Bible (12:7–9), Satan—the devil—originally was an angel who led a rebellion in Heaven. As a result, he and his followers, called the fallen angels, were cast out of Heaven.
3. **bailiff's** (BAY LIHFS): A bailiff is a minor local official.
4. **magnanimous** (MAG NAN UH MUHS): generous; noble.

C QUICK CHECK

How do Pelayo and Elisenda react to the fact that this man has wings? What do they think he is?

_____

_____

_____

_____

_____

D QUICK CHECK

What is the neighbor's explanation for the old man's wings?

_____

_____

_____

A **VOCABULARY**

Selection Vocabulary

Why do you think the previous onlookers are described as *frivolous*, or not properly serious?

_____

_____

_____

_____

_____

B **QUICK CHECK**

What are some things the people think the angel should become?

_____

_____

_____

_____

60
angel, without the slightest reverence,[5] tossing him things to eat through the openings in the wire as if he weren't a supernatural creature but a circus animal.

Father Gonzaga arrived before seven o'clock, alarmed at the strange news. By that time onlookers less frivolous than those at dawn had already arrived and they were making all kinds of conjectures[6] concerning the captive's future. **A** The simplest among them thought that he should be named mayor of the world. Others of sterner mind felt that he should be promoted to the rank of five-star general in order to win all wars. Some visionaries hoped that he could be put to stud in order to implant
70
on earth a race of winged wise men who could take charge of the universe. **B** But Father Gonzaga, before becoming a priest, had been a robust woodcutter. Standing by the wire, he reviewed his catechism[7] in an instant and asked them to open the door so that he could take a close look at that pitiful man who looked more like a huge decrepit hen among the fascinated chickens. He was lying in a corner drying his open wings in the sunlight among the fruit peels and breakfast leftovers that the early risers had thrown him. Alien to the impertinences[8] of the world, he only lifted his antiquarian[9] eyes and murmured something in
80
his dialect when Father Gonzaga went into the chicken coop and said good morning to him in Latin. The parish priest had his first suspicion of an impostor when he saw that he did not understand the language of God or know how to greet His ministers. Then he noticed that seen close up, he was much too human: He had an unbearable smell of the outdoors, the back side of his wings was strewn with parasites and his main feathers had been mistreated by terrestrial[10] winds, and nothing about

---

5. **reverence** (REV UHR UHNS): attitude or display of deep respect and awe.
6. **conjectures** (KUHN JEHK CHURZ): guesses not completely supported by evidence.
7. **catechism** (KAT UH KIHZ UHM): book of religious doctrine, consisting of a series of questions and answers.
8. **impertinences** (IHM PUR TUH NEHNS EHZ): insults; disrespectful acts or remarks.
9. **antiquarian** (AN TUH KWAR EE UHN): ancient.
10. **terrestrial** (TUH REHS TREE UHL): earthly.

him measured up to the proud dignity of angels. **C** Then he came out of the chicken coop and in a brief sermon warned the

90 curious against the risks of being ingenuous.[11] He reminded them that the devil had the bad habit of making use of carnival tricks in order to confuse the unwary. He argued that if wings were not the essential element in determining the difference between a hawk and an airplane, they were even less so in the recognition of angels. Nevertheless, he promised to write a letter to his bishop so that the latter would write to his primate[12] so that the latter would write to the Supreme Pontiff[13] in order to get the final verdict from the highest courts.

His prudence fell on sterile hearts. The news of the captive

100 angel spread with such rapidity that after a few hours the courtyard had the bustle of a marketplace, and they had to call in troops with fixed bayonets to disperse the mob that was about to knock the house down. Elisenda, her spine all twisted from sweeping up so much marketplace trash, then got the idea of fencing in the yard and charging five cents admission to see the angel. **D**

The curious came from far away. A traveling carnival arrived with a flying acrobat, who buzzed over the crowd several times, but no one paid any attention to him because his wings were not

110 those of an angel but, rather, those of a sidereal[14] bat. The most unfortunate invalids on earth came in search of health: a poor woman who since childhood had been counting her heartbeats and had run out of numbers; a Portuguese man who couldn't sleep because the noise of the stars disturbed him; a sleepwalker who got up at night to undo the things he had done while awake; and many others with less serious ailments. In the midst of that shipwreck disorder that made the earth tremble, Pelayo and Elisenda were happy with fatigue, for in less than a week they

---

11. **ingenuous** (IHN JEHN YOO UHS): too trusting; tending to believe too readily.
12. **primate:** here, an archbishop or highest-ranking bishop in a country or province.
13. **Supreme Pontiff:** pope, head of the Roman Catholic Church.
14. **sidereal** (SY DIHR EE UHL): relating to the stars or constellations.

C **READING FOCUS**

What are some of the **details** the writer uses to describe the old man in this paragraph?

_____

_____

_____

_____

_____

D **LITERARY FOCUS**

How is Elisenda's behavior **ironic?**

_____

_____

_____

_____

_____

_____

_____

_____

A LANGUAGE COACH

A **suffix** is a group of letters that is added to the end of a word to change its meaning. For example, the word *showed* contains the suffix –ed. Identify the suffix and the root of the word *hellish*. What do you think this word means?

_____

_____

_____

B VOCABULARY

Academic Vocabulary

What is *significant*, or important, about the fact that the angel is patient with everyone except when they try to burn him with a branding iron?

_____

_____

_____

_____

_____

C VOCABULARY

Word Study

The adjective *passive* means "calm" or "without emotion." Knowing this, what might the noun *passivity* mean?

_____

_____

_____

had crammed their rooms with money and the line of pilgrims
120   waiting their turn to enter still reached beyond the horizon.

The angel was the only one who took no part in his own act. He spent his time trying to get comfortable in his borrowed nest, befuddled by the hellish heat of the oil lamps and sacramental candles that had been placed along the wire. **A** At first they tried to make him eat some mothballs, which, according to the wisdom of the wise neighbor woman, were the food prescribed for angels. But he turned them down, just as he turned down the papal[15] lunches that the penitents[16] brought him, and they never found out whether it was because he was an angel or because
130   he was an old man that in the end he ate nothing but eggplant mush. His only supernatural virtue seemed to be patience. Especially during the first days, when the hens pecked at him, searching for stellar[17] parasites that proliferated[18] in his wings, and the cripples pulled out feathers to touch their defective parts with, and even the most merciful threw stones at him, trying to get him to rise so they could see him standing. The only time they succeeded in arousing him was when they burned his side with an iron for branding steers, for he had been motionless for so many hours that they thought he was dead. He awoke with
140   a start, ranting in his hermetic[19] language and with tears in his eyes, and he flapped his wings a couple of times, which brought on a whirlwind of chicken dung and lunar dust and a gale of panic that did not seem to be of this world. **B** Although many thought that his reaction had been one not of rage but of pain, from then on they were careful not to annoy him, because the majority understood that his passivity was not that of a hero taking his ease but that of a cataclysm[20] in repose. **C**

Father Gonzaga held back the crowd's frivolity[21] with formulas of maidservant inspiration while awaiting the arrival

---

15. **papal** (PAY PUHL): here, fit for the pope.
16. **penitents** (PEHN UH TUHNTS): people who repent their sins.
17. **stellar** (STEHL UHR): having to do with the stars.
18. **proliferated** (PROH LIHF UH RAYT IHD): quickly increased in number.
19. **hermetic** (HUR MEHT IHK): difficult to understand; mysterious.
20. **cataclysm** (KAT UH KLIHZ UHM): disaster; sudden, violent event.
21. **frivolity** (FRIH VAHL UH TEE): silly behavior.

Art by Sergio Bustamante/photograph © 2003 Clint Clemens

D **LITERARY ANALYSIS**

How do the letters from Rome relate to Father Gonzaga's unhappiness?

_____

_____

_____

_____

_____

_____

_____

_____

150 of a final judgment on the nature of the captive. But the mail from Rome showed no sense of urgency. They spent their time finding out if the prisoner had a navel, if his dialect had any connection with Aramaic,[22] how many times he could fit on the head of a pin, or whether he wasn't just a Norwegian with wings. Those meager letters might have come and gone until the end of time if a providential[23] event had not put an end to the priest's tribulations.[24] **D**

160 It so happened that during those days, among so many other carnival attractions, there arrived in town the traveling show of the woman who had been changed into a spider for having disobeyed her parents. The admission to see her was not only less than the admission to see the angel, but people were permitted to ask her all manner of questions about her absurd

---

22. **Aramaic:** ancient Middle Eastern language spoken by Jesus and his disciples.
23. **providential** (PRAHV uh DEHN shuhl): fortunate; like something caused by a divine act.
24. **tribulations** (TRIHB yuh LAY shuhnz): conditions of great unhappiness, sometimes caused by oppression.

A **LANGUAGE COACH**

What is the meaning of *fright*? Adding the **suffix** *–ful* creates the word *frightful*. What does it mean? What part of speech is it?

_____

_____

_____

_____

B **VOCABULARY**

Word Study

The word *rent* has more than one meaning. What meaning is used here? What is another, more common, meaning?

_____

_____

_____

_____

_____

_____

C **LITERARY FOCUS**

Underline two sentences in this paragraph that introduce more elements of **magic realism** into the story.

state and to examine her up and down so that no one would ever doubt the truth of her horror. She was a frightful tarantula the size of a ram and with the head of a sad maiden. **A** What was most heart-rending, however, was not her outlandish shape but the sincere affliction[25] with which she recounted the details of her misfortune. While still practically a child, she had sneaked out of her parents' house to go to a dance, and while she was coming back through the woods after having danced all night without permission, a fearful thunderclap rent the sky in two and through the crack came the lightning bolt of brimstone that changed her into a spider. **B** Her only nourishment came from the meatballs that charitable souls chose to toss into her mouth. A spectacle like that, full of so much human truth and with such a fearful lesson, was bound to defeat without even trying that of a haughty angel who scarcely deigned to look at mortals. Besides, the few miracles attributed to the angel showed a certain mental disorder, like the blind man who didn't recover his sight but grew three new teeth, or the paralytic who didn't get to walk but almost won the lottery, or the leper whose sores sprouted sunflowers. Those consolation miracles, which were more like mocking fun, had already ruined the angel's reputation when the woman who had been changed into a spider finally crushed him completely. **C** That was how Father Gonzaga was cured forever of his insomnia and Pelayo's courtyard went back to being as empty as during the time it had rained for three days and crabs walked through the bedrooms.

The owners of the house had no reason to lament. With the money they saved they built a two-story mansion with balconies and gardens and high netting so that crabs wouldn't get in during the winter, and with iron bars on the windows so that angels wouldn't get in. Pelayo also set up a rabbit warren close to town and gave up his job as bailiff for good, and Elisenda bought some satin pumps with high heels and many dresses of iridescent silk, the kind worn on Sunday by the most desirable women in those times. The chicken coop was the only thing that

---

25. **affliction** (UH FLIHK SHUHN): suffering; distress.

didn't receive any attention. If they washed it down with creolin

200 and burned tears of myrrh[26] inside it every so often, it was not

in homage to the angel but to drive away the dung-heap stench

that still hung everywhere like a ghost and was turning the new

house into an old one. At first, when the child learned to walk,

they were careful that he not get too close to the chicken coop.

But then they began to lose their fears and got used to the smell,

and before the child got his second teeth, he'd gone inside the

chicken coop to play, where the wires were falling apart. The

angel was no less standoffish with him than with other mortals,

but he tolerated the most ingenious infamies[27] with the patience

210 of a dog who had no illusions. They both came down with

chickenpox at the same time. The doctor who took care of the

child couldn't resist the temptation to listen to the angel's heart,

and he found so much whistling in the heart and so many sounds

in his kidneys that it seemed impossible for him to be alive. What

surprised him most, however, was the logic of his wings. They

seemed so natural on that completely human organism that he

couldn't understand why other men didn't have them too. **D**

　　When the child began school, it had been some time since

the sun and rain had caused the collapse of the chicken coop.

220 The angel went dragging himself about here and there like a stray

dying man. They would drive him out of the bedroom with a

broom and a moment later find him in the kitchen. He seemed to

be in so many places at the same time that they grew to think that

he'd been duplicated, that he was reproducing himself all through

the house, and the exasperated and unhinged Elisenda shouted

that it was awful living in that hell full of angels. **E** He could

scarcely eat and his antiquarian eyes had also become so foggy

that he went about bumping into posts. All he had left were the

bare cannulae[28] of his last feathers. Pelayo threw a blanket over

230 him and extended him the charity of letting him sleep in the shed,

and only then did they notice that he had a temperature at night

and was delirious with the tongue twisters of an old Norwegian.

26. **myrrh** (MUHR): sweet-smelling substance used in making perfume.
27. **infamies** (IHN FUH MEEZ): disrespectful acts; insults.
28. **cannulae** (KAN YOO LEE): here, tubes that hold the feathers.

D **READING FOCUS**

Which **details** in this paragraph suggest how human this angel really is?

_____

_____

_____

_____

_____

_____

E **LITERARY FOCUS**

What is **ironic** about Elisenda's words in this sentence?

_____

_____

_____

_____

_____

_____

_____

_____

_____

_____

_____

_____

_____

_____

_____

A QUICK CHECK

What are some of the ways in which the angel seems to be getting sick or possibly dying?

_____
_____
_____
_____
_____

B LITERARY ANALYSIS

In many traditions, myths, and religions, angels are messengers from God who arrive with some purpose (to be a "guardian angel," for example). For what purpose do you think the angel comes to Pelayo and Elisenda?

_____
_____
_____
_____
_____
_____
_____
_____
_____
_____

That was one of the few times they became alarmed, for they thought he was going to die and not even the wise neighbor woman had been able to tell them what to do with dead angels. **A**

And yet he not only survived his worst winter but seemed improved with the first sunny days. He remained motionless for several days in the farthest corner of the courtyard, where no one would see him, and at the beginning of December some large, stiff feathers began to grow on his wings, the feathers of a scarecrow, 240 which looked more like another misfortune of decrepitude.[29] But he must have known the reason for those changes, for he was quite careful that no one should notice them, that no one should hear the sea chanteys that he sometimes sang under the stars. One morning Elisenda was cutting some bunches of onions for lunch when a wind that seemed to come from the high seas blew into the kitchen. Then she went to the window and caught the angel in his first attempts at flight. They were so clumsy that his fingernails opened a furrow in the vegetable patch and he was on the point of knocking the shed down with the ungainly flapping that slipped 250 on the light and couldn't get a grip on the air. But he did manage to gain altitude. Elisenda let out a sigh of relief, for herself and for him, when she saw him pass over the last houses, holding himself up in some way with the risky flapping of a senile vulture. She kept watching him even when she was through cutting the onions and she kept on watching until it was no longer possible for her to see him, because then he was no longer an annoyance in her life but an imaginary dot on the horizon of the sea. **B**

---

29. **decrepitude** (DIH KREHP UH TOOD): feebleness; weakness usually due to old age.

Applying Your Skills

A Very Old Man with Enormous Wings

VOCABULARY DEVELOPMENT

DIRECTIONS: Match the vocabulary word on the left with the best definition on the right.

_____ **1.** stench		**a.** silly
_____ **2.** impeded		**b.** inadequate
_____ **3.** frivolous		**c.** blocked
_____ **4.** prudence		**d.** stink
_____ **5.** meager		**e.** carefulness

LITERARY FOCUS: MAGIC REALISM AND IRONY

DIRECTIONS: On a separate sheet of paper, write a brief paragraph discussing the story's use of **magic realism** and **irony**. What was realistic about the story? What elements of the story are fantastic? How did the author's merging of the fantastic and the realistic impact the story? What are some examples of irony in the story?

READING FOCUS: ANALYZING DETAILS

DIRECTIONS: Complete the following chart by reviewing the story and selecting three **details** that appeal to any three of the five senses.

Senses	Details from story
1.	
2.	
3.	

SKILLS FOCUS

Literary Skills
Understand magical realism and irony.

Reading Skills
Analyze details.

R.M.S. Titanic

by Hanson W. Baldwin

A Fireman's Story

by Harry Senior

From a Lifeboat

by Mrs. D.H. Bishop

INFORMATIONAL TEXT FOCUS: PRIMARY AND SECONDARY SOURCES

Authors who write about historical events use **primary sources** and **secondary sources**. A primary source is a report of an event from a witness. Examples include autobiographies and personal letters. A secondary source contains information that has been summarized from several other sources. Biographies, textbooks, and newspaper articles are all secondary sources.

Primary sources can be **subjective**—the information may be clouded by a person's opinions. Writers of secondary sources (like news journalists) usually try to be **objective**, or attempt to write factual pieces without adding their opinions.

SELECTION VOCABULARY

ascertain (AS UHR TAYN) *v.:* find out with certainty; determine.
   The captain needed to ascertain if the ship had indeed hit an iceberg.

corroborated (KUH RAHB UH RAYT IHD) *v.:* supported; upheld the truth of.
   Several accounts corroborated the report that the lifeboats were not filled.

perfunctory (PUHR FUHNGK TUHR EE) *adj.:* done with little care or thought; indifferent.
   The efforts to gather more people into the lifeboats were perfunctory at best.

pertinent (PUR TUH NUHNT) *adj.:* having some connection with the subject.
   Baldwin tried to select only pertinent information from the dozens of accounts.

SKILLS FOCUS

Informational Text Skills
Understand the difference between subjective primary sources and objective secondary sources.

WORD STUDY

DIRECTIONS: Write one sentence of your own that correctly uses two of the selection vocabulary words from the list above.

_____

_____

R.M.S. TITANIC

by Hanson W. Baldwin

> **BACKGROUND**
> The R.M.S. *Titanic* was a giant luxury cruise ship that left
> Southampton, England, to sail to New York in April, 1912.
> The ship hit an iceberg and sunk. Around 1,500 people died.
> The following article from 1934 describes the tragedy. The
> author researched ship's logs, interviews, and other records to
> write the article.

I

The White Star liner *Titanic*, largest ship the world had ever
known, sailed from Southampton on her maiden voyage to New
York on April 10, 1912. The paint on her strakes[1] was fair and
bright; she was fresh from Harland and Wolff's Belfast yards,
strong in the strength of her forty-six thousand tons of steel,
bent, hammered, shaped, and riveted through the three years
of her slow birth. **A**

There was little fuss and fanfare at her sailing; her sister
ship, the *Olympic*—slightly smaller than the *Titanic*—had been
in service for some months and to her had gone the thunder of
the cheers.

But the *Titanic* needed no whistling steamers or shouting
crowds to call attention to her superlative qualities. **B** Her
bulk dwarfed the ships near her as longshoremen singled up
her mooring lines and cast off the turns of heavy rope from the
dock bollards.[2] She was not only the largest ship afloat, but was
believed to be the safest. Carlisle, her builder, had given her

---

1. **strakes:** single lines of metal plating extending the whole length of
a ship.
2. **bollards** (BAHL UHRDZ): strong posts on a pier or wharf for holding
a ship's mooring ropes.

"R.M.S. Titanic" by Hanson W. Baldwin from Harper's Magazine, January 1934. Copyright ©
1934 by Hanson W. Baldwin. Reproduced by permission of **Curtis Brown Ltd.**

A | QUICK CHECK

How long did it take to build
the *Titanic*?

_____

_____

B | VOCABULARY

Word Study
Look up the word *superlative*
in the dictionary. Write at
least two synonyms (words
with similar meanings) for
superlative.

_____

_____

_____

A QUICK CHECK

What reasons did people have for thinking the *Titanic* was unsinkable?

_____

_____

_____

_____

_____

_____

B VOCABULARY

Word Study

Ominous means "suggesting evil or harm; threatening." It is in the same word family as *omen*. Find *omen* in a dictionary. What does it mean? How does its definition relate to the definition of *ominous*?

© Ralph White/Corbis

double bottoms and had divided her hull into sixteen watertight compartments, which made her, men thought, unsinkable. She had been built to be and had been described as a gigantic lifeboat. **A** Her designers' dreams of a triple-screw[3] giant, a luxurious, floating hotel, which could speed to New York at twenty-three knots, had been carefully translated from blueprints and mold loft lines at the Belfast yards into a living reality.

The *Titanic's* sailing from Southampton, though quiet, was not wholly uneventful. As the liner moved slowly toward the end of her dock that April day, the surge of her passing sucked away from the quay[4] the steamer *New York*, moored just to seaward of the *Titanic's* berth. There were sharp cracks as the manila mooring lines of the *New York* parted under the strain. The frayed ropes writhed and whistled through the air and snapped down among the waving crowd on the pier; the *New York* swung toward the *Titanic's* bow, was checked and dragged back to the dock barely in time to avert a collision. Seamen muttered, thought it an ominous start. **B**

Past Spithead and the Isle of Wight the *Titanic* steamed. She called at Cherbourg at dusk and then laid her course for Queenstown. At 1:30 P.M. on Thursday, April 11, she stood out of Queenstown harbor, screaming gulls soaring in her wake, with 2,201 persons—men, women, and children—aboard.

Occupying the Empire bedrooms and Georgian suites of the first-class accommodations were many well-known men and women—Colonel John Jacob Astor and his young bride; Major Archibald Butt, military aide to President Taft, and his friend Frank D. Millet, the painter; John B. Thayer, vice president of the Pennsylvania Railroad, and Charles M. Hays, president of the Grand Trunk Railway of Canada; W. T. Stead, the English

---

3. **triple-screw:** three-propellered.
4. **quay** (KEE): dock.

journalist; Jacques Futrelle, French novelist; H. B. Harris, theatrical manager, and Mrs. Harris; Mr. and Mrs. Isidor Straus; and J. Bruce Ismay, chairman and managing director of the White Star Line.

Down in the plain wooden cabins of the steerage class were 706 immigrants to the land of promise, and trimly stowed in the great holds was a cargo valued at $420,000: oak beams, sponges, wine, calabashes,[5] and an odd miscellany of the common and the rare.

The *Titanic* took her departure on Fastnet Light[6] and, heading into the night, laid her course for New York. She was due at quarantine[7] the following Wednesday morning.

Sunday dawned fair and clear. The *Titanic* steamed smoothly toward the west, faint streamers of brownish smoke trailing from her funnels. The purser held services in the saloon in the morning; on the steerage deck aft[8] the immigrants were playing games and a Scotsman was puffing "The Campbells Are Coming" on his bagpipes in the midst of the uproar. **C**

At 9:00 A.M. a message from the steamer Caronia sputtered into the wireless shack:

Captain, *Titanic*—Westbound steamers report bergs growlers and field ice 42 degrees N. from 49 degrees to 51 degrees W. 12th April.

Compliments—Barr. **D**

It was cold in the afternoon; the sun was brilliant, but the *Titanic*, her screws turning over at seventy-five revolutions per minute, was approaching the Banks.[9]

---

5. **calabashes** (KAL UH BASH UHZ): large smoking pipes made from the necks of gourds.
6. **Fastnet Light:** lighthouse at the southwestern tip of Ireland. After the Fastnet Light there is only open sea until the coast of North America.
7. **quarantine** (KWAR UHN TEEN): place where a ship is held in port after arrival to determine whether its passengers and cargo are free of communicable diseases. Quarantine can also be used to mean the length of time a ship is held.
8. **aft:** in the rear of a ship.
9. **Banks:** Grand Banks, shallow waters near the southeast coast of Newfoundland.

C READING FOCUS

Do you think the information in this paragraph is **objective** or **subjective**? Why?

_____

_____

_____

_____

_____

_____

D READING FOCUS

After having read this far, do you think that this entire selection is a **primary** or **secondary source**? Give a reason for your answer.

_____

_____

_____

_____

_____

_____

A LITERARY ANALYSIS

Why do you think Second Operator Bride didn't write down and pass along the message from the *Californian*?

_____

_____

_____

_____

_____

B LANGUAGE COACH

Based on **context clues**, or clues from the surrounding text, figure out which meaning of the word *bitter* is being used in this sentence and write it below.

_____

_____

_____

C READING FOCUS

Is this description of Second Officer Lightoller **subjective** or **objective**? Give a reason to support your answer.

_____

_____

_____

_____

_____

In the Marconi cabin[10] Second Operator Harold Bride, earphones clamped on his head, was figuring accounts; he did not stop to answer when he heard MWL, Continental Morse for the nearby Leyland liner, *Californian*, calling the *Titanic*. The *Californian* had some message about three icebergs; he didn't bother then to take it down. **A** About 1:42 P.M. the rasping spark of those days spoke again across the water. It was the Baltic, calling the *Titanic*, warning her of ice on the steamer track. Bride took the message down and sent it up to the bridge.[11] The officer-of-the-deck glanced at it; sent it to the bearded master of the *Titanic*, Captain E. C. Smith,[12] a veteran of the White Star service. It was lunchtime then; the captain, walking along the promenade deck, saw Mr. Ismay, stopped, and handed him the message without comment. Ismay read it, stuffed it in his pocket, told two ladies about the icebergs, and resumed his walk. Later, about 7:15 P.M., the captain requested the return of the message in order to post it in the chart room for the information of officers.

Dinner that night in the Jacobean dining room was gay. It was bitter on deck, but the night was calm and fine; the sky was moonless but studded with stars twinkling coldly in the clear air. **B**

After dinner some of the second-class passengers gathered in the saloon, where the Reverend Mr. Carter conducted a "hymn singsong." It was almost ten o'clock and the stewards were waiting with biscuits and coffee as the group sang:

O, hear us when we cry to Thee
For those in peril on the sea.

On the bridge Second Officer Lightoller—short, stocky, efficient—was relieved at ten o'clock by First Officer Murdoch. **C** Lightoller had talked with other officers about the proximity of ice; at least five wireless ice warnings had reached the ship; lookouts had been cautioned to be alert; captains and

---

10. **Marconi cabin:** room where messages were received and sent by radio.
11. **bridge:** raised structure on a ship. The ship is controlled from the bridge.
12. Smith's initials were actually E. J., not E. C.

officers expected to reach the field at any time after 9:30 P.M. At twenty-two knots, its speed unslackened, the *Titanic* plowed on through the night. **D**

Lightoller left the darkened bridge to his relief and turned in. Captain Smith went to his cabin. The steerage was long since quiet; in the first and second cabins lights were going out; voices were growing still; people were asleep. Murdoch paced back and forth on the bridge, peering out over the dark water, glancing

120 now and then at the compass in front of Quartermaster Hichens at the wheel. **E**

In the crow's-nest, lookout Frederick Fleet and his partner, Leigh, gazed down at the water, still and unruffled in the dim, starlit darkness. Behind and below them the ship, a white shadow with here and there a last winking light; ahead of them a dark and silent and cold ocean.

There was a sudden clang. "Dong-dong. Dong-dong. Dong-dong. Dong!" The metal clapper of the great ship's bell struck out 11:30. Mindful of the warnings, Fleet strained his

130 eyes, searching the darkness for the dreaded ice. But there were only the stars and the sea.

In the wireless room, where Phillips, first operator, had relieved Bride, the buzz of the *Californian's* set again crackled into the earphones:

Californian: "Say, old man, we are stuck here, surrounded by ice."

Titanic: "Shut up, shut up; keep out. I am talking to Cape Race; you are jamming my signals."

Then, a few minutes later—about 11:40 . . .

II

140 Out of the dark she came, a vast, dim, white, monstrous shape, directly in the *Titanic's* path. For a moment Fleet doubted his eyes. But she was a deadly reality, this ghastly thing. **F** Frantically, Fleet struck three bells—something dead ahead. He snatched the telephone and called the bridge:

D **VOCABULARY**

Word Study

If you're not sure what *unslackened* means, examine the prefix *un–* and think about what the root word *slack* means. Write a definition below.

_____

_____

_____

_____

E **READING FOCUS**

The author probably got this exchange between the *Californian* and the *Titanic* from a radio communication transcript (a written copy of something that was said). Would this be a **primary** or **secondary source**?

_____

F **LANGUAGE COACH**

Use **context clues** to determine the meaning of the word *ghastly*. Write the definition in your own words.

_____

_____

_____

_____

A **VOCABULARY**

Word Study

Starboard, *port*, and *astern*
are nautical terms—words
that are related to ships.
Look up these words in
a dictionary. Write their
definitions below.

_____

_____

_____

_____

_____

_____

B **QUICK CHECK**

How did Murdoch try to
avoid hitting the iceberg?

_____

_____

_____

_____

_____

_____

_____

"Iceberg! Right ahead!"

The first officer heard but did not stop to acknowledge the
message.

"Hard-a-starboard!"

Hichens strained at the wheel; the bow swung slowly to
150   port. The monster was almost upon them now.

Murdoch leaped to the engine-room telegraph. Bells
clanged. Far below in the engine room those bells struck the first
warning. Danger! The indicators on the dial faces swung round
to "Stop!" Then "Full speed astern!" A Frantically the engineers
turned great valve wheels; answered the bridge bells . . .

There was a slight shock, a brief scraping, a small list to
port. Shell ice—slabs and chunks of it—fell on the foredeck.
Slowly the *Titanic* stopped.

Captain Smith hurried out of his cabin.

160   "What has the ship struck?"

Murdoch answered, "An iceberg, sir. I hard-a-starboarded
and reversed the engines, and I was going to hard-a-port around
it, but she was too close. I could not do any more. I have closed
the watertight doors." B

Fourth Officer Boxhall, other officers, the carpenter, came
to the bridge. The captain sent Boxhall and the carpenter below
to ascertain the damage.

A few lights switched on in the first and second cabins;
sleepy passengers peered through porthole glass; some casually
170   asked the stewards:

"Why have we stopped?"

"I don't know, sir, but I don't suppose it is anything much."

In the smoking room a quorum[13] of gamblers and their prey
were still sitting round a poker table; the usual crowd of kibitzers[14]
looked on. They had felt the slight jar of the collision and had seen
an eighty-foot ice mountain glide by the smoking-room windows,

---

13. **quorum** (KWAWR UHM): number of people required for a particular
activity—in this case, for a game.
14. **kibitzers** (KIHB IHT SUHRZ): talkative onlookers who often give
unwanted advice.

but the night was calm and clear, the *Titanic* was "unsinkable"; they hadn't bothered to go on deck.

But far below, in the warren of passages on the starboard side forward, in the forward holds and boiler rooms, men could see that the *Titanic's* hurt was mortal. 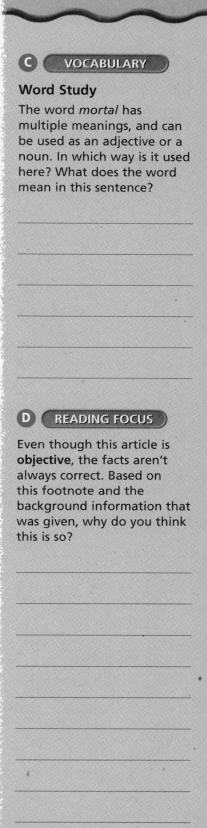 In No. 6 boiler room, where the red glow from the furnaces lighted up the naked, sweaty chests of coal-blackened firemen, water was pouring through a great gash about two feet above the floor plates. This was no slow leak; the ship was open to the sea; in ten minutes there were eight feet of water in No. 6. Long before then the stokers had raked the flaming fires out of the furnaces and had scrambled through the watertight doors in No. 5 or had climbed up the long steel ladders to safety. When Boxhall looked at the mailroom in No. 3 hold, twenty-four feet above the keel, the mailbags were already floating about in the slushing water. In No. 5 boiler room a stream of water spurted into an empty bunker. All six compartments forward of No. 4 were open to the sea; in ten seconds the iceberg's jagged claw had ripped a three-hundred-foot slash in the bottom of the great *Titanic*.[15]

Reports came to the bridge; Ismay in dressing gown ran out on deck in the cold, still, starlit night, climbed up the bridge ladder.

"What has happened?"

Captain Smith: "We have struck ice."

"Do you think she is seriously damaged?"

Captain Smith: "I'm afraid she is."

Ismay went below and passed Chief Engineer William Bell, fresh from an inspection of the damaged compartments. Bell corroborated the captain's statement; hurried back down the

---

15. An underwater expedition to the Titanic wreck in 1986 led by the explorer Dr. Robert Ballard revealed loosened or buckled seams in the ship's hull but no three-hundred-foot gash. Ballard concluded that the collision of the ship with the iceberg caused the buckling of the seams and a separation of the hull's plates, which in turn allowed water to enter the ship and sink it. This theory explains why survivors said they barely felt the fatal collision when it occurred.

C VOCABULARY

Word Study

The word *mortal* has multiple meanings, and can be used as an adjective or a noun. In which way is it used here? What does the word mean in this sentence?

D READING FOCUS

Even though this article is **objective**, the facts aren't always correct. Based on this footnote and the background information that was given, why do you think this is so?

A (VOCABULARY)

Selection Vocabulary

Corroborated means "supported; upheld the truth of." Explain how Bell corroborated what the captain had said.

_____

_____

_____

_____

_____

_____

_____

B (QUICK CHECK)

What are some reasons why none of the passengers knew the *Titanic* was sinking?

_____

_____

_____

_____

_____

_____

_____

glistening steel ladders to his duty. **A** Man after man followed him—Thomas Andrews, one of the ship's designers, Archie Frost, the builder's chief engineer, and his twenty assistants—men who had no posts of duty in the engine room but whose traditions called them there.

On deck, in corridor and stateroom, life flowed again. Men, women, and children awoke and questioned; orders were given to uncover the lifeboats; water rose into the firemen's quarters; half-dressed stokers streamed up on deck. But the passengers—most of them—did not know that the *Titanic* was sinking. The shock of the collision had been so slight that some were not awakened by it; the *Titanic* was so huge that she must be unsinkable; the night was too calm, too beautiful, to think of death at sea. **B**

Captain Smith half ran to the door of the radio shack. Bride, partly dressed, eyes dulled with sleep, was standing behind Phillips, waiting.

"Send the call for assistance."

The blue spark danced: "CQD—CQD—CQD—CQ—"[16]

Miles away Marconi men heard. Cape Race heard it, and the steamships *La Provence* and *Mt. Temple.*

The sea was surging into the *Titanic's* hold. At 12:20 the water burst into the seamen's quarters through a collapsed fore-and-aft wooden bulkhead. Pumps strained in the engine rooms—men and machinery making a futile fight against the sea. Steadily the water rose.

The boats were swung out—slowly, for the deckhands were late in reaching their stations; there had been no boat drill, and many of the crew did not know to what boats they were assigned. Orders were shouted; the safety valves had lifted, and steam was blowing off in a great rushing roar. In the chart house Fourth Officer Boxhall bent above a chart, working rapidly with pencil and dividers.

---

16. **CQD:** call by radio operators, inviting others to communicate with them.

240   12:25 A.M. Boxhall's position is sent out to a fleet of vessels: "Come at once; we have struck a berg."

To the Cunarder *Carpathia* (Arthur Henry Rostron, Master, New York to Liverpool, fifty-eight miles away): "It's a CQD, old man. Position 41–46N.; 50–14 W."

The blue spark dancing: "Sinking; cannot hear for noise of steam."

12:30 A.M. The word is passed: "Women and children in the boats." Stewards finish waking their passengers below; life preservers are tied on; some men smile at the precaution. "The
250   *Titanic* is unsinkable." The *Mt. Temple* starts for the *Titanic*; the *Carpathia*, with a double watch in her stokeholds, radios, "Coming hard." The CQD changes the course of many ships—but not of one; the operator of the *Californian*, nearby, has just put down his earphones and turned in.

The CQD flashes over land and sea from Cape Race to New York; newspaper city rooms leap to life and presses whir.

On the *Titanic*, water creeps over the bulkhead between Nos. 5 and 6 firerooms. She is going down by the head; the engineers—fighting a losing battle—are forced back foot by
260   foot by the rising water. Down the promenade deck, Happy Jock Hume, the bandsman, runs with his instrument.

12:45 A.M. Murdoch, in charge on the starboard side, eyes tragic, but calm and cool, orders boat No. 7 lowered. **C** The women hang back; they want no boat ride on an ice-strewn sea; the *Titanic* is unsinkable. The men encourage them, explain that this is just a precautionary measure: "We'll see you again at breakfast." There is little confusion; passengers stream slowly to the boat deck. In the steerage the immigrants chatter excitedly.

270   A sudden sharp hiss—a streaked flare against the night; Boxhall sends a rocket toward the sky. It explodes, and a parachute of white stars lights up the icy sea. "God! Rockets!" The band plays ragtime.

No. 8 is lowered, and No. 5. Ismay, still in dressing gown, calls for women and children, handles lines, stumbles in the

C READING FOCUS

Is this sentence about Murdoch **subjective** or **objective**, or both? Explain your answer.

_____

_____

_____

_____

way of an officer, is told to "get the hell out of here." Third Officer Pitman takes charge of No. 5; as he swings into the boat, Murdoch grasps his hand. "Goodbye and good luck, old man."

No. 6 goes over the side. There are only twenty-eight people in a lifeboat with a capacity of sixty-five. **A**

A light stabs from the bridge; Boxhall is calling in Morse flashes, again and again, to a strange ship stopped in the ice jam five to ten miles away. Another rocket drops its shower of sparks above the ice-strewn sea and the dying ship.

1:00 A.M. Slowly the water creeps higher; the fore ports of the *Titanic* are dipping into the sea. Rope squeaks through blocks; lifeboats drop jerkily seaward. Through the shouting on the decks comes the sound of the band playing ragtime.

The "Millionaires' Special" leaves the ship—boat No. 1, with a capacity of forty people, carries only Sir Cosmo and Lady Duff Gordon and ten others. Aft, the frightened immigrants mill and jostle and rush for a boat. An officer's fist flies out; three shots are fired in the air, and the panic is quelled. . . . Four Chinese sneak unseen into a boat and hide in the bottom.

1:20 A.M. Water is coming into No. 4 boiler room. Stokers slice and shovel as water laps about their ankles—steam for the dynamos, steam for the dancing spark! As the water rises, great ash hoes rake the flaming coals from the furnaces. Safety valves pop; the stokers retreat aft, and the watertight doors clang shut behind them.

The rockets fling their splendor toward the stars. The boats are more heavily loaded now, for the passengers know the *Titanic* is sinking. **B** Women cling and sob. The great screws aft are rising clear of the sea. Half-filled boats are ordered to come alongside the cargo ports and take on more passengers, but the ports are never opened—and the boats are never filled. Others pull for the steamer's light miles away but never reach it; the lights disappear; the unknown ship steams off.

The water rises and the band plays ragtime.

1:30 A.M. Lightoller is getting the port boats off; Murdoch, the starboard. As one boat is lowered into the sea, a boat officer fires his gun along the ship's side to stop a rush from the lower decks. A woman tries to take her Great Dane into a boat with her; she is refused and steps out of the boat to die with her dog. Millet's "little smile which played on his lips all through the voyage" plays no more; his lips are grim, but he waves goodbye and brings wraps for the women.

320   Benjamin Guggenheim, in evening clothes, smiles and says, "We've dressed up in our best and are prepared to go down like gentlemen."

1:40 A.M. Boat 14 is clear, and then 13, 16, 15, and C. The lights still shine, but the Baltic hears the blue spark say, "Engine room getting flooded." **C**

The Olympia signals, "Am lighting up all possible boilers as fast as can."

Major Butt helps women into the last boats and waves goodbye to them. Mrs. Straus puts her foot on the gunwale

330   of a lifeboat; then she draws back and goes to her husband: "We have been together many years; where you go, I will go." Colonel John Jacob Astor puts his young wife in a lifeboat, steps back, taps cigarette on fingernail: "Goodbye, dearie; I'll join you later." **D**

1:45 A.M. The foredeck is under water; the fo'c'sle[17] head almost awash; the great stern is lifted high toward the bright stars; and still the band plays. Mr. and Mrs. Harris approach a lifeboat arm in arm.

Officer: "Ladies first, please."

340   Harris bows, smiles, steps back: "Of course, certainly; ladies first."

Boxhall fires the last rocket, then leaves in charge of boat No. 2.

2:00 A.M. She is dying now; her bow goes deeper, her stern higher. But there must be steam. Below in the stokeholds the sweaty firemen keep steam up for the flaring lights and

---

17. fo'c'sle (FOHK SUHL): forecastle, front upper deck of a ship.

C QUICK CHECK

What is the "blue spark"? Go back and re-read some of the story to help you find the answer.

_____

_____

_____

_____

D LITERARY ANALYSIS

What do you think Colonel Astor means when he tells his wife, "I'll join you later"?

_____

_____

_____

_____

A READING FOCUS

Why is the information in this sentence **objective**?

_____

_____

_____

_____

_____

_____

B VOCABULARY

Word Study

Companionways is a compound word, a word that is formed by joining two words. It means "stairs or ladders within a ship." Circle two more compound words on this page.

C VOCABULARY

Word Study

The word *brain* has multiple meanings and can be used as a noun and as a verb. How is it being used here and what does it mean?

_____

_____

_____

_____

_____

_____

_____

the dancing spark. The glowing coals slide and tumble over the slanted grate bars; the sea pounds behind that yielding bulkhead. But the spark dances on.

The Asian hears Phillips try the new signal—SOS.

350 Boat No. 4 has left now; boat D leaves ten minutes later. Jacques Futrelle clasps his wife: "For God's sake, go! It's your last chance; go!" Madame Futrelle is half forced into the boat. It clears the side.

There are about 660 people in the boats and 1,500 still on the sinking *Titanic*. **A**

On top of the officers' quarters, men work frantically to get the two collapsibles stowed there over the side. Water is over the forward part of A deck now; it surges up the companionways toward the boat deck. **B** In the radio shack,

360 Bride has slipped a coat and life jacket about Phillips as the first operator sits hunched over his key, sending—still sending—"41–46 N.; 50–14 W. CQD—CQD—SOS—SOS—"

The captain's tired white face appears at the radio-room door. "Men, you have done your full duty. You can do no more. Now, it's every man for himself." The captain disappears—back to his sinking bridge, where Painter, his personal steward, stands quietly waiting for orders. The spark dances on. Bride turns his back and goes into the inner cabin. As he does so, a stoker, grimed with coal, mad with fear, steals into the shack and reaches

370 for the life jacket on Phillips's back. Bride wheels about and brains him with a wrench. **C**

2:10 A.M. Below decks the steam is still holding, though the pressure is falling—rapidly. In the gymnasium on the boat deck, the athletic instructor watches quietly as two gentlemen ride the bicycles and another swings casually at the punching bag. Mail clerks stagger up the boat-deck stairways, dragging soaked mail sacks. The spark still dances. The band still plays—but not ragtime:

Nearer my God to Thee.

380 Nearer to Thee . . .

A few men take up the refrain; others kneel on the slanting decks to pray. Many run and scramble aft, where hundreds are clinging above the silent screws on the great uptilted stern. **D** The spark still dances and the lights still flare; the engineers are on the job. The hymn comes to its close. Bandmaster Hartley, Yorkshireman violinist, taps his bow against a bulkhead, calls for "Autumn" as the water curls about his feet, and the eight musicians brace themselves against the ship's slant. People are leaping from the decks into the nearby water—the icy water. A

390 woman cries, "Oh, save me, save me!" A man answers, "Good lady, save yourself. Only God can save you now." The band plays "Autumn":

> God of Mercy and Compassion!
>
> Look with pity on my pain . . .

The water creeps over the bridge where the *Titanic's* master stands; heavily he steps out to meet it.

2:17 A.M. "CQ—" The Virginian hears a ragged, blurred CQ, then an abrupt stop. The blue spark dances no more. The lights flicker out; the engineers have lost their battle. **E**

400 2:18 A.M. Men run about blackened decks; leap into the night; are swept into the sea by the curling wave that licks up the *Titanic's* length. Lightoller does not leave the ship; the ship leaves him; there are hundreds like him, but only a few who live to tell of it. The funnels still swim above the water, but the ship is climbing to the perpendicular; the bridge is under and most of the foremast; the great stern rises like a squat leviathan.[18] Men swim away from the sinking ship; others drop from the stern.

The band plays in the darkness, the water lapping
410 upward:

> Hold me up in mighty waters,
>
> Keep my eyes on things above, **F**
>
> Righteousness, divine atonement,
>
> Peace and everlas . . .

---

18. **leviathan** (LUH VY UH THUHN): biblical sea monster, perhaps a whale.

D (QUICK CHECK)

What are some of the people who do not make it onto the lifeboats doing?

_____

_____

_____

E (LITERARY ANALYSIS)

What do you think it means that "the engineers have lost their battle"? What evidence is there that they have failed at something?

_____

_____

_____

_____

_____

F (LITERARY ANALYSIS)

Why do you think the band played while the ship was sinking?

_____

_____

_____

_____

_____

_____

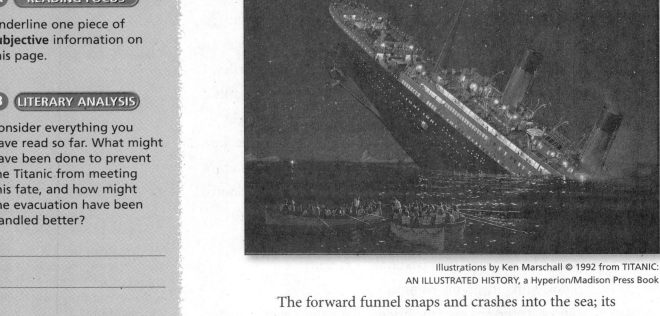

Illustrations by Ken Marschall © 1992 from TITANIC: AN ILLUSTRATED HISTORY, a Hyperion/Madison Press Book

The forward funnel snaps and crashes into the sea; its steel tons hammer out of existence swimmers struggling in the freezing water. Streams of sparks, of smoke and steam, burst from the after funnels. The ship upends to 50—to 60 degrees.

Down in the black abyss of the stokeholds, of the engine
420   rooms, where the dynamos have whirred at long last to a stop, the stokers and the engineers are reeling against the hot metal, the rising water clutching at their knees. The boilers, the engine cylinders, rip from their bed plates; crash through bulkheads; rumble—steel against steel.

The *Titanic* stands on end, poised briefly for the plunge. Slowly she slides to her grave—slowly at first, and then more quickly—quickly—quickly.

2:20 A.M. The greatest ship in the world has sunk. From the calm, dark waters, where the floating lifeboats move, there
430   goes up, in the white wake of her passing, "one long continuous moan." **A** **B**

III

The boats that the *Titanic* had launched pulled safely away from the slight suction of the sinking ship, pulled away from the screams that came from the lips of the freezing men and women in the water. The boats were poorly manned and badly equipped, and they had been unevenly loaded. Some carried so few seamen that women bent to the oars. Mrs. Astor tugged at an oar handle; the Countess of Rothes took a tiller. Shivering stokers in sweaty, coal-blackened singlets and light trousers steered in some boats; stewards in white coats rowed in others. Ismay was in the last boat that left the ship from the starboard side; with Mr. Carter of Philadelphia and two seamen he tugged at the oars. In one of the lifeboats an Italian with a broken wrist—disguised in a woman's shawl and hat—huddled on the floorboards, ashamed now that fear had left him. In another rode the only baggage saved from the *Titanic*—the carryall of Samuel L. Goldenberg, one of the rescued passengers.

There were only a few boats that were heavily loaded; most of those that were half empty made but perfunctory efforts to pick up the moaning swimmers, their officers and crew fearing they would endanger the living if they pulled back into the midst of the dying. Some boats beat off the freezing victims; fear-crazed men and women struck with oars at the heads of swimmers. One woman drove her fist into the face of a half-dead man as he tried feebly to climb over the gunwale. Two other women helped him in and staunched the flow of blood from the ring cuts on his face. **C**

One of the collapsible boats, which had floated off the top of the officers' quarters when the *Titanic* sank, was an icy haven for thirty or forty men. **D** The boat had capsized as the ship sank; men swam to it, clung to it, climbed upon its slippery bottom, stood knee-deep in water in the freezing air. Chunks of ice swirled about their legs; their soaked clothing clutched their bodies in icy folds. Colonel Archibald Gracie was cast up there, Gracie who had leaped from the stern as the *Titanic* sank; young Thayer who had seen his father die; Lightoller who had twice been sucked down with the ship and twice blown to the surface by a belch of air; Bride, the second operator, and Phillips, the first. There were many stokers, half

440

450

460

470

C VOCABULARY

Academic Vocabulary

What ideas about the lifeboat passengers can you *derive*, or obtain, from this paragraph?

_____

_____

_____

_____

_____

_____

D VOCABULARY

Word Study

Use a dictionary to find the meaning of *haven*, and then write a synonym for *haven* below.

_____

naked; it was a shivering company. They stood there in the icy sea, under the far stars, and sang and prayed—the Lord's Prayer. After a while a lifeboat came and picked them off, but Phillips was dead then or died soon afterward in the boat. **A**

Only a few of the boats had lights; only one—No. 2—had a light that was of any use to the *Carpathia*, twisting through the ice field to the rescue. Other ships were "coming hard" too; one, the *Californian*, was still dead to opportunity.

The blue sparks still danced, but not the *Titanic's*. *La Provence*
480 to *Celtic*: "Nobody has heard the *Titanic* for about two hours."

It was 2:40 when the *Carpathia* first sighted the green light from No. 2 boat; it was 4:10 when she picked up the first boat and learned that the *Titanic* had foundered.[19] The last of the moaning cries had just died away then.

Captain Rostron took the survivors aboard, boatload by boatload. He was ready for them, but only a small minority of them required much medical attention. Bride's feet were twisted and frozen; others were suffering from exposure; one died, and seven were dead when taken from the boats, and were buried
490 at sea.

It was then that the fleet of racing ships learned they were too late; the *Parisian* heard the weak signals of MPA, the *Carpathia*, report the death of the *Titanic*. It was then—or soon afterward, when her radio operator put on his earphones—that the *Californian*, the ship that had been within sight as the *Titanic* was sinking, first learned of the disaster.

And it was then, in all its white-green majesty, that the *Titanic's* survivors saw the iceberg, tinted with the sunrise, floating idly, pack ice jammed about its base, other bergs heaving slowly
500 nearby on the blue breast of the sea. **B**

IV

But it was not until later that the world knew, for wireless then was not what wireless is today, and garbled messages had

---

19. **foundered:** filled with water, so that it sank; generally, collapsed; failed.

nourished a hope that all of the *Titanic's* company were safe. Not until Monday evening, when P.A.S. Franklin, vice president of the International Mercantile Marine Company, received relayed messages in New York that left little hope, did the full extent of the disaster begin to be known. Partial and garbled lists of the survivors; rumors of heroism and cowardice; stories spun out of newspaper imagination, based on a few bare facts and many

510 false reports, misled the world, terrified and frightened it. **C** It was not until Thursday night, when the *Carpathia* steamed into the North River, that the full truth was pieced together.

Flashlights flared on the black river when the *Carpathia* stood up to her dock. Tugs nosed about her, shunted her toward Pier 54. Thirty thousand people jammed the streets; ambulances and stretchers stood on the pier; coroners and physicians waited.

In midstream the Cunarder dropped over the *Titanic's* lifeboats; then she headed toward the dock. Beneath the customs

520 letters on the pier stood relatives of the 711 survivors, relatives of the missing—hoping against hope. The *Carpathia* cast her lines ashore; stevedores[20] looped them over bollards. The dense throngs stood quiet as the first survivor stepped down the gangway. **D** The woman half staggered—led by customs guards—beneath her letter. A "low wailing" moan came from the crowd; fell, grew in volume, and dropped again.

Thus ended the maiden voyage of the *Titanic*. The lifeboats brought to New York by the *Carpathia*, a few deck chairs and gratings awash in the ice field off the Grand Bank eight hundred

530 miles from shore, were all that was left of the world's greatest ship. **E**

V

The aftermath of weeping and regret, of recriminations and investigations, dragged on for weeks. Charges and countercharges were hurled about; the White Star Line was

---

20. **stevedores** (STEE VUH DAWRZ): persons who load and unload ships.

C VOCABULARY

Word Study

Heroism and *cowardice* are antonyms—they have opposite meanings. Knowing this, write a definition of *heroism*. Then, write one example of heroism that you have read about in this story.

_____

_____

_____

_____

_____

_____

D LANGUAGE COACH

Using **context clues**, define *throngs* in your own words. Use a dictionary to check your answer.

_____

_____

_____

_____

E QUICK CHECK

According to the text, what remained after the *Titanic* sank?

_____

_____

_____

_____

Selection Vocabulary

Pertinent means "having some connection with the subject." Why were Senator Smith's questions not pertinent to the proceedings?

_____

_____

_____

_____

_____

_____

_____

_____

_____

bitterly criticized; Ismay was denounced on the floor of the Senate as a coward but was defended by those who had been with him on the sinking *Titanic* and by the Board of Trade investigation in England.

540 It was not until weeks later, when the hastily convened Senate investigation in the United States and the Board of Trade report in England had been completed, that the whole story was told. The Senate investigating committee, under the chairmanship of Senator Smith, who was attacked in both the American and the British press as a "backwoods politician," brought out numerous pertinent facts, though its proceedings verged at times on the farcical.[21] Senator Smith was ridiculed for his lack of knowledge of the sea when he asked witnesses, "Of what is an iceberg composed?" and "Did any of the passengers take refuge in the watertight compartments?" **A** The senator seemed par-
550 ticularly interested in the marital status of Fleet, the lookout, who was saved. Fleet, puzzled, growled aside, "Wot questions they're arskin' me!"

The report of Lord Mersey, wreck commissioner in the British Board of Trade's investigation, was tersely damning.

The *Titanic* had carried boats enough for 1,178 persons, only one third of her capacity. Her sixteen boats and four collapsibles had saved but 711 persons; 400 people had needlessly lost their lives. The boats had been but partly loaded; officers in
560 charge of launching them had been afraid the falls[22] would break or the boats buckle under their rated loads; boat crews had been slow in reaching their stations; launching arrangements were confused because no boat drill had been held; passengers were loaded into the boats haphazardly because no boat assignments had been made.

But that was not all. Lord Mersey found that sufficient warnings of ice on the steamer track had reached the *Titanic*,

---

21. **farcical** (FAHR SIH KUHL): absurd; ridiculous; like a farce (an exaggerated comedy).
22. **falls**: chains used for hoisting.

that her speed of twenty-two knots was "excessive under the circumstances," that "in view of the high speed at which the vessel was running it is not considered that the lookout was sufficient," and that her master made "a very grievous mistake"— but should not be blamed for negligence. **B** Captain Rostron of the *Carpathia* was highly praised. "He did the very best that could be done." The *Californian* was damned. The testimony of her master, officers, and crew showed that she was not, at the most, more than nineteen miles away from the sinking *Titanic* and probably no more than five to ten miles distant. She had seen the *Titanic's* lights; she had seen the rockets; she had not received the CQD calls because her radio operator was asleep. She had attempted to get in communication with the ship she had sighted by flashing a light, but vainly.

"The night was clear," reported Lord Mersey, "and the sea was smooth. When she first saw the rockets, the *Californian* could have pushed through the ice to the open water without any serious risk and so have come to the assistance of the *Titanic*. Had she done so she might have saved many if not all of the lives that were lost.

"She made no attempt." **C**

B QUICK CHECK

What were some of the criticisms of the *Titanic's* preparedness and its crew's actions during the disaster?

_____

_____

_____

_____

_____

C READING FOCUS

Would you say this article is mostly a **subjective** or **objective** account of what happened to the *Titanic*? Explain your answer and give examples from the text.

_____

_____

_____

_____

_____

_____

_____

_____

_____

_____

_____

A Fireman's Story

by Harry Senior

> **BACKGROUND**
> The lifeboats of the "unsinkable" *Titanic* carried fewer than
> one third of the approximately 2,200 people aboard. A
> large number of the 1,517 people who died in the disaster
> were poor passengers who were far below deck, in steerage.
> This is an eyewitness account from a survivor.

A **READING FOCUS**

Is this selection a **primary** or
secondary source? How can
you tell?

_____

_____

_____

_____

B **VOCABULARY**

Academic Vocabulary

What is *significant*, or
important, about the fact
that three of the people
in the lifeboat were
millionaires?

_____

_____

_____

_____

I was in my bunk when I felt a bump. One man said, "Hello. She
has been struck." I went on deck and saw a great pile of ice on
the well deck before the forecastle, but we all thought the ship
would last some time, and we went back to our bunks. Then one
of the firemen came running down and yelled, "All muster for
the lifeboats." I ran on deck, and the captain said, "All firemen
keep down on the well deck. If a man comes up, I'll shoot
him." **A**

10   Then I saw the first lifeboat lowered. Thirteen people were
on board, eleven men and two women. Three were millionaires,
and one was Ismay [J. Bruce Ismay, managing director of the
White Star Line; a survivor]. **B**

Then I ran up onto the hurricane deck and helped to throw
one of the collapsible boats onto the lower deck. I saw an Italian
woman holding two babies. I took one of them and made the
woman jump overboard with the baby, while I did the same with
the other. When I came to the surface, the baby in my arms was
dead. I saw the woman strike out in good style, but a boiler burst
on the *Titanic* and started a big wave. When the woman saw that
20   wave, she gave up. Then, as the child was dead, I let it sink too.

© Mary Evans Picture Library/Alamy

I swam around for about half an hour, and was swimming on my back when the *Titanic* went down. I tried to get aboard a boat, but some chap hit me over the head with an oar. There were too many in her. I got around to the other side and climbed in. **C** **D**

C QUICK CHECK

How is this selection different from the selection "R.M.S. Titanic"?

D READING FOCUS

Does Senior's recollection of the sinking seem **objective** or **subjective**? Why?

_____

_____

_____

_____

_____

_____

_____

_____

FROM A LIFEBOAT

by Mrs. D.H. Bishop

> **BACKGROUND**
> Mrs. D.H. Bishop was a survivor of the *Titanic* disaster.
> She was 25 years old at the time of the wreck and was
> traveling in first class. She was on her way home to
> Michigan from Europe. In the following account, she tells
> what she remembers about the sinking ship as she sat in a
> lifeboat at a safe distance from the ship.

A **LITERARY ANALYSIS**

Why do you think people
on board did not realize
how great the danger was
at first?

_____

_____

_____

_____

_____

_____

We did not begin to understand the situation till we were perhaps a mile or more away from the *Titanic*. Then we could see the rows of lights along the decks begin to slant gradually upward from the bow.

10 Very slowly, the lines of light began to point downward at a greater and greater angle. The sinking was so slow that you could not perceive the lights of the deck changing their position. The slant seemed to be greater about every quarter of an hour. That was the only difference.

In a couple of hours, though, she began to go down more 20 rapidly. Then the fearful sight began. The people in the ship were just beginning to realize how great their danger was. **A** When the forward part of the ship dropped suddenly at a faster rate,

© Don Lynch Collection

© Stockbyte/Punchstock

so that the upward slope became marked, there was a sudden rush of passengers on all the decks toward the stern. It was like a wave. We could see the great black mass of people in the steerage sweeping to the rear part of the boat and breaking through into the upper decks. At the distance of about a mile, we could distinguish everything through the night, which was perfectly clear. We could make out the increasing excitement on board the 30 boat as the people, rushing to and fro, caused the deck lights to disappear and reappear as they passed in front of them.

This panic went on, it seemed for an hour. Then suddenly the ship seemed to shoot up out of the water and stand there perpendicularly. It seemed to us that it stood upright in the water for a four full minutes. **B**

Then it began to slide gently downward. Its speed increased as it went down headfirst, so that the stern shot down with a rush.

The lights continued to burn till it sank. We could see the people packed densely in the stern till it was gone. . . .

40 As the ship sank, we could hear the screaming a mile away. Gradually it became fainter and fainter and died away. Some of the lifeboats that had room for more might have gone to their rescue, but it would have meant that those who were in the water would have swarmed aboard and sunk them. **C**

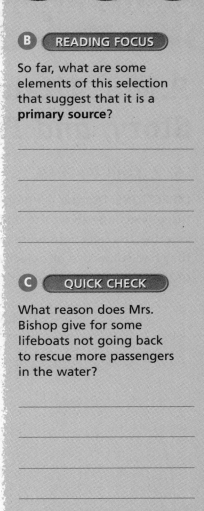

B READING FOCUS

So far, what are some elements of this selection that suggest that it is a **primary source**?

_____

_____

_____

_____

C QUICK CHECK

What reason does Mrs. Bishop give for some lifeboats not going back to rescue more passengers in the water?

_____

_____

_____

_____

R.M.S. Titanic, A Fireman's Story, *and* From a Lifeboat

USE A VENN DIAGRAM

DIRECTIONS: Use the Venn diagram below to compare and contrast the three selections about the sinking of the Titanic. Include information about whether the selections were **primary sources** or **secondary sources**, and whether they had **subjective** or **objective** information. List differences in the outside sections of the circles, and put similarities in the sections where the circles overlap.

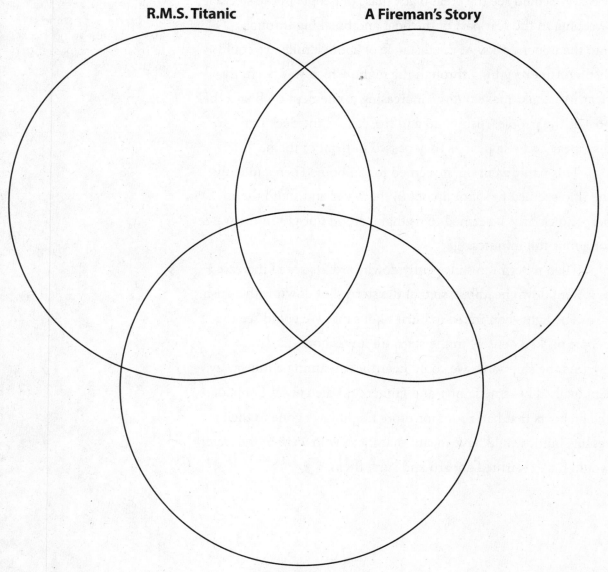

R.M.S. Titanic

A Fireman's Story

From a Lifeboat

Applying Your Skills

R.M.S. Titanic, A Fireman's Story, *and* From a Lifeboat

VOCABULARY DEVELOPMENT

DIRECTIONS: Circle the word that is a synonym (word with a similar meaning) of each italicized vocabulary word below.

1. *pertinent:*   attentive   constant   relevant

2. *perfunctory:*   disinterested   pierced   simple

3. *corroborated:*   rotten   proved   sectioned

4. *ascertain:*   explain   discover   unsure

INFORMATIONAL TEXT FOCUS: PRIMARY AND SECONDARY SOURCES

DIRECTIONS: Complete the chart below by providing four **objective** details and four **subjective** details from these three readings. Identify the selection in which each detail is found.

Objective details	Subjective details
1.	5.
2.	6.
3.	7.
4.	8.

SKILLS FOCUS

Informational Text Skills
Understand the difference between subjective primary sources and objective secondary sources.

Collection 4

VOCABULARY REVIEW

DIRECTIONS: Match each vocabulary word in the left column with the correct definition in the right column.

_____	1. derive	**a.**	challenging authority
_____	2. contrition	**b.**	good judgment
_____	3. stench	**c.**	full of meaning; important
_____	4. ascertain	**d.**	tiny
_____	5. function	**e.**	having some connection with the subject
_____	6. defiant	**f.**	find out with certainty; determine
_____	7. impeded	**g.**	bad smell
_____	8. corroborated	**h.**	disbelieving; skeptical
_____	9. interact	**i.**	obtain from a source or origin
_____	10. inquisitive	**j.**	regret or sense of guilt at having done wrong
_____	11. frivolous	**k.**	act upon each other
_____	12. perfunctory	**l.**	not properly serious; silly
_____	13. significant	**m.**	done with little thought; indifferent
_____	14. minute	**n.**	questioning or curious
_____	15. prudence	**o.**	act in a specific manner; work
_____	16. pertinent	**p.**	supported; upheld the truth of
_____	17. incredulous	**q.**	not full or rich
_____	18. meager	**r.**	obstructed; blocked

Skills Review

Collection 4

LANGUAGE COACH

Sometimes a writer will provide clues about a word's meaning in a text. These are called **context clues**. Context clues may include the word's definition, a synonym (word with a similar meaning), or an antonym (word with the opposite meaning).

DIRECTIONS: Look at the sentences below. For each sentence, underline the context clues that help you figure out the meaning of the italicized vocabulary word.

1. The portions at the restaurant were so *meager* that I was still hungry after lunch.

2. The fallen branch *impeded* our car, and we couldn't get by.

3. The child was *defiant* and refused to clean up her room as her parents had asked her to.

4. The bug on the ground was so *minute* that I could barely see it.

5. I don't know why he told a story about the first day of school, because it was not *pertinent* to my question about what he did this past summer.

ORAL LANGUAGE ACTIVITY

In "From a Lifeboat" and "A Fireman's Story," you read the firsthand stories of two eyewitnesses to the *Titanic* disaster. Even though both Mrs. Bishop and Harry Senior lived through the same event, their memories of the experience were different.

DIRECTIONS: Pick a partner with whom you have shared a similar experience, such as a place you both have visited, a book you both have read, or an event in your school or community you both have witnessed. Take a few minutes to make some notes about what you remember, and then take turns telling each other about the experience aloud. Just as in the *Titanic* selections, you should tell your story using the first person pronoun "I" and include as much detail as you can remember.

After you both are finished telling your tales to each other, discuss the ways in which your stories are similar and different. Be sure to talk about the fact that just because you were both sharing an account of the same thing or event, you likely did not experience it the same way.

Form and Style

Fish Pond, 1993 (oil on linen), Culler, Pat/The Bridgeman
Art Library International

Literary and Academic Vocabulary for Collection 5

component (KUHM POH NUHNT) *n.:* a necessary or essential part; element.
Diction is one component of style.

subsequent (SUHB SUH KWUHNT) *adj.:* coming next; following.
In subsequent paragraphs, Lahiri describes how her feelings changed over the years.

equivalent (IH KWIHV UH LUHNT) *adj.:* equal in value, strength, or force.
Synonyms have equivalent meanings but sometimes different connotations.

technique (TEHK NEEK) *n.:* method used to accomplish something.
Andy Harris uses a dangerous technique to reach Camp Four: He slides down the ice bulge on his behind.

mood (MOOD) *n.:* atmosphere created by a writer's language.
The mood of the satire was silly and upbeat.

journalist (JUHR NUH LIHST) *n.:* a writer of a newspaper or magazine article who presents facts, statistics, and statements by other people in a straightforward manner.
The journalist went to the scene of the crime to gather facts about the robbery from the police.

memoir (MEHM WAWR) *n.:* a type of autobiography that deals with a significant event or period in a writer's life.
Jacob's memoir focused on his early childhood experiences.

diction (DIHK SHUN) *n.:* a writer's word choice.
The diction of my college roommate's physics paper was too difficult for me to understand.

Typhoid Fever

by Frank McCourt

LITERARY FOCUS: STYLE—DICTION, TONE, AND VOICE

Great writers have their own **style**, which is their own distinct way of writing. The following elements are part of a writer's style:

- **diction**, or the words the writer chooses

- **sentence structure**, or the way words in a sentence are arranged, which may be simple or complex

- the **tone**, or attitude, a writer takes toward his or her subject

- **voice**, which is how writers use written language to express themselves in a unique way

READING FOCUS: EVALUATING WORD CHOICE

In "Typhoid Fever," Frank McCourt's **word choices** highlight the differences among the different characters. For example, some characters speak formally, while other's speak informally. Analyzing McCourt's word choice will help you figure out his attitude toward the characters.

Use the Skill   While you read "Typhoid Fever," use the chart below to list examples of word choice for each character's speech. An example is given.

Character	Example
Patricia Madigan	"You won't be able to stop marching and saluting."

SKILLS FOCUS

Literary Skills
Understand the elements of style, including diction, tone, and voice.

Reading Skills
Evaluate word choice.

Vocabulary Development

Typhoid Fever

SELECTION VOCABULARY

internal (IHN TUR NUHL) *adj.:* on the inside.
    Many diseases affect internal organs.

relapse (RIH LAPS) *n.:* the process of slipping back into a former state.
    The nurse thinks that singing and talking might lead to Frankie's relapse.

induced (ihn DOOST) *v.* used as *adj.:* persuaded; led on.
    Induced by Frankie, Seamus learned the rest of "The Highwayman."

potent (POH TUHNT) *adj.:* powerful.
    The potent words of Shakespeare and Alfred Noyes help Frankie find humor and beauty in an otherwise dismal place.

clamoring (KLAM UHR IHNG) *v.:* crying out; demanding.
    Frankie imagined a group of sick children clamoring for his chocolate bar.

WORD STUDY

DIRECTIONS: Fill in the blanks in the sentences below with the correct word from the selection vocabulary list above.

1. There are possibly some illegal dealings going on inside the government, so the government agency members decided to launch an _____ investigation into the matter.

2. The rotten eggs gave off a _____ stench.

3. The scream Gwen let out when she saw a dinosaur step on her car was _____ by fear.

4. Fran was overwhelmed by working at the day-care center because all of the toddlers were _____ for attention.

5. I was feeling so much better that I decided to exercise yesterday, but now I feel sick again, so I fear I've had a _____.

TYPHOID FEVER

from "Angela's Ashes" by Frank McCourt

> ### BACKGROUND
> "Angela's Ashes" is Frank McCourt's memoir of growing up in Ireland in the 1930s and 1940s. People living in slums at the time often caught diseases such as typhoid fever. In Ireland, people with these illnesses were isolated in "fever hospitals." When he was ten, McCourt caught typhoid fever and was sent to a fever hospital.

A LITERARY FOCUS

Describe the **diction** and **sentence structure** in this opening section. Why do you think the author used this **style**?

_____

_____

_____

_____

_____

_____

_____

_____

_____

Yoo hoo, are you there, typhoid boy?

The room next to me is empty till one morning a girl's voice says, Yoo hoo, who's there?

I'm not sure if she's talking to me or someone in the room beyond.

Yoo hoo, boy with the typhoid, are you awake?

I am.

Are you better?

I am.

10   Well, why are you here?

I don't know. I'm still in the bed. They stick needles in me and give me medicine.

What do you look like?

I wonder, What kind of a question is that? I don't know what to tell her.

Yoo hoo, are you there, typhoid boy?

I am. **A**

What's your name?

Frank.

20   That's a good name. My name is Patricia Madigan. How old are you?

Courtesy of David Prifti

B QUICK CHECK

What are the names of
the two characters in this
passage? How old are they?
What else do you know
about them at this point?

_____

_____

_____

_____

_____

_____

_____

_____

Ten.

Oh. She sounds disappointed.

But I'll be eleven in August, next month.

Well, that's better than ten. I'll be fourteen in September.
Do you want to know why I'm in the Fever Hospital?

I do.

I have diphtheria and something else.

What's something else?

30   They don't know. They think I have a disease from foreign
parts because my father used to be in Africa. I nearly died. Are
you going to tell me what you look like?

I have black hair.

You and millions.

I have brown eyes with bits of green that's called hazel.

You and thousands.

I have stitches on the back of my right hand and my two feet
where they put in the soldier's blood. **B**

Oh, did they?

A **READING FOCUS**

Think about the **word choice** for Patricia's speech in her conversation with Frank. How would you describe the way she speaks?

_____

_____

_____

_____

_____

B **VOCABULARY**

Word Study

Habit has multiple meanings. Sister Rita is a nun and wears a nun's outfit. Knowing this, what do you think *habit* means in this context?

_____

_____

_____

C **VOCABULARY**

Selection Vocabulary

In this sentence, *apparatus* means "group of organs." Knowing this, what do you think *internal* means?

_____

_____

40   They did.

You won't be able to stop marching and saluting. **A**

There's a swish of habit and click of beads and then Sister Rita's voice. **B** Now, now, what's this? There's to be no talking between two rooms especially when it's a boy and a girl. Do you hear me, Patricia?

I do, Sister.

Do you hear me, Francis?

I do, Sister.

You could be giving thanks for your two remarkable
50   recoveries. You could be saying the rosary.[1] You could be reading *The Little Messenger of the Sacred Heart*[2] that's beside your beds. Don't let me come back and find you talking.

She comes into my room and wags her finger at me. Especially you, Francis, after thousands of boys prayed for you at the Confraternity.[3] Give thanks, Francis, give thanks.

She leaves and there's silence for awhile. Then Patricia whispers, Give thanks, Francis, give thanks, and say your rosary, Francis, and I laugh so hard a nurse runs in to see if I'm all right. She's a very stern nurse from the County Kerry and she
60   frightens me. What's this, Francis? Laughing? What is there to laugh about? Are you and that Madigan girl talking? I'll report you to Sister Rita. There's to be no laughing for you could be doing serious damage to your internal apparatus. **C**

She plods out and Patricia whispers again in a heavy Kerry accent, No laughing, Francis, you could be doin' serious damage to your internal apparatus. Say your rosary, Francis, and pray for your internal apparatus.

Mam visits me on Thursdays. I'd like to see my father, too, but I'm out of danger, crisis time is over, and I'm allowed only
70   one visitor. Besides, she says, he's back at work at Rank's Flour

---

1. **rosary** (ROH ZUHR EE): set of prayers that Roman Catholics recite while holding a string of beads.
2. ***The Little Messenger of the Sacred Heart***: religious publication for children.
3. **Confraternity**: here, a religious organization made up of nonclergy, or laypersons.

Mills and please God this job will last a while with the war on and the English desperate for flour. **D** She brings me a chocolate bar and that proves Dad is working. She could never afford it on the dole.[4] He sends me notes. He tells me my brothers are all praying for me, that I should be a good boy, obey the doctors, the nuns, the nurses, and don't forget to say my prayers. He's sure St. Jude pulled me through the crisis because he's the patron saint of desperate cases and I was indeed a desperate case.

80   Patricia says she has two books by her bed. One is a poetry book and that's the one she loves. The other is a short history of England and do I want it? She gives it to Seamus, the man who mops the floors every day, and he brings it to me. He says, I'm not supposed to be bringing anything from a dipteria room to a typhoid room with all the germs flying around and hiding between the pages and if you ever catch dipteria on top of the typhoid they'll know and I'll lose my good job and be out on the street singing patriotic songs with a tin cup in my hand, which I could easily do because there isn't a song ever written about Ireland's sufferings I don't know and a few songs about the joy of

90 whiskey too. **E**

    Oh, yes, he knows Roddy McCorley. He'll sing it for me right enough but he's barely into the first verse when the Kerry nurse rushes in. What's this, Seamus? Singing? Of all the people in this hospital you should know the rules against singing. I have a good mind to report you to Sister Rita.

    Ah, don't do that, nurse.

    Very well, Seamus. I'll let it go this one time. You know the singing could lead to a relapse in these patients.

    When she leaves he whispers he'll teach me a few songs

100 because singing is good for passing the time when you're by yourself in a typhoid room. He says Patricia is a lovely girl the way she often gives him sweets from the parcel her mother sends every fortnight.[5] He stops mopping the floor and calls to Patricia

---

4. **dole** (DOHL): government payment to the unemployed; also, money or food given to those in need.
5. **fortnight:** chiefly British for "two weeks."

D **LITERARY FOCUS**

Why do you think the author used this particular **sentence structure** here? What does it tell us about the **tone** of the passage?

_____

_____

_____

_____

_____

_____

_____

_____

_____

E **READING FOCUS**

Look at Seamus' **word choice** compared to that of the other characters. What does this tell us about him?

_____

_____

_____

_____

_____

_____

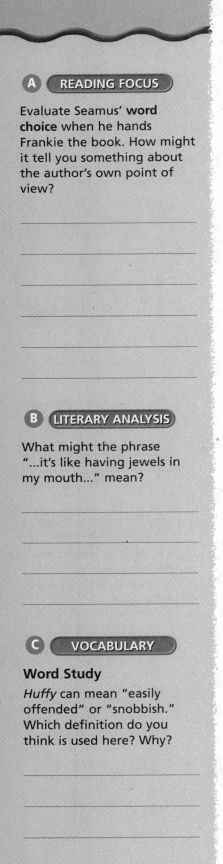

in the next room, I was telling Frankie you're a lovely girl, Patricia, and she says, You're a lovely man, Seamus. He smiles because he's an old man of forty and he never had children but the ones he can talk to here in the Fever Hospital. He says, Here's the book, Frankie. Isn't it a great pity you have to be reading all about England after all they did to us, that there isn't a history of

110 Ireland to be had in this hospital. **A**

The book tells me all about King Alfred and William the Conqueror and all the kings and queens down to Edward, who had to wait forever for his mother, Victoria, to die before he could be king. The book has the first bit of Shakespeare I ever read.

> _I do believe, induced by potent_
>   _circumstances,_
> _That thou art mine enemy._

The history writer says this is what Catherine, who is a wife of Henry the Eighth, says to Cardinal Wolsey, who is trying to

120 have her head cut off. I don't know what it means and I don't care because it's Shakespeare and it's like having jewels in my mouth when I say the words. **B** If I had a whole book of Shakespeare they could keep me in the hospital for a year.

Patricia says she doesn't know what induced means or potent circumstances and she doesn't care about Shakespeare, she has her poetry book and she reads to me from beyond the wall a poem about an owl and a pussycat that went to sea in a green boat with honey and money and it makes no sense and when I say that Patricia gets huffy and says that's the last poem

130 she'll ever read to me. **C** She says I'm always reciting the lines from Shakespeare and they make no sense either. Seamus stops mopping again and tells us we shouldn't be fighting over poetry because we'll have enough to fight about when we grow up and get married. Patricia says she's sorry and I'm sorry too so she reads me part of another poem[6] which I have to remember so

---

6. **part . . . poem:** The reference is to "The Highwayman" by the British poet Alfred Noyes (1880–1958). The poem is based on a true story about a highwayman who fell in love with an innkeeper's daughter in eighteenth-century England. Highwaymen, who robbed wealthy stagecoach passengers, were at that time popular romantic figures.

I can say it back to her early in the morning or late at night when
there are no nuns or nurses about,

> *The wind was a torrent of darkness among the gusty trees,*
> *The moon was a ghostly galleon tossed upon cloudy seas,*

140
> *The road was a ribbon of moonlight over the purple moor,*
> *And the highwayman came riding—*
>> *Riding—riding—*
> *The highwayman came riding, up to the old inn door.*
> *He'd a French cocked-hat on his forehead, a bunch of lace at*
> *his chin,*
> *A coat of the claret velvet, and breeches of brown doeskin,*
> *They fitted with never a wrinkle. His boots were up to the*
> *thigh.*
> *And he rode with a jeweled twinkle,*

150
>> *His pistol butts a-twinkle,*
> *His rapier hilt a-twinkle, under the jeweled sky.*

Every day I can't wait for the doctors and nurses to leave me
alone so I can learn a new verse from Patricia and find out what's
happening to the highwayman and the landlord's red-lipped
daughter. I love the poem because it's exciting and almost as
good as my two lines of Shakespeare. The redcoats are after the
highwayman because they know he told her, I'll come to thee by
moonlight, though hell should bar the way.

160
    I'd love to do that myself, come by moonlight for Patricia in
the next room not giving a hoot though hell should bar the way.
She's ready to read the last few verses when in comes the nurse
from Kerry shouting at her, shouting at me, I told ye there was to
be no talking between rooms. Diphtheria is never allowed to talk
to typhoid and visa versa. I warned ye. And she calls out, Seamus,
take this one. Take the by. Sister Rita said one more word out
of him and upstairs with him. We gave ye a warning to stop the
blathering but ye wouldn't. Take the by, Seamus, take him.

    Ah, now, nurse, sure isn't he harmless. 'Tis only a bit o'
poetry.

170
    Take that by, Seamus, take him at once. **D**

D **LITERARY FOCUS**

What is the author's **tone**
toward the nurse? Explain
your answer.

_____

_____

_____

_____

_____

B (LITERARY ANALYSIS)

What does Sister Rita's attitude toward the poem about the highwayman reveal about her character?

_____

_____

_____

_____

_____

_____

_____

_____

He bends over me and whispers, Ah, I'm sorry, Frankie. Here's your English history book. He slips the book under my shirt and lifts me from the bed. He whispers that I'm a feather. I try to see Patricia when we pass through her room but all I can make out is a blur of dark head on a pillow. **A**

Sister Rita stops us in the hall to tell me I'm a great disappointment to her, that she expected me to be a good boy after what God had done for me, after all the prayers said by hundreds of boys at the Confraternity, after all the care from the nuns and nurses of the Fever Hospital, after the way they let my mother and father in to see me, a thing rarely allowed, and this is how I repaid them lying in the bed reciting silly poetry back and forth with Patricia Madigan knowing very well there was a ban on all talk between typhoid and diphtheria. She says I'll have plenty of time to reflect on my sins in the big ward upstairs and I should beg God's forgiveness for my disobedience reciting a pagan[7] English poem about a thief on a horse and a maiden with red lips who commits a terrible sin when I could have been praying or reading the life of a saint. She made it her business to read that poem so she did and I'd be well advised to tell the priest in confession. **B**

The Kerry nurse follows us upstairs gasping and holding on to the banister. She tells me I better not get the notion she'll be running up to this part of the world every time I have a little pain or a twinge.

There are twenty beds in the ward, all white, all empty. The nurse tells Seamus put me at the far end of the ward against the wall to make sure I don't talk to anyone who might be passing the door, which is very unlikely since there isn't another soul on this whole floor. She tells Seamus this was the fever ward during the Great Famine[8] long ago and only God knows how many died here brought in too late for anything but a wash before they were buried and there are stories of cries and moans in the far reaches

180

190

200

---

7. **pagan** (PAY GUHN): here, non-Christian.
8. **Great Famine:** the great famine in Ireland from 1845 to 1849, when failed potato crops resulted in the starvation and death of about one million people.

of the night. She says 'twould break your heart to think of what the English did to us, that if they didn't put the blight[9] on the potato they didn't do much to take it off. No pity. No feeling at all for the people that died in this very ward, children suffering and dying here while the English feasted on roast beef and guzzled the best of wine in their big houses, little children with their
210 mouths all green from trying to eat the grass in the fields beyond, God bless us and save us and guard us from future famines. **C**

Seamus says 'twas a terrible thing indeed and he wouldn't want to be walking these halls in the dark with all the little green mouths gaping at him. The nurse takes my temperature, 'Tis up a bit, have a good sleep for yourself now that you're away from the chatter with Patricia Madigan below who will never know a gray hair.

She shakes her head at Seamus and he gives her a sad shake back.

220 Nurses and nuns never think you know what they're talking about. If you're ten going on eleven you're supposed to be simple like my uncle Pat Sheehan who was dropped on his head. You can't ask questions. You can't show you understand what the nurse said about Patricia Madigan, that she's going to die, and you can't show you want to cry over this girl who taught you a lovely poem which the nun says is bad. **D**

The nurse tells Seamus she has to go and he's to sweep the lint from under my bed and mop up a bit around the ward. Seamus tells me she's a right oul' witch for running to Sister Rita
230 and complaining about the poem going between the two rooms, that you can't catch a disease from a poem unless it's love ha ha and that's not bloody likely when you're what? ten going on eleven? He never heard the likes of it, a little fella shifted upstairs for saying a poem and he has a good mind to go to the Limerick Leader and tell them print the whole thing except he has this job and he'd lose it if ever Sister Rita found out. Anyway, Frankie, you'll be outa here one of these fine days and you can read all

---

9. **blight** (BLYT): kind of plant disease.

C LANGUAGE COACH

A **connotation** is the feeling or association attached to a word. What are the connotations of the words *feasted* and *guzzled*? How does the use of these words help you understand the nurse's attitude toward the English?

_____

_____

_____

_____

_____

_____

_____

D LITERARY FOCUS

Based on the **tone** of this paragraph, what do you think is the author's opinion about how children are treated by nurses and nuns?

_____

_____

_____

_____

_____

_____

_____

Why do you think Frankie wants to know what happens in the poem about the highwayman?

_____

_____

_____

_____

_____

_____

_____

_____

_____

the poetry you want though I don't know about Patricia below, I don't know about Patricia, God help us.

240   He knows about Patricia in two days because she got out of the bed to go to the lavatory when she was supposed to use a bedpan and collapsed and died in the lavatory. Seamus is mopping the floor and there are tears on his cheeks and he's saying, 'Tis a dirty rotten thing to die in a lavatory when you're lovely in yourself. She told me she was sorry she had you reciting that poem and getting you shifted from the room, Frankie. She said 'twas all her fault.

It wasn't, Seamus.

I know and didn't I tell her that. **A**

250   Patricia is gone and I'll never know what happened to the highwayman and Bess, the landlord's daughter. I ask Seamus but he doesn't know any poetry at all especially English poetry. He knew an Irish poem once but it was about fairies and had no sign of a highwayman in it. Still he'll ask the men in his local pub where there's always someone reciting something and he'll bring it back to me. **B** Won't I be busy meanwhile reading my short history of England and finding out all about their perfidy.[10] That's what Seamus says, perfidy, and I don't know what it means and he doesn't know what it means but if it's something the English do it must be terrible.

260   He comes three times a week to mop the floor and the nurse is there every morning to take my temperature and pulse. The doctor listens to my chest with the thing hanging from his neck. They all say, And how's our little soldier today? A girl with a blue dress brings meals three times a day and never talks to me. Seamus says she's not right in the head so don't say a word to her.

The July days are long and I fear the dark. There are only two ceiling lights in the ward and they're switched off when the tea tray is taken away and the nurse gives me pills. The nurse tells

270   me go to sleep but I can't because I see people in the nineteen beds in the ward all dying and green around their mouths where they tried to eat grass and moaning for soup Protestant soup any

---

10. **perfidy** (PUHR FUH DEE): treachery; betrayal.

soup and I cover my face with the pillow hoping they won't come and stand around the bed clawing at me and howling for bits of the chocolate bar my mother brought last week. **C**

No, she didn't bring it. She had to send it in because I can't have any more visitors. Sister Rita tells me a visit to the Fever Hospital is a privilege and after my bad behavior with Patricia Madigan and that poem I can't have the privilege anymore. She says I'll be going home in a few weeks and my job is to concentrate on getting better and learn to walk again after being in bed for six weeks and I can get out of bed tomorrow after breakfast. I don't know why she says I have to learn how to walk when I've been walking since I was a baby but when the nurse stands me by the side of the bed I fall to the floor and the nurse laughs, See, you're a baby again.

I practice walking from bed to bed back and forth back and forth. I don't want to be a baby. I don't want to be in this empty ward with no Patricia and no highwayman and no red-lipped landlord's daughter. I don't want the ghosts of children with green mouths pointing bony fingers at me and clamoring for bits of my chocolate bar. **D** **E**

Seamus says a man in his pub knew all the verses of the highwayman poem and it has a very sad end. Would I like him to say it because he never learned how to read and he had to carry the poem in his head? He stands in the middle of the ward leaning on his mop and recites,

Tlot-tlot, *in the frosty silence!* Tlot-tlot, *in the echoing night!*
Nearer he came and nearer! Her face was like a light!
Her eyes grew wide for a moment; she drew one last deep breath,
Then her fingers moved in the moonlight,
Her musket shattered the moonlight,
Shattered her breast in the moonlight and warned him—with her death.

He hears the shot and escapes but when he learns at dawn how Bess died he goes into a rage and returns for revenge only to be shot down by the redcoats.

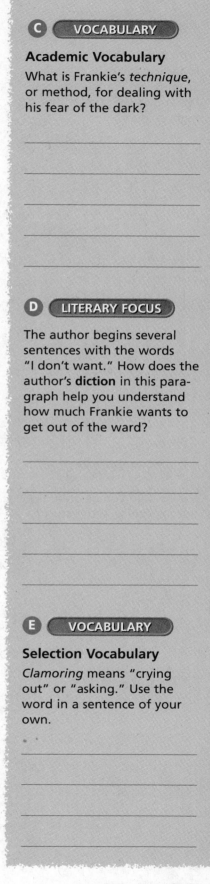

C VOCABULARY

Academic Vocabulary
What is Frankie's *technique*, or method, for dealing with his fear of the dark?

_____
_____
_____
_____

D LITERARY FOCUS

The author begins several sentences with the words "I don't want." How does the author's **diction** in this paragraph help you understand how much Frankie wants to get out of the ward?

_____
_____
_____
_____

E VOCABULARY

Selection Vocabulary
Clamoring means "crying out" or "asking." Use the word in a sentence of your own.

_____
_____
_____
_____

Why do you think that it is particularly painful for Seamus and Frankie to know the end of the story of the highwayman?

_____
_____
_____
_____
_____
_____
_____
_____
_____

B **LITERARY FOCUS**

How would you describe the author's **voice** in this story?

_____
_____
_____
_____
_____
_____
_____
_____
_____
_____

310 *Blood-red were his spurs in the golden noon; wine-red was his velvet coat,*

When they shot him down on the highway,

Down like a dog on the highway,

And he lay in his blood on the highway,

with a bunch of lace at his

320 *throat.*

Seamus wipes his sleeve across his face and sniffles. He says, There was no call at all to shift you up here away from Patricia when you didn't even know what happened to the highwayman and Bess. **A** 'Tis a very sad

330 story and when I said it to my wife she wouldn't stop crying the whole night till we went to bed. She said there was no call for them redcoats to shoot that highwayman, they are responsible for half the troubles of the world and they never had any pity

340 on the Irish, either. Now if you want to know any more poems, Frankie, tell me and I'll get them from the pub and bring 'em back in my head. **B**

Courtesy of David Prifti

Applying Your Skills

Typhoid Fever

VOCABULARY DEVELOPMENT

DIRECTIONS: A choice of three possible synonyms is given for each vocabulary word. Select the one that is closest in meaning to the original word.

1. potent

    a. predict

    b. powerful

    c. lame

2. clamoring

    a. rejoicing

    b. rejecting

    c. bellowing

3. induced

    a. caused

    b. reduced

    c. withered

LITERARY FOCUS: STYLE—DICTION, TONE, AND VOICE

DIRECTIONS: Diction, sentence structure, tone, and **voice** all contribute to a writer's individual **style**. Work with a partner to review "Typhoid Fever." Find one example of each of these elements of style in McCourt's writing. Read the passages aloud to each other and then compare your choices with other classmates.

READING FOCUS: EVALUATING WORD CHOICE

DIRECTIONS: For each character listed below, write an example of their speech taken from the story. Then explain what the **word choice** reveals about that character's personality.

Character	Example of speech	What this shows
Frankie		
Patricia		
Seamus		

SKILLS FOCUS

Literary Skills
Understand the elements of style, including diction, tone, and voice.

Reading Skills
Evaluate word choice.

from Into Thin Air

by Jon Krakauer

LITERARY FOCUS: STYLE

A writer's **style** is the way that he or she uses language. Sentence structure and mood are two important elements of style. **Sentence structure** is the way the writer arranges and combines words to make meaningful sentences. For example, a writer might use short sentences to create excitement during an action-filled paragraph. Long sentences might be used to describe an elaborate setting.

Mood is the atmosphere that a writer creates with his or her language. Just like the mood of a person, the mood of a story can change very suddenly. For example, it might be joyful and then become dark and gloomy.

READING FOCUS: IDENTIFYING CAUSE AND EFFECT

A **cause** is the reason why something happens in a story. The result of what has happened is called the **effect**. A single effect may have more than one cause, and just one cause may lead to many effects.

Use the Skill As you read "Into Thin Air," look for the causes of the various events of the story, especially the tragedies that occur during the climb and later on top of the mountain. Record them in the chart below. An example is given. Add more rows if needed.

SKILLS FOCUS

Literary Skills
Examine an author's writing style by studying sentence structure and mood.

Reading Skills
Identify cause-and-effect relationships.

Cause	Effect
Mount Everest is very high up. The air is thin at high elevations.	Krakauer has difficulty concentrating.

Vocabulary Development

from Into Thin Air

SELECTION VOCABULARY

deteriorate (DIH TIHR EE UH RAYT) *v.:* get worse.

> Storm clouds blew in, and the weather started to deteriorate rapidly.

benign (BIH NYN) *adj.:* not dangerous.

> The clouds appeared benign, but the storm was on its way.

crucial (KROO SHUHL) *adj.:* very important.

> Oxygen is crucial for humans; they cannot survive without it.

jeopardize (JEHP UHR DYZ) *v.:* put in danger or at risk.

> Eating too much junk food can jeopardize your health because junk food does not supply the vitamins that your body needs.

tenuous (TEHN YOO UHS) *adj.:* thin or slight; weak; fragile.

> The climbers had only a tenuous grip on reality because their brains were not functioning properly.

WORD STUDY

DIRECTIONS: Context clues are words and phrases in a sentence that help you find the meaning of an unfamiliar word. In the sample sentences above, underline the words or phrases that help you determine the meaning of each vocabulary word.

from INTO THIN AIR

by Jon Krakauer

> **BACKGROUND**
> Mount Everest is the tallest mountain in the world. The first successful climb to the top was in 1953 by Edmund Hillary and Tenzing Norgay. Hundreds have died attempting to make it to the top. Here, Jon Krakauer writes of a particularly deadly day in the history of Everest.

Straddling the top of the world, one foot in Tibet and the other in Nepal, I cleared the ice from my oxygen mask, hunched a shoulder against the wind, and stared absently at the vast sweep of earth below. I understood on some dim, detached level that it was a spectacular sight. I'd been fantasizing about this moment, and the release of emotion that would accompany it, for many months. But now that I was finally here, standing on the summit of Mount Everest, I just couldn't summon the energy to care. **A**

It was the afternoon of May 10. I hadn't slept in 57 hours.
10 The only food I'd been able to force down over the preceding three days was a bowl of Ramen soup and a handful of peanut M&M's. Weeks of violent coughing had left me with two separated ribs, making it excruciatingly painful to breathe. Twenty-nine thousand twenty-eight feet[1] up in the troposphere,[2] there was so little oxygen reaching my brain that my mental capacity was that of a slow child. Under the circumstances, I was incapable of feeling much of anything except cold and tired. **B**

---

1. In 1999, after this article was written, scientists using sophisticated equipment determined the elevation of Everest to be 29,035 feet, not 29,028 feet, as previously believed.
2. **troposphere** (TROH PUHS FEER): portion of the atmosphere directly below the stratosphere (it extends from six to eight miles above the earth's surface).

© Scott Fischer/Woodfin Camp and Associates

C LITERARY ANALYSIS

Why might Krakauer be worried about approaching clouds?
_____
_____
_____
_____
_____
_____

I'd arrived on the summit a few minutes after Anatoli Boukreev,[3] a Russian guide with an American expedition, and
20   just ahead of Andy Harris, a guide with the New Zealand–based commercial team that I was a part of and someone with whom I'd grown to be friends during the last six weeks. I snapped four quick photos of Harris and Boukreev striking summit poses, and then turned and started down. My watch read 1:17 P.M. All told, I'd spent less than five minutes on the roof of the world.

After a few steps, I paused to take another photo, this one looking down the Southeast Ridge, the route we had ascended. Training my lens on a pair of climbers approaching the summit, I saw something that until that moment had escaped my
30   attention. To the south, where the sky had been perfectly clear just an hour earlier, a blanket of clouds now hid Pumori, Ama Dablam, and the other lesser peaks surrounding Everest. **C**

Days later—after six bodies had been found, after a search for two others had been abandoned, after surgeons had amputated[4] the gangrenous[5] right hand of my teammate Beck

---

3. **Anatoli Boukreev:** Boukreev was killed in an avalanche about a year and a half later, on December 25, 1997, while climbing Annapurna in the Himalayas.
4. **amputated:** surgically removed, usually a limb or another body part.
5. **gangrenous** (GANG GRUH NUHS): affected by the decay of tissue resulting from a lack of blood supply.

A **LITERARY FOCUS**

What is the **mood** at the beginning of this paragraph? Describe how the mood changes throughout the paragraph.

_____

_____

_____

_____

_____

_____

_____

_____

B **LITERARY FOCUS**

Look at the **sentence structure** in this paragraph. Count the number of words in each sentence. Why do you think the author chose sentences of this length?

_____

_____

_____

_____

_____

_____

_____

Weathers—people would ask why, if the weather had begun to deteriorate, had climbers on the upper mountain not heeded the signs? Why did veteran Himalayan guides keep moving upward, leading a gaggle of amateurs, each of whom had paid as much as $65,000 to be ushered safely up Everest, into an apparent death trap?

Nobody can speak for the leaders of the two guided groups involved, for both men are now dead. But I can attest that nothing I saw early on the afternoon of May 10 suggested that a murderous storm was about to bear down on us. To my oxygen-depleted mind, the clouds drifting up the grand valley of ice known as the Western Cwm looked innocuous, wispy, insubstantial. Gleaming in the brilliant midday sun, they appeared no different from the harmless puffs of convection condensation that rose from the valley almost daily. As I began my descent, I was indeed anxious, but my concern had little to do with the weather. A check of the gauge on my oxygen tank had revealed that it was almost empty. I needed to get down, fast. **A**

The uppermost shank of the Southeast Ridge is a slender, heavily corniced fin[6] of rock and wind-scoured snow that snakes for a quarter-mile toward a secondary pinnacle known as the South Summit. Negotiating the serrated[7] ridge presents few great technical hurdles, but the route is dreadfully exposed. After 15 minutes of cautious shuffling over a 7,000-foot abyss,[8] I arrived at the notorious Hillary Step, a pronounced notch in the ridge named after Sir Edmund Hillary, the first Westerner to climb the mountain, and a spot that does require a fair amount of technical maneuvering. As I clipped into a fixed rope and prepared to rappel[9] over the lip, I was greeted by an alarming sight. **B**

---

6. **corniced** (KAWR NIHST) **fin:** ridge with an overhanging mass of snow or ice deposited by the wind.
7. **serrated:** notched like a saw.
8. **abyss** (UH BIHS): deep crack or opening in the earth's surface.
9. **rappel** (RA PEHL): descend a mountain by means of a double rope arranged around the climber's body so that he or she can control the slide downward.

Thirty feet below, some 20 people were queued up[10] at the base of the Step, and three climbers were hauling themselves up the rope that I was attempting to descend. I had no choice but to unclip from the line and step aside.

The traffic jam comprised climbers from three separate expeditions: the team I belonged to, a group of paying clients under the leadership of the celebrated New Zealand guide Rob Hall; another guided party headed by American Scott Fischer; and a nonguided team from Taiwan. Moving at the snail's pace that is the norm above 8,000 meters, the throng labored up the Hillary Step one by one, while I nervously bided my time. **C**

Harris, who left the summit shortly after I did, soon pulled up behind me. Wanting to conserve whatever oxygen remained in my tank, I asked him to reach inside my backpack and turn off the valve on my regulator, which he did. For the next ten minutes I felt surprisingly good. My head cleared. I actually seemed less tired than with the gas turned on. Then, abruptly, I felt like I was suffocating. My vision dimmed and my head began to spin. I was on the brink of losing consciousness.

Instead of turning my oxygen off, Harris, in his hypoxically[11] impaired state, had mistakenly cranked the valve open to full flow, draining the tank. I'd just squandered the last of my gas going nowhere. **D** There was another tank waiting for me at the South Summit, 250 feet below, but to get there I would have to descend the most exposed terrain on the entire route without benefit of supplemental oxygen.

But first I had to wait for the crowd to thin. I removed my now useless mask, planted my ice ax into the mountain's frozen hide, and hunkered on the ridge crest. As I exchanged banal[12] congratulations with the climbers filing past, inwardly I was frantic: "Hurry it up, hurry it up!" I silently pleaded. "While you

70

80

90

C **LANGUAGE COACH**

Based on the **context clues** in this paragraph, what do you think *throng* means?

_____

_____

_____

_____

D **READING FOCUS**

What was the **effect** of Harris's error?

_____

_____

_____

_____

_____

_____

---

10. **queued** (KYOOD) **up:** lined up.
11. **hypoxically:** characterized by hypoxia, a condition resulting from a decrease in the oxygen reaching body tissues. Hypoxia is a common condition at very high altitudes.
12. **banal** (BUH NAL): everyday; commonplace.

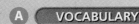

guys are messing around here, I'm losing brain cells by the millions!"

100   Most of the passing crowd belonged to Fischer's group, but near the back of the parade two of my teammates eventually appeared: Hall and Yasuko Namba. Girlish and reserved, the 47-year-old Namba was 40 minutes away from becoming the oldest woman to climb Everest and the second Japanese woman to reach the highest point on each continent, the so-called Seven Summits.

Later still, Doug Hansen—another member of our expedition, a postal worker from Seattle who had become my closest friend on the mountain—arrived atop the Step. "It's in the bag!" I yelled over the wind, trying to sound more upbeat than I felt. Plainly

110   exhausted, Doug mumbled something from behind his oxygen mask that I didn't catch, shook my hand weakly, and continued plodding upward.

The last climber up the rope was Fischer, whom I knew casually from Seattle, where we both lived. His strength and drive were legendary—in 1994 he'd climbed Everest without using bottled oxygen—so I was surprised at how slowly he was moving and how hammered he looked when he pulled his mask aside to say hello. "Bruuuuuuce!" he wheezed with forced cheer, employing his trademark, fratboyish greeting. When I asked how he was

120   doing, Fischer insisted he was feeling fine: "Just dragging a little today for some reason. No big deal." With the Hillary Step finally clear, I clipped into the strand of orange rope, swung quickly around Fischer as he slumped over his ice ax, and rappelled over the edge.

It was after 2:30 when I made it down to the South Summit. By now tendrils of mist were wrapping across the top of 27,890-foot Lhotse and lapping at Everest's summit pyramid. No longer did the weather look so benign. **B** I grabbed a fresh oxygen cylinder, jammed it onto my regulator, and hurried down into

130   the gathering cloud.

Four hundred vertical feet above, where the summit was still washed in bright sunlight under an immaculate cobalt sky, my compadres[13] were dallying,[14] memorializing their arrival at the apex of the planet with photos and high-fives—and using up precious ticks of the clock. None of them imagined that a horrible ordeal was drawing nigh. None of them suspected that by the end of that long day, every minute would matter. . . . **C**

At 3 P.M., within minutes of leaving the South Summit, I descended into clouds ahead of the others. Snow started to fall. In the flat, diminishing light, it became hard to tell where the mountain ended and where the sky began. It would have been very easy to blunder off the edge of the ridge and never be heard from again. The lower I went, the worse the weather became.

When I reached the Balcony again, about 4 P.M., I encountered Beck Weathers standing alone, shivering violently. Years earlier, Weathers had undergone radial keratotomy to correct his vision. A side effect, which he discovered on Everest and consequently hid from Hall, was that in the low barometric pressure at high altitude, his eyesight failed. Nearly blind when he'd left Camp Four in the middle of the night but hopeful that his vision would improve at daybreak, he stuck close to the person in front of him and kept climbing. **D**

Upon reaching the Southeast Ridge shortly after sunrise, Weathers had confessed to Hall that he was having trouble seeing, at which point Hall declared, "Sorry, pal, you're going down. I'll send one of the Sherpas[15] with you." Weathers countered that his vision was likely to improve as soon as the sun crept higher in the sky; Hall said he'd give Weathers 30 minutes to find out—after that, he'd have to wait there at 27,500 feet for Hall and the rest of the group to come back down. Hall didn't want Weathers descending alone. **E** "I'm dead serious about this," Hall admonished his client. "Promise me that you'll sit right here until I return."

---

13. **compadres** (KUHM PAH DRAYZ): close friends; in this case, fellow members of the climbing team.
14. **dallying:** wasting time.
15. **Sherpas:** members of a Tibetan people living on the southern slopes of the Himalayas. As experienced mountain climbers, Sherpas are often hired to assist or act as guides for mountaineering.

C LITERARY FOCUS

Underline the sentences in this paragraph in which the **mood** is joyous. Circle the sentences in which the mood is dark and threatening.

D QUICK CHECK

Why was Weathers "nearly blind"?

_____

_____

_____

_____

_____

E LITERARY ANALYSIS

What might have happened if Weathers were to have climbed down the mountain by himself?

_____

_____

_____

_____

_____

A VOCABULARY

Selection Vocabulary

Underline the phrases and sentences in this paragraph that show that the weather has *deteriorated*, or gotten worse.

B LANGUAGE COACH

Based on the **context clues** in this paragraph, what do you think is the meaning of *appalling*?

_____

_____

_____

_____

"I crossed my heart and hoped to die," Weathers recalls now, "and promised I wouldn't go anywhere." Shortly after noon, Hutchison, Taske, and Kasischke[16] passed by with their Sherpa escorts, but Weathers elected not to accompany them. "The weather was still good," he explains, "and I saw no reason to break my promise to Rob."

170   By the time I encountered Weathers, however, conditions were turning ugly. "Come down with me," I implored, "I'll get you down, no problem." He was nearly convinced, until I made the mistake of mentioning that Groom was on his way down, too. In a day of many mistakes, this would turn out to be a crucial one. "Thanks anyway," Weathers said. "I'll just wait for Mike. He's got a rope; he'll be able to short-rope[17] me." Secretly relieved, I hurried toward the South Col, 1,500 feet below.

These lower slopes proved to be the most difficult part of the descent. Six inches of powder snow blanketed outcroppings

180   of loose shale. Climbing down them demanded unceasing concentration, an all but impossible feat in my current state. By 5:30, however, I was finally within 200 vertical feet of Camp Four, and only one obstacle stood between me and safety: a steep bulge of rock-hard ice that I'd have to descend without a rope. But the weather had deteriorated into a full-scale blizzard. Snow pellets born on 70-mph winds stung my face; any exposed skin was instantly frozen. The tents, no more than 200 horizontal yards away, were only intermittently visible through the whiteout. **A** There was zero margin for error. Worried about making a critical

190   blunder, I sat down to marshal my energy.

Suddenly, Harris appeared out of the gloom and sat beside me.[18] At this point there was no mistaking that he was in appalling shape. **B** His cheeks were coated with an armor of frost, one eye was frozen shut, and his speech was slurred. He was frantic to

---

16. Stuart Hutchison, Dr. John Taske, and Lou Kasischke were three clients on Rob Hall's team.
17. **short-rope:** assist a weak or injured climber by hauling him or her.
18. After writing this article, Krakauer discovered through conversations with Martin Adams (a client on Scott Fischer's team) that the person he thought was Harris was, in fact, Martin Adams.

reach the tents. After briefly discussing the best way to negotiate the ice, Harris started scooting down on his butt, facing forward. "Andy," I yelled after him, "it's crazy to try it like that!" He yelled something back, but the words were carried off by the screaming wind. A second later he lost his purchase[19] and was rocketing
200   down on his back.

Two hundred feet below, I could make out Harris's motionless form. I was sure he'd broken at least a leg, maybe his neck. But then he stood up, waved that he was OK, and started stumbling toward camp, which was for the moment in plain sight, 150 yards beyond.

I could see three or four people shining lights outside the tents. I watched Harris walk across the flats to the edge of camp, a distance he covered in less than ten minutes. When the clouds closed in a moment later, cutting off my view, he was within
210   30 yards of the tents. I didn't see him again after that, but I was certain that he'd reached the security of camp, where Sherpas would be waiting with hot tea. Sitting out in the storm, with the ice bulge still standing between me and the tents, I felt a pang of envy. I was angry that my guide hadn't waited for me.

Twenty minutes later I was in camp. I fell into my tent with my crampons still on, zipped the door tight, and sprawled across the frost-covered floor. I was drained, more exhausted than I'd ever been in my life. But I was safe. Andy was safe. The others would be coming into camp soon. We'd done it. We'd climbed
220   Mount Everest. **C**

It would be many hours before I learned that everyone had in fact not made it back to camp—that one teammate was already dead and that 23 other men and women were caught in a desperate struggle for their lives. . . .

Meanwhile, Hall and Hansen were still on the frightfully exposed summit ridge, engaged in a grim struggle of their own. The 46-year-old Hansen, whom Hall had turned back just below this spot exactly a year ago, had been determined to bag the

---

19. **purchase:** firm hold.

Describe the **sentence structure** in this paragraph. Why do you think the author chooses to use this structure here?

_____

_____

_____

_____

_____

_____

_____

What do you think **causes** someone to continue to climb even if he or she is in life-threatening danger?

_____

_____

_____

_____

_____

230 summit this time around. "I want to get this thing done and out of my life," he'd told me a couple of days earlier. "I don't want to have to come back here."

Indeed Hansen had reached the top this time, though not until after 3 P.M., well after Hall's predetermined turnaround time. Given Hall's conservative, systematic nature, many people wonder why he didn't turn Hansen around when it became obvious that he was running late. It's not far-fetched to speculate that because Hall had talked Hansen into coming back to Everest this year, it would have been especially hard for him to deny Hansen the summit a second time—especially when all of

240 Fischer's clients were still marching blithely toward the top.

"It's very difficult to turn someone around high on the mountain," cautions Guy Cotter, a New Zealand guide who summited Everest with Hall in 1992 and was guiding the peak for him in 1995 when Hansen made his first attempt. "If a client sees that the summit is close and they're dead set on getting there, they're going to laugh in your face and keep going up." **A**

In any case, for whatever reason, Hall did not turn Hansen around. Instead, after reaching the summit at 2:10 P.M., Hall waited for more than an hour for Hansen to arrive and then

250 headed down with him. Soon after they began their descent, just below the top, Hansen apparently ran out of oxygen and collapsed. "Pretty much the same thing happened to Doug in '95," says Ed Viesturs, an American who guided the peak for Hall that year. "He was fine during the ascent, but as soon as he started down he lost it mentally and physically. He turned into a real zombie, like he'd used everything up."

At 4:31 P.M., Hall radioed Base Camp to say that he and Hansen were above the Hillary Step and urgently needed oxygen. Two full bottles were waiting for them at the South Summit; if

260 Hall had known this he could have retrieved the gas fairly quickly and then climbed back up to give Hansen a fresh tank. But Harris, in the throes of his oxygen-starved dementia,[20] overheard

---

20. **dementia** (DIH MEHN SHUH): mental impairment.

the 4:31 radio call while descending the Southeast Ridge and broke in to tell Hall that all the bottles at the South Summit were empty. So Hall stayed with Hansen and tried to bring the helpless client down without oxygen, but could get him no farther than the top of the Hillary Step. **B**

Cotter, a very close friend of both Hall and Harris, happened to be a few miles from Everest Base Camp at the time, guiding an expedition on Pumori. Overhearing the radio conversations between Hall and Base Camp, he called Hall at 5:36 and again at 5:57, urging his mate to leave Hansen and come down alone. . . . Hall, however, wouldn't consider going down without Hansen.

There was no further word from Hall until the middle of the night. At 2:46 A.M. on May 11, Cotter woke up to hear a long, broken transmission, probably unintended: Hall was wearing a remote microphone clipped to the shoulder strap of his backpack, which was occasionally keyed on by mistake. **C** In this instance, says Cotter, "I suspect Rob didn't even know he was transmitting. I could hear someone yelling—it might have been Rob, but I couldn't be sure because the wind was so loud in the background. He was saying something like 'Keep moving! Keep going!' presumably to Doug, urging him on."

If that was indeed the case, it meant that in the wee hours of the morning Hall and Hansen were still struggling from the Hillary Step toward the South Summit, taking more than 12 hours to traverse a stretch of ridge typically covered by descending climbers in half an hour.

Hall's next call to Base Camp was at 4:43 A.M. He'd finally reached the South Summit but was unable to descend farther, and in a series of transmissions over the next two hours he sounded confused and irrational. "Harold[21] was with me last night," Hall insisted, when in fact Harris had reached the South Col at sunset. "But he doesn't seem to be with me now. He was very weak."

270

280

290

---

21. **Harold:** Andy Harris's nickname.

B READING FOCUS

What **causes** Hall to not retrieve the full oxygen tanks?

_____

_____

_____

C LANGUAGE COACH

Based on the **context clues** in this sentence, what does *unintended* mean?

_____

_____

_____

Mackenzie[22] asked him how Hansen was doing. "Doug," Hall replied, "is gone." That was all he said, and it was the last mention he ever made of Hansen.

On May 23, when Breashears and Viesturs, of the IMAX 300 team,[23] reached the summit, they found no sign of Hansen's body but they did find an ice ax planted about 50 feet below the Hillary Step, along a highly exposed section of ridge where the fixed ropes came to an end. It is quite possible that Hall managed to get Hansen down the ropes to this point, only to have him lose his footing and fall 7,000 feet down the sheer Southwest Face, leaving his ice ax jammed into the ridge crest where he slipped. A

During the radio calls to Base Camp early on May 11, Hall revealed that something was wrong with his legs, that he was no 310 longer able to walk and was shaking uncontrollably. This was very disturbing news to the people down below, but it was amazing that Hall was even alive after spending a night without shelter or oxygen at 28,700 feet in hurricane-force wind and minus-100-degree windchill.

At 5 A.M., Base Camp patched through a call on the satellite telephone to Jan Arnold, Hall's wife, seven months pregnant with their first child in Christchurch, New Zealand. Arnold, a respected physician, had summited Everest with Hall in 1993 and entertained no illusions about the gravity of her 320 husband's predicament. B "My heart really sank when I heard his voice," she recalls. "He was slurring his words markedly. He sounded like Major Tom[24] or something, like he was just floating away. I'd been up there; I knew what it could be like in bad weather. Rob and I had talked about the impossibility of being

---

22. **Mackenzie:** Dr. Caroline Mackenzie was Base Camp doctor for Rob Hall's team.
23. **IMAX team:** another team of climbers, who were shooting a $5.5-million giant-screen movie about Mount Everest. The movie was released in 1998.
24. **Major Tom:** reference to the David Bowie song "Space Oddity," which is about an astronaut, Major Tom, who is lost in space.

rescued from the summit ridge. As he himself had put it, 'You might as well be on the moon.'"

By that time, Hall had located two full oxygen bottles, and after struggling for four hours trying to de-ice his mask, around 8:30 A.M. he finally started breathing the life-sustaining gas.

330 Several times he announced that he was preparing to descend, only to change his mind and remain at the South Summit. The day had started out sunny and clear, but the wind remained fierce, and by late morning the upper mountain was wrapped with thick clouds. Climbers at Camp Two reported that the wind over the summit sounded like a squadron of 747s, even from 8,000 feet below. . . .

Throughout that day, Hall's friends begged him to make an effort to descend from the South Summit under his own power. At 3:20 P.M., after one such transmission from Cotter, Hall began

340 to sound annoyed. "Look," he said, "if I thought I could manage the knots on the fixed ropes with me frostbitten hands, I would have gone down six hours ago, pal. Just send a couple of the boys up with a big thermos of something hot—then I'll be fine." **C**

At 6:20 P.M., Hall was patched through a second time to Arnold in Christchurch. "Hi, my sweetheart," he said in a slow, painfully distorted voice. "I hope you're tucked up in a nice warm bed. How are you doing?"

"I can't tell you how much I'm thinking about you!" Arnold replied. "You sound so much better than I expected. . . . Are you

350 warm, my darling?"

"In the context of the altitude, the setting, I'm reasonably comfortable," Hall answered, doing his best not to alarm her.

"How are your feet?"

"I haven't taken me boots off to check, but I think I may have a bit of frostbite."

"I'm looking forward to making you completely better when you come home," said Arnold. "I just know you're going to be rescued. Don't feel that you're alone. I'm sending all my positive energy your way!" Before signing off, Hall told his wife, "I love

360 you. Sleep well, my sweetheart. Please don't worry too much." **D**

C READING FOCUS

What **caused** Hall to be unable to descend on his own?

_____

_____

_____

_____

_____

_____

_____

D LITERARY FOCUS

Describe the **mood** of the story during the conversation between Hall and his wife.

_____

_____

_____

_____

_____

A **VOCABULARY**

Word Study
Which word in this sentence is a synonym for *carapace*, which appears in line 380?

_____

_____

B **LITERARY FOCUS**

What **mood** does Hutchison's descriptions of Namba and Weathers create?

_____

_____

_____

_____

_____

_____

These would be the last words anyone would hear him utter. Attempts to make radio contact with Hall later that night and the next day went unanswered. Twelve days later, when Breashears and Viesturs climbed over the South Summit on their way to the top, they found Hall lying on his right side in a shallow ice-hollow, his upper body buried beneath a drift of snow.

370 Early on the morning of May 11, when I returned to Camp Four, Hutchison, standing in for Groom, who was unconscious in his tent, organized a team of four Sherpas to locate the bodies of our teammates Weathers and Namba. The Sherpa search party, headed by Lhakpa Chhiri, departed ahead of Hutchison, who was so exhausted and befuddled that he forgot to put his boots on and left camp in his light, smooth-soled liners. Only when Lhakpa Chhiri pointed out the blunder did Hutchison return for his boots. Following Boukreev's directions, the Sherpas had no trouble locating the two bodies at the edge of the Kangshung Face.

380 The first body turned out to be Namba, but Hutchison couldn't tell who it was until he knelt in the howling wind and chipped a three-inch-thick carapace of ice from her face. To his shock, he discovered that she was still breathing. Both her gloves were gone, and her bare hands appeared to be frozen solid. Her eyes were dilated.[25] The skin on her face was the color of porcelain. "It was terrible," Hutchison recalls. "I was overwhelmed. She was very near death. I didn't know what to do."

He turned his attention to Weathers, who lay 20 feet away. His face was also caked with a thick armor of frost. **A** Balls of ice the size of grapes were matted to his hair and eyelids. After cleaning the frozen detritus[26] from his face, Hutchison
390 discovered that he, too, was still alive: "Beck was mumbling something, I think, but I couldn't tell what he was trying to say. His right glove was missing and he had terrible frostbite. He was as close to death as a person can be and still be breathing." **B**

---

25. **dilated:** made wider; here, referring to the pupil of the eye.
26. **detritus** (DEE TRYT uhs): debris.

Badly shaken, Hutchison went over to the Sherpas and asked Lhakpa Chhiri's advice. Lhakpa Chhiri, an Everest veteran respected by Sherpas and sahibs[27] alike for his mountain savvy, urged Hutchison to leave Weathers and Namba where they lay. Even if they survived long enough to be dragged back to Camp Four, they would certainly die before they could be carried down to Base Camp, and attempting a rescue would needlessly jeopardize the lives of the other climbers on the Col, most of whom were going to have enough trouble getting themselves down safely.

Hutchison decided that Chhiri was right. There was only one choice, however difficult: Let nature take its inevitable course with Weathers and Namba, and save the group's resources for those who could actually be helped. It was a classic act of triage.[28] When Hutchison returned to camp at 8:30 A.M. and told the rest of us of his decision, nobody doubted that it was the correct thing to do.

Later that day a rescue team headed by two of Everest's most experienced guides, Pete Athans and Todd Burleson, who were on the mountain with their own clients, arrived at Camp Four. Burleson was standing outside the tents about 4:30 P.M. when he noticed someone lurching slowly toward camp. The person's bare right hand, naked to the wind and horribly frostbitten, was outstretched in a weird, frozen salute. Whoever it was reminded Athans of a mummy in a low-budget horror film. The mummy turned out to be none other than Beck Weathers, somehow risen from the dead.

A couple of hours earlier, a light must have gone on in the reptilian core of Weathers' comatose[29] brain, and he regained consciousness. **C** "Initially I thought I was in a dream," he recalls. "Then I saw how badly frozen my right hand was, and that helped bring me around to reality. Finally I woke up enough

---

27. **sahibs** (SAH IHBZ): term used by Sherpas to refer to the paying members of the expeditions.
28. **triage** (TREE AHZH): assigning of priorities of medical care based on chances for survival.
29. **comatose**: deeply unconscious due to injury or disease.

C QUICK CHECK

What had been the last we knew of Weathers?

to recognize that the cavalry[30] wasn't coming so I better do something about it myself."

Although Weathers was blind in his right eye and able to focus his left eye within a radius of only three or four feet, he started walking into the teeth of the wind, deducing correctly that camp lay in that direction. If he'd been wrong he would have stumbled immediately down the Kangshung Face, the edge of which was a few yards in the opposite direction. Ninety minutes later he encountered "some unnaturally smooth, bluish-looking rocks," which turned out to be the tents of Camp Four. **A**

The next morning, May 12, Athans, Burleson, and climbers from the IMAX team short-roped Weathers down to Camp Two. On the morning of May 13, in a hazardous helicopter rescue, Weathers and Gau[31] were evacuated from the top of the icefall

430

---

30. **cavalry:** soldiers on horseback or motorized transport; an allusion to the idea that troops were not coming to the rescue.
31. **Gau:** "Makalu" Gau Ming-Ho, leader of the Taiwanese National Expedition, another team climbing on Everest.

440   by Lieutenant Colonel Madan Khatri Chhetri of the Nepalese army. A month later, a team of Dallas surgeons would amputate Weathers' dead right hand just below the wrist and use skin grafts to reconstruct his left hand.

       After helping to load Weathers and Gau into the rescue chopper, I sat in the snow for a long while, staring at my boots, trying to get some grip, however tenuous, on what had happened over the preceding 72 hours. Then, nervous as a cat, I headed down into the icefall for one last trip through the maze of decaying seracs.[32]

450   I'd always known, in the abstract, that climbing mountains was a dangerous pursuit. But until I climbed in the Himalayas this spring, I'd never actually seen death at close range. And there was so much of it: Including three members of an Indo-Tibetan team who died on the north side just below the summit in the same May 10 storm and an Austrian killed some days later, 11 men and women lost their lives on Everest in May 1996, a tie with 1982 for the worst single-season death toll in the peak's history. . . .[33] **B**

       Climbing mountains will never be a safe, predictable, rule-
460 bound enterprise. It is an activity that idealizes risk-taking; its most celebrated figures have always been those who stuck their necks out the farthest and managed to get away with it. **C** Climbers, as a species, are simply not distinguished by an excess of common sense. And that holds especially true for Everest climbers: When presented with a chance to reach the planet's highest summit, people are surprisingly quick to abandon prudence altogether. "Eventually," warns Tom Hornbein, 33 years after his ascent of the West Ridge, "what happened on Everest this season is certain to happen again." **D**

---

32. seracs: pointed masses of ice.
33. It was actually the worst death toll on record. After Krakauer wrote this article, a twelfth death was discovered.

B **VOCABULARY**

Academic Vocabulary
The number of deaths in May 1996 was *equivalent*, or equal, to that of the number in 1982, according to Krakauer. What were some of the reasons this count was so high?

_____

_____

_____

C **LITERARY ANALYSIS**

What does Krakauer mean in this sentence?

_____

_____

_____

_____

D **LITERARY FOCUS**

Describe the **mood** of the final paragraph. What feeling are you left with at the end of the story?

_____

_____

_____

_____

_____

from Into Thin Air   **233**

from Into Thin Air

USE A CAUSE-AND-EFFECT CHART

DIRECTIONS: You can use a cause-and-effect chart to record events and the reasons for them. Fill in the boxes on the left with **causes** of important events from "Into Thin Air." Then, fill in each of the four boxes on the right with details of these events (**effects**).

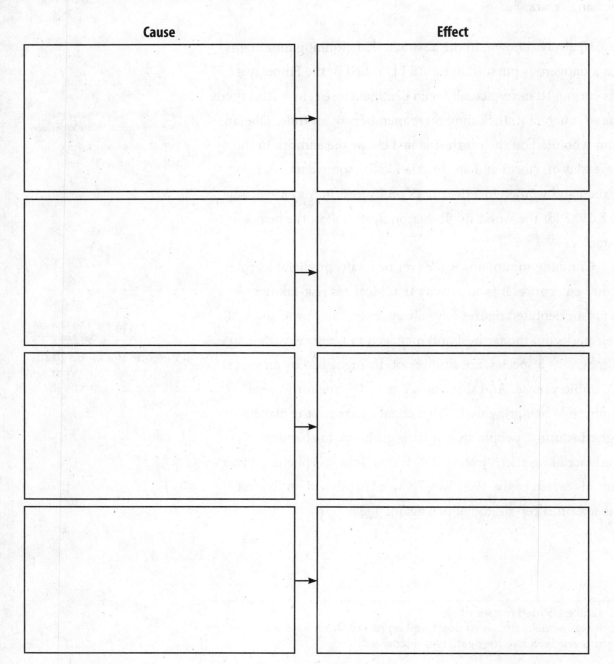

Cause

Effect

Applying Your Skills

from Into Thin Air

VOCABULARY DEVELOPMENT

DIRECTIONS: Complete the following sentences with the correct vocabulary words from the Word Box:

Word Box

deteriorate

benign

crucial

jeopardize

tenuous

1. It is _____ that you look carefully both ways before you cross the street so that you don't get hit by a car.

2. I was relieved when my doctor told me that a strange freckle I had was _____ and that I had nothing to worry about.

3. The building was already old and falling apart, but after an entire summer of rain, it really began to _____.

4. Mark feared he would fail his history test because his knowledge of the Civil War was _____ at best.

5. I would never _____ my friend's safety by allowing her to ride in my car without her seatbelt on.

LITERARY FOCUS: STYLE

DIRECTIONS: Mood is one important part of a writer's individual **style**. On a separate sheet of paper, write a paragraph describing how the mood of the selection from "Into Thin Air" changes throughout the story.

READING FOCUS: IDENTIFYING CAUSE AND EFFECT

DIRECTIONS: Complete the chart by filling in the missing **cause** or **effect** from "Into Thin Air."

Cause	Effect
1.	Krakauer was "drained, more exhausted than [he'd] ever been in his life."
Beck Weathers had a procedure done on his eyes, and there was a side effect when he was at a high altitude.	2.
3.	Krakauer had to interrupt his descent and step aside to allow others to pass; his tank was rapidly running out of oxygen.

SKILLS FOCUS

Literary Skills
Examine an author's writing style by studying sentence structure and mood.

Reading Skills
Identify cause-and-effect relationships.

from 102 Minutes

by Jim Dwyer and Kevin Flynn

and And of Clay Are We Created

by Isabel Allende, translated by Margaret Sayers Peden

LITERARY FOCUS: THEMES ACROSS GENRES

Some experiences are so common that writers throughout history have explored them in a variety of **genres**, or types of literature. Writers express their insights about these subjects in the form of **themes** (recurring ideas) in fiction and **main ideas** in nonfiction. Note how the writers of the following selections explore similar subjects and express similar ideas in two different genres.

READING FOCUS: ANALYZING AN AUTHOR'S PURPOSE

What writers say and how they say it depends on their **purpose**, or reason, for writing. The writer may want to persuade, entertain, or inform the reader. A writer's purpose also affects the genre in which they choose to write. For example, if a writer's purpose is to persuade the reader, he or she may choose to write a newspaper editorial.

Use the Skill   While you read "*from* 102 Minutes: The Untold Story of the Fight to Survive Inside the Twin Towers" and "And of Clay Are We Created," use a chart like the one below to keep track of details that tell about the author's purpose.

"*from* 102 Minutes"	"And of Clay Are We Created"
Detail: 3 of 5 officers killed **Purpose:** to show role of luck in Jimeno's rescue	

SKILLS FOCUS

Literary Skills
Understand themes across genres.

Reading Skills
Analyze an author's purpose.

Vocabulary Development

from 102 Minutes and And of Clay Are We Created

SELECTION VOCABULARY

extricate (EHKS TRUH KAYT) *v.:* set free; release.

Crews worked for hours to extricate the men buried under the rubble.

tenacity (TIH NAS UH TEE) *n.:* stubborn persistence and determination.

Rolf Carlé showed tenacity during the rescue attempt.

equanimity (EE KWUH NIHM UH TEE) *n.:* calmness; composure.

Trapped in the mud, Azucena displayed equanimity.

fortitude (FAWR TUH TOOD) *n.:* strength to endure pain or danger.

Both the girl and the man showed fortitude throughout the ordeal.

resignation (REHZ IHG NAY SHUHN) *n.:* passive acceptance; submission.

Determined to save Azucena, Rolf showed no signs of resignation.

WORD STUDY

DIRECTIONS: The sentences below use the selection vocabulary words incorrectly. Re-write the sentences so that the vocabulary words are used correctly.

1. When the prize fighter gave up, he showed great *fortitude*.

   _____

2. To climb to the top of a tall mountain, one needs no *tenacity* whatsoever.

   _____

3. I needed the butterflies for my collection, so I decided to *extricate* them.

   _____

4. Ritchie was in a nervous mood—all day he showed *equanimity*.

   _____

5. With a sigh of *resignation*, Candice accepted the job she had been wanting all her life.

   _____

from 102 MINUTES: THE UNTOLD STORY OF THE FIGHT TO SURVIVE INSIDE THE TWIN TOWERS

by Jim Dwyer and Kevin Flynn

BACKGROUND

On September 11, 2001, terrorists flew two airplanes into the Twin Towers of the World Trade Center in New York City. Both towers collapsed, killing or trapping many people. Reporters Jim Dwyer and Kevin Flynn interviewed survivors for their book. This selection tells what happened to two members of the Port Authority (a government commission that manages bridges, tunnels, airports, and other facilities of a port or city).

A **READING FOCUS**

Based on what you have read so far, try to identify one of the authors' **purposes** for writing the selection.

_____

_____

_____

_____

_____

_____

11:00 A.M. GROUND ZERO

Will Jimeno found himself buried but alive, pinned below the burning ground at the center of the trade center plaza. A load of concrete had fallen onto his lap, and a cinder-block wall rested on one of his feet. The oxygen tank strapped to his back also was wedged into rubble, fixing him in a semblance of a seated position, bent at a forty-five-degree angle. Of the four other Port Authority police officers who had been running with him through the concourse, pushing a cart full of rescue gear, only one, Sgt. John McLoughlin, was still alive. Two members of their
10 group had been killed immediately by the collapse of the south tower. A third officer, Dominick Pezzulo, had managed to free himself and was picking at the rubble around Jimeno when the collapse of the north tower killed him. **A**

From "Epilogue" from *102 Minutes: The Untold Story of the Fight to Survive inside the Twin Towers* by Jim Dwyer and Kevin Flynn. Copyright © 2005 by Jim Dwyer and Kevin Flynn. Reproduced by permission of **Henry Holt** and **Company, LLC.**

© Yoni Brook/Corbis

B LITERARY FOCUS

The **genre** of this selection is nonfiction, meaning that it is true, but it might seem to be a work of fiction at first glance. In what ways is this selection like a typical fiction story?

_____

_____

_____

_____

_____

_____

_____

C LITERARY FOCUS

Based on what you have read so far, what do you think might be the **main idea** of this story?

_____

_____

_____

_____

_____

_____

_____

_____

_____

_____

_____

Now Jimeno was slumped in the hole, talking occasionally with McLoughlin, who was even deeper in the heap than Jimeno. The two men had no view of each other.

"Can you see sky?" McLoughlin asked.

"No sky, but light," Jimeno replied.

The sergeant worked his radio. No one answered.

20 McLoughlin, who over the years had led elevator rescues at the trade center and rappelled[1] into the blind shafts, told Jimeno that the rescue operations would have to pull back for a day, until the scene was stable. They were on their own. **B** **C**

All across the northeastern United States, people were essentially on their own, stepping into the first minutes of a new

---

1. rappelled (RA PEHLD): descended a wall or shaft by using a rope to make a series of short drops.

A **LITERARY ANALYSIS**

What does this paragraph suggest about the causes of the events of September 11, 2001?

_____

_____

_____

_____

_____

_____

_____

_____

B **VOCABULARY**

Word Study

Look at the words *fundamentalism, globalism, capitalism,* and *modernism.* Generally, the suffix *–ism* is used to make a word into a noun. Here, it is used to create nouns that refer to a theory or school of thought. Write two more words that have the suffix *–ism*.

_____

_____

epoch[2] without the protections of an old world order whose institutions and functions seemed to have turned instantly decrepit.[3] So a consideration of the events of September 11, 2001, could begin at any one of numerous spots across the globe, at

30 almost any moment over the preceding four decades: the end of the Cold War;[4] the collapse of the Soviet Union;[5] any hour of any year in the unfinished history of the Middle East; in the often empty and petty exercise of authority in the capital of the world's only superpower; at the boiling, nihilistic[6] springs of religious fundamentalism[7] that not only have endured but have thrived as forces in opposition to globalism, capitalism, modernism. **A B**

Those historic currents, and others, merged and crashed on the morning of September 11 at the two towers of the World Trade Center, and at the Pentagon, and in a field in Pennsylvania.

40 The particulars of the era that had just passed—the expectations of protection, the habits of defense, the sense of safety—seemed to have fossilized[8] from one breath to the next. What happened in New York City that morning was replicated through all the arms of government, differing only in details, duration, and cost.

An hour or so after the collapse, Will Jimeno, buried beneath the plaza, heard a voice coming through the same hole where the light was entering. The voice wanted to know if a particular person was down in the hole. Jimeno could not quite make out the name, but he was delighted by the sound of another

50 human voice.

---

2. **epoch** (EHP UHK): particular period of time or of history.
3. **decrepit** (DIH KREHP IHT): broken down; weakened.
4. **Cold War:** state of hostility and rivalry between the United States and the Soviet Union, as well as their allies, which began after World War II and ended by 1991.
5. **collapse of the Soviet Union:** The Soviet Union, established in 1922, was dissolved in 1991 after the republics that made up the union achieved independence.
6. **nihilistic** (NY UH LIHS TIHK): characterized by a destructive, violent rejection of established beliefs, such as those of religion and morality.
7. **religious fundamentalism:** religious movement or viewpoint that promotes a return to basic religious principles and the strict following of these principles.
8. **fossilized** (FAHS UH LYZD): become out-of-date.

"No, but Jimeno and McLoughlin, PAPD are down here," he yelled.

The voice did not answer, but moved off, and they heard no more from him.

Balls of fire tumbled into their tidy space, a gust of wind or a draft steering them away, the fire spending itself before it could find another morsel of fuel. **C** Jimeno, thirty-three years old, felt that death was near. His wife, Allison, and their four-year-old daughter, Bianca, would be sad, but proud, he thought. The Jimenos' second child was due at the end of November. So he prayed.

Please, God, let me see my little unborn child.

Jimeno tried to make a bargain. He might die, but surely there was a way he could do something for this child.

Somehow in the future, he prayed, let me touch this baby. Then shots rang out.

The fireballs had apparently heated up the gun of the late Dominick Pezzulo. The rounds pinged off pipes and concrete, erratic and unpredictable, until the last of the ammunition was gone. **D**

With his one free arm, Jimeno reached his gun belt for something to dig with. He had graduated from the Port Authority Police Academy in January and was issued the standard police tools, but he already owned his own handcuffs—a pair made by Smith & Wesson, bought when he was a security guard in a store, arresting shoplifters. He scraped at the rubble with them, but the cuffs slipped out of his hands, and he could not find them again.

No one had heard from Chuck Sereika, and by midmorning, the messages had piled up on his telephone answering machine and in his e-mail. Can't believe it. Hope you're okay. Our hearts are with you.

Sereika woke up. He had slept through everything, not a whisper of trouble in his apartment in midtown Manhattan. The e-mails told him something awful had happened, then news on his computer spelled it out, and as he blinked into the new world,

60

70

80

Spending is a word with **multiple meanings**. Usually it refers to using money to buy things. What do you think it means in this sentence? Write down your guess and use a dictionary to check your answer.

_____

_____

_____

_____

D **QUICK CHECK**

Why does a gun go off?

_____

_____

_____

_____

_____

_____

_____

_____

_____

_____

_____

_____

_____

B **VOCABULARY**

Academic Vocabulary

What happened to Sereika *subsequent* to, or following, the loss of his paramedic license?

_____

_____

_____

_____

_____

© John Labriola/AP Photo

he heard the messages on his answering machine. His sister had called.

"I love you," she said. "I know you're down there helping."

Actually, he had been moping. In his closet, he found a

90 paramedic[9] sweatshirt and a badge he had not used for years. He had lost his paramedic license, let it lapse after he squandered too many days and nights carousing. **A** He had gone into rehab programs, slipped, then climbed back on the wagon. He had fought his way back to sobriety, but the paramedic work was behind him. **B** He still had the sweatshirt, though, and no one had taken the badge away. Maybe he could do some splints and bandages. He walked outside. Midtown Manhattan was teeming with people, a stream of humanity trooping in the middle of avenues, the subways shut down and scarcely a bus to be seen.

100 The only way to move was on foot, and by the tens of thousands, people were walking north, or over to the river for ferries, or into Penn Station for a commuter train that would take them east to Long Island or west to New Jersey.

9.   **paramedic (PAR** UH **MEHD** IHK**):** of or relating to a person trained to provide emergency medical care.

Sereika walked a few blocks from his apartment to St. Luke's-Roosevelt Hospital Center. Then he hitched rides on ambulances going downtown. **C**

Seven World Trade Center—a forty-seven-story building—collapsed at 5:20 that afternoon. The firefighters had decided to let the fire there burn itself out. There was no one inside.
110 Against all that had happened, the loss of even such an enormous building seemed like a footnote.

David Karnes had arrived downtown not long after its collapse, and as far as he could see, the searches were confined entirely to the periphery of the complex, picking through the rubble at the edges for signs of life. **D** Other structures were now burning—the low-rise building at 4 World Trade Center was shooting flames—and all hands were staying clear of the ruins of the two towers and the plaza between them.

Karnes had started the morning in a business suit, working
120 as an accountant for Deloitte and Touche in Wilton, Connecticut. After the attacks, he drove from Connecticut to Long Island and went to a storage facility where he kept his Marine kit. His utility trousers and jacket were freshly pressed, though his commitment had ended months earlier. Trim as a whip, he slipped into them, drove to a barber, and ordered a high and tight haircut. He stopped at his church and asked for prayers with the pastor, then with the top down on his new convertible, drove straight for lower Manhattan.

He found the rescue workers in shock, depressed, doing
130 little by way of organized searches. Karnes spotted another Marine, a man named Sergeant Thomas, no first name.

"Come on, Sergeant," Karnes said. "Let's take a walk."

Not another soul was around them. They swept across the broken ground, yelling, "United States Marines. If you can hear us, yell or tap."

No one answered. They moved forward, deeper into the rubble. The fires roared at 4 World Trade Center. They plowed across the jagged, fierce ground. **E**

C LITERARY FOCUS

In what ways is Sereika's story and behavior consistent with the **main idea** of being "on one's own"?

_____
_____
_____
_____

D VOCABULARY

Word Study

Periphery comes from the Greek word *periphéreia,* meaning "outer surface." Knowing this, write a definition for *periphery.*

_____
_____
_____
_____

E READING FOCUS

Has your guess about the authors' **purpose** for writing this selection changed? Why or why not?

_____
_____
_____
_____
_____
_____

140 Lost in thought, waiting for release, Will Jimeno listened to the trade center complex ripping itself apart. He had gotten tired of shouting at phantoms. He asked McLoughlin to put out a radio message that Officer Jimeno wanted his newborn baby to be named Olivia. **A** The sergeant was in excruciating pain, his legs crushed. There was nothing to do, Jimeno thought, except wait until they sent out rescue parties in the morning. If they lived that long.

Then came the voice.

"United States Marines. If you can hear us, yell or tap."

What? That was a person.

150 Jimeno shouted with every bit of strength he had.

"Right here! Jimeno and McLoughlin, PAPD! Here!"

"Keep yelling," Karnes said.

It took a few minutes, but Karnes found the hole.

"Don't leave," Jimeno pleaded.

"I'm not going anywhere," Karnes said.

Karnes pulled out his cell phone and dialed 911, but the call did not go through. He tried again, without success. How could he get help, without leaving Jimeno and McLoughlin? Maybe the problem was with phone lines downtown, and he could find

160 an electronic bridge via someone outside the city. He dialed his sister in a suburb of Pittsburgh and got through. She called the local police. They were able to reach the New York police. The message had traveled 300 miles from the pile to Pennsylvania, then 300 miles back to police headquarters, but the NYPD finally learned that a few blocks away, two cops were buried in the middle of the pile, and a United States Marine was standing by to direct the rescuers. **B**

Chuck Sereika had been wandering the edge of that pile as evening approached, when he heard people yelling that

170 someone had been found in the center of the place. Sereika set out, walking part of the way with a firefighter. They could see the flames roaring from the remains of 4 World Trade Center, an eight-story building. The fire-fighter peeled away. By himself, Sereika stumbled and climbed, until he found Dave Karnes

standing alone. **C** From the surface, he could see nothing of Will Jimeno, but he could hear him. Sereika squeezed his way into a crevice, inching his way down the rubble, finally spotting Jimeno's hand.

"Hey," Sereika said.

180 "Don't leave me," Jimeno said.

Sereika felt for a pulse. A good, strong distal pulse,[10] a basic in emergency care.

"Don't leave me," Jimeno said.

"We're not going to leave you," Sereika said. He pawed at the rubble and found Jimeno's gun, which he passed up to Karnes. Then he sent word for oxygen and an intravenous setup.[11] Two emergency service police officers, Scott Strauss and Paddy McGee, soon arrived, and Sereika handed rocks and rubble back to them. A fire-man, Tom Ascher, arrived with a hose to fight off

190 the flames. They could hear McLoughlin calling out for help.

We will get there, they promised.

The basics of trauma care are simple: provide fluids and oxygen. Simple—except that in the hole at the trade center, they could not take the next step in the classic formula: "load and go." First they had to extricate Jimeno, a highly delicate proposition. **D**

Sereika could hear 4 World Trade Center groaning to its bones. To shift large pieces off Jimeno risked starting a new slide. There was room in the hole only for one person at a time, and Sereika was basically on top of him. It was not unlike working

200 under the dash-board of a car, except the engine was on fire and the car was speeding and about to crash. The space was filled with smoke. Strauss and McGee were carefully moving the rubble, engineering on the fly, so that they could shift loads without bringing more debris down on themselves or on Jimeno and McLoughlin. Tools were passed from the street along a line of helpers. A handheld air chisel. Shears. When the

---

10. **distal pulse:** *Distal* means "away from the center of the body." Here, *distal pulse* refers to the pulse in the wrist.
11. **intravenous setup:** equipment used to administer medicine or other substances directly into a vein.

C **LITERARY FOCUS**

How is the **main idea** of the selection reinforced by this part of the story?

_____

_____

_____

_____

_____

_____

D **VOCABULARY**

Selection Vocabulary

Extricate means "set free; release." Why do you think that extricating Jimeno was "a highly delicate proposition"?

_____

_____

_____

_____

_____

_____

Hurst jaws of life[12] tool arrived, the officers wanted to use it to lift one particularly heavy section, but they could not quite get solid footing on the rubble. Sereika, the lapsed paramedic, 210 immediately sized up the problem and shimmed rubble into place for the machine to rest on. **A**

The work inched forward, treacherous and hot and slow.

After four hours, at 11 P.M., Will Jimeno was freed. They loaded him into a basket, slid him up the path to the surface. That left only John McLoughlin, deeper still, but none of the group in and around the hole could go on. They called down a fresh team that would work until the morning before they finally pulled him out, not long before the last survivor from stairway B, Genelle Guzman, would also be reached.

220 Aboveground, the men who had gone into the hole with Will Jimeno found they could barely walk. Smoke reeked from the hair on their heads, soot packed every pore on their skin. Sereika stumbled up from the crevice in time to see Jimeno in his basket being passed along police officers and firefighters who had set up a line, scores of people deep, across the jagged, broken ground.

---

12. **Hurst jaws of life:** tool used to remove victims from collapsed concrete and steel structures.

He could not keep up with his patient. He could just about get himself to the sidewalk. He had worked for hours alongside the other men, first names only, and Sereika was employed by

230   no official agency, no government body. Once they left the hole, the men lost track of each other. Just as people had come to work by themselves hours earlier, at the start of the day—an entire age ago—now Chuck Sereika was starting for home on his own. His old paramedic shirt torn, he plodded north in the late-summer night, alone, scuffling down streets blanketed by the dust that had been the World Trade Center. **B** **C**

B **READING FOCUS**

Now that you have read the entire selection, what do you think is the authors' **purpose** for writing the selection? Why?

_____

_____

_____

_____

_____

_____

_____

_____

_____

C **LITERARY FOCUS**

What is the **main idea** of the entire selection? How is the main idea used in the conclusion of the story?

_____

_____

_____

_____

_____

_____

_____

_____

AND OF CLAY ARE WE CREATED

by Isabel Allende, translated by Margaret Sayers Peden

BACKGROUND

This selection by is fictional, but it is based on a real event. In 1985, a volcano erupted in Colombia. The heat of the volcano melted sheets of ice, resulting in mudslides. More than 23,000 people were killed. The media focused much attention on a thirteen-year-old girl trapped in the mud. In this story, the girl is called Azucena, and her rescuer is named Rolf Carlé.

A **READING FOCUS**

Based on what you have read so far, what do you think is the author's **purpose** for writing this story?

_____

_____

_____

_____

_____

_____

_____

"And of Clay Are We Created" from *The Stories of Eva Luna* by Isabel Allende, translated by Margaret Sayers Peden. Copyright © 1989 by Isabel Allende; English translation copyright © 1991 by Macmillan Publishing Company. Reproduced by permission of **Scribner, an imprint of Simon & Schuster Adult Publishing Group** and electronic format by permission of **Agencia Literaria Carmen Balcells, S.A. [NO WEB]**

They discovered the girl's head protruding from the mudpit, eyes wide open, calling soundlessly. She had a First Communion name, Azucena.[1] Lily. In that vast cemetery where the odor of death was already attracting vultures from far away, and where the weeping of orphans and wails of the injured filled the air, the little girl obstinately clinging to life became the symbol of the tragedy. The television cameras transmitted so often the unbearable image of the head budding like a black squash from the clay that there was no one who did not recognize her and

10 know her name. And every time we saw her on the screen, right behind her was Rolf Carlé,[2] who had gone there on assignment, never suspecting that he would find a fragment of his past, lost thirty years before. **A**

First a subterranean[3] sob rocked the cotton fields, curling them like waves of foam. Geologists had set up their seismographs[4] weeks before and knew that the mountain had awakened again. For some time they had predicted that the heat

---

1. **Azucena** (AH SOO SAY NUH): Spanish for "lily."
2. **Rolf Carlé** (ROHLF KAHR LAY).
3. **subterranean** (suhb tuh RAY nee uhn): underground.
4. **seismographs** (SYZ MUH GRAFS): instruments that measure and record earthquakes and other tremors.

© Corbis

of the eruption could detach the eternal ice from the slopes of the volcano, but no one heeded their warnings; they sounded like the tales of frightened old women. The towns in the valley went about their daily life, deaf to the moaning of the earth, until that fateful Wednesday night in November when a prolonged roar announced the end of the world, and walls of snow broke loose, rolling in an avalanche of clay, stones, and water that descended on the villages and buried them beneath unfathomable meters of telluric[5] vomit. **B** As soon as the survivors emerged from the paralysis of that first awful terror, they could see that houses, plazas, churches, white cotton plantations, dark coffee forests, cattle pastures—all had disappeared. Much later, after soldiers and volunteers had arrived to rescue the living and try to assess the magnitude of the cataclysm,[6] it was calculated that beneath the mud lay more than twenty thousand human beings and an indefinite number of animals putrefying in a viscous soup.[7] Forests and rivers had also been swept away, and there was nothing to be seen but an immense desert of mire.[8]

When the station called before dawn, Rolf Carlé and I were together. I crawled out of bed, dazed with sleep, and went to prepare coffee while he hurriedly dressed. He stuffed his gear in the green canvas backpack he always carried, and we said goodbye, as we had so many times before. I had no presentiments. I sat in the kitchen, sipping my coffee and

5. **telluric** (TEH LUR IHK): of or from the earth.
6. **cataclysm** (KAT UH KLIHZ UHM): disaster; great upheaval causing sudden, violent changes.
7. **putrefying in a viscous soup**: rotting in a thick mixture.
8. **mire** (MYR): deep mud.

B LITERARY ANALYSIS

Why do you think the people of the town ignored the warnings?

_____

_____

_____

_____

_____

_____

_____

_____

A LITERARY FOCUS

At this point, can you guess what the **theme** of this story might be? Explain your answer.

_____

_____

_____

_____

_____

B VOCABULARY

Selection Vocabulary

Use context clues to write a meaning for *equanimity*. Underline clues in the text that helped you find the meaning.

_____

_____

_____

C LITERARY ANALYSIS

Why do you think Rolf would need protection "from his own emotions"?

_____

_____

_____

_____

_____

_____

planning the long hours without him, sure that he would be back the next day. **A**

He was one of the first to reach the scene, because while other reporters were fighting their way to the edges of that morass[9] in jeeps, bicycles, or on foot, each getting there however he could, Rolf Carlé had the advantage of the television heli-copter, which flew him over the avalanche. We watched on our screens the footage captured by his assistant's camera, in which he was up to his knees in muck, a microphone in his hand, in the midst of a bedlam[10] of lost children, wounded survivors, corpses, and devastation. The story came to us in his calm voice. For years he had been a familiar figure in newscasts, reporting live at the scene of battles and catastrophes with awesome tenacity. Nothing could stop him, and I was always amazed at his equanimity in the face of danger and suffering; it seemed as if nothing could shake his fortitude or deter his curiosity. **B** Fear seemed never to touch him, although he had confessed to me that he was not a courageous man, far from it. I believe that the lens of the camera had a strange effect on him; it was as if it transported him to a different time from which he could watch events without actually participating in them. When I knew him better, I came to real-ize that this fictive distance seemed to protect him from his own emotions. **C**

Rolf Carlé was in on the story of Azucena from the begin-ning. He filmed the volunteers who discovered her, and the first persons who tried to reach her; his camera zoomed in on the girl, her dark face, her large desolate eyes, the plastered-down tangle of her hair. The mud was like quicksand around her, and anyone attempting to reach her was in danger of sinking. They threw a rope to her that she made no effort to grasp until they shouted to her to catch it; then she pulled a hand from the mire and tried to move, but immediately sank a little deeper. Rolf threw down his knapsack and the rest of his equipment and waded into the

---

9. **morass** (MUH RAS): bog; swamp.
10. **bedlam** (BEHD LUHM): place or situation filled with noise and confusion (from the name of an old insane asylum in London).

quagmire, commenting for his assistant's microphone that it was cold and that one could begin to smell the stench of corpses.

"What's your name?" he asked the girl, and she told him her flower name. "Don't move, Azucena," Rolf Carlé directed, and kept talking to her, without a thought for what he was saying, just to distract her, while slowly he worked his way forward in mud up to his waist. **D** The air around him seemed as murky as the mud.

It was impossible to reach her from the approach he was attempting, so he retreated and circled around where there seemed to be firmer footing. When finally he was close enough, he took the rope and tied it beneath her arms, so they could pull her out. He smiled at her with that smile that crinkles his eyes and makes him look like a little boy; he told her that everything was fine, that he was here with her now, that soon they would have her out. He signaled the others to pull, but as soon as the cord tensed, the girl screamed. They tried again, and her shoulders and arms appeared, but they could move her no farther; she was trapped. Someone suggested that her legs might be caught in the collapsed walls of her house, but she said it was not just rubble, that she was also held by the bodies of her brothers and sisters clinging to her legs.

"Don't worry, we'll get you out of here," Rolf promised. Despite the quality of the transmission, I could hear his voice break, and I loved him more than ever. Azucena looked at him, but said nothing.

During those first hours Rolf Carlé exhausted all the resources of his ingenuity to rescue her. He struggled with poles and ropes, but every tug was an intolerable torture for the imprisoned girl. It occurred to him to use one of the poles as a lever but got no result and had to abandon the idea. He talked a couple of soldiers into working with him for a while, but they had to leave because so many other victims were calling for help. The girl could not move, she barely could breathe, but she did not seem desperate, as if an ancestral resignation allowed her to accept her fate. **E** The reporter, on the other hand, was

D LITERARY ANALYSIS

Why do you think Rolf was trying to distract Azucena?

_____

_____

_____

_____

_____

E READING FOCUS

So far, what details might lead you to think that one of the author's **purposes** for writing is to have the reader feel sympathy for Azucena's predicament?

_____

_____

_____

_____

_____

_____

_____

_____

_____

A QUICK CHECK

What are some ways Rolf tries to rescue Azucena?

_____

_____

_____

_____

_____

_____

B LITERARY ANALYSIS

What do you think it means that "time had stagnated and reality had been irreparably distorted"?

_____

_____

_____

_____

_____

_____

_____

_____

_____

_____

_____

determined to snatch her from death. Someone brought him a tire, which he placed beneath her arms like a life buoy, and then laid a plank near the hole to hold his weight and allow him to stay closer to her. As it was impossible to remove the rubble blindly, he tried once or twice to dive toward her feet, but emerged frustrated, covered with mud, and spitting gravel. He concluded that he would have to have a pump to drain the water, and radioed a request for one, but received in return a message that there was no available transport and it could not be sent

120   until the next morning. **A**

"We can't wait that long!" Rolf Carlé shouted, but in the pandemonium[11] no one stopped to commiserate. Many more hours would go by before he accepted that time had stagnated and reality had been irreparably distorted. **B**

A military doctor came to examine the girl, and observed that her heart was functioning well and that if she did not get too cold she could survive the night.

"Hang on, Azucena, we'll have the pump tomorrow," Rolf Carlé tried to console her.

130   "Don't leave me alone," she begged.

"No, of course I won't leave you."

Someone brought him coffee, and he helped the girl drink it, sip by sip. The warm liquid revived her and she began telling him about her small life, about her family and her school, about how things were in that little bit of world before the volcano had erupted. She was thirteen, and she had never been outside her village. Rolf Carlé, buoyed by a premature optimism, was convinced that everything would end well: the pump would arrive, they would drain the water, move the rubble, and Azucena

140   would be transported by helicopter to a hospital where she would recover rapidly and where he could visit her and bring her gifts. He thought, She's already too old for dolls, and I don't know what would please her; maybe a dress. I don't know much about women, he concluded, amused, reflecting that although he had known many women in his lifetime, none had taught him these

---

11. **pandemonium** (PAN DUH MOH NEE UHM): wild disorder; great confusion.

details. To pass the hours he began to tell Azucena about his travels and adventures as a newshound, and when he exhausted his memory, he called upon imagination, inventing things he thought might entertain her. From time to time she dozed, but he

150   kept talking in the darkness, to assure her that he was still there and to overcome the menace of uncertainty. **C**

     That was a long night.

Many miles away, I watched Rolf Carlé and the girl on a television screen. I could not bear the wait at home, so I went to National Television, where I often spent entire nights with Rolf editing programs. **D** There, I was near his world, and I could at least get a feeling of what he lived through during those three decisive days. I called all the important people in the city, senators, commanders of the armed forces, the North American

160   ambassador, and the president of National Petroleum, begging them for a pump to remove the silt, but obtained only vague promises. I began to ask for urgent help on radio and television, to see if there wasn't someone who could help us. Between calls I would run to the newsroom to monitor the satellite transmissions that periodically brought new details of the catastrophe. While reporters selected scenes with most impact for the news report, I searched for footage that featured Azucena's mudpit. The screen reduced the disaster to a single plane and accentuated the tremendous distance that separated me from Rolf Carlé;

170   nonetheless, I was there with him. **E** The child's every suffering hurt me as it did him; I felt his frustration, his impotence. Faced with the impossibility of communicating with him, the fantastic idea came to me that if I tried, I could reach him by force of mind and in that way give him encouragement. I concentrated until I was dizzy—a frenzied and futile activity. At times I would be overcome with compassion and burst out crying; at other times, I was so drained I felt as if I were staring through a telescope at the light of a star dead for a million years.

     I watched that hell on the first morning broadcast,

180   cadavers of people and animals awash in the current of new

C QUICK CHECK

What does Rolf realize about himself as a result of talking to Azucena?

_____
_____
_____
_____
_____

D LANGUAGE COACH

The word *bear* has **multiple meanings**. When the word is a noun, it refers to a large animal, but in this sentence, *bear* is a verb. What do you think the word means here?

_____
_____
_____

E READING FOCUS

What **purpose** might the author have for writing this paragraph?

_____
_____
_____
_____
_____
_____

B VOCABULARY

Word Study

The root of *embodying* is *embody*, which means "express, personify, or give concrete form to." What does it mean that Azucena had been given the responsibility of embodying the horror of what had happened?

_____

_____

_____

_____

_____

_____

_____

_____

rivers formed overnight from the melted snow. Above the mud rose the tops of trees and the bell towers of a church where several people had taken refuge and were patiently awaiting rescue teams. Hundreds of soldiers and volunteers from the Civil Defense were clawing through rubble searching for survivors, while long rows of ragged specters awaited their turn for a cup of hot broth. Radio networks announced that their phones were jammed with calls from families offering shelter to orphaned children. Drinking water was in scarce

190   supply, along with gasoline and food. Doctors, resigned to amputating arms and legs without anesthesia, pled that at least they be sent serum and painkillers and antibiotics; most of the roads, however, were impassable, and worse were the bureaucratic obstacles that stood in the way. To top it all, the clay contaminated by decomposing bodies threatened the living with an outbreak of epidemics. **A**

     Azucena was shivering inside the tire that held her above the surface. Immobility and tension had greatly weakened her, but she was conscious and could still be heard

200   when a microphone was held out to her. Her tone was humble, as if apologizing for all the fuss. Rolf Carlé had a growth of beard, and dark circles beneath his eyes; he looked near exhaustion. Even from that enormous distance I could sense the quality of his weariness, so different from the fatigue of other adventures. He had completely forgotten the camera; he could not look at the girl through a lens any longer. The pictures we were receiving were not his assistant's but those of other reporters who had appropriated Azucena, bestowing on her the pathetic responsibility of embodying the horror of

210   what had happened in that place. **B** With the first light Rolf tried again to dislodge the obstacles that held the girl in her tomb, but he had only his hands to work with; he did not dare use a tool for fear of injuring her. He fed Azucena a cup of the cornmeal mush and bananas the Army was distributing, but she immediately vomited it up. A doctor stated that she had a fever, but added that there was little he could do: Antibiotics

were being reserved for cases of gangrene.[12] A priest also passed by and blessed her, hanging a medal of the Virgin around her neck. By evening a gentle, persistent drizzle began

220 to fall.

"The sky is weeping," Azucena murmured, and she, too, began to cry.

"Don't be afraid," Rolf begged. "You have to keep your strength up and be calm. Everything will be fine. I'm with you, and I'll get you out somehow."

Reporters returned to photograph Azucena and ask her the same questions, which she no longer tried to answer. In the meanwhile, more television and movie teams arrived with spools of cable, tapes, film, videos, precision lenses, recorders,

230 sound consoles, lights, reflecting screens, auxiliary motors, cartons of supplies, electricians, sound technicians, and cameramen: Azucena's face was beamed to millions of screens around the world. And all the while Rolf Carlé kept pleading for a pump. The improved technical facilities bore results, and National Television began receiving sharper pictures and clearer sound; the distance seemed suddenly compressed, and I had the horrible sensation that Azucena and Rolf were by my side, separated from me by impenetrable glass. I was able to follow events hour by hour; I knew everything my love did to wrest

240 the girl from her prison and help her endure her suffering; I overheard fragments of what they said to one another and could guess the rest; I was present when she taught Rolf to pray, and when he distracted her with the stories I had told him in a thousand and one nights beneath the white mosquito netting of our bed. **C**

When darkness came on the second day, Rolf tried to sing Azucena to sleep with old Austrian folk songs he had learned from his mother, but she was far beyond sleep. They spent most of the night talking, each in a stupor of exhaustion and hunger,

250 and shaking with cold. That night, imperceptibly, the unyielding

---

12. **gangrene** (GANG GREEN): death or decay of flesh, usually caused by disease.

Academic Vocabulary
What different *techniques*, or methods, has Rolf used to keep Azucena distracted and calm?

_____

_____

_____

_____

_____

_____

A **LITERARY ANALYSIS**

Why does the narrator think that Rolf is finally able to talk about his past traumas?

_____

_____

_____

_____

_____

_____

_____

_____

_____

B **LITERARY FOCUS**

What **theme** do you think the writer is touching on with the phrase "to flee from himself"? Think about what Rolf is going through as a universal experience that many people go through during their lives.

_____

_____

_____

_____

_____

_____

_____

_____

floodgates that had contained Rolf Carlé's past for so many years began to open, and the torrent of all that had lain hidden in the deepest and most secret layers of memory poured out, leveling before it the obstacles that had blocked his consciousness for so long. He could not tell it all to Azucena; she perhaps did not know there was a world beyond the sea or time previous to her own; she was not capable of imagining Europe in the years of the war. So he could not tell her of defeat, nor of the afternoon the Russians had led them to the concentration camp to bury prisoners dead

260 from starvation. Why should he describe to her how the naked bodies piled like a mountain of firewood resembled fragile china? How could he tell this dying child about ovens and gallows? Nor did he mention the night that he had seen his mother naked, shod in stiletto-heeled red boots, sobbing with humiliation. There was much he did not tell, but in those hours he relived for the first time all the things his mind had tried to erase. Azucena had surrendered her fear to him and so, without wishing it, had obliged Rolf to confront his own. **A** There, beside that hellhole of mud, it was impossible for Rolf to flee from himself any longer,

270 and the visceral[13] terror he had lived as a boy suddenly invaded him. **B** He reverted to the years when he was the age of Azucena, and younger, and, like her, found himself trapped in a pit without escape, buried in life, his head barely above ground; he saw before his eyes the boots and legs of his father, who had removed his belt and was whipping it in the air with the never-forgotten hiss of a viper coiled to strike. Sorrow flooded through him, intact and precise, as if it had lain always in his mind, waiting. He was once again in the armoire[14] where his father locked him to punish him for imagined misbehavior, there where for eternal hours he had

280 crouched with his eyes closed, not to see the darkness, with his hands over his ears, to shut out the beating of his heart, trembling, huddled like a cornered animal. Wandering in the mist of his memories he found his sister Katharina, a sweet, retarded child who spent her life hiding, with the hope that her father would

---

13. **visceral** (VIHS UHR UHL): intuitive, emotional; not intellectual.
14. **armoire** (AHR MWAHR): large cupboard for holding clothes.

forget the disgrace of her having been born. With Katharina, Rolf crawled beneath the dining room table, and with her hid there under the long white tablecloth, two children forever embraced, alert to footsteps and voices. Katharina's scent melded with his own sweat, with aromas of cooking, garlic, soup, freshly baked bread, and the unexpected odor of putrescent[15] clay. **C** His sister's hand in his, her frightened breathing, her silk hair against his cheek, the candid gaze of her eyes. Katharina . . . Katharina materialized before him, floating on the air like a flag, clothed in the white tablecloth, now a winding sheet, and at last he could weep for her death and for the guilt of having abandoned her. He understood then that all his exploits as a reporter, the feats that had won him such recognition and fame, were merely an attempt to keep his most ancient fears at bay, a stratagem[16] for taking refuge behind a lens to test whether reality was more tolerable from that perspective. **D** He took excessive risks as an exercise of courage, training by day to conquer the monsters that tormented him by night. But he had come face to face with the moment of truth; he could not continue to escape his past. He was Azucena; he was buried in the clayey mud; his terror was not the distant emotion of an almost forgotten childhood, it was a claw sunk in his throat. In the flush of his tears he saw his mother, dressed in black and clutching her imitation-crocodile pocketbook to her bosom, just as he had last seen her on the dock when she had come to put him on the boat to South America. She had not come to dry his tears, but to tell him to pick up a shovel: the war was over and now they must bury the dead.

"Don't cry. I don't hurt anymore. I'm fine," Azucena said when dawn came.

"I'm not crying for you," Rolf Carlé smiled. "I'm crying for myself. I hurt all over."

The third day in the valley of the cataclysm began with a pale light filtering through storm clouds. The President of the Republic visited the area in his tailored safari jacket to confirm

---

15. **putrescent** (PYOO TREHS UHNT): rotting.
16. **stratagem** (STRAT UH JUHM): plan or scheme for achieving some goal.

C VOCABULARY

Word Study

Aromas comes from the Latin word *aroma,* meaning "sweet odor." How do the descriptions in this sentence illustrate what Rolf is thinking?

_____

_____

_____

_____

_____

D LITERARY ANALYSIS

Summarize what Rolf has come to understand about himself in this section.

_____

_____

_____

_____

_____

_____

_____

_____

_____

_____

A QUICK CHECK

What does the president do in response to the disaster?

_____

_____

_____

_____

_____

_____

B LITERARY ANALYSIS

How do you think the narrator, from just watching the television screen, was able to tell that Rolf's "defenses had crumbled" and to tell "the precise moment at which Rolf gave up the fight"?

_____

_____

_____

_____

_____

_____

_____

_____

_____

_____

that this was the worst catastrophe
320 of the century; the country was in mourning; sister nations had offered aid; he had ordered a state of siege; the Armed Forces would be merciless, anyone caught stealing or committing other offenses would be shot on sight. He added that it was impossible to remove all the corpses or count the thousands who had disappeared; the entire valley would be declared holy ground,
330 and bishops would come to celebrate a solemn mass for the souls of the victims. He went to the Army field tents to offer relief in the form of vague promises to crowds of the rescued, then to the improvised hospital to offer a word of encouragement to doctors and nurses worn down from so many hours of tribulations.[17] **A** Then he asked to be taken to see Azucena, the little girl the whole world had seen. He waved to her with a limp statesman's hand, and microphones recorded his emotional voice and paternal tone as he told her that her courage had served as an example to the nation. Rolf Carlé interrupted to ask for a pump,
340 and the President assured him that he personally would attend to the matter. I caught a glimpse of Rolf for a few seconds kneeling beside the mudpit. On the evening news broadcast, he was still in the same position; and I, glued to the screen like a fortuneteller to her crystal ball, could tell that something fundamental had changed in him. I knew somehow that during the night his defenses had crumbled and he had given in to grief; finally he was vulnerable. The girl had touched a part of him that he himself had no access to, a part he had never shared with me. Rolf had wanted to console her, but it was Azucena who had
350 given him consolation.

I recognized the precise moment at which Rolf gave up the fight and surrendered to the torture of watching the girl die. **B** I was with them, three days and two nights, spying on them from

---

17. **tribulations** (TRIHB YUH LAY SHUHNZ): miseries; sufferings.

the other side of life. I was there when she told him that in all her thirteen years no boy had ever loved her and that it was a pity to leave this world without knowing love. Rolf assured her that he loved her more than he could ever love anyone, more than he loved his mother, more than his sister, more than all the women who had slept in his arms, more than he loved me, his life companion, who would have given anything to be trapped in that well in her place, who would have exchanged her life for Azucena's, and I watched as he leaned down to kiss her poor forehead, consumed by a sweet, sad emotion he could not name. I felt how in that instant both were saved from despair, how they were freed from the clay, how they rose above the vultures and helicopters, how together they flew above the vast swamp of corruption and laments. How, finally, they were able to accept death. Rolf Carlé prayed in silence that she would die quickly, because such pain cannot be borne.

370   By then I had obtained a pump and was in touch with a general who had agreed to ship it the next morning on a military cargo plane. But on the night of that third day, beneath the unblinking focus of quartz lamps and the lens of a hundred cameras, Azucena gave up, her eyes locked with those of the friend who had sustained her to the end. Rolf Carlé removed the life buoy, closed her eyelids, held her to his chest for a few moments, and then let her go. She sank slowly, a flower in the mud.

You are back with me, but you are not the same man. I often accompany you to the station and we watch the videos of Azucena again; you study them intently, looking for something you could have done to save her, something you did not think of in time. Or maybe you study them to see yourself as if in a mirror, naked. Your cameras lie forgotten in a closet; you do not write or sing; you sit long hours before the window, staring at the mountains. Beside you, I wait for you to complete the voyage into yourself, for the old wounds to heal. I know that when you return from your nightmares, we shall again walk hand in hand, as before. **C D E**

360

380

How did Azucena's death change Rolf?

_____

_____

_____

_____

D **LITERARY FOCUS**

What do you think is the **theme** of the entire selection? How does it compare to the **main idea** of the previous selection?

_____

_____

_____

_____

_____

_____

_____

E **READING FOCUS**

What do you think is the author's **purpose** for writing the selection?

_____

_____

_____

_____

_____

_____

from 102 Minutes
and And of Clay Are We Created

USE A VENN DIAGRAM

DIRECTIONS: Use the Venn diagram below to compare and contrast the **main idea** from "*from* 102 Minutes" and the **theme** from "And of Clay Are We Created." List differences in the outside sections of the ovals, and list similarities in the sections where the ovals overlap.

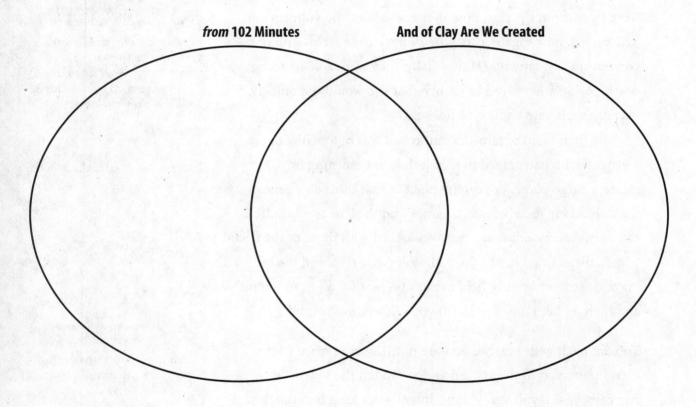

from **102 Minutes**   **And of Clay Are We Created**

Applying Your Skills

from 102 Minutes *and* And of Clay Are We Created

VOCABULARY DEVELOPMENT

DIRECTIONS: Fill in each blank with the correct vocabulary word from the Word Box.

Word Box
extricate
tenacity
equanimity
fortitude
resignation

1. Showing great _____, she finished the long SAT test in record time.

2. With a sigh of _____, Martha reluctantly accepted the terms of the deal.

3. The zookeeper survived the snakebite with great _____.

4. I was really impressed with the mayor's _____ during the crisis—it helped keep the citizens calm.

5. After the bird's wing healed completely, it was time to _____ it from the animal hospital.

LITERARY FOCUS: THEMES ACROSS GENRES

DIRECTIONS: Think about the **theme** or **main idea** of helping others. Was there a time in your life in which you helped someone? What **genre** might you use to tell that story? Would you write fiction, as in "And of Clay Are We Created," or nonfiction, as in "*from* 102 Minutes"? Write a paragraph that summarizes what you would write about and how you would write it.

READING FOCUS: ANALYZING AN AUTHOR'S PURPOSE

DIRECTIONS: Under each selection's detail, give a reason why the authors might have included the detail.

"*from* 102 Minutes"	"And of Clay Are We Created"
Detail: Karnes found the rescue workers in shock, depressed, doing little by way of organized searches. **Purpose:**	**Detail:** The child's suffering hurt me as it did him; I felt his frustration, his impotence. **Purpose:**

SKILLS FOCUS

Literary Skills
Understand themes across genres.

Reading Skills
Analyze an author's purpose.

from The 9/11 Report

by Sid Jacobson and Ernie Colón

INFORMATIONAL TEXT FOCUS: GENERATING RESEARCH QUESTIONS

Doing research involves asking questions and searching for answers. Creating answerable questions guides you in your research. When you come up with a research subject, think about what you want to know more about. Then follow these guidelines to come up with good research questions:

- Stick to a narrow topic. Try to find the **main idea** of your topic to keep your questions focused.

- Do not ask *yes* or *no* questions. Instead, ask the **5W-How? questions**— those that begin with *who, what, when, where, why,* and *how.* These questions will help you find specific information.

SELECTION VOCABULARY

unprecedented (UHN PREHS UH DEHN TIHD) *adj.:* never done before; new.
The severity of the attacks was unprecedented on American soil.

integrated (IHN TUH GRAYTED) *v.* used as *adj.:* made up of elements that work together; combined.
The response teams needed an integrated communications system.

WORD STUDY

DIRECTIONS: On the blank line next to each sentence, write "Yes" if the vocabulary word is used correctly. Write "No" if it is used incorrectly, and rewrite the sentence so that it is correct.

1. A Presidential election is *unprecedented* in U.S. history. _____

_____

_____

2. The *integrated* government agencies worked together flawlessly to help the victims of the disaster. _____

_____

_____

SKILLS FOCUS

Informational Text Skills
Generate research questions.

from THE 9/11 REPORT

by Sid Jacobson and Ernie Colón

BACKGROUND

On September 11, 2001, four passenger airplanes were hijacked by terrorists. Two planes were flown into the World Trade Center in New York City, one crashed into the Pentagon in Washington, D.C., and another crashed in an open field in Pennsylvania. Thousands of people were killed in the attacks. In December 2002, President George W. Bush created a special group, called a commission, to investigate all matters surrounding the 9/11 attacks. Their report was issued in July 2004.

ABOUT THE 9/11 REPORT

From Text to Graphics

In 2006, fellow cartoonists Ernie Colón and Sid Jacobson decided to adapt *The 9/11 Report* into a graphic form.

"Our desire to adapt *The 9/11 Report* arose from the desire to render the complex accessible. After both of us struggled with the verbal labyrinth of the original report, we decided there must be a better way. Then it occurred to us . . . that visually adapting the information in the report—comics, the graphic medium—was the better way. We could tell the story graphically to make it more easily understood. . . . What was more, we could make it more informative, more available, and, to be frank, more likely to be read in its entirety." **A**

Tips for Reading Graphic Texts

When reading graphic texts, it's important to look at the images and read the accompanying text. Here are some tips for reading graphic texts:

- Read the panels as you would a printed page. Read from left to right and from the top of the page to the bottom.
- Read one panel at a time. First, read the text in the panel. Then, study the illustration.
- Look carefully at the faces of the characters. Think about what their facial expressions or body language tells you.
- Ask yourself, "What do the pictures add to the text?"

Terms to Know

Knowing the meanings of these abbreviations will help you understand the text.

FDNY: Fire Department of New York
WTC: World Trade Center
NYPD: New York Police Department
PAPD: Port Authority Police Department
The following excerpt from *The 9/11 Report* is from Chapter 9: "Heroism and Horror."

A | READING FOCUS

How might the **main idea** of the 9/11 Report be easier to understand in graphic form?

_____

_____

_____

_____

_____

_____

_____

_____

_____

_____

_____

_____

_____

_____

A LANGUAGE COACH

A **prefix** is a group of letters added to the beginning of a word to change its meaning. *Unprecedented* and *unprepared* have the same prefix, *un–*. This prefix means "not." *Unprecedented* is the opposite of *precedented* (done before) and *unprepared* means the opposite of *prepared* (in a state of readiness). List three other words with the prefix *un–*.

_____

_____

_____

B VOCABULARY

Academic Vocabulary

Illustrations and words are both *components*, or essential parts, of comics. What do the illustrations and text on this page tell you?

_____

_____

_____

_____

_____

_____

_____

_____

THE 9/11 REPORT

A Graphic Adaptation
by Sid Jacobson and Ernie Colón

Based on the Final Report of the National Commission
on Terrorist Attacks Upon the United States

SEPTEMBER 11, 2001, WAS A DAY OF UNPRECEDENTED SHOCK AND SUFFERING IN THE HISTORY OF THE UNITED STATES. THE NATION WAS UNPREPARED. HOW DID THIS HAPPEN, AND HOW CAN WE AVOID SUCH TRAGEDY AGAIN? TEN COMMISSIONERS WERE GIVEN A SWEEPING MANDATE TO FIND ANSWERS AND OFFER RECOMMENDATIONS. ON JULY 22, 2004, THEY ISSUED THEIR REPORT... **A**

With a foreword by the Chair and
Vice Chair of the 9/11 Commission,
Thomas H. Kean and Lee H. Hamilton **B**

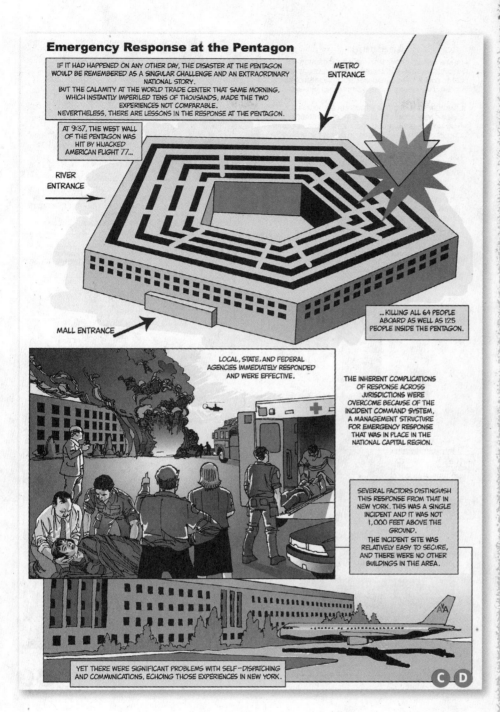

Emergency Response at the Pentagon

IF IT HAD HAPPENED ON ANY OTHER DAY, THE DISASTER AT THE PENTAGON WOULD BE REMEMBERED AS A SINGULAR CHALLENGE AND AN EXTRAORDINARY NATIONAL STORY.
BUT THE CALAMITY AT THE WORLD TRADE CENTER THAT SAME MORNING, WHICH INSTANTLY IMPERILED TENS OF THOUSANDS, MADE THE TWO EXPERIENCES NOT COMPARABLE.
NEVERTHELESS, THERE ARE LESSONS IN THE RESPONSE AT THE PENTAGON.

METRO ENTRANCE

AT 9:37, THE WEST WALL OF THE PENTAGON WAS HIT BY HIJACKED AMERICAN FLIGHT 77...

RIVER ENTRANCE

...KILLING ALL 64 PEOPLE ABOARD AS WELL AS 125 PEOPLE INSIDE THE PENTAGON.

MALL ENTRANCE

LOCAL, STATE, AND FEDERAL AGENCIES IMMEDIATELY RESPONDED AND WERE EFFECTIVE.

THE INHERENT COMPLICATIONS OF RESPONSE ACROSS JURISDICTIONS WERE OVERCOME BECAUSE OF THE INCIDENT COMMAND SYSTEM, A MANAGEMENT STRUCTURE FOR EMERGENCY RESPONSE THAT WAS IN PLACE IN THE NATIONAL CAPITAL REGION.

SEVERAL FACTORS DISTINGUISH THIS RESPONSE FROM THAT IN NEW YORK. THIS WAS A SINGLE INCIDENT AND IT WAS NOT 1,000 FEET ABOVE THE GROUND.
THE INCIDENT SITE WAS RELATIVELY EASY TO SECURE, AND THERE WERE NO OTHER BUILDINGS IN THE AREA.

YET THERE WERE SIGNIFICANT PROBLEMS WITH SELF-DISPATCHING AND COMMUNICATIONS, ECHOING THOSE EXPERIENCES IN NEW YORK.

C D

C QUICK CHECK

What reason does the commission give as to why the attack on the Pentagon was not treated as a larger national event?

_____

_____

_____

_____

_____

_____

D READING FOCUS

Come up with at least three **5W-How? questions** that you might ask about the attack on the Pentagon.

_____

_____

_____

_____

_____

_____

_____

_____

_____

_____

Selection Vocabulary

Use context clues to figure out the meaning of the word *integrated* in this sentence. Write a definition below.

_____

_____

_____

B **LITERARY ANALYSIS**

You already know from this page that the WTC "lacked any plan for evacuating the upper floors" in a situation where the stairwells were unusable. How else might people have escaped?

_____

_____

_____

_____

_____

_____

C **QUICK CHECK**

Name one of the suggestions that the commission is making.

_____

_____

_____

_____

Analysis

IN NEW YORK, THE FDNY, NYPD, THE PORT AUTHORITY, WTC EMPLOYEES, AND THE WTC OCCUPANTS THEMSELVES DID THEIR BEST TO COPE WITH AN UNIMAGINABLE CATASTROPHE FOR WHICH THEY WERE UNPREPARED IN TERMS OF TRAINING AND MIND-SET.

IT HAS BEEN ESTIMATED THAT BETWEEN 16,400 AND 18,800 CIVILIANS WERE IN THE WTC AS OF 8:46 ON SEPTEMBER 11. AT MOST, 2,152 INDIVIDUALS DIED AT THE WTC COMPLEX WHO WERE NOT RESCUE WORKERS OR ON THE TWO PLANES.

OUT OF THIS NUMBER, 1,942 WERE AT OR ABOVE THE IMPACT ZONES. THIS DATA STRONGLY SUPPORTS THAT THE EVACUATION WAS A SUCCESS FOR CIVILIANS BELOW THE IMPACT.

THE EVACUATION WAS AIDED BY CHANGES MADE BY THE PORT AUTHORITY IN RESPONSE TO THE 1993 BOMBING, REDUCING EVACUATION TIME FROM MORE THAN FOUR HOURS TO UNDER AN HOUR ON SEPTEMBER 11.

THE CIVILIANS AT OR ABOVE THE IMPACT ZONE HAD THE SMALLEST HOPE OF SURVIVAL. THEIR ONLY HOPE WAS A SWIFT AIR RESCUE, BUT THIS WAS IMPOSSIBLE.

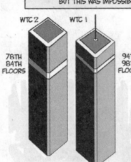

WTC 2 — 78TH 84TH FLOORS

WTC 1 — 94TH 98TH FLOORS

THE WTC LACKED ANY PLAN FOR EVACUATION OF THE UPPER FLOORS IN THE EVENT ALL STAIRWELLS WERE IMPASSABLE.

ONE LESSON IS THE NEED TO INTEGRATE THEM INTO THE RESPONSE SYSTEM AND INVOLVE THEM IN PROVIDING UP-TO-DATE ASSISTANCE AND INFORMATION.

INDIVIDUALS SHOULD KNOW THE EXACT LOCATION OF EVERY STAIRWELL AND HAVE ACCESS AT ALL TIMES TO FLASHLIGHTS.

THOUGH MAYOR GIULIANI'S EMERGENCY DIRECTIVE OF JULY 2001 WAS FOLLOWED TO SOME DEGREE ...

WE'VE GOT TO GET OUT OF HERE!

THE "FIRST" RESPONDERS ON 9/11 WERE PRIVATE-SECTOR CIVILIANS. BECAUSE 85% OF OUR NATION'S INFRASTRUCTURE IS CONTROLLED BY THE PRIVATE SECTOR, CIVILIANS ARE LIKELY TO BE THE FIRST RESPONDERS IN ANY FUTURE CATASTROPHE. THEREFORE, THE COMMISSION MAKES THE FOLLOWING CONCLUSIONS.

NO DECISION HAS BEEN CRITIZED MORE THAN THAT OF BUILDING PERSONNEL NOT TO EVACUATE THE SOUTH TOWER AFTER THE NORTH WAS HIT.

LESS UNDERSTANDABLE TO THE COMMISSION WAS THE INSTRUCTION TO SOME CIVILIANS WHO HAD REACHED THE LOBBY TO RETURN TO THEIR OFFICES!

NYPD 911 OPERATORS AND FDNY DISPATCH WERE NOT ADEQUATELY INTEGRATED AND GAVE OUT WRONG DIRECTIONS. A

SORRY, THIS IS RESERVED FOR FIRE TRUCKS ONLY.

...IT IS CLEAR THAT THE RESPONSE LACKED THE KIND OF INTEGRATED COMMUNICATION AND UNIFIED COMMAND CONTEMPLATED IN THE DIRECTIVE. B C

Of the NYPD, the FDNY, and the PAPD, which group experienced the fewest command and communication problems?

_____

_____

_____

_____

E READING FOCUS

Which of the **5W–How? questions** might be most important when considering the lack of sharing of information among the NYPD, NYFD, and PAPD? Explain your answer.

_____

_____

_____

_____

_____

_____

_____

_____

_____

_____

_____

_____

_____

_____

from **The 9/11 Report**

USE A COMPARISON TABLE

DIRECTIONS: Fill out the chart below. In the first column, write facts that you knew about 9/11 before you read the selection. In the middle column, write facts you learned from the graphic report. In the last column, explain what else you want to learn about the subject.

Knew	Learned	Want to learn

Applying Your Skills

from The 9/11 Report

VOCABULARY DEVELOPMENT

DIRECTIONS: A choice of three synonyms is given for each word. Select the one that is closest in meaning to the original word.

1. jurisdictions
  a. decisions
  b. areas
  c. judges

2. unprecedented
  a. common
  b. delayed
  c. exceptional

3. integrated
  a. cooperative
  b. segregated
  c. inside

INFORMATIONAL TEXT FOCUS: GENERATING RESEARCH QUESTIONS

DIRECTIONS: Suppose you were doing additional research on 9/11, beyond the selection you just read. Think of **5W-How questions** that will help you in your research. These questions should cover topics not fully explained in the selection you just read and should be focused on clarifying the **main ideas** of the selection.

1. Who _____

2. What _____

3. Where _____

4. When _____

5. Why _____

6. How _____

SKILLS FOCUS

Informational Text Skills
Generate research questions.

Collection 5

VOCABULARY REVIEW

DIRECTIONS: Fill in each blank with the correct vocabulary word from the Word Box. Some words will not be used.

Word Box

benign

clamoring

component

crucial

deteriorate

equanimity

equivalent

extricate

fortitude

induced

integrated

internal

jeopardize

potent

relapse

resignation

subsequent

technique

tenacity

tenuous

unprecedented

1. The conductor has a clear and beautiful conducting _____; it's no wonder the orchestra can follow his every gesture.

2. An engine is an absolutely necessary _____ because a car won't run without one.

3. If my parents leave for vacation, the condition of the kitchen will _____ because I'm not good at cleaning up after myself.

4. The teacher gave the class an _____ surprise when she announced that everyone would receive $5 for coming to class on time.

5. If that medicine isn't strong enough for your headache, I can find you something more _____.

6. If you don't have the _____ to take your sisters to the mall and wait there on the busiest shopping day of the year, then I'll do it.

7. I didn't want to _____ my chances of getting into college, so I studied very hard for the entrance exam.

8. During a disaster, it is _____ that rescue workers reach the victims immediately.

9. The house was so cold that it wasn't long before we started _____ for somebody to turn up the heat.

10. Although the spaceship looked mostly fine from the outside, it had suffered heavy _____ damage during the battle.

Skills Review

Collection 5

LANGUAGE COACH

DIRECTIONS: Many words have **multiple meanings**. They even might have different parts of speech (noun, verb, adjective, and adverb). Fill in the chart below with two different meanings of each given word. Be sure to include the part of speech for each definition. Use a dictionary if you need help.

Word	Definition 1	Definition 2
bear		
lean		
address		
state		
long		

WRITING ACTIVITY

DIRECTIONS: Remember that researching a topic involves first coming up with helpful research questions. Pick a topic that interests you and about which you don't already know a great deal. Write a paragraph about how you would begin to research the topic. In your paragraph, first narrow down the topic. Then tell what you already know about the subject. Finally, come up with **5W-How? questions** that would help you in your research.

Persuasion

9th November, 2002, Crook, P.J./Private Collection/
The Bridgeman Art Library International

Literary and Academic Vocabulary for Collection 6

---

challenge (CHAL uhnj) *v.:* call to a contest or fight; dare.

I challenge you to think of a way to raise money for the hurricane victims.

debate (DIH BAYT) *n.:* discussion of opposing arguments.

Our team won the final debate in the competition.

demonstrate (DEHM uhn strayt) *v.:* to show or prove by using evidence.

I will demonstrate how to tie shoes for the children.

evident (EHV uh duhnt) *adj.:* easy to understand; obvious.

It's evident from all of her trophies that she is a great athlete.

anecdotes (AN uhk dohts) *n.:* short, personal stories.

I told two anecdotes about my childhood during my interview.

tone (TOHN) *n.:* attitude.

The writer's tone was sarcastic and critical.

There Comes a Time When People Get Tired

by Martin Luther King, Jr.

Eulogy for Martin Luther King, Jr.

by Robert F. Kennedy

LITERARY FOCUS: PERSUASION: APPEALS TO EMOTION

Sometimes writing is more persuasive, or convincing, when it appeals to your **emotions,** or feelings, rather than your logic. Emotional appeals may encourage readers to feel sympathy for victims or outrage for injustices. Emotional appeals often contain **loaded words** (words with strong emotional associations, or **connotations**) and **anecdotes** (short, often personal, stories). As you read the following selections, look for emotional appeals in each speech.

READING FOCUS: SUMMARIZING

When you a read a speech, a good way to keep track of the writer's message is to summarize its most important ideas. To **summarize**, look for the main ideas and supporting details. Then, combine the main ideas to create one statement that explains the author's argument.

Use the Skill As you read, organize the texts' ideas in a chart like the one below to determine the authors' arguments.

SKILLS FOCUS

Literary Skills
Analyze emotional appeals in a text.

Reading Skills
Summarize an author's main ideas.

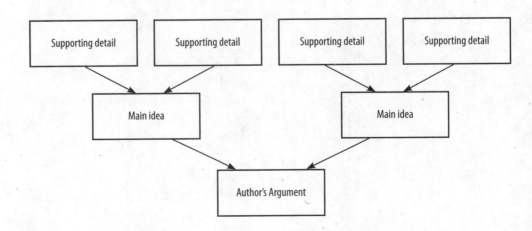

Vocabulary Development

There Comes a Time When People Get Tired *and* Eulogy for Martin Luther King, Jr.

SELECTION VOCABULARY

integrity (IHN TEHG RUH TEE) *n.:* honesty and sincerity.
> The protesters were not troublemakers but people of integrity who believed in their cause.

advocating (AD VUH KAYT IHNG) *v.:* recommending; speaking in favor of.
> Martin Luther King, Jr., was advocating nonviolent forms of protest.

utopian (YOO TOH PEE UHN) *adj.:* extremely idealistic but impractical.
> His utopian plans would never have worked in the real world.

coercion (KOH UHR SHUHN) *n.:* use of force or forceful persuasion.
> Sometimes a little coercion is necessary to change unfair laws.

WORD STUDY

DIRECTIONS: Write "Yes" after each sentence if the vocabulary word is used correctly. Write "No" if it is used incorrectly, and rewrite the sentence so that the word is used correctly.

1. Judges are expected to be fair and honest, making it important that they exercise *integrity* both inside and outside of the courtroom. _____

   _____

2. The author was *advocating* a new system for testing high school students.
   _____

   _____

3. The police officer wore his *utopian* with pride. _____

   _____

4. Eventually, the frustrated babysitter resorted to using *coercion* to control the children by threatening to call their parents. _____

   _____

THERE COMES A TIME WHEN PEOPLE GET TIRED

by Martin Luther King, Jr.

> **BACKGROUND**
> On December 1, 1955, an African American woman named Rosa Parks was arrested in Montgomery, Alabama, for refusing to give up her bus seat to a white person. Soon after this happened, Martin Luther King, Jr., a civil rights leader, organized a boycott to protest segregation. For over a year, thousands of people refused to ride the buses in Montgomery until the rules changed. King gave this speech a few days after Parks was arrested.

My friends, we are certainly very happy to see each of you out this evening. We are here this evening for serious business. We are here in a general sense because first and foremost we are American citizens and we are determined to apply our citizenship to the
10 fullness of its meaning. We are here also because of our love for democracy, because of our deep-seated belief that democracy transformed from thin paper to thick action is the greatest form of government on earth. **A**

© Don Cravens/Time & Life Pictures/Getty Images

From "There Comes a Time When People Get Tired" (Address to First Montgomery Improvement Association [MIA] Mass Meeting, at Holt Street Baptist Church, December 5, 1955, Montgomery, Alabama) by Martin Luther King, Jr. Copyright © 1963 by Martin Luther King, Jr.; copyright renewed © 1991 by Coretta Scott King. Reproduced by permission of **The Estate of Martin Luther King, Jr., c/o Writers House as agent for the proprietor, New York, NY.**

But we are here in a specific sense because of the bus situation in Montgomery.[1] We are here because we are determined to get the situation corrected. This situation is not at all new. The problem has existed over endless years. For many years now, Negroes in Montgomery and so many other areas have

20 been inflicted with the paralysis of crippling fear on buses in our community. On so many occasions, Negroes have been intimidated and humiliated and oppressed because of the sheer fact that they were Negroes. I don't have time this evening to go into the history of these numerous cases. Many of them now are lost in the thick fog of oblivion but at least one stands before us now with glaring dimensions. **B**

Just the other day, just last Thursday to be exact, one of the finest citizens in Montgomery—not one of the finest Negro citizens, but one of the finest citizens in Montgomery—was taken

30 from a bus and carried to jail and arrested because she refused to get up to give her seat to a white person. Now the press would have us believe that she refused to leave a reserved section for Negroes but I want you to know this evening that there is no reserved section. The law has never been clarified at that point. Now I think I speak with legal authority—not that I have any legal authority, but I think I speak with legal authority behind me—that the law, the ordinance, the city ordinance has never been totally clarified. **C**

Mrs. Rosa Parks is a fine person. And, since it had to happen,

40 happen, I'm happy that it happened to a person like Mrs. Parks, for nobody can doubt the boundless outreach of her integrity. Nobody can doubt the height of her character nobody can doubt the depth of her Christian commitment and devotion to the teachings of Jesus. **D** And I'm happy, since it had to happen, it happened to a person that nobody can call a disturbing factor in the community. Mrs. Parks is a fine Christian person, unassuming, and yet there is integrity and character there. And just because she refused to get up, she was arrested.

---

1. **bus situation in Montgomery:** reference to the Montgomery bus boycott by African Americans, which began after the arrest of Rosa Parks on December 1, 1955.

B LITERARY FOCUS

Circle the **loaded words** in this paragraph. Choose one of those words and describe its **connotations**.

_____

_____

_____

_____

C LITERARY FOCUS

What are King's legal reasons for supporting Rosa Parks? Do these reasons appeal to your logic or to your **emotions**?

_____

_____

_____

_____

D VOCABULARY

Word Study
Height has multiple meanings. Find the word in a dictionary. Which meaning is used in this sentence?

_____

_____

_____

_____

Selection Vocabulary

Advocating means "speaking in favor of." What is a synonym (word with a similar meaning) for *advocating*?

_____

_____

B **READING FOCUS**

Summarize the main idea and supporting details of this paragraph.

_____

_____

_____

_____

_____

50 And you know, my friends, there comes a time when people get tired of being trampled over by the iron feet of oppression. There comes a time, my friends, when people get tired of being plunged across the abyss of humiliation, where they experience the bleakness of nagging despair. There comes a time when people get tired of being pushed out of the glittering sunlight of life's July and left standing amid the piercing chill of an alpine November. There comes a time.

We are here, we are here this evening because we are tired now. And I want to say that we are not here advocating violence. **A** We have never done that. I want it to be known
60 throughout Montgomery and throughout this nation that we are Christian people. We believe in the Christian religion. We believe in the teachings of Jesus. The only weapon that we have in our hands this evening is the weapon of protest. That's all.

And certainly, certainly, this is the glory of America, with all of its faults. This is the glory of our democracy. If we were incarcerated behind the iron curtains of a Communistic[2] nation, we couldn't do this. If we were dropped in the dungeon of a totalitarian regime,[3] we couldn't do this. But the great glory of American democracy is the right to protest for right. My friends,
70 don't let anybody make us feel that we are to be compared in our actions with the Ku Klux Klan or with the White Citizens Council.[4] There will be no crosses burned at any bus stops in Montgomery. There will be no white persons pulled out of their homes and taken out on some distant road and lynched for not cooperating. There will be nobody among us who will stand up and defy the Constitution of this nation. We only assemble here because of our desire to see right exist. My friends, I want it to be known that we're going to work with grim and bold determination to gain justice on the buses in this city. **B**

---

2. **Communistic:** Under Communism, a government suppresses political opposition and limits individual freedoms.
3. **totalitarian regime:** a government that suppresses all opposition by force.
4. **Ku Klux Klan . . . White Citizens Council:** white supremacist groups.

80 And we are not wrong; we are not wrong in what we are doing. If we are wrong, the Supreme Court of this nation is wrong. If we are wrong, the Constitution of the United States is wrong. If we are wrong, God Almighty is wrong. If we are wrong, Jesus of Nazareth was merely a utopian dreamer that never came down to Earth. **C** If we are wrong, justice is a lie, love has no meaning. And we are determined here in Montgomery to work and fight until justice runs down like water and righteousness like a mighty stream. **D**

I want to say that in all of our actions, we must stick

90 together. Unity is the great need of the hour and if we are united we can get many of the things that we not only desire but which we justly deserve. And don't let anybody frighten you. We are not afraid of what we are doing because we are doing it within the law. There is never a time in our American democracy that we must ever think we are wrong when we protest. We reserve that right. When labor all over this nation came to see that it would be trampled over by capitalistic power, it was nothing wrong with labor getting together and organizing and protesting for its rights. We, the disinherited of this land, we who have been oppressed so

100 long, are tired of going through the long night of captivity. And now we are reaching out for the daybreak of freedom and justice and equality. **E**

May I say to you, my friends, as I come to a close, and just giving some idea of why we are assembled here, that we must keep—and I want to stress this, in all of our doings, in all of our deliberations here this evening and all of the week and while, whatever we do, we must keep God in the forefront. Let us be Christian in all of our actions. But I want to tell you this evening that it is not enough for us to talk about love, love is one of the

110 pivotal points of the Christian faith. There is another side called justice. And justice is really love in calculation. Justice is love correcting that which revolts against love.

The Almighty God himself is not only, not the God just standing out saying through Hosea,[5] "I love you, Israel." He's also

---

5. **Hosea:** a Hebrew prophet who lived during the eighth century B.C.

C **LANGUAGE COACH**

The word *utopian* has an interesting origin. Sir Thomas More wrote a book called "Utopia" in 1516. A *utopia* is an impossibly perfect world. More made up the name for his imaginary island by combining the Greek *ou* (not) and *topos* (place). Why do you think he chose to combine these two particular words?

_____

_____

_____

D **LITERARY FOCUS**

In this paragraph, do you think that King is appealing to his listeners' **emotions** more than to their logic? Explain your answer.

_____

_____

_____

_____

E **VOCABULARY**

Academic Vocabulary

How does King *demonstrate*, or show, his strong leadership abilities in this paragraph?

_____

_____

_____

Selection Vocabulary

Using context clues, write a definition for *coercion*. How is coercion different from *persuasion*?

_____

_____

_____

_____

_____

What **anecdote** does King use in this final paragraph?

_____

_____

_____

_____

_____

_____

_____

_____

© Don Cravens/Time & Life Pictures/Getty Images

the God that stands up before the nations and said: "Be still and know that I'm God, that if you don't obey me I will break the backbone of your power and slap you out of the orbits of your international and national relationships." Standing beside love is always justice, and we are only using the tools of justice. Not only

120   are we using the tools of persuasion, but we've come to see that we've got to use the tools of coercion. **A** Not only is this thing a process of education, but it is also a process of legislation.

And as we stand and sit here this evening and as we prepare ourselves for what lies ahead, let us go out with the grim and bold determination that we are going to stick together. We are going to work together. Right here in Montgomery, when the history books are written in the future, somebody will have to say, "There lived a race of people, a black people (Yes sir), 'fleecy locks and black complexion' (Yes), a people who had the moral

130   courage to stand up for their rights. [applause] And thereby they injected a new meaning into the veins of history and of civilization." And we're going to do that. God grant that we will do it before it is too late. As we proceed with our program, let us think of these things. **B**

EULOGY FOR MARTIN LUTHER KING, JR.

by Robert F. Kennedy

> **BACKGROUND**
>
> In 1968, Senator Robert F. Kennedy, the brother of the late President John F. Kennedy, was making his own run for the presidency. On April 4, he was campaigning in Indianapolis, Indiana, when he received news of the assassination of Martin Luther King, Jr. As someone who also believed in equality, Kennedy was moved to deliver this eulogy (a speech that honors a person who has died) for the civil rights leader just hours after King's death.

I have bad news for you, for all of our fellow citizens, and people who love peace all over the world, and that is that Martin Luther King was shot and killed tonight.

Martin Luther King dedicated his life to love and to justice for his fellow human beings, and he died because of that effort.

In this difficult day, in this difficult time for the United States, it is perhaps well to ask what kind of a nation we are and what direction we want to move in. For those of you who are black—considering the evidence there evidently is that there
10 were white people who were responsible—you can be filled with bitterness, with hatred, and a desire for revenge. We can move in that direction as a country, in great polarization—black people amongst black, white people amongst white, filled with hatred toward one another. **A**

Or we can make an effort, as Martin Luther King did, to understand and to comprehend, and to replace that violence, that stain of bloodshed that has spread across our land, with an effort to understand with compassion and love.

A (**LITERARY FOCUS**)

Do you think Kennedy is appealing more to **emotion** or to logic in the first three paragraphs? Provide details that support your answer.

_____

_____

_____

_____

_____

_____

_____

© Flip Schulke/Corbis

A **LITERARY FOCUS**

Underline Kennedy's **anecdote**. What effect do you think it has on the listeners?

_____

_____

_____

_____

B **QUICK CHECK**

According to Kennedy, what is needed in the United States?

_____

_____

_____

_____

20 For those of you who are black and are tempted to be filled with hatred and distrust at the injustice of such an act, against all white people, I can only say that I feel in my own heart the same kind of feeling. I had a member of my family killed, but he was killed by a white man. But we have to make an effort in the United States, we have to make an effort to understand, to go beyond these rather difficult times. **A**

My favorite poet was Aeschylus.[1] He wrote: "In our sleep, pain which cannot forget falls drop by drop upon the heart until, in our own despair, against our will, comes wisdom through the awful grace of God."

30 What we need in the United States is not division; what we need in the United States is not hatred; what we need in the United States is not violence or lawlessness; but love and wisdom, and compassion toward one another, and a feeling of justice toward those who still suffer within our country, whether they be white or they be black. **B**

So I shall ask you tonight to return home, to say a prayer for the family of Martin Luther King, that's true, but more importantly to say a prayer for our own country, which all of us love—a prayer for understanding and that compassion of which

40 I spoke.

---

1. **Aeschylus:** Greek poet who lived during the sixth century B.C.

We can do well in this country. We will have difficult times; we've had difficult times in the past; we will have difficult times in the future. It is not the end of violence; it is not the end of lawlessness; it is not the end of disorder.

But the vast majority of white people and the vast majority of black people in this country want to live together, want to improve the quality of our life, and want justice for all human beings who abide in our land. **C**

Let us dedicate ourselves to what the Greeks wrote so many years ago: to tame the savageness of man and make gentle the life of this world.

Let us dedicate ourselves to that, and say a prayer for our country and for our people. **D**

C VOCABULARY

Academic Vocabulary
How does the speech make Kennedy's commitment to the civil rights movement *evident,* or obvious?

_____

_____

_____

_____

D READING FOCUS

Summarize Kennedy's speech in three sentences or less.

_____

_____

_____

_____

_____

_____

_____

_____

_____

There Comes a Time When People Get Tired *and* Eulogy for Martin Luther King, Jr.

USE AN EMOTIONAL APPEAL CHART

DIRECTIONS: Both selections you just read—"There Comes a Time When People Get Tired" and "Eulogy for Martin Luther King, Jr."—include emotional appeals. Choose one of the two selections. In the chart below, list five **loaded words** from that selection. On the right, describe the **connotations** that are associated with each word.

The selection I chose:	
Loaded words	**Connotations**
1.	
2.	
3.	
4.	
5.	

Applying Your Skills

There Comes a Time When People Get Tired *and* Eulogy for Martin Luther King, Jr.

VOCABULARY DEVELOPMENT

DIRECTIONS: Complete each sentence with the correct vocabulary word from the Word Box. One word will not be used.

Word Box
integrity
advocating
utopian
coercion

1. Boycotts were an effective means of _____ during the civil rights movement.

2. Martin Luther King, Jr., was not _____ violence as a means to gain equality.

3. The protestors showed _____ by standing up for their beliefs.

LITERARY FOCUS: PERSUASION: APPEALS TO EMOTION

DIRECTIONS: Complete the chart below by deciding if the following quotation from "Eulogy for Martin Luther King, Jr." appeals more to **emotion** or to logic. Include a brief explanation of your answer.

Quotation	Emotional or logical?
"What we need in the United States is not division; what we need in the United States is not hatred; what we need in the United States is not violence or lawlessness; but love and wisdom…" (lines 30–33)	

READING FOCUS: SUMMARIZING

DIRECTIONS: Summarize the first paragraph of "There Comes a Time When People Get Tired" on the lines below.

_____

_____

_____

SKILLS FOCUS

Literary Skills
Analyze emotional appeals in a text.

Reading Skills
Summarize an author's main ideas.

from Cesar's Way
by Cesar Millan
Pack of Lies
by Mark Derr

LITERARY FOCUS: ARGUMENTS: PRO AND CON

When a writer presents an argument, he or she will give an opinion. To support his or her opinion, the writer might use **logical appeals**, or reasons backed up by evidence (facts, statistics, examples, and experts' opinions). A writer may also use **emotional appeals**, such as loaded words and anecdotes, and use a particular **tone** (attitude) to convince a reader to think a certain way. As you read the following two selections, determine which argument you think is more **credible**, or believable.

READING FOCUS: QUESTIONING

As you read a persuasive selection, it helps to **ask questions**. Asking questions will help you identify the strengths and weaknesses of a writer's arguments.

Use the Skill   While you read "*from* Cesar's Way" and "Pack of Lies," make a chart like the one below for each selection, and record your questions. As you read, fill in the answers to your questions, or indicate that more information is needed to answer the question by putting a check mark in that column.

Title: *"from* Cesar's Way"		
Questions	**Answers**	**More information needed**
Is there proof that dogs have a "pack instinct"?		

SKILLS FOCUS

Literary Skills
Understand arguments.

Reading Skills
Ask questions about an author's argument.

Vocabulary Development

from Cesar's Way *and* Pack of Lies

SELECTION VOCABULARY

primal (PRY MUHL) *adj.:* first in importance; essential.

Everyone's safety is my primal concern on this trip.

submissive (SUHB MIHS IHV) *adj.:* obedient; under another's control.

Unlike leaders of packs, followers are submissive.

intimidation (IHN TIHM UH DAY SHUHN) *n.:* inspiring fear; using threats or fear to influence behavior.

Some trainers use intimidation instead of rewards to train dogs.

punitive (PYOO NUH TIHV) *adj.:* punishing; seeking to punish.

Frightening a dog is a punitive form of training.

aggression (UH GREHSH UHN) *n.:* habit of attacking; unfriendly, destructive behavior.

Aggression can cause a dog to harm a person or another dog.

WORD STUDY

DIRECTIONS: Fill in the blanks in the following sentences with the correct word from the selection vocabulary list above.

1. The _____ reason for the dog's odd behavior was fear.

2. We hired a dog trainer because our dog showed too much _____ around other dogs.

3. The bully has a history of aggression. He also uses _____ to frighten the younger kids on the playground.

4. The judge's decision was unnecessarily _____, I thought.

5. Don't be so _____; stick up for yourself!

from CESAR'S WAY

by Cesar Millan

> **BACKGROUND**
> Cesar Millan is well-known to many dog owners as a dog training expert. In 2006, he published a book called *Cesar's Way: The Natural, Everyday Guide to Understanding and Correcting Common Dog Problems.* The following selection is from the chapter titled "Power of the Pack."

 VOCABULARY

Selection Vocabulary
Use context clues to write a definition for *primal.* Underline the context clues that helped you.

_____

_____

_____

A dog's pack is his life force. The pack instinct is his primal instinct. **A** His status in the pack is his self, his identity. The pack is all important to a dog because if anything threatens the pack's harmony, it threatens each individual dog's harmony. If something threatens the pack's survival, it threatens the very survival of every dog in it. The need to keep the pack stable and running smoothly is a powerful motivating force in every dog— even in a pampered poodle that has never met another dog or left the confines of your backyard. Why? It's deeply ingrained in
10 his brain. Evolution and Mother Nature took care of that.

It's vital for you to understand that your dog views all his interactions with other dogs, with you, and even with other animals in your household in the "pack" context. Humans—in fact, all primates—are pack animals, too. In fact, dog packs are really not so different from the human equivalent of packs. We call our packs families. Clubs. Football teams. Churches. Corporations. Governments. Sure, we think of our social groups as infinitely more complicated than dogs' groups, but are they really all that different? When you break it down, the basics
20 are the same: every one of the "packs" I've mentioned has a

"Power of the Pack" from *Cesar's Way* by Cesar Millan and Melissa Jo Peltier. Copyright © 2006 by Cesar Millan and Melissa Jo Peltier. Reproduced by permission of **Crown Publishers, a division of Random House, Inc.** and electronic format by permission of **Trident Media Group, LLC.**

hierarchy,[1] or it doesn't work. There is a father or mother, a chairman, a quarterback, a minister, a CEO, a president. Then there are varying levels of status for the people under him or her. That's how a pack of canines[2] works, too.

The concept of pack and pack leader is directly related to the way in which dogs interact with us when we bring them into our homes. **B**

The Natural Pack

If you study a wolf pack in the wild, you'll observe a natural rhythm to its days and nights. First, the animals in the pack
30 walk, sometimes up to ten hours a day, to find food and water. Then they eat. If they kill a deer, the pack leader gets the biggest piece, but everyone cooperates in sharing the rest. They'll eat until the entire deer is gone—not just because they don't have Saran Wrap in the wild, but because they don't know when there's going to be another deer again. What they eat today may have to hold them for a long time. That's where the expression "wolfing down" food comes from, and you'll see it in your own dog's behavior much of the time. Wolves don't necessarily eat just when they're hungry; they eat when the food is there. Their
40 bodies are designed to conserve. It's the root of your own dog's often seemingly insatiable appetite. **C**

Only after wolves and wild dogs have finished their daily work do they play. That's when they celebrate. And in nature, they usually go to sleep exhausted. Not once, while watching the dogs on my grandfather's farm, did I ever see a sleeping dog having nightmares, the way domestic dogs in America do. Their ears would twitch, their eyes would move, but there was no whimpering or whining or moaning. They were so completely worn out from their day's work and play that they slept
50 peacefully, every night.

---

1. **hierarchy** (HY UH RAHR KEE): structure in which the members of a group are ranked based on ability or status.
2. **canines** (KAY NYNZ): members of the family of mammals that includes dogs, wolves, and foxes.

B READING FOCUS

Remember that it's good to **ask questions** as you read to help identify strengths and weaknesses of the writer's argument. What questions do you have so far?

_____

_____

_____

_____

_____

C QUICK CHECK

Why do dogs seem to eat even when they're not hungry?

_____

_____

_____

from **Cesar's Way**   **289**

A **QUICK CHECK**

How do puppies learn to be cooperative members of a pack?

_____

_____

_____

_____

B **QUICK CHECK**

What two factors play a role in what makes a dog a pack leader?

_____

_____

_____

_____

Every pack has its rituals. These include traveling, working for food and water, eating, playing, resting, and mating. Most important, the pack always has a pack leader. The rest of the animals are followers. Within the pack, the animals fall into their own order of status, usually determined by that animal's inborn energy level. The leader determines—and enforces—the rules and boundaries by which the members will live.

A puppy's first pack leader is his mother. From birth, puppies learn how to be cooperative members of a pack oriented
60 society. At about three or four months, after they're weaned, they fall into the regular pack structure, and take their cues from the pack leader, not their mother. In packs of wolves and wild dogs, the leader is often a male, because the hormone[3] testosterone— present in male puppies from the time they are very small— seems to be a cue to dominance behaviors. A

Though hormones are part of what makes a pack leader, energy plays an even greater role. When humans live in households with more than one dog, the dominant dog can be either male or female. The gender doesn't matter, only the inborn
70 energy level, and who establishes dominance. In many packs, there is an "alpha couple," a male and female pair who seem to run things between them. B

---

3. **hormone** (HAWR MOHN): substance produced by the body that affects an organ or other tissue.

In the wild, pack leaders are born, not made. They don't take classes to become leaders; they don't fill out applications and go on interviews. Leaders develop early and they show their dominant qualities quite young. It's that all-important energy we discussed earlier that separates the pack leader from the follower. A pack leader must be born with high or very high energy. The energy must also be dominant energy, as well as calm-assertive[4]

80 energy. Medium- and low-energy dogs do not make natural pack leaders. Most dogs—like most humans—are born to be followers, not leaders. Being a pack leader isn't only about dominance, it's also about responsibility. Think about our own species, and the percentage of people who would like to have the power and perks of the president, or the money and goodies of a Bill Gates.[5] Then tell those people that the trade-off is that they will have to work around the clock, 24-7, almost never see their families, and rarely take weekends off. Tell them they'll be financially responsible for thousands of people, or responsible for the national security of

90 hundreds of millions of people. How many people would choose those leadership roles after being presented with such daunting realities? I believe most people would choose comfortable but simpler lives over great power and wealth—if they truly understood the work and sacrifice that leadership costs. **C**

Similarly, in a dog's world, the pack leader has the responsibility for the survival of all the pack members. The leader leads the pack to food and water. He decides when to hunt; decides who eats, how much, and when; decides when to rest and when to sleep and when to play. The leader sets all the

100 regulations and structures that the other pack members must live by. A pack leader has to have total confidence and know what he's doing. And just as in the human world, most dogs are born to follow rather than do all the work it takes to maintain the position of pack leader. **D** Life is easier and less stressful for

---

4. **calm-assertive** (UH SUR TIHV): Millan uses this term to mean relaxed but confident and in control.
5. **Bill Gates:** cofounder of the giant computer company Microsoft and one of the wealthiest people in the world.

C **LITERARY FOCUS**

In lines 82–94, is the writer making a **logical appeal** or an **emotional appeal** to make a point about responsibility? Explain your answer.

_____

_____

_____

_____

_____

_____

D **LITERARY ANALYSIS**

Do you agree with the argument that most humans are born to follow? Why or why not?

_____

_____

_____

_____

_____

_____

_____

them when they live within the rules, boundaries, and limitations that the pack leader has set for them. . . .

To Lead or to Follow?

To dogs, there are only two positions in a relationship: leader and follower. Dominant and submissive. **A** It's either black or white. There is no in-between in their world. When a dog lives with a human, in order for the human to be able to control the dog's behavior, she must make the commitment to take on the role of pack leader, 100 percent of the time. It's that simple. . . .

A dog will usually accept a human as its pack leader if that human projects the correct calm-assertive energy, sets solid rules, boundaries, and limitations, and acts responsibly in the cause of the pack's survival. **B** This doesn't mean that we can't still be uniquely human pack leaders. Just as dogs shouldn't have to give up what's unique about them to live with us, we shouldn't have to give up what's so special about being human. We are, for instance, the only pack leaders who are going to love the dogs in the way we humans define love. Their canine pack leader will not buy them squeaky toys or throw birthday parties for them. Their canine pack leader won't directly reward their good behavior. He won't turn around and say, "Gee, guys, thanks for following me ten miles." It's expected that they do that! A mother dog won't say, "You know, you pups have behaved so well today. Let's go to the beach!" In their natural world, the reward is in the process. (That's a concept we humans could sometimes do well to remember.) For a dog there's a reward in simply fitting in with the pack and helping to ensure its survival. Cooperation automatically results in the primal rewards of food, water, play, and sleep. Rewarding our dogs with treats and the things that they love is one way we can bond with them and reinforce good behavior. But if we don't project strong leadership energy before we give rewards, we're never going to have a truly functional "pack." **C**

Who's Top Dog in Your House?

Once my clients start to grasp the concept of the pack and the pack leader, they usually ask me, "How can I tell who's the pack leader in my house?" The answer is very simple: who controls the dynamics of your relationship?

There are dozens and dozens of different ways in which your dog will tell you, loud and clear, who's the dominant one between the two of you. If he jumps on you when you come home from work in the evening, he's not just happy to see you. He is the pack leader. If you open the door to go for a walk and he exits ahead of you, it's not just because he loves his walks so much. He is the pack leader. If he barks at you and then you feed him, it's not "cute." He is the pack leader. If you are sleeping and he wakes you up at five in the morning pawing you to say "Let me out; I gotta pee," then he's showing you even before the sun comes up who's running the house. Whenever he makes you do anything, he is the pack leader. Simple as that.

Most of the time dogs are the pack leaders of the human world because the human will say, "Isn't that adorable? He's trying to tell me something." There it is, that old Lassie syndrome again, "What's that, Lassie? Gramps fell down the well?"[6] Yes, in this case, human, your dog is trying to tell you something—he's trying to remind you that he is the leader and you are his follower. **D**

So, when you wake up on your own terms, you are the pack leader. When you open the door on own your terms, you are the pack leader. When you exit the house ahead of your dog, you are the pack leader. When you are the one who makes the decisions in the household, then you are the pack leader. And I'm not talking about 80 percent of the time. I'm talking about 100 percent of the time. **E** If you give only 80 percent

---

6. **Lassie syndrome . . . the well:** In a much-loved TV show that aired from 1954 until the early 1970s, Lassie, a collie dog, helped rescue people. The character originally appeared in a 1938 short story, and over the years she has been the subject of books, movies, and a second TV series.

D **LITERARY FOCUS**

Discuss the ways in which the author uses **emotional appeals** in this paragraph.

_____

_____

_____

_____

E **READING FOCUS**

What **questions** do you have for the writer at this point in his argument?

_____

_____

_____

_____

_____

_____

Why must any correction to a dog's behavior be given at the exact moment that a bad behavior occurs?

_____

_____

_____

_____

Academic Vocabulary

How does Jada Pinkett Smith's size *demonstrate*, or show, that anyone can be a "pack leader" to a dog?

_____

_____

_____

_____

_____

_____

leadership, your dog will give you 80 percent following. And the other 20 percent of the time he will run the show. If you give your dog any opportunity for him to lead you, he will take it.

Leading Is a Full-time Job

170   Dogs need leadership, from the day they're born to the day they die. They instinctively need to know what their position is in regard to us. Usually owners have a position for their dogs in their hearts but not in their "packs." That's when the dogs take over. They take advantage of a human who loves them but offers no leadership. Dogs don't reason. They don't think, "Gee, it's so great that this person loves me. It makes me feel so good, I'll never attack another dog again." You can't say to a dog like you'd say to a child, "Unless you behave, you're not going to the dog park tomorrow." A dog can't make that connection. Any show

180   of leadership you give dogs must be given at the moment of the behavior that needs correction. **A**

In your household, anybody can be a pack leader. In fact, it is vital that all the humans in the house be the dog's pack leader—from the smallest infant to the oldest adult. Male or female. Everybody must get with the program. I go to many households where the dog respects one person, but runs roughshod over the rest of the family. This can be another recipe for disaster. In my family, I am the dogs' pack leader, but so are my wife and two sons. Andre and Calvin can walk through

190   my pack dogs at the Dog Psychology Center without the dogs so much as blinking an eye. The boys learned pack leadership from watching me, but all children can be taught how to assert leadership with animals.

Pack leadership doesn't hinge on size or weight or gender or age. Jada Pinkett Smith weighs maybe 110 pounds soaking wet, but she was able to handle four Rottweilers at once even better than her husband was. **B** Will Smith[7] was good with the dogs and they respected him, but Jada really put in the time

_____

7.   **Jada Pinkett Smith . . . Will Smith:** well-known actors who are married to each other.

© Alan Weissman

C VOCABULARY

Word Study

In this sentence, *cements* is used as a verb that means "joins together." Think of a synonym (word with a similar meaning) for the verb *cement*. Use a thesaurus if you need help.

and energy needed to be a strong pack leader. She's gone with
200   me to the beach and the mountains, where I take the pack out
for off-leash walks.

Leading a dog on a walk—as evidenced by the dogs who live
with the homeless—is the best way to establish pack leadership.
It's a primal activity that creates and cements those pack leader–
follower bonds. **C** As simple as it sounds, it's one of the keys to
creating stability in the mind of your dog.

In dogs that are trained for specific jobs, the pack leader
doesn't even need to be out in front. In Siberian husky dogsled
teams, though the human pack leader is at the back of the sled,
210   it's she who is running the sled. Dogs who live with handicapped
people—people in wheelchairs, the blind, people with special
needs—often have to take the physical lead in some situations.

But the person they are helping is always the one in control. It's a beautiful thing to watch a service dog who lives with a handicapped person. Often, the two seem to have a kind of supernatural connection between them—a sixth sense. They are so in tune with each other that the dog can often sense what that person needs before being given a command. That's the kind of bond dogs in packs have with one another. Their communication 220 is unspoken, and it comes from the security they have within the pack structure.

With the proper calm-assertive energy, pack leadership, and discipline, you, too, can have this sort of deep connection with your dog. In order to accomplish this, however, it's important to be aware of the things you may be inadvertently doing that are contributing to your dog's problems. **A** **B**

PACK OF LIES

from The New York Times
by Mark Derr

BACKGROUND
Mark Derr has written two books about dogs. In this article for *The New York Times*, he criticizes some of Cesar Millan's dog-training methods.

With a compelling personal story as the illegal immigrant made good because of his uncanny[1] ability to understand dogs, Cesar Millan has taken the world of canine behavior—or rather misbehavior—by storm. He has the top-rated program, "Dog Whisperer," on the National Geographic Channel, a best-selling book and a devoted following, and he has been the subject of several glowing magazine articles.

He is even preparing to release his own "Illusion" collar and leash set, named for his wife and designed to better allow people
10 to walk their dogs the "Cesar way"—at close heel, under strict control.

Essentially, National Geographic and Cesar Millan have cleverly repackaged and promoted a simplistic view of the dog's social structure and constructed around it a one-size-fits-all, cookie-cutter approach to dog training. In Mr. Millan's world, dog behavioral problems result from a failure of the human to be the "pack leader," to dominate the dog (a wolf by any other name) completely. **C**

While Mr. Millan rejects hitting and yelling at dogs
20 during training, his confrontational methods include physical

---

1. uncanny (UHN KAN EE): so remarkable as to seem unnatural or not normal.

"Pack of Lies" by Mark Derr from *The New York Times*, August 31, 2006. Copyright © 2006 by The New York Times. Reproduced by permission of **The New York Times Syndication Sales.**

> **C LITERARY FOCUS**
> Circle any loaded words in the first three paragraphs. How does the **tone** of these paragraphs tell you that Derr will be critical of Cesar Millan in this article?
>
> _____
> _____
> _____
> _____
> _____

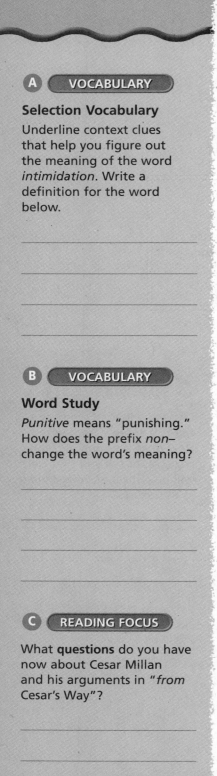

A **VOCABULARY**

Selection Vocabulary
Underline context clues that help you figure out the meaning of the word *intimidation*. Write a definition for the word below.

_____

_____

_____

_____

B **VOCABULARY**

Word Study
Punitive means "punishing." How does the prefix *non*– change the word's meaning?

_____

_____

_____

_____

C **READING FOCUS**

What **questions** do you have now about Cesar Millan and his arguments in *"from Cesar's Way"*?

_____

_____

_____

_____

_____

and psychological intimidation, like finger jabs, choke collars, extended sessions on a treadmill and what is called flooding, or overwhelming the animal with the thing it fears. **A** Compared with training devices still in use—whips and cattle prods, for example—these are mild, but combined with a lack of positive reinforcement[2] or rewards, they place Mr. Millan firmly in a long tradition of punitive dog trainers.

Mr. Millan brings his pastiche[3] of animal behaviorism and pop psychology into millions of homes a week. He's a charming,

30 one-man wrecking ball directed at 40 years of progress in understanding and shaping dog behavior and in developing nonpunitive, reward-based training programs, which have led to seeing each dog as an individual, to understand what motivates it, what frightens it and what its talents and limitations are. **B** Building on strengths and working around and through weaknesses, these trainers and specialists in animal behavior often work wonders with their dogs, but it takes time.

Mr. Millan supposedly delivers fast results. His mantra[4] is "exercise, discipline, affection," where discipline means "rules,

40 boundaries, limitations." Rewards are absent and praise scarce, presumably because they will upset the state of calm submission Mr. Millan wants in his dogs. Corrections abound as animals are forced to submit or face their fear, even if doing so panics them.

Mr. Millan builds his philosophy from a simplistic conception of the dog's "natural" pack, controlled by a dominant alpha animal (usually male). In his scheme, that leader is the human, which leads to the conclusion that all behavior problems in dogs derive from the failure of the owner or owners to dominate. **C** (Conveniently, by this logic, if Mr. Millan's

50 intervention doesn't produce lasting results, it is the owner's fault.) . . .

---

2. **positive reinforcement**: rewards designed to encourage good behavior.
3. **pastiche** (PAS TEESH): confused mixture.
4. **mantra** (MAHN TRUH): word or phrase repeated over and over, as in a prayer or a request for guidance.

The notion of the "alpha pack leader" dominating all other pack members is derived from studies of captive packs of unrelated wolves and thus bears no relationship to the social structure of natural packs, according to L. David Mech, one of the world's leading wolf experts. In the wild, the alpha wolves are merely the breeding pair, and the pack is generally comprised of their juvenile offspring and pups.

60 "The typical wolf pack," Dr. Mech wrote in The Canadian Journal of Zoology in 1999, "is a family, with the adult parents guiding the activities of a group in a division-of-labor system." In a natural wolf pack, "dominance contests with other wolves are rare, if they exist at all," he writes. **D**

That's a far cry from the dominance model that Mr. Millan attributes to the innate need of dogs by way of wolves.

Unlike their wolf forebears,[5] dogs exist in human society. They have been selectively bred for 15,000 or more years to live with people. Studies have shown that almost from birth they are attentive to people, and that most are eager to please, given 70 proper instruction and encouragement. **E**

But sometimes the relationship goes very wrong, and it is time to call on a professional.

Aggression is perhaps the most significant of the behavioral problems that may afflict more than 20 percent of the nation's 65 million dogs, because it can lead to injury and death. Mr. Millan often treats aggression by forcing the dog to exercise extensively on a treadmill, by asserting his authority by rolling it on its back in the "alpha rollover," and through other forms of intimidation, including exposure to his pack of dogs.

80 Forcefully rolling a big dog on its back was once recommended as a way to establish dominance, but it is now recognized as a good way to get bitten. People are advised not to try it. In fact, many animal behaviorists believe that in the long run meeting aggression with aggression breeds more aggression.

D LITERARY FOCUS

How does Derr's use of quotes from L. David Mech strengthen the **credibility** of Derr's own arguments?

_____

_____

_____

_____

E LITERARY FOCUS

What evidence does Derr give to oppose Millan's argument that dogs are just like wolves in their pack behavior? Is it a **logical appeal** or an **emotional appeal**? How do you know?

_____

_____

_____

_____

_____

_____

---

5. **forebears** (FAWR BAIRZ): ancestors.

Academic Vocabulary

In this paragraph, how does Derr *challenge*, or call into question, Millan's argument about dog aggression?

_____

_____

_____

_____

What **questions** do you have about the strengths and weaknesses of Derr's arguments? Do you think his arguments are convincing?

_____

_____

_____

_____

_____

_____

_____

_____

_____

_____

_____

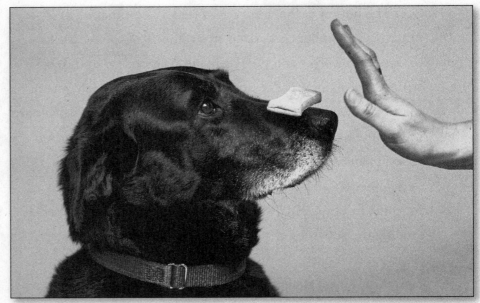

© Tim McGuire/Corbis

More important, aggression often has underlying medical causes that might not be readily apparent—hip dysplasia[6] or some other hidden physical ailment that causes the dog to bite out of pain; hereditary forms of sudden rage that require a medical history and genealogy to diagnose; inadequate blood

90 flow to the brain or a congenital brain malformation that produces aggression and can only be uncovered through a medical examination. Veterinary behaviorists, having found that many aggressive dogs suffer from low levels of serotonin,[7] have had success in treating such dogs with fluoxetine (the drug better known as Prozac). **A**

Properly treating aggression, phobias, anxiety and fears from the start can literally save time Mr. Millan's quick fix might make for good television and might even produce lasting results in some cases. But it flies in the face of what professional

100 animal behaviorists—either trained and certified veterinarians or ethologists[8]—have learned about normal and abnormal behavior in dogs. **B**

---

6. **hip dysplasia:** disease affecting the hip joint, common among certain dog breeds.
7. **serotonin** (SEHR OH TOH NUHN): chemical produced by the body that affects the brain and other organs.
8. **ethologists** (EE THOL UH JIHSTS): scientists who study animal behavior.

Applying Your Skills

from Cesar's Way and Pack of Lies

VOCABULARY DEVELOPMENT

DIRECTIONS: Circle the antonym (word with opposite meaning) of each vocabulary word.

1. **submissive**

   a. shy   **b.** defiant   **c.** cooperative

2. **punitive**

   a. harsh   **b.** deadly   **c.** rewarding

3. **aggression**

   a. peacefulness   **b.** hostility   **c.** active

LITERARY FOCUS: ARGUMENTS: PRO AND CON

DIRECTIONS: Answer the following questions about **logical** and **emotional appeals** in "*from* Cesar's Way" and "Pack of Lies."

1. What is an example of a logical appeal in "*from* Cesar's Way"?

   _____

2. What is an example of a logical appeal in "Pack of Lies"?

   _____

3. What is an example of an emotional appeal in "*from* Cesar's Way"?

   _____

4. What is an example of an emotional appeal in "Pack of Lies"?

   _____

READING FOCUS: QUESTIONING

DIRECTIONS: Look back at the chart you made from the Preparing to Read page. Write a short paragraph that summarizes what you learned from one of the **questions** that you were able to answer after reading the selection.

Literary Skills
Understand arguments.

Reading Skills
Ask questions about an author's argument.

Skills Review

Collection 6

VOCABULARY REVIEW

DIRECTIONS: Write "Yes" on the blank next to each sentence in which the vocabulary word is used correctly. Write "No" if the word is used incorrectly, and rewrite the sentence so that it is used correctly.

1. Giving a dog treats is a *punitive* form of training. _____

_____

2. He's been frowning and complaining all day, so it's *evident* that he's in a bad mood. _____

_____

3. I knew from her *integrity* that she was lying. _____

_____

4. The *coercion* wasn't running properly, so we took it to the mechanic. _____

_____

5. I knew that the main character in the story was going to *challenge* his enemy to a duel. _____

_____

6. The dog showed *submissive* behavior by following all of my commands. _____

_____

7. In her book, the author created a *utopian* world full of war, violence, and death. _____

_____

8. I tried to *demonstrate* finger painting to the class. _____

_____

9. Her *intimidation* demeanor puts everyone at ease. _____

_____

10. The writer's *advocating* arguments about dog training were weak. _____

_____

11. The dog's *aggression* told me that it would be well-behaved around children. _____

_____

12. The *debate* between the two students was very interesting and both of them had convincing arguments. _____

_____

Skills Review

Collection 6

LANGUAGE COACH

DIRECTIONS: Knowing the meaning of a word's **prefix** (letters added to the beginning of a word that change the word's meaning) can help you better understand the word. Study the meanings of the prefixes below. Then write a definition for each word. Check your answers in a dictionary.

Word	Prefix and its meaning	Meaning of word
nondescript	*non–:* not	1.
disconnect	*dis–:* away, not, negative	2.
multipurpose	*multi–:* many	3.
antifreeze	*anti–:* against, opposite	4.
megaphone	*mega–:* great, million	5.
autograph	*auto–:* self	6.
malformation	*mal–:* bad, badly	7.
compress	*com–:* with, together	8.

ORAL LANGUAGE ACTIVITY

DIRECTIONS: In the two selections "*from* Cesar's Way" and "Pack of Lies," you learned that a writer who is presenting an opinion may provide evidence in the form of **logical appeals** and **emotional appeals.**

Try to convince a partner of your opinion about a current event in your school or community. Try to use both logical and emotional appeals in your argument. Your partner should ask questions that will help identify the strengths and weaknesses of your case. Then, switch roles and do the exercise again.

© Eduardo Muñoz/Sicardi Gallery, Texas

Literary and Academic Vocabulary for Collection 7

_____

transform (TRANS FAWRM) *v.:* change.

A poem can transform ordinary objects into unusual images.

literal (LIHT UHR UHL) *adj.:* interpreting words the usual way.

A literal interpretation of a metaphor may not always make sense.

evoke (IH VOHK) *v.:* bring out; call forth.

For some people, the grandmother's condition in the poem may evoke sadness.

complement (KAHM PLUH MUHNT) *v.:* complete; fulfill a lack of any kind.

The title and introduction complement the poem.

smile (SIHM UH LEE) *n.:* figure of speech that uses a connective word such as *like, as, than,* or *resembles* to compare things that seem to have little or nothing in common.

I used the simile, "a smile is like a sunny day," in my poem.

metaphor (MEHT UH FOHR) *n.:* kind of comparison between unlike things that does not use a connective word such as *like, as,* or *than.*

My sister is so smart that people use the metaphor, "she's a walking encyclopedia," to describe her.

visualizing (VIHJ OO UHL Y ZIHNG) *n.:* translating words into images with the imagination.

While the teacher read the story to the class, we were visualizing the vivid details.

Same Song

by Pat Mora

LITERARY FOCUS: IMAGERY AND ALLUSION

Poets use words to create an image, or representation, of something that can be seen, heard, tasted, smelled, or felt. The language that is used to appeal to your senses is called **imagery**. Imagery helps you "see" something in your own imagination. For example, when you read the words "red wheelbarrow," you form a picture of this object in your mind's eye.

In this poem, the speaker makes an **allusion**, or indirect reference, to a classic fairy tale. If you recognize the allusion, be aware of the image it instantly forms in your mind. Allusions may refer to literature, history, myths, religion, politics, sports, science, or the arts.

Use the Skill On the blank lines below, write a short paragraph that describes something from your life, such as your daily routine. In the description, make an allusion to a story you have heard or read. The allusion does not have to be a direct comparision.

_____
_____
_____
_____
_____
_____
_____
_____
_____
_____
_____
_____
_____
_____
_____

SKILLS FOCUS

Literary Skills
Understand imagery and allusion.

Same Song

READING FOCUS: VISUALIZING

Poetry often contains images with startling details. You may never before have noticed a certain angle of light or the echo of a door slamming. **Visualizing** is the process of "seeing" in your mind the detailed images that the poet is describing. Taking time to visualize as you read can help you both understand and enjoy a poem.

Use the Skill   As you read "Same Song," use the chart below to record the images from the poem. Take note of the sense or senses the images appeal to. One example is given.

Images	Senses
"squeezes into faded jeans"	touch, sight

Reading Skills
Understand visualization as a strategy for comprehension.

SAME SONG

by Pat Mora

© Elizabeth Barakah Hodges/Superstock

A LITERARY FOCUS

What **allusion** is the author using in line 10? Why do you think she includes it in the poem?

_____

_____

_____

_____

B READING FOCUS

What descriptive words help you **visualize** the son's workout?

_____

_____

_____

C VOCABULARY

Academic Vocabulary

Why do you think the son and daughter are trying to *transform*, or change, themselves?

_____

_____

_____

While my sixteen-year-old son sleeps,

my twelve-year-old daughter

stumbles into the bathroom at six A.M.

plugs in the curling iron

5   squeezes into faded jeans

curls her hair carefully

strokes Aztec Blue shadow on her eyelids

smooths Frosted Mauve blusher on her cheeks

outlines her mouth in Neon Pink

10 peers into the mirror, mirror on the wall **A**

frowns at her face, her eyes, her skin,

not fair.

At night this daughter

stumbles off to bed at nine

15 eyes half-shut while my son

jogs a mile in the cold dark

then lifts weights in the garage

curls and bench presses

expanding biceps, triceps, pectorals,

20 one-handed push-ups, one hundred sit-ups **B**

peers into that mirror, mirror and frowns too. **C**

"Same Song" from *Borders* by Pat Mora. Copyright © 1986 by **Arte Publico Press-University of Houston, Houston, TX.** Reproduced by permission of the publisher.

Applying Your Skills

Same Song

LITERARY FOCUS: IMAGERY AND ALLUSION

DIRECTIONS: In the chart below, list the sense or senses that the **imagery** in the left column appeals to.

Imagery	Sense(s)
The lamb had a snow-white fleece.	1.
The ice creaked as I walked across the frozen pond.	2.
The puppy's fur was soft and cuddly.	3.
The aroma of freshly baked bread made my stomach rumble.	4.
I always get a sharp pain in my knee when I work out too long.	5.
The chocolate cake was a little too sweet for my liking.	6.

READING FOCUS: VISUALIZING

DIRECTIONS: Choose a few lines from "Same Song" and write a paragraph that describes in detail what you "see" in your mind's eye when you **visualize** the details.

_____

_____

_____

_____

_____

_____

_____

Literary Skills
Understand imagery and allusion.

Reading Skills
Use visualization as a strategy for comprehension.

Shall I Compare Thee to a Summer's Day?

by William Shakespeare

LITERARY FOCUS: SONNET

The poetic form that was often used by William Shakespeare is the **English sonnet**, also called the **Shakespearean sonnet**. It has fourteen lines divided into three **quatrains** (rhyming four-line stanzas) and a **couplet** (a pair of rhyming lines) at the end. Each quatrain makes a different point or gives an example, and the couplet sums up the whole poem. As you read this sonnet, note how the speaker expresses passionate feelings within the very strict rules of the English sonnet.

READING FOCUS: READING A POEM

As you read "Shall I Compare Thee to a Summer's Day?" don't be discouraged if you don't understand its meaning right away. Try a few of these methods to help you figure out its meaning: look for punctuation that tells you where thoughts end and begin; rearrange sentences to put words in the traditional order; and **paraphrase**, or restate in your own words, the lines of the poem.

Use the Skill As you read "Shall I Compare Thee to a Summer's Day?" use the chart below to keep track of the paraphrasing you do as you read the sonnet.

Line 1	Should I compare you to a day during the summer?

SKILLS FOCUS

Literary Skills
Analyze an English sonnet.

Reading Skills
Paraphrase while reading a poem.

Vocabulary Development

Shall I Compare Thee to a Summer's Day?

SELECTION VOCABULARY

temperate (TEHM PUHR IHT) *adj.:* not too hot or too cold; mild; moderate in behavior; self-restrained.

The speaker says his love's personality is more temperate than summer weather.

complexion (KUHM PLEHK SHUHN) *n.:* appearance of the skin, especially the face.

The speaker observes that time can dim a person's beautiful complexion.

WORD STUDY

DIRECTIONS: Write "Yes" next to each sentence if the vocabulary word is used correctly. Write "No" if it is used incorrectly. If you write "No," rewrite the sentence so it is correct.

1. The *temperate* weather made it the perfect day for a picnic. _____

_____

2. She is very photogenic, because she has a clear, beautiful *complexion*. _____

_____

3. I found this science chapter much too *complexion*. _____

_____

4. She took her child's *temperate* to see if he had a fever. _____

_____

SHALL I COMPARE THEE TO A SUMMER'S DAY?

by William Shakespeare

Shall I compare thee to a summer's day?
Thou art more lovely and more temperate.
Rough winds do shake the darling buds of May,
And summer's lease[1] hath all too short a date. **A**

5 Sometime too hot the eye of heaven shines,
And often is his gold complexion dimmed; **B**
And every fair from fair sometime declines,
By chance, or nature's changing course, untrimmed;[2]
But thy eternal summer shall not fade,

10 Nor lose possession of that fair thou ow'st,[3]
Nor shall Death brag thou wand'rest in his shade,
When in eternal lines to time thou grow'st:
　　So long as men can breathe or eyes can see,
　　So long lives this, and this gives life to thee. **C**

A **READING FOCUS**

Paraphrase the first quatrain (lines 1–4).

_____

_____

_____

_____

B **LANGUAGE COACH**

Dim, the root of *dimmed,* means "not bright." Think of an antonym (word with the opposite meaning) for *dim.*

_____

C **LITERARY FOCUS**

Identify the ways in which "Shall I Compare Thee to a Summer's Day?" qualifies as an **English sonnet**.

_____

_____

_____

_____

Springtime, 1956, Zardarian, Hovannes/Tretyakov Gallery, Moscow, Russia/The Bridgeman Art Library International

1. **lease** (LEES): allotted time.
2. **untrimmed** (UHN TRIHMD): without trimmings or decorations.
3. **thou ow'st**: you own.

Applying Your Skills

Shall I Compare Thee to a Summer's Day?

VOCABULARY DEVELOPMENT

DIRECTIONS: Circle the synonym (word with a similar meaning) of each vocabulary word.

1. **temperate**

    a. humid   **b.** mild   **c.** threatening

2. **complexion**

    a. appearance   **b.** intricacy   **c.** manner

LITERARY FOCUS: SONNET

DIRECTIONS: Use the chart below to identify the main idea of each **quatrain** and the main idea of the **couplet** of "Shall I Compare Thee to a Summer's Day."

Section of poem	Main idea
Quatrain 1	**1.**
Quatrain 2	**2.**
Quatrain 3	**3.**
Couplet	**4.**

READING FOCUS: READING A POEM

DIRECTIONS: Paraphrase the following lines from the sonnet.

Line from poem	My paraphrase
"Sometimes too hot the eye of heaven shines," (line 5)	**1.**
"But thy eternal summer shall not fade," (line 9)	**2.**

SKILLS FOCUS

Literary Skills
Analyze an English sonnet.

Reading Skills
Paraphrase while reading a poem.

since feeling is first

by E. E. Cummings

LITERARY FOCUS: METAPHOR

Poets often use metaphors to enrich their poems. A **metaphor** is a comparison between two things that are not at all alike. By making such a comparison, a surprising connection can be revealed. A metaphor is more direct than a simile (which uses comparison words such as *like* or *as*). A metaphor says that something *is* another thing. In this poem, Cummings compares love and death to something unusual.

READING FOCUS: ANALYZING WORD CHOICE

When writers try to communicate a specific idea, they will choose their words very carefully. Two words might mean basically the same thing but have different feelings attached to them. Consider the different feelings associated with *large* and *gigantic*, for example. **Analyzing word choice** will help you grasp the deeper meaning of the poem.

Use the Skill As you read "since feeling is first," use the chart below to record key words in the poem. Then list the feelings that you associate with each word.

Words	Associations

SKILLS FOCUS

Literary Skills
Understand metaphors.

Reading Skills
Analyze word choice.

Vocabulary Development

since feeling is first

SELECTION VOCABULARY

syntax (SIHN TAKS) *n.:* sentence structure; relationship of words in a sentence.
> *E. E. Cummings's syntax in the poem is unusual.*

gesture (JEHS CHUHR) *n.:* a movement, usually by part of the body; an action.
> *The flutter of eyelids is an example of a gesture.*

parenthesis (PUH REHN THUH SIHS) *n.:* a curved line used in pairs to set off words or phrases, usually comments or explanations, in a sentence.
> *Although the poet uses the word* parenthesis, *the poem does not actually include a parenthesis.*

WORD STUDY

DIRECTIONS: Rewrite each of the following sentences, replacing the italicized word with one of the vocabulary words from above so that the sentence makes sense.

1. Put a *period* before and after the explanation to set it off from the rest of the sentence.

   _____

   _____

2. During the argument, the woman used her hand to *shout* a rude comment.

   _____

   _____

3. That poet's *capitalization* is so boring and predictable; I prefer the complexities of a poet like E. E. Cummings.

   _____

   _____

SINCE FEELING IS FIRST

by E. E. Cummings

> **BACKGROUND**
> E. E. Cummings (1894–1962) liked to used lowercase letters, space his words across the page, and punctuate in his own style. The themes in his poetry are familiar, though—the joy, wonder, and mystery of life and the miracle of individual identity.

 A VOCABULARY

Selection Vocabulary

Syntax means "sentence structure." What is unusual about Cummings's syntax in this poem?

_____

_____

_____

_____

_____

since feeling is first
who pays any attention
to the syntax of things
will never wholly kiss you; **A**

5   wholly to be a fool
while Spring is in the world

© Tel Aviv Museum of Art, Lovers (1929) by Marc Chagall. Oil on Canvas, 55x38, Collection of the Tel Aviv Museum of Art, Gift of Mr. Oscar Fischer, Tel Aviv, c. 1940.

my blood approves,

and kisses are a better fate

than wisdom

10 lady i swear by all flowers. Don't cry

—the best gesture of my brain is less than

your eyelids' flutter which says **B**

we are for each other:then

laugh,leaning back in my arms

15 for life's not a paragraph

And death i think is no parenthesis **C** **D**

B **READING FOCUS**

Analyze word choice in this line. What feelings do you associate with the word *flutter*?

_____

_____

_____

C **LITERARY FOCUS**

Cummings ends his poem with two powerful **metaphors**. What do you think he is trying to say?

_____

_____

_____

D **LANGUAGE COACH**

The plural of *parenthesis* is *parentheses* (PUH REHN THUH SEEZ). Notice that the *-es* at the end of the word is pronounced "eez." The plural form of words that end in *–sis* have a different pronunciation than other plural words that end in *–es* such as *places*, pronounced PLAY SIHZ. What would be the plural form and pronunciation of *crisis*?

_____

_____

since feeling is first

USE A CONCEPT MAP

DIRECTIONS: Use the concept map below to analyze a **metaphor** from "since feeling is first." In the first oval, write the word that is being compared to something else. In the middle oval, write what it is being compared to. In the last oval, write what you think the metaphor means, or what Cummings is trying to say by using the metaphor.

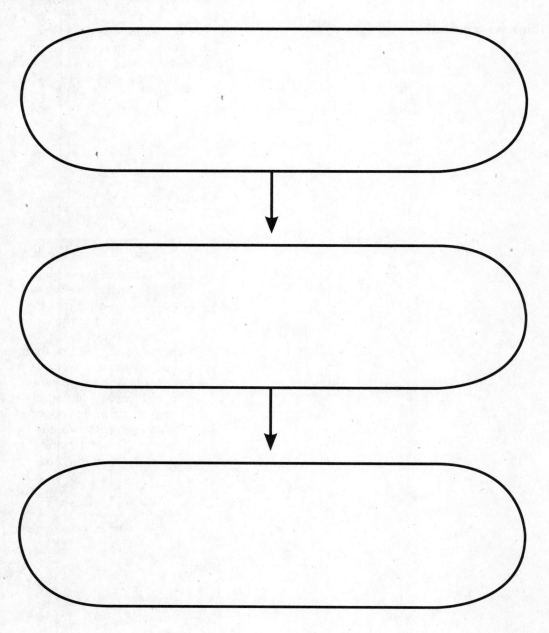

Applying Your Skills

since feeling is first

VOCABULARY DEVELOPMENT

DIRECTIONS: Complete the following sentences with the correct words from the Word Box. One word will be not used.

<table>
<tr><td rowspan="3">

Word Box

syntax

gesture

parenthesis

</td><td>1. I thought the candidate's offer to shake the hand of her competitor was a nice _____ on her part.</td></tr>
<tr><td>2. The teacher was impressed with the level of creativity in the young poet's _____.</td></tr>
</table>

LITERARY FOCUS: METAPHOR

DIRECTIONS: Write two **metaphors** of your own in the chart below. Remember that metaphors are direct comparisons and do not use connecting words such as *as*, *than*, or *like*. In the first column, write your metaphor. In the second column, explain what your metaphor means.

Metaphor	Meaning
1.	
2.	

READING FOCUS: ANALYZING WORD CHOICE

DIRECTIONS: Analyze the list of words taken from the poem "since feeling is first" in the chart below. In the second column, write a synonym for each word (use a thesaurus if you need help). Then explain how the mood of the poem would have been different if it had been written with the synonyms instead.

Words from poem	Synonyms	How mood would change
fool	1.	
wisdom	2.	

SKILLS FOCUS

Literary Skills
Understand metaphors.

Reading Skills
Analyze word choice.

We Real Cool

by Gwendolyn Brooks

LITERARY FOCUS: SOUND EFFECTS

Poets often use sound effects, or the sounds of words, to help them bring their poems to life. Types of sound effects include **alliteration** (the repetition of the same or similar consonant sounds at the beginning of words), rhyme, rhythm, repetition, and **onomatopoeia** (when the sound of the word suggests its meaning, such as *buzz*).

Use the Skill   Look at the list of words and phrases below. In the second column, tell what type of sound effect is being used for each example.

Word or phrase	Type of sound effect
Peter Piper picked a peck of pickled peppers.	1.
thud	2.
A fly landed on my eye!	3.

SKILLS FOCUS

Literary Skills
Understand
sound effects.

Preparing to Read

We Real Cool

READING FOCUS: READING ALOUD

Reading a poem aloud to yourself or to a partner is a great way to hear all of the sound effects. The sounds of the words add to the meaning and enjoyment of a poem.

Use the Skill   As you read "We Real Cool," use the chart below to record the sound effects in the poem. First write the phrase from the poem and then name the sound effect it illustrates.

Phrase	Sound effect
Lurk late	Alliteration

Reading Skills
Read aloud.

WE REAL COOL

The Pool Players Seven at the Golden Shovel

by Gwendolyn Brooks

BACKGROUND

Gwendolyn Brooks (1917–2000) wrote "We Real Cool" after seeing some youths playing pool at a neighborhood pool hall during the school day.

A **LITERARY FOCUS**

What is an example of **alliteration** from the poem?

B **READING FOCUS**

Read the poem aloud. Describe how you read the last two lines.

C **VOCABULARY**

Academic Vocabulary

What mood is *evoked*, or called forth, in this poem?

We real cool. We
Left school. We

Lurk late. We
Strike straight. We
5   Sing sin. We
Thin gin. We
Jazz June. We **A**
Die soon. **B** **C**

© The Granger Collection, NY

"We Real Cool" from *Blacks* by Gwendolyn Brooks. Copyright © 1991 by Gwendolyn Brooks. Published by Third World Press, Chicago, 1991. Reproduced by permission of **Brooks Permissions**.

Applying Your Skills

We Real Cool

LITERARY FOCUS: SOUND EFFECTS

DIRECTIONS: Use the chart below to come up with your own sound effects. In the second column, give one example each of **alliteration**, rhyme, repetition, and **onomatopoeia**.

Sound effect	Example
alliteration	1.
rhyme	2.
repetition	3.
onomatopoeia	4.

READING FOCUS: READING ALOUD

DIRECTIONS: Read "We Real Cool" **aloud** a couple of times and then write a short paragraph explaining how you think the sound effects add to the poem's meaning. What might the sounds of the words tell you about where the pool players live? How does reading aloud help you better understand the poem?

_____

_____

_____

_____

_____

_____

_____

_____

_____

Literary Skills
Understand sound effects.

Reading Skills
Read aloud.

Skills Review

Collection 7

VOCABULARY REVIEW

DIRECTIONS: Review and practice the vocabulary words by filling in the blanks with the correct words from the Word Box. One word will not be used. Then, use the remaining vocabulary word from the Word Box to write a sentence of your own.

Word Box

complement
complexion
evoke
gesture
literal
parenthesis
syntax
temperate
transform

1. Mr. and Mrs. Rose have a great marriage—they _____ each other perfectly.

2. The teacher warned us that the memorial service might _____ sadness and tears.

3. If you are too _____ in your interpretation of a poem, you might miss its beauty.

4. By drinking the potion, the mad scientist could _____ himself into the creature in just a few seconds.

5. The _____ weather conditions allowed us to hike the Grand Canyon without any problems.

6. I hope my _____ clears up before our pictures are taken.

7. The baseball coach made a hand _____ to let the pitcher know what kind of pitch to throw.

8. The teacher marked up my essay because the _____ was incorrect.

9. _____

_____

Skills Review

Collection 7

LANGUAGE COACH

DIRECTIONS: Look at the list of word pairs below. On the blank lines, tell whether the word pairs are synonyms (words with similar meanings) or **antonyms** (words with opposite meanings).

1. ignore, acknowledge _____

2. mourn, grieve _____

3. temperate, severe _____

4. gigantic, miniscule _____

5. arrogant, modest _____

6. believable, credible _____

7. complement, complete _____

8. correct, inaccurate _____

9. bitter, pleasant _____

10. sufficient, enough _____

WRITING ACTIVITY

DIRECTIONS: Select three of the poems you read in this collection and write a brief (two or three sentences) summary for each. Remember that the goal of a summary is to provide the most important points of a piece of writing. First identify the main idea of the poem—the poet's reason for writing it. Then write a few supporting details that support your choice for the main idea. Use examples from the poems. Be sure to consider all aspects of the poem, such as imagery, form, figures of speech, sound effects, rhyme, and word choice.

Elements of Drama

Museo Nazionale del Bargello, Florence,
Italy/Eric Lessing/Art Resource, NY

Literary and Academic Vocabulary Collection 8

highlight (HY LYT) *v.:* to make a subject or idea stand out so people will pay attention.

An antagonist sometimes serves to highlight the good qualities of the protagonist.

predominant (PREE DAHM UH NUHNT) *adj.:* more powerful, common, or noticeable than others.

Blue is the predominant color in the painting.

principal (PRIHN SUH PUHL) *adj.:* most important.

Conflict is the principal element in a tragedy.

criteria (KRY TIHR EE UH) *n.:* rules or standards for making a judgment; test.

Theater reviewers have many criteria about what makes a good play.

tragedy (TRA JUH DEE) *n.:* play, novel, or other narrative that ends unhappily for the main character.

If you're going to see a tragedy, I won't go with you; I can't stand plays with sad endings.

foil (FOYL) *n.:* character used to contrast with another character.

Oscar is a good foil for Felix; Oscar is messy, while Felix is very neat.

The Tragedy of Julius Caesar, Act I, Scene 2 *and* Act III, Scene 2

by William Shakespeare

LITERARY FOCUS: TRAGEDY

Shakespeare tells us in the title of his play that "The Tragedy of Julius Caesar" is a tragedy. A **tragedy** is a play, novel, or other narrative that involves serious and important events and ends unhappily for the main character. Shakespeare's tragedies share these characteristics:

- The main character is often high-ranking and respected, not an ordinary man or woman.

- The main character, the tragic hero, has a **tragic flaw**—a defect in character or judgment that directly causes the character's downfall. Other characters may also have tragic flaws.

- The play ends unhappily, with the deaths of one or more characters, including the main character.

Use the Skill As you read "The Tragedy of Julius Caesar", think about Caesar's personality and try to determine what characteristic causes his downfall. Keep track of Caesar's actions and what they say about his personality on the chart below.

Caesar's actions	Caesar's personality

SKILLS FOCUS

Literary Skills
Understand the characteristics of a tragedy.

Vocabulary Development

The Tragedy of Julius Caesar, Act I, Scene 2 *and* Act III, Scene 2

READING FOCUS: READING A PLAY

Reading one of Shakespeare's plays requires a high level of alertness. You must not only read the lines but also *between* the lines. Use the characters' words and actions to **make inferences,** or educated guesses, about what the characters are really thinking and feeling. For instance, Cassius is usually kind to Caesar, but he secretly hates Caesar. Think about the characters' motives as you work to determine what they are really thinking and saying throughout the play.

Reading a play aloud will also give you a better understanding of the characters' relationships. When you read aloud, think about the tone and volume the characters would be using. You should adjust your delivery (persentation) depending on whether the character is giving a speech to a crowd or whispering a secret to a friend.

Finally, **paraphrasing** (restating information in your own words) can help you comprehend difficult passages. One example of paraphrasing Shakespeare's difficult language is provided below:

Original text	Paraphrase
"Yet if my name were liable to fear, / I do not know the man I should avoid / So soon as that spare Cassius. He reads much, / He is a great observer, and he looks / Quite through the deeds of men." (lines 199–203)	If I feared any men, I would fear Cassius the most. He is intelligent and insightful. He can look through men's actions to determine their true feelings and motives.

SKILLS FOCUS

Reading Skills
Read Shakespeare aloud and paraphrase.

The Tragedy of Julius Caesar, Act I, Scene 2

by William Shakespeare

BACKGROUND

At the time this story takes place, Rome has been a republic, with elected leaders, for 450 years. However, some Romans worry that Julius Caesar, a successful general, is becoming too powerful. Caesar has conquered many lands for the Roman Republic and has gained much popularity with the Roman plebeians, or commoners. Some elected officials want to get rid of Caesar before the plebeians try to make him king. Act I, Scene 2 opens with a ceremonial footrace. Caesar instructs Antony, a strong young man running in the race, to touch his wife, Calphurnia, as he passes. Caesar believes this will cure Calphurnia's sterility, as she not yet been able to bear Caesar a child.

A LANGUAGE COACH

Shakespeare's dialogue is mostly written as poetry and does not always reflect how people spoke during his lifetime. In addition, many of the words he uses are rarely used today. One example of this is *doth,* a word which means "does." How might this sentence be written in modern, nonpoetic English?

_____

_____

_____

ACT I, SCENE 2

Scene 2. *A public place.*

Enter CAESAR, ANTONY (*dressed for the race*), CALPHURNIA, PORTIA, DECIUS, CICERO, BRUTUS, CASSIUS, CASCA, *a* SOOTHSAYER;[1] *after them,* MARULLUS *and* FLAVIUS

Caesar.

1   Calphurnia!

Casca.   Peace, ho! Caesar speaks.

Caesar.   Calphurnia!

Calphurnia. Here, my lord.

Caesar.

       Stand you directly in Antonius' way

       When he doth run his course. **A** Antonius!

5 **Antony.** Caesar, my lord?

---

1. **soothsayer:** a person who foretells the future.

Caesar.

Forget not in your speed, Antonius,

To touch Calphurnia; for our elders say

The barren, touchèd in this holy chase,

Shake off their sterile curse.

Antony.   I shall remember:

10   When Caesar says "Do this," it is performed. **B**

Caesar.

Set on, and leave no ceremony out. **C**

Soothsayer.   Caesar!

Caesar.   Ha! Who calls?

Casca.

Bid every noise be still; peace yet again!

Caesar.

15   Who is it in the press² that calls on me?

I hear a tongue, shriller than all the music,

Cry "Caesar." Speak; Caesar is turned to hear.

Soothsayer.

Beware the ides of March.³

Caesar.   What man is that?

Brutus.

A soothsayer bids you beware the ides of March.

Caesar.

20   Set him before me; let me see his face.

Cassius.

Fellow, come from the throng; look upon Caesar.

Caesar.

What say'st thou to me now? Speak once again.

Soothsayer.

Beware the ides of March.

Caesar.

He is a dreamer, let us leave him. Pass. **D**

[*Sennet.*⁴ *Exeunt all except* BRUTUS *and* CASSIUS.]

---

2. **press:** crowd.
3. **ides** (YDZ) **of March:** March 15.
4. **Sennet** (SEHN IHT): flourish, or fanfare of trumpets announcing a ceremonial entrance or exit.

B (LITERARY ANALYSIS)

What do Antony's words suggest about his character?

_____

_____

_____

C (LANGUAGE COACH)

What do you think "Set on, and leave no ceremony out" means in Shakespeare's language?

_____

_____

D (LITERARY FOCUS)

The Soothsayer warns Caesar about the Ides of March, but Caesar immediately dismisses him. How might this reveal a **tragic flaw**?

_____

_____

_____

_____

_____

_____

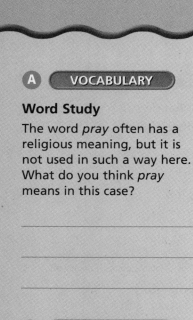

A **VOCABULARY**

Word Study

The word *pray* often has a religious meaning, but it is not used in such a way here. What do you think *pray* means in this case?

_____

_____

_____

B **READING FOCUS**

Paraphrase what Cassius says in lines 32–36.

_____

_____

_____

_____

C **READING FOCUS**

Make inferences about what Brutus is really thinking from his response.

_____

_____

_____

_____

Cassius.

25   Will you go see the order of the course?

Brutus. Not I.

Cassius. I pray you do. **A**

Brutus.

   I am not gamesome: I do lack some part

   Of that quick spirit that is in Antony.

30   Let me not hinder, Cassius, your desires;

   I'll leave you.

Cassius.

   Brutus, I do observe you now of late;

   I have not from your eyes that gentleness

   And show of love as I was wont to have;

35   You bear too stubborn and too strange a hand[5]

   Over your friend that loves you. **B**

Brutus.   Cassius,

   Be not deceived: if I have veiled my look,

   I turn the trouble of my countenance

   Merely[6] upon myself. Vexèd I am

40   Of late with passions of some difference,[7]

   Conceptions only proper to myself,

   Which give some soil,[8] perhaps, to my behaviors;

   But let not therefore my good friends be grieved

   (Among which number, Cassius, be you one)

45   Nor construe[9] any further my neglect

   Than that poor Brutus, with himself at war,

   Forgets the shows of love to other men. **C**

Cassius.

   Then, Brutus, I have much mistook your passion,[10]

   By means whereof this breast of mine hath buried

---

5. **You . . . hand:** Cassius is comparing Brutus's treatment of him to the way a trainer treats a horse.
6. **Merely:** wholly.
7. **passions of some difference:** conflicting feelings or emotions.
8. **give some soil:** stain or mar.
9. **construe** (KUHN STROO): to interpret.
10. **passion:** feeling.

© Suzanne Worthington/Royal Shakespeare Company

50   Thoughts of great value, worthy cogitations.[11]

      Tell me, good Brutus, can you see your face?

Brutus.

      No, Cassius; for the eye sees not itself

      But by reflection, by some other things.

Cassius.

      'Tis just:[12]

55   And it is very much lamented, Brutus,

      That you have no such mirrors as will turn

      Your hidden worthiness into your eye,

      That you might see your shadow.[13] I have heard

      Where many of the best respect[14] in Rome

60   (Except immortal Caesar), speaking of Brutus,

      And groaning underneath this age's yoke,

      Have wished that noble Brutus had his eyes.

Brutus.

      Into what dangers would you lead me, Cassius,

      That you would have me seek into myself

65   For that which is not in me?

---

11. **worthy cogitations** (KOJ UH TAY SHUHNZ): reflections of great value.
12. **just:** true.
13. **shadow:** reflection (of what others think of him).
14. **respect:** reputation.

D **LITERARY ANALYSIS**

What does Brutus mean here?

_____

_____

_____

_____

_____

_____

E **QUICK CHECK**

What is Cassius saying about Brutus here?

_____

_____

_____

_____

_____

_____

_____

_____

F **READING FOCUS**

Read aloud Brutus's response. How would you deliver these lines?

_____

_____

_____

_____

_____

_____

LANGUAGE COACH

Here, Shakespeare uses *glass* to mean "mirror." What does Cassius mean when he says that he will be Brutus's mirror?

_____

_____

_____

_____

_____

_____

_____

_____

_____

B **QUICK CHECK**

What does Brutus suspect the people are cheering about? How does he feel about this?

_____

_____

_____

_____

_____

_____

_____

Cassius.

    Therefore, good Brutus, be prepared to hear;

    And since you know you cannot see yourself

    So well as by reflection, I, your glass[15]

    Will modestly discover to yourself

70   That of yourself which you yet know not of. **A**

    And be not jealous on[16] me, gentle Brutus:

    Were I a common laughter,[17] or did use

    To stale with ordinary oaths my love

    To every new protester,[18] if you know

75   That I do fawn on men and hug them hard,

    And after scandal them;[19] or if you know

    That I profess myself in banqueting

    To all the rout,[20] then hold me dangerous.

[*Flourish*[21] *and shout.*]

Brutus.

    What means this shouting? I do fear the people

    Choose Caesar for their king.

80 **Cassius.**   Ay, do you fear it?

    Then must I think you would not have it so.

Brutus.

    I would not, Cassius, yet I love him well.

    But wherefore do you hold me here so long?

    What is it that you would impart to me?

85   If it be aught toward the general good,

    Set honor in one eye and death i' th' other,

    And I will look on both indifferently;[22]

    For let the gods so speed me, as I love

    The name of honor more than I fear death. **B**

---

15. **glass:** mirror.
16. **jealous on:** suspicious of.
17. **common laughter:** butt of a joke; object of mockery.
18. **To stale . . . new protestor:** In other words, if he swore to love everyone who came along.
19. **scandal them:** ruin them by gossip.
20. **rout** (ROWT): common people, the mob.
21. **flourish** (FLUR IHSH): brief, elaborate music of trumpets.
22. **indifferently:** impartially; fairly.

Cassius.

90 I know that virtue to be in you, Brutus,

As well as I do know your outward favor.[23]

Well, honor is the subject of my story.

I cannot tell what you and other men

Think of this life, but for my single self,

95 I had as lief[24] not be, as live to be

In awe of such a thing as I myself.

I was born free as Caesar; so were you:

We both have fed as well, and we can both

Endure the winter's cold as well as he: **C**

100 For once, upon a raw and gusty day,

The troubled Tiber chafing with[25] her shores,

Caesar said to me "Dar'st thou, Cassius, now

Leap in with me into this angry flood,

And swim to yonder point?" Upon the word,

105 Accout'red as I was, I plungèd in

And bade him follow: so indeed he did.

The torrent roared, and we did buffet it

With lusty sinews, throwing it aside

And stemming it with hearts of controversy.[26]

110 But ere we could arrive the point proposed,

Caesar cried "Help me, Cassius, or I sink!"

I, as Aeneas,[27] our great ancestor,

Did from the flames of Troy upon his shoulder

The old Anchises bear, so from the waves of Tiber

115 Did I the tired Caesar. **D** **E** And this man

Is now become a god, and Cassius is

---

23. **outward favor:** appearance.
24. **as lief** (LEEF): just as soon.
25. **chafing** (CHAYF IHNG): with raging against (the river was rough with waves and currents).
26. **hearts of controversy** (KAHN TRUH VUHR SEE): hearts full of aggressive feelings, or fighting spirit.
27. **Aeneas** (IH NEE UHS): legendary forefather of the Roman people who, in Virgil's *Aeneid*, fled from the burning city of Troy carrying his old father on his back. (In many accounts of the legend, Romulus and Remus were descendants of Aeneas.)

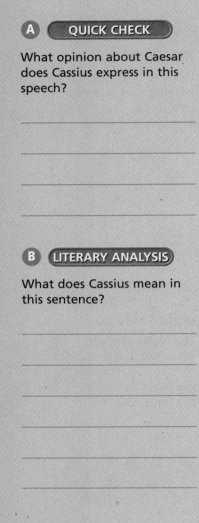

A QUICK CHECK

What opinion about Caesar does Cassius express in this speech?

_____

_____

_____

_____

B LITERARY ANALYSIS

What does Cassius mean in this sentence?

_____

_____

_____

_____

_____

_____

_____

A wretched creature, and must bend his body

If Caesar carelessly but nod on him.

He had a fever when he was in Spain,

120   And when the fit was on him, I did mark

How he did shake; 'tis true, this god did shake.

His coward lips did from their color fly,

And that same eye whose bend doth awe the world

Did lose his luster; I did hear him groan;

125   Ay, and that tongue of his, that bade the Romans

Mark him and write his speeches in their books,

Alas, it cried, "Give me some drink, Titinius,"

As a sick girl. Ye gods! It doth amaze me,

A man of such a feeble temper should

130   So get the start of the majestic world,

And bear the palm[28] alone. **A**

[_Shout. Flourish._]

Brutus.

Another general shout?

I do believe that these applauses are

For some new honors that are heaped on Caesar.

Cassius.

135   Why, man, he doth bestride the narrow world

Like a Colossus,[29] and we petty men

Walk under his huge legs and peep about

To find ourselves dishonorable graves.

Men at some time are masters of their fates:

140   The fault, dear Brutus, is not in our stars,[30]

But in ourselves, that we are underlings. **B**

Brutus and Caesar: what should be in that "Caesar"?

Why should that name be sounded more than yours?

---

28. **bear the palm:** hold the palm branch, an award given to a victorious general.

29. **Colossus** (KUH LAHS UHS): huge statue of Helios that was said to straddle the entrance to the harbor at Rhodes, an island in the Aegean Sea. The statue, so huge that ships passed under its legs, was one of the Seven Wonders of the Ancient World. It was destroyed by an earthquake in 224 B.C.

30. **stars:** Elizabethans believed that one's life was governed by the stars or constellation one was born under.

145   Write them together, yours is as fair a name;

Sound them, it doth become the mouth as well;

Weigh them, it is as heavy; conjure with 'em,

"Brutus" will start a spirit as soon as "Caesar."

Now, in the names of all the gods at once,

Upon what meat doth this our Caesar feed,

150   That he is grown so great? Age, thou art shamed!

Rome, thou hast lost the breed of noble bloods! **C**

When went there by an age, since the great flood,[31]

But it was famed with more than with one man?

When could they say (till now) that talked of Rome,

155   That her wide walks encompassed but one man?

Now is it Rome indeed, and room[32] enough,

When there is in it but one only man.

O, you and I have heard our fathers say,

There was a Brutus once that would have brooked[33]

160   Th' eternal devil to keep his state in Rome

As easily as a king.[34] **D**

Brutus.

That you do love me, I am nothing jealous;

What you would work me to, I have some aim;[35]

How I have thought of this, and of these times,

165   I shall recount hereafter. For this present,

I would not so (with love I might entreat you)

Be any further moved. What you have said

I will consider; what you have to say

I will with patience hear, and find a time

170   Both meet[36] to hear and answer such high things.

C **READING FOCUS**

Read aloud lines 142–151. How would you deliver these lines?

_____

_____

_____

_____

_____

D **LITERARY FOCUS**

You already know that this play is a **tragedy**. What do you think will cause a tragic ending for Caesar?

_____

_____

_____

_____

_____

_____

---

31. the great flood: according to Greek myth, the flood sent by Zeus to drown all the wicked people on Earth. Only the faithful couple Deucalion and Pyrrha were saved.

32. Rome . . . room: a pun; both words were pronounced room in Shakespeare's day.

33. brooked: put up with.

34. Th' eternal . . . king: This refers to the ancestor of Brutus who, in the sixth century B.C., helped to expel the last king from Rome and set up the Republic.

35. aim: idea.

36. meet: appropriate.

Word Study

The verb *repute* is related to the noun *reputation*, which is the way others view a person. Knowing this, what do you think *repute* means, and what does Brutus mean in this sentence?

_____

_____

_____

_____

_____

_____

_____

_____

B **LITERARY ANALYSIS**

How does Cassius feel about Caesar? Has he changed Brutus's opinion of Caesar?

_____

_____

_____

_____

_____

_____

_____

Till then, my noble friend, chew upon this:

Brutus had rather be a villager

Than to repute himself a son of Rome

Under these hard conditions as this time

Is like to lay upon us. A

175 **Cassius.** I am glad

That my weak words have struck but thus much show

Of fire from Brutus. B

[*Enter* CAESAR *and his* TRAIN.]

Brutus.

The games are done, and Caesar is returning.

Cassius.

As they pass by, pluck Casca by the sleeve,

180 And he will (after his sour fashion) tell you

What hath proceeded worthy note today.

Brutus.

I will do so. But look you, Cassius,

The angry spot doth glow on Caesar's brow,

And all the rest look like a chidden[37] train:

185 Calphurnia's cheek is pale, and Cicero

Looks with such ferret[38] and such fiery eyes

As we have seen him in the Capitol,

Being crossed in conference by some senators.

Cassius.

Casca will tell us what the matter is.

190 **Caesar.** Antonius.

Antony. Caesar?

Caesar.

Let me have men about me that are fat,

Sleek-headed men, and such as sleep a-nights.

Yond Cassius has a lean and hungry look;

195 He thinks too much: such men are dangerous.

Antony.

Fear him not, Caesar, he's not dangerous;

---

37. **chidden** (CHIHD UHN): rebuked; corrected.
38. **ferret:** weasel-like animal, usually considered crafty.

He is a noble Roman, and well given.[39]

Caesar.

Would he were fatter! But I fear him not.

Yet if my name were liable to fear,

200　I do not know the man I should avoid

So soon as that spare Cassius. **C** He reads much,

He is a great observer, and he looks

Quite through the deeds of men.[40] He loves no plays,

As thou dost, Antony; he hears no music;

205　Seldom he smiles, and smiles in such a sort[41]

As if he mocked himself, and scorned his spirit

That could be moved to smile at anything.

Such men as he be never at heart's ease

Whiles they behold a greater than themselves,

210　And therefore are they very dangerous.

I rather tell thee what is to be feared

Than what I fear; for always I am Caesar.

Come on my right hand, for this ear is deaf,

And tell me truly what thou think'st of him.

[*Sennet. Exeunt* CAESAR *and his* TRAIN.]

Casca.

215　You pulled me by the cloak; would you speak with me?

Brutus.

Ay, Casca; tell us what hath chanced today, **D**

That Caesar looks so sad.[42]

Casca.

Why, you were with him, were you not?

Brutus.

I should not then ask Casca what had chanced.

220　**Casca.** Why, there was a crown offered him; and being

offered him, he put it by[43] with the back of his hand,

thus; and then the people fell a-shouting.

---

39. well given: inclined to support Caesar.

40. he looks . . . of men: In other words, he looks through what men do to search out their feelings and motives.

41. sort: way; manner.

42. sad: serious.

43. put it by: pushed it aside.

C (**LITERARY FOCUS**)

Caesar says he is suspicious of Cassius but that he is not "liable to fear." How does this connect to Caesar's **tragic flaw**?

_____

_____

_____

_____

_____

_____

_____

_____

_____

_____

D (**LANGUAGE COACH**)

In Shakespeare's language, Brutus says, "tell us what hath chanced today." Translate this line to modern English.

_____

_____

_____

_____

_____

_____

Brutus. What was the second noise for?

Casca. Why, for that too.

Cassius.

225   They shouted thrice; what was the last cry for?

Casca. Why, for that too.

Brutus. Was the crown offered him thrice?

Casca. Ay, marry,[44] was't, and he put it by thrice, every
        time gentler than other; and at every putting-by mine
230   honest neighbors shouted. **A**

Cassius.

        Who offered him the crown?

Casca. Why, Antony.

Brutus.

        Tell us the manner of it, gentle Casca.

Casca. I can as well be hanged as tell the manner of it:
235   it was mere foolery; I did not mark it. I saw Mark
        Antony offer him a crown—yet 'twas not a crown
        neither, 'twas one of these coronets[45]—and, as I told
        you, he put it by once; but for all that, to my thinking,
        he would fain[46] have had it. Then he offered it to him
240   again; then he put it by again; but to my thinking, he
        was very loath to lay his fingers off it. And then he
        offered it the third time. He put it the third time by;
        and still as he refused it, the rabblement hooted, and
        clapped their chopt[47] hands, and threw up their
245   sweaty nightcaps,[48] and uttered such a deal of
        stinking breath because Caesar refused the crown,
        that it had, almost, choked Caesar; for he swounded[49]
        and fell down at it. **B** And for mine own part, I durst not
        laugh, for fear of opening my lips and receiving the
250   bad air.

---

44. **marry:** a mild oath meaning "by the Virgin Mary."
45. **coronets** (KAWR uh NEHTZ): small crowns.
46. **fain** (FAYN): happily.
47. **chopt:** chapped (raw and rough from hard work and the weather).
48. **nightcaps:** Casca is mockingly referring to the hats of the workingmen.
49. **swounded** (SWOON dihd): swooned or fainted.

© Donald Cooper/Royal Shakespeare Company/Photostage

C **READING FOCUS**

What **inferences** can you make about Cassius from what he says here? Does he mean exactly what he says?

_____

_____

_____

_____

_____

_____

_____

_____

Cassius.

But, soft,[50] I pray you; what, did Caesar swound?

Casca. He fell down in the market place, and foamed

at mouth, and was speechless.

Brutus.

'Tis very like he hath the falling-sickness.[51]

Cassius.

255   No, Caesar hath it not; but you, and I,

And honest Casca, we have the falling-sickness. **C**

Casca. I know not what you mean by that, but I am

sure Caesar fell down. If the tag-rag people[52] did not

clap him and hiss him, according as he pleased and

260   displeased them, as they use to do the players in the

theater, I am no true man.

Brutus.

What said he when he came unto himself?

---

50. **soft:** wait a minute.
51. **falling-sickness:** old term for the disease we now call epilepsy, which
    is marked by seizures and momentary loss of consciousness.
52. **tag-rag people:** contemptuous, or scornful, reference to the
    commoners in the crowd.

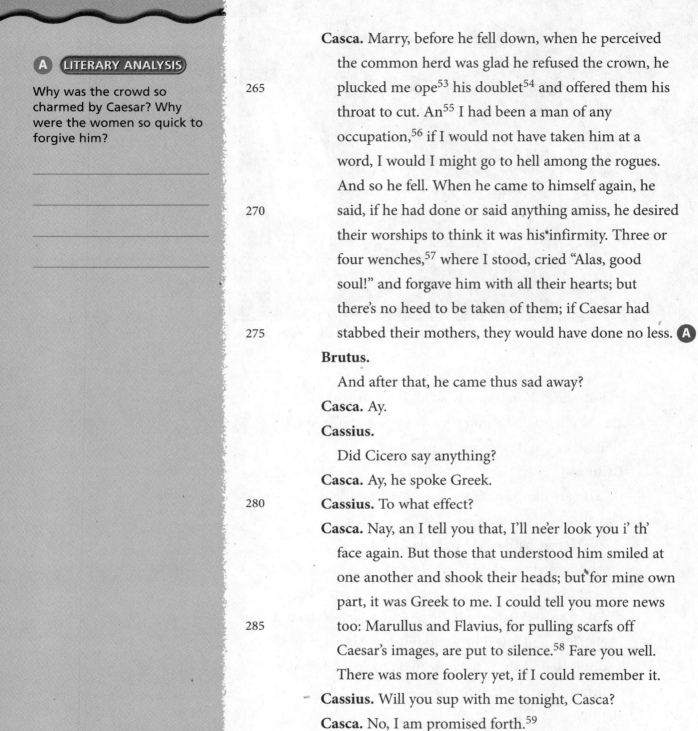

Why was the crowd so charmed by Caesar? Why were the women so quick to forgive him?

_____

_____

_____

_____

265

Casca. Marry, before he fell down, when he perceived the common herd was glad he refused the crown, he plucked me ope[53] his doublet[54] and offered them his throat to cut. An[55] I had been a man of any occupation,[56] if I would not have taken him at a word, I would I might go to hell among the rogues. And so he fell. When he came to himself again, he

270

said, if he had done or said anything amiss, he desired their worships to think it was his infirmity. Three or four wenches,[57] where I stood, cried "Alas, good soul!" and forgave him with all their hearts; but there's no heed to be taken of them; if Caesar had

275

stabbed their mothers, they would have done no less. **A**

Brutus.

And after that, he came thus sad away?

Casca. Ay.

Cassius.

Did Cicero say anything?

Casca. Ay, he spoke Greek.

280

Cassius. To what effect?

Casca. Nay, an I tell you that, I'll ne'er look you i' th' face again. But those that understood him smiled at one another and shook their heads; but for mine own part, it was Greek to me. I could tell you more news

285

too: Marullus and Flavius, for pulling scarfs off Caesar's images, are put to silence.[58] Fare you well. There was more foolery yet, if I could remember it.

Cassius. Will you sup with me tonight, Casca?

Casca. No, I am promised forth.[59]

290

Cassius. Will you dine with me tomorrow?

---

53. **plucked me ope:** plucked open.
54. **doublet:** close-fitting jacket.
55. **An:** if.
56. **man of any occupation:** working man.
57. **wenches:** girls or young women.
58. **put to silence:** silenced, perhaps being dismissed from their positions as tribunes or by being exiled.
59. **forth:** previously (he has other plans).

Casca. Ay, if I be alive, and your mind hold, and your
dinner worth the eating.

Cassius. Good; I will expect you.

Casca. Do so. Farewell, both.   [*Exit.*]

Brutus.

295   What a blunt fellow is this grown to be!

            He was quick mettle[60] when he went to school.

Cassius.

            So is he now in execution

            Of any bold or noble enterprise,

            However he puts on this tardy form.[61] **B**

300   This rudeness[62] is a sauce to his good wit,[63]

            Which gives men stomach to disgest[64] his words

            With better appetite.

Brutus.

            And so it is. For this time I will leave you.

            Tomorrow, if you please to speak with me,

305   I will come home to you; or if you will,

            Come home to me, and I will wait for you.

Cassius.

            I will do so. Till then, think of the world.[65]

                                    [*Exit* BRUTUS.]

            Well, Brutus, thou art noble; yet I see

            Thy honorable mettle may be wrought

310   From that it is disposed;[66] therefore it is meet

            That noble minds keep ever with their likes;

            For who so firm that cannot be seduced? **C**

            Caesar doth bear me hard,[67] but he loves Brutus.

            If I were Brutus now and he were Cassius,

---

60. **quick mettle:** lively of disposition.
61. **tardy form:** sluggish appearance.
62. **rudeness:** rough manner.
63. **wit:** intelligence.
64. **disgest:** to digest.
65. **the world:** the state of affairs in Rome.
66. **Thy honorable . . . disposed:** In other words, he may be persuaded against his better nature to join the conspirators.
67. **bear me hard:** has a grudge (hard feelings) against me.

B QUICK CHECK

What do Brutus and Cassius say about Casca in lines 295–299?

_____

_____

_____

C QUICK CHECK

In lines 308–312, what does Cassius say about Brutus?

_____

_____

_____

_____

_____

_____

_____

315 He should not humor[68] me. I will this night,

In several hands,[69] in at his windows throw,

As if they came from several citizens,

Writings, all tending to the great opinion

That Rome holds of his name; wherein obscurely

320 Caesar's ambition shall be glancèd at.[70]

And after this, let Caesar seat him sure;[71]

For we will shake him, or worse days endure. A   [*Exit.*]

WHAT HAPPENS NEXT In the final scene of Act One, Cicero and Casca meet on a stormy night. Casca tells Cicero of supernatural events. When Cicero leaves, Cassius arrives. He interprets the strange events as divine warnings that Caesar will destroy the Republic. Cassius wants Casca to help him oppose Caesar. When Cinna agrees to the plot, Cassius urges him to persuade Brutus to join them. The three conspirators—Casca, Cassius, and Cinna—agree to meet with other men to advance their cause.

In Act Two, Brutus decides Caesar should be killed. Though he is a close personal friend of Caesar, he feels the Roman people will be treated very badly as Caesar's power grows. The conspirators—Cassius, Casca, Cinna, now joined by Decius, Metellus Cimber, and Trebonius—meet with Brutus and agree to exclude Cicero from the conspiracy. Cassius argues that Mark Antony should be killed along with Caesar. Brutus reasons that this is unnecessary.

Bad omens continue to warn of coming danger. Caesar's wife and close advisors feel he will put himself at risk by attending that morning's senate session. But Decius, one of the conspirators, finally convinces Caesar not to stay home. Caesar decides to go to the Capitol.

At the beginning of Act Three, a man hands Caesar a note warning of the plot against him, but he refuses to read

---

68. **humor:** to influence by flattery.
69. **hands:** varieties of handwriting.
70. **glancèd at:** touched on.
71. **seat him sure:** make his position secure.

it. Caesar enters the Capitol. Trebonious takes Antony aside so he will not interfere. The conspirators surround Caesar and suddenly, from behind, Casca stabs him. Caesar falls and dies. Antony flees, and then comes back to pay tribute to his fallen friend. Antony pretends to make peace with the murderers and asks to speak at Caesar's funeral. In private, Antony speaks to Caesar's corpse, asking forgiveness for having been gentle with his killers. A servant enters and announces that Octavius Caesar, Caesar's adopted son and heir, is coming to Rome. The servant and Antony exit, carrying Caesar's body.

ACT III, SCENE 2

Scene 2. *The Forum*

Enter BRUTUS *and goes into the pulpit, and* CASSIUS, *with the* PLEBEIANS.[72]

Plebeians.

We will be satisfied! Let us be satisfied!

Brutus.

Then follow me, and give me audience, friends.

325 Cassius, go you into the other street

And part the numbers.

Those that will hear me speak, let 'em stay here;

Those that will follow Cassius, go with him;

And public reasons shall be renderèd

330 Of Caesar's death. **B**

First Plebeian.   I will hear Brutus speak.

Second Plebeian.

I will hear Cassius, and compare their reasons,

When severally we hear them renderèd. **C**

                        [*Exit* CASSIUS, *with some of the* PLEBEIANS.]

Third Plebeian.

The noble Brutus is ascended. Silence!

Brutus. Be patient till the last.

335 Romans, countrymen, and lovers, hear me for my cause,

and be silent, that you may hear. Believe me for mine

---

72. **plebeians:** the common people.

C LANGUAGE COACH

Shakespeare often adds accent marks to words in order to emphasize, or stress, syllables that are normally unstressed or not fully pronounced. Here, *rendered* (REHN DUHRD) has an accent mark that charges the pronunciation to (REHN DUHR EHD). Why do you think Shakespeare does this?

A READING FOCUS

How would you deliver the opening lines of this speech if you were **reading it aloud**?

_____

_____

_____

_____

_____

_____

_____

B LITERARY ANALYSIS

What reason does Brutus give for killing Caesar? Does this seem ironic? Why?

_____

_____

_____

_____

_____

_____

_____

_____

_____

honor, and have respect to mine honor, that you may believe. Censure[73] me in your wisdom, and awake your senses,[74] that you may the better judge. **A** If there be any

340   in this assembly, any dear friend of Caesar's, to him I say that Brutus' love to Caesar was no less than his. If then that friend demand why Brutus rose against Caesar, this is my answer: Not that I loved Caesar less, but that I loved Rome more. **B** Had you rather Caesar were living,

345   and die all slaves, than that Caesar were dead, to live all free men? As Caesar loved me, I weep for him; as he was fortunate, I rejoice at it; as he was valiant, I honor him; but, as he was ambitious, I slew him. There is tears, for his love; joy, for his fortune; honor, for his valor; and

350   death, for his ambition. Who is here so base, that would be a bondman?[75] If any, speak; for him have I offended. Who is here so rude,[76] that would not be a Roman? If any, speak; for him have I offended. Who is here so vile, that will not love his country? If any, speak; for him have I

355   offended. I pause for a reply.

All. None, Brutus, none!

Brutus. Then none have I offended. I have done no more to Caesar than you shall do to Brutus. The question of his death is enrolled[77] in the Capitol; his glory not extenuated,[78]

360   wherein he was worthy, nor his offenses enforced,[79] for which he suffered death.

[*Enter* MARK ANTONY, *with* CAESAR's *body.*]

Here comes his body, mourned by Mark Antony, who, though he had no hand in his death, shall receive the benefit of his dying, a place in the commonwealth, as

---

73. **censure:** judge.
74. **senses:** reasoning powers.
75. **bondman:** slave.
76. **rude:** rough and uncivilized.
77. In other words, there is a record of the reasons he was killed.
78. **extenuated:** lessened.
79. **enforced:** exaggerated.

365   which of you shall not? With this I depart, that, as I
           slew my best lover for the good of Rome, I have the
           same dagger for myself, when it shall please my
           country to need my death.

All.   Live, Brutus! Live, live!

First Plebeian.

           Bring him with triumph home unto his house.

Second Plebeian.

370   Give him a statue with his ancestors.

Third Plebeian.

           Let him be Caesar.

Fourth Plebeian.   Caesar's better parts[80]

           Shall be crowned in Brutus.

First Plebeian.

           We'll bring him to his house with shouts and clamors. **C**

Brutus. My countrymen—

375 **Second Plebeian.**   Peace! Silence! Brutus speaks.

First Plebeian.   Peace, ho!

Brutus.

           Good countrymen, let me depart alone,

           And, for my sake, stay here with Antony.

           Do grace to Caesar's corpse, and grace his speech[81]

380   Tending to Caesar's glories, which Mark Antony

           By our permission, is allowed to make.

           I do entreat you, not a man depart,

           Save I alone, till Antony have spoke.   [*Exit.*] **D**

First Plebeian.

           Stay, ho! And let us hear Mark Antony.

Third Plebeian.

385   Let him go up into the public chair;[82]

           We'll hear him. Noble Antony, go up.

Antony.

           For Brutus' sake, I am beholding to you.

---

80. **better parts:** better qualities.
81. **grace his speech:** listen respectfully to Antony's funeral oration.
82. **public chair:** pulpit or rostrum.

C   **QUICK CHECK**

How does the crowd react to Brutus's speech?

_____

_____

_____

_____

D   **LITERARY FOCUS**

Although Caesar is dead, "The Tragedy of Julius Caesar" is still a **tragedy** for the other characters. What might still happen that makes this play end unhappily? Explain.

_____

_____

_____

_____

_____

_____

_____

_____

_____

_____

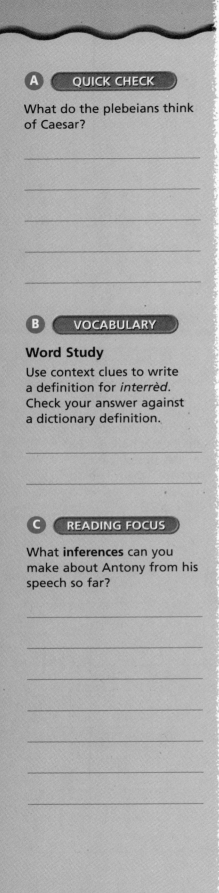

Fourth Plebeian.

> What does he say of Brutus?

Third Plebeian.   He says, for Brutus' sake,

> He finds himself beholding to us all.

Fourth Plebeian.

390   'Twere best he speak no harm of Brutus here!

First Plebeian.

> This Caesar was a tyrant.

Third Plebeian.   Nay, that's certain.

> We are blest that Rome is rid of him. **A**

Second Plebeian.

> Peace! Let us hear what Antony can say.

Antony.

> You gentle Romans—

All.   Peace, ho! Let us hear him.

Antony.

395   Friends, Romans, countrymen, lend me your ears;

> I come to bury Caesar, not to praise him.

> The evil that men do lives after them,

> The good is oft interrèd with their bones;

> So let it be with Caesar. **B** The noble Brutus

400   Hath told you Caesar was ambitious.

> If it were so, it was a grievous fault,

> And grievously hath Caesar answered[83] it.

> Here, under leave of Brutus and the rest

> (For Brutus is an honorable man,

405   So are they all, all honorable men),

> Come I to speak in Caesar's funeral.

> He was my friend, faithful and just to me;

> But Brutus says he was ambitious,

> And Brutus is an honorable man. **C**

410   He hath brought many captives home to Rome,

> Whose ransoms did the general coffers[84] fill;

> Did this in Caesar seem ambitious?

---

83. **answered:** paid the penalty for.
84. **general coffers:** public funds.

When that the poor have cried, Caesar hath wept;

Ambition should be made of sterner stuff.

415   Yet Brutus says he was ambitious;

And Brutus is an honorable man.

You all did see that on the Lupercal

I thrice presented him a kingly crown,

Which he did thrice refuse. Was this ambition?

420   Yet Brutus says he was ambitious;

And sure he is an honorable man.

I speak not to disprove what Brutus spoke,

But here I am to speak what I do know.

You all did love him once, not without cause;

425   What cause withholds you then to mourn for him?

O judgment, thou art fled to brutish beasts,

And men have lost their reason! Bear with me;

My heart is in the coffin there with Caesar,

And I must pause till it come back to me. **D**

First Plebeian.

430   Methinks there is much reason in his sayings.

Second Plebeian.

If thou consider rightly of the matter,

Caesar has had great wrong.

Third Plebeian. Has he, masters?

I fear there will a worse come in his place.

Fourth Plebeian.

Marked ye his words? He would not take the crown,

435   Therefore 'tis certain he was not ambitious.

First Plebeian.

If it be found so, some will dear abide it.⁸⁵ **E**

Second Plebeian.

Poor soul, his eyes are red as fire with weeping.

Third Plebeian.

There's not a nobler man in Rome than Antony.

Fourth Plebeian.

Now mark him, he begins again to speak.

---

85. **dear abide it:** pay dearly for it.

D LITERARY ANALYSIS

Underline instances in which Antony repeatedly calls Brutus an "honorable man." What effect does this repetition have?

_____

_____

_____

_____

_____

_____

E LITERARY FOCUS

Based on this line and other responses from the plebeians, do you think **tragedy** will continue to plague the play's main characters?

_____

_____

_____

_____

Antony.

440   But yesterday the word of Caesar might

    Have stood against the world; now lies he there,

    And none so poor to[86] do him reverence.

    O masters! If I were disposed to stir

    Your hearts and minds to mutiny and rage,

445   I should do Brutus wrong and Cassius wrong,

    Who, you all know, are honorable men.

    I will not do them wrong; I rather choose

    To wrong the dead, to wrong myself and you,

    Than I will wrong such honorable men. **A**

450   But here's a parchment with the seal of Caesar;

    I found it in his closet; 'tis his will.

    Let but the commons hear this testament,

    Which, pardon me, I do not mean to read,

    And they would go and kiss dead Caesar's wounds,

455   And dip their napkins[87] in his sacred blood;

    Yea, beg a hair of him for memory,

    And dying, mention it within their wills,

    Bequeathing it as a rich legacy

    Unto their issue.[88]

Fourth Plebeian.

460   We'll hear the will; read it, Mark Antony.

All. The will, the will! We will hear Caesar's will!

Antony.

    Have patience, gentle friends, I must not read it.

    It is not meet you know how Caesar loved you. **B**

    You are not wood, you are not stones, but men;

465   And being men, hearing the will of Caesar,

    It will inflame you, it will make you mad.

    'Tis good you know not that you are his heirs;

    For if you should, O, what would come of it?

---

86. **so poor to:** so low in rank as to.
87. **napkins:** handkerchiefs.
88. **issue:** children; heirs.

© Royal Shakespeare Company/Lebrecht Music Collection

C READING FOCUS

How does Antony convince the crowd that he should read Caesar's will? What can you **infer** about Antony's personality from this?

_____

_____

_____

_____

_____

_____

Fourth Plebeian.

> Read the will! We'll hear it, Antony!

470 > You shall read us the will, Caesar's will!

Antony.

> Will you be patient? Will you stay awhile?
>
> I have o'ershot myself[89] to tell you of it.
>
> I fear I wrong the honorable men
>
> Whose daggers have stabbed Caesar; I do fear it.

Fourth Plebeian.

475 > They were traitors. Honorable men!

All. The will! The testament!

Second Plebeian. They were villains, murderers! The
> will! Read the will!

Antony.

> You will compel me then to read the will?

480 > Then make a ring about the corpse of Caesar,
>
> And let me show you him that made the will.
>
> Shall I descend? And will you give me leave?

All. Come down.

Second Plebeian. Descend.

> [ANTONY _comes down._]

---

89. o'ershot myself: gone farther than I intended.

The Tragedy of Julius Caesar, Act III, Scene 2   **351**

A **READING FOCUS**

How would you deliver Antony's speech so far if you were **reading the play aloud**?

_____

_____

_____

_____

_____

_____

B **READING FOCUS**

Paraphrase lines 512–513.

_____

_____

_____

_____

_____

_____

_____

_____

Third Plebeian. You shall have leave.

485 **Fourth Plebeian.** A ring! Stand round.

First Plebeian.

    Stand from the hearse, stand from the body!

Second Plebeian.

    Room for Antony, most noble Antony!

Antony.

    Nay, press not so upon me; stand far off.

All. Stand back! Room! Bear back.

Antony.

490   If you have tears, prepare to shed them now.

    You all do know this mantle; I remember

    The first time ever Caesar put it on:

    'Twas on a summer's evening, in his tent,

    That day he overcame the Nervii.[90]

495   Look, in this place ran Cassius' dagger through;

    See what a rent the envious[91] Casca made;

    Through this the well-belovèd Brutus stabbed,

    And as he plucked his cursèd steel away,

    Mark how the blood of Caesar followed it,

500   As rushing out of doors, to be resolved

    If Brutus so unkindly knocked, or no;

    For Brutus, as you know, was Caesar's angel. **A**

    Judge, O you gods, how dearly Caesar loved him!

    This was the most unkindest cut of all;

505   For when the noble Caesar saw him stab,

    Ingratitude, more strong than traitors' arms,

    Quite vanquished him. Then burst his mighty heart;

    And, in his mantle muffling up his face,

    Even at the base of Pompey's statue[92]

510   (Which all the while ran blood) great Caesar fell.

    O, what a fall was there, my countrymen!

    Then I, and you, and all of us fell down,

    Whilst bloody treason flourished over us. **B**

90. **Nervii:** one of the tribes conquered by Caesar, in 57 B.C.
91. **envious** (EHN VEE UHS): spiteful.
92. **statue:** pronounced in three syllables for meter's sake.

O, now you weep, and I perceive you feel

515   The dint[93] of pity; these are gracious drops.

Kind souls, what weep you when you but behold

Our Caesar's vesture[94] wounded? Look you here,

Here is himself, marred as you see with traitors.

First Plebeian. O piteous spectacle!

520   **Second Plebeian.** O noble Caesar!

Third Plebeian. O woeful day!

Fourth Plebeian. O traitors, villains!

First Plebeian. O most bloody sight!

Second Plebeian. We will be revenged.

525   **All.** Revenge! About! Seek! Burn! Fire! Kill! Slay! Let

not a traitor live! **C**

Antony. Stay, countrymen.

First Plebeian. Peace there! Hear the noble Antony.

Second Plebeian. We'll hear him, we'll follow him,

530   we'll die with him!

Antony.

Good friends, sweet friends, let me not stir you up

To such a sudden flood of mutiny.

They that have done this deed are honorable.

What private griefs[95] they have, alas, I know not,

535   That made them do it. They are wise and honorable,

And will, no doubt, with reasons answer you.

I come not, friends, to steal away your hearts;

I am no orator, as Brutus is;

But (as you know me all) a plain blunt man

540   That love my friend, and that they know full well

That gave me public leave to speak of him.

For I have neither writ, nor words, nor worth,

Action, nor utterance, nor the power of speech

To stir men's blood; I only speak right on.

545   I tell you that which you yourselves do know,

---

93. **dint:** stroke.
94. **vesture:** clothing.
95. **griefs:** grievances.

Copyright © by Holt, Rinehart and Winston. All rights reserved.

C **LITERARY FOCUS**

Some people think the moment when the mob turns on the assassins is the **tragedy's** turning point. Why might this be the turning point?

_____

_____

_____

_____

_____

_____

_____

_____

Show you sweet Caesar's wounds, poor poor dumb mouths, A

And bid them speak for me. But were I Brutus,

And Brutus Antony, there were an Antony

Would ruffle up your spirits, and put a tongue

550 In every wound of Caesar that would move

The stones of Rome to rise and mutiny. B

All.

We'll mutiny.

First Plebeian. We'll burn the house of Brutus.

Third Plebeian.

Away, then! Come, seek the conspirators.

Antony.

Yet hear me, countrymen. Yet hear me speak.

All.

555 Peace, ho! Hear Antony, most noble Antony!

Antony.

Why, friends, you go to do you know not what:

Wherein hath Caesar thus deserved your loves?

Alas, you know not; I must tell you then:

You have forgot the will I told you of. C

All.

560 Most true, the will! Let's stay and hear the will.

Antony.

Here is the will, and under Caesar's seal.

To every Roman citizen he gives,

To every several[96] man, seventy-five drachmas.[97]

Second Plebeian.

Most noble Caesar! We'll revenge his death!

565 **Third Plebeian.** O royal Caesar!

Antony. Hear me with patience.

All. Peace, ho!

---

96. **several:** individual.
97. **drachmas** (DRAK muhz): silver coins (Greek currency).

Antony.

    Moreover, he hath left you all his walks,

    His private arbors, and new-planted orchards,

570   On this side Tiber; he hath left them you,

    And to your heirs forever: common pleasures,[98]

    To walk abroad and recreate yourselves.

    Here was a Caesar! When comes such another?

First Plebeian.

    Never, never! Come, away, away!

575   We'll burn his body in the holy place,

    And with the brands fire the traitors' houses.

    Take up the body.

Second Plebeian. Go fetch fire.

Third Plebeian. Pluck down benches.

580 **Fourth Plebeian.** Pluck down forms, windows,[99]

    anything!

[*Exeunt* PLEBEIANS *with the body.*]

Antony.

    Now let it work: Mischief, thou art afoot,

    Take thou what course thou wilt.

[*Enter* SERVANT.]

How now, fellow?

Servant.

    Sir, Octavius is already come to Rome.

Antony. Where is he?

Servant.

585   He and Lepidus are at Caesar's house.

Antony.

    And thither will I straight to visit him;

    He comes upon a wish. Fortune is merry,

    And in this mood will give us anything. **D**

Servant.

    I heard him say, Brutus and Cassius

D (LANGUAGE COACH)

In his writings, Shakespeare often uses personification, or the assignment of human qualities to nonhuman objects or ideas. What is Antony personifying in these lines?

---

98. **common pleasures:** public recreation areas.
99. **forms, windows:** long benches and shutters.

590 Are rid[100] like madmen through the gates of Rome.

Antony.

Belike[101] they had some notice of the people,

How I had moved them. Bring me to Octavius. **A**

[*Exeunt.*]

FINAL SUMMARY In Act Four, Antony, Octavius, and Lepidus form the Second Triumvirate and meet in Rome. They make plans to fight against the armies being organized by Brutus and Cassius.

Brutus and Cassius argue over ambition and honor, but make amends. They agree to march toward Philippi to meet the advancing armies of Octavius and Antony. That night, Caesar's ghost appears to Brutus. The ghost calls itself "thy evil spirit" and says they will meet again at Philippi.

In Act Five, Brutus and Cassius meet Octavius and Antony at Philippi. The opposing generals argue bitterly. In battle, Cassius mistakenly believes the enemy has won. Instead of surrendering, he kills himself. When Titinius and Massala discover Cassius dead, Titinius kills himself with Cassius's sword. Brutus and the others find the bodies of Cassius and Titinius, pay their respects, and then prepare for battle. Antony sends his soldiers to search for Brutus. Brutus and his forces are weary from battle. Brutus tells his men it is time for him to die. As Strato holds his sword, Brutus runs onto it, killing himself. When they capture Brutus's army, Antony, Octavius, Messala, Lucilius, and others come upon the leader's corpse. Antony delivers a brief speech over the body of Brutus, stating that while others killed Caesar out of personal envy, Brutus acted in what he felt were the best interests of the Roman people. As the battle ends, Octavius promises a proper funeral for Brutus. Octavius and his friends celebrate their victory.

---

100. Are rid: have ridden.
101. Belike: probably.

Applying Your Skills

The Tragedy of Julius Caesar, Act I, Scene 2 *and* Act III, Scene 2

LITERARY FOCUS: TRAGEDY

DIRECTIONS: On a separate sheet of paper, write a paragraph that explains how "The Tragedy of Julius Caesar" reflects the elements of a **tragedy**. Include specific examples from the text.

READING FOCUS: READING A PLAY

DIRECTIONS: Complete the chart below by **paraphrasing** the following portions of speeches by Brutus and Antony:

Speech	Paraphrase
Brutus: "Had you rather Caesar were living, and die all slaves, than that Caesar were dead, to live all free men? As Caesar loved me, I weep for him; as he was fortunate, I rejoice at it; as he was valiant, I honor him; but, as he was ambitious, I slew him." (Lines 344–348)	1.
Antony: "Friends, Romans, countrymen, lend me your ears; / I come to bury Caesar, not to praise him. / The evil that men do lives after them, / The good is oft interrèd with their bones; / So let it be with Caesar. The noble Brutus / Hath told you Caesar was ambitious. / If it were so, it was a grievous fault, / And grievously hath Caesar answered it." (Lines 395–402)	2.

Literary Skills
Understand the characteristics of a tragedy.

Reading Skills
Read Shakespeare aloud and paraphrase.

A Big-Name Brutus in a Caldron of Chaos

by Ben Brantley

INFORMATIONAL TEXT FOCUS: EVALUATING AN ARGUMENT

When you read a movie or book review in a newspaper, the professional reviewer or critic is trying to convince you, the reader, of his or her views and opinions. Determine the critic's **intent**, or purpose, by asking yourself the following questions:

- What is the critic's standards for a quality piece of work? What do they need to see in order to give a good review?

- What evidence does the critic provide in support of his or her opinions? This can include informed judgments, examples, or facts.

- How thorough is the evidence? A good review gives many details to support the opinion.

SELECTION VOCABULARY

carnage (KAHR NIHJ) *n.:* slaughter of a great number of people; butchery.
The survivors of the battle described the carnage on both sides.

inaudible (IHN AW DUH BUHL) *adj.:* impossible to hear.
After yelling through three performances, the actor's voice was almost inaudible.

conspirators (KUHN SPIHR UH TUHRZ) *n.:* people who help plan a crime; traitors.
Each conspirator in the plot was caught.

WORD STUDY

DIRECTIONS: The following words were created from the vocabulary words above. Based on the definitions of the original words, what do you think each new word means? Use a dictionary to check your answers.

1. conspiratorial *adj.* _____

2. inaudibly *adv.* _____

SKILLS FOCUS

Informational Text Skills
Evaluate an argument.

A BIG-NAME BRUTUS IN A CALDRON OF CHAOS

by Ben Brantley

> **BACKGROUND**
>
> Ben Brantley is a theater critic for the *New York Times*. This selection is his review for the 2005 Broadway revival of Shakespeare's play "The Tragedy of Julius Caesar." The character of Brutus was played by Oscar winner Denzel Washington. "The Tragedy of Julius Caesar." had not been performed on Broadway since 1950.

Those cruel forces of history known as the dogs of war are on a rampage at the Belasco Theater during a carnage-happy production of Shakespeare's "Julius Caesar." **A** Dripping blood and breathing smoke, these specters[1] are chewing up and spitting out everything in their path: friends, Romans, countrymen, blank verse, emotional credibility, a man who would be king and even the noblest movie star of them all, he whom the masses call Denzel.

That's Denzel Washington, the two-time Academy Award winner. He's the reason theater-goers are lining up to see this show. This play hasn't drawn such crowds in New York since Al Pacino gnawed his way through Mark Antony's funeral oration at the Public Theater 17 years ago. Mr. Washington has taken on the quieter but meatier role of Brutus. **B**

As the most important passenger on Daniel Sullivan's fast, bumpy ride of a production, Mr. Washington does not embarrass himself, as leading citizens of Hollywood have been known to do

10

---

1. **specters** (SPEHK TUHRZ): ghosts.

A **LITERARY ANALYSIS**

Based on this sentence and the title, do you think this review will be positive or negative?

_____

_____

B **VOCABULARY**

Academic Vocabulary

Why do you think the author *highlights*, or points out, Washington's popularity as the reason many people are seeing this play?

_____

_____

_____

_____

"A Big-Name Brutus in a Caldron of Chaos" by Ben Brantley from *The New York Times*, April 4, 2005. Coyright © 2005 by **The New York Times Company**. Reproduced by premission of the publisher.

Copyright © by Holt, Rinehart and Winston. All rights reserved.

A Big-Name Brutus in a Caldron of Chaos   **359**

A **LANGUAGE COACH**

What does the word *unsettled* mean? If you remove the **prefix** *un–*, what does the resulting new word mean?

_____

_____

_____

_____

B **VOCABULARY**

Selection Vocabulary
Use context clues to write a definition for *inaudible*. Is this something an actor should try to be? Explain.

_____

_____

_____

_____

_____

_____

C **READING FOCUS**

To determine the reviewer's **intent**, what are some of the reviewer's standards for a good performance of the role of Brutus? How does Washington meet these standards, if at all?

_____

_____

_____

_____

_____

on Broadway. But even in the glow of fame, he can't help getting lost amid the mismatched crowd and the heavy topical artillery
20 assembled here.

This is regrettable, since Mr. Washington would appear an inspired choice. The character Brutus anticipates Hamlet in divided feelings about bloody deeds. And among leading American film actors, Mr. Washington has all but cornered the market on advanced ambivalence. Whether playing smugly evil ("Training Day") or raggedly heroic ("The Manchurian Candidate"), he gives off a grave, unsettled air. **A** His world seems to be a symphony of mixed signals. Casting him as "poor Brutus, with himself at war," must have seemed like a no-brainer.

30 In several shining sequences, Mr. Washington justifies his presence in this production. It is telling, however, that such moments usually occur during monologues. These scenes require little or no interaction with others. In the second-act soliloquy in which Brutus considers the planned assassination of the tyrant Caesar (William Sadler), Mr. Washington is filled with the uneasiness of a good man struggling against instinct.

He has the tired, open face of someone long battered by doubt. This same quality is surprisingly and affectingly carried over into the speech Brutus makes to the frightened mob
40 after Caesar has been slain. You can sense why the people like Brutus. You can also understand why they will soon be putty in the hands of the more flamboyant and assured Mark Antony (Eamonn Walker).

This Brutus, however, so often seems plagued less by moral and philosophical uncertainty than by a kind of insecurity. Mr. Washington's voice becomes rushed and soft and sometimes inaudible. **B** And when other characters are looking to the mighty Brutus for guidance amid chaos, Mr. Washington looks more apologetic than anything else. **C**

50 Under the circumstances, it's hard to blame him. Mr. Sullivan is an agile director whose credits include "Proof" and "A Moon for the Misbegotten." But he has populated his "Julius Caesar" with performers who seem to have arrived from different planets

© UPI Photo/Ezio Petersen/Landov

in the great galaxy of show business. On the one hand, you have the naturalistic actors[2] like Mr. Washington. They speak Shakespearean speech with the equivalent of an easygoing shrug. On the other hand, you have fiercely classical interpreters who are going for Tragedy with a capital *T*, such as the excellent Colm Feore (as Cassius) and Jessica Hecht (as Portia, Brutus's wife).

60   Then there is Mr. Walker, whose Mark Antony combines fierceness with incomprehensibility. You have Jack Willis, who plays Casca as a jaunty backroom gossip. Mr. Sadler, a scrappy man with the air of a gangster, portrays the title character as if the play were titled "Little Caesar." And Kelly AuCoin gives young Octavius Caesar (Julius's great nephew) the cockiness of a lead singer in a boy band.

The overall effect is bewildering, like a free-for-all concert in which opera, jazz, light rock and musical comedy are all performed. **D** Points of emotional connection among the
70 characters are mostly nonexistent. **E**

There is little sense of the crucial, shifting relationships among the conspirators. When Mr. Feore's Cassius and Mr. Washington's Brutus fight and make up on the fields of battle,

---

2. **naturalistic actors:** Naturalistic acting tries to capture everyday ways of speaking and behaving.

D VOCABULARY

Word Study
Bewildering means "extremely confusing." Think of a synonym (word with a similar meaning) for *bewildering*. Use a thesaurus if you need help.

_____

E READING FOCUS

What can you infer as being one of the reviewer's standards for a successful production of play? How does this standard connect with the reviewer's **intent** in writing this article?

_____
_____
_____
_____
_____
_____

What methods are used to set the play in modern times?

_____

_____

_____

_____

_____

B READING FOCUS

What is Brantley's **intent** with this review? Is he recommending the play or not? How thorough do you think the evidence is?

_____

_____

_____

_____

_____

_____

_____

_____

_____

_____

_____

_____

_____

the impression is of scenes from different films spliced together. Everyone manages to convey intensity, but rarely with any specificity of character.

Mr. Sullivan, perhaps of necessity, shifts the burden of interpretation to the staging. Designed by Ralph Funicello (sets), Jess Goldstein (costumes), and Mimi Jordan Sherin (lighting),
80 the production has a war-is-still-hell look. It will be familiar to anyone who has spent time at the National Theater in London or the New York Shakespeare Festival in Central Park.

The setting is a ravaged, vaguely Balkan-looking ancient city. Armed thugs lurk in shadows. Soldiers sport berets and guerrilla fatigues. Plaster falls to the sound of exploding bombs. Accessories include photo I.D. tags and metal detectors. How the conspirators manage to bypass the latter in smuggling daggers becomes a matter of distracting stage business involving a battered briefcase. **A**
90 Mr. Sullivan keeps things moving, though the general impression is blurry, like a landscape seen through the window of a speeding train. In the second half of the show, blood spurts in geysers. There is one especially grisly decapitation. And the suicides of Brutus and Cassius are rendered in gut-churning detail. But without having come to know these tragic losers, you may find it hard to work up sentiment about their demises, however grisly.

Mr. Washington's Brutus bites the dust with convincing bravado. But it says much about this production that his final
100 invocation of the ghost of Caesar ("I killed not thee with half so good a will") is muffled by the noise of his death throes. **B**

A Big-Name Brutus in a Caldron of Chaos

VOCABULARY DEVELOPMENT

DIRECTIONS: Fill in the blanks in the following sentences with the correct vocabulary words from the Word Box.

Word Box

carnage

inaudible

conspirators

1. During the battle that was fought near my home, I saw a horrible scene of _____.

2. The men who aided the bank robbers were eventually tried in a court of law as _____.

3. Magda whispered throughout the entire movie, thinking she was completely _____ to others, but she wasn't.

INFORMATIONAL TEXT FOCUS: EVALUATING AN ARGUMENT

DIRECTIONS: Use the table below to evaluate Ben Brantley's overall **intent** in reviewing this production of "The Tragedy of Julius Caesar." State one of his arguments, and then give his criteria, or standards, and his evidence for that argument. Then, on the lines below, explain whether or not you thought his argument was convincing, and why.

Argument	Criteria	Evidence

_____

_____

_____

SKILLS FOCUS

Informational Text Skills
Evaluate an argument.

Collection 8

VOCABULARY REVIEW

DIRECTIONS: Write the letter of each definition in the second column next to the correct selection or academic vocabulary word in the first column.

Vocabulary Words	Definitions
1. _____ carnage	**a.** more powerful, common or noticeable than others.
2. _____ conspirators	**b.** rules or standards for making a judgment; test.
3. _____ criteria	**c.** slaughter of a great number of people; butchery.
4. _____ highlight	**d.** most important.
5. _____ inaudible	**e.** to make a subject or idea stand out so people will pay attention.
6. _____ predominant	**f.** impossible to hear.
7. _____ principal	**g.** people who help plan a crime; traitors.

Skills Review

Collection 8

DIRECTIONS: A **prefix** is a letter or a group of letters that is added to the beginning of a word in order to change the word's meaning. Look at the chart below. Either a word, a word with a prefix, or the meaning of a word with a prefix is missing. Fill in the missing information. Use a dictionary if needed. The first row has been completed as an example.

Word	Word with prefix	Definition of word with prefix
audible	inaudible	"impossible to hear"
		"impossible to predict"
	antisocial	
school		"a school for children too young to attend kindergarten"
		"not functioning normally"
	disrespect	

ORAL LANGUAGE ACTIVITY

DIRECTIONS: A strong, critical review gives both an opinion and some evidence that supports it. Work with a partner and find something that you both have either seen, heard, read, or played (for example, a movie, a piece of music, a play, a video game or a book). Take turns giving an oral review of the work. As part of your review, you must state what your criteria, or standards, for quality are. For example, what qualities are usually present in books that you like? Also be sure to include enough evidence to support your opinion. If you didn't care for the acting in a movie, for example, talk specifically about certain performances and what in particular you didn't like. Your evidence must be thorough or else your review won't stand up to challenges and questioning from your partner.

The Hero's Story

© Robert Dale/Images.com/Corbis

Literary and Academic Vocabulary for Collection 9

---

recurring (RIH KUR IHNG) *v.* used as *adj.:* coming up again, being repeated.
   The heroic quest is a recurring theme in myths.

exhibit (EHG ZIHB IHT) *v.:* to show, display, or indicate.
   He did not want to exhibit his true feelings for Diana.

retain (RIH TAYN) *v.:* to continue to have or hold.
   She was able to retain her lead in the race.

recount (RIH KOWNT) *v.:* to tell or give an account of.
   My grandmother will recount her experiences as a nurse during the Korean War in her autobiography.

myth (MIHTH) *n.:* traditional story rooted in a particular culture that serves to explain beliefs, rituals, or nature.
   My favorite myth explains why tigers have stripes.

legend (LEH JUHND) *n.:* story about extraordinary events based on a real historical event or person.
   Although many of the things in the legend were too wild to have actually happened, much of the story is based on facts.

archetype (AHR KUH TYP) *n.:* type of plot, character, or image that appears throughout literature.
   The idea of a child becoming an adult is a very famous archetype that has been used many times in books and movies.

Theseus

retold by Edith Hamilton

LITERARY FOCUS: MYTHS AND HEROES

A **myth** is a traditional story that tries to explain the beliefs, rituals, or mysteries of the culture from which it came. Myths demonstrate through storytelling the values of a particular culture.

Myths may explain anything from what stars are to why the seasons change to how an animal got its name. A **hero** is the main character of a myth. While heroes might have supernatural powers, they are nevertheless noticeably human. Heroes love, suffer, feel, think, and learn, just like you. Typically, a myth involving a hero will include a quest that the hero undertakes, which is a difficult journey or test. Once completed, the hero will have learned something new about himself or herself.

READING FOCUS: SUMMARIZING

Summarizing is the process of retelling a text in your own words, including only the key points and events. Summarizing can help you identify what parts of the story are most important.

Use the Skill   While you read "Theseus," keep track of the myth's main events in the chart below.

Main events
Theseus is the son of Aegeus, and was raised by his mother.

Literary Skills
Analyze the components of a myth.

Reading Skills
Summarize what you read.

Vocabulary Development

Theseus

SELECTION VOCABULARY

acknowledged (AK NAHL IHJD) *adj.:* admitted; recognized to be true.

Once Theseus proved he was King Aegeus's son, he became the acknowledged prince.

endear (EHN DEER) *v.:* inspire affection.

Theseus was able to endear himself to the Atheneans by being a good and fair ruler.

afflicted (UH FLIHKT IHD) *adj.:* upset; saddened.

King Aegeus was so afflicted at the sight of the black sail that he killed himself.

prosperous (PRAHS PUHR UHS) *adj.:* wealthy.

Citizens lived comfortably in the prosperous state of Athens.

consent (KUHN SEHNT) *v.:* agree.

Theseus would not consent to becoming king.

WORD STUDY

DIRECTIONS: For each sentence, write "Yes" if the vocabulary word is used correctly. Write "No" if it is used incorrectly. If your answer is "No," rewrite the sentence so that the word is used correctly.

1. I *consent* my cousin a gift for her birthday. _____

_____

2. The *prosperous* businessman owned two homes. _____

_____

3. His bad attitude did not *endear* him to me. _____

_____

4. She was overjoyed and *afflicted* when she won the race. _____

_____

5. He was very *acknowledged* on the subject of the Civil War. _____

_____

THESEUS

retold by Edith Hamilton

> ### BACKGROUND
> Ancient Greece is known for being the place where democracy was born. The mythical Greek hero Theseus is credited with founding the first democratic city-state in Athens. According to myth, Theseus is the son of Aegeus, king of Athens, and Aethra, princess of Troizen, a city in southern Greece.

A **LANGUAGE COACH**

Look at the word *Athenian*. An Athenian is a person from Athens. What is the suffix of this word? What do you think the suffix means? List some other words that use this suffix.

_____

_____

_____

_____

_____

_____

_____

_____

The great Athenian hero was Theseus. **A** He had so many adventures and took part in so many great enterprises that there grew up a saying in Athens, "Nothing without Theseus."

He was the son of the Athenian king, Aegeus. He spent his youth, however, in his mother's home, a city in southern Greece. Aegeus went back to Athens before the child was born, but first he placed in a hollow a sword and a pair of shoes and covered them with a great stone. He did this with the knowledge of his wife and told her that whenever the boy—if it was a boy—grew

10 strong enough to roll away the stone and get the things beneath it, she could send him to Athens to claim him as his father. The child was a boy, and he grew up strong far beyond others, so that when his mother finally took him to the stone he lifted it with no trouble at all. She told him then that the time had come for him to seek his father, and a ship was placed at his disposal by his grandfather. But Theseus refused to go by water, because the voyage was safe and easy. His idea was to become a great hero as quickly as possible, and easy safety was certainly not the way to do that. Hercules, who was the most magnificent of all the heroes

20 of Greece, was always in his mind, and the determination to be

"Theseus" from *Mythology* by Edith Hamilton. Copyright © 1942 by Edith Hamilton; copyright renewed © 1969 by Dorian Fielding Reid and Dorian Fielding Reid. Reproduced by permission of **Little, Brown and Company, (Inc.)**, and electronic format by permission of **Alice R. Abbott**.

Museo Archeologico Nazionale, Naples, Italy/Erich Lessing/Art Resource, NY

just as magnificent himself. This was quite natural, since the two were cousins. **B**

He steadfastly refused, therefore, the ship his mother and grandfather urged on him, telling them that to sail on it would be a contemptible[1] flight from danger, and he set forth to go to Athens by land. The journey was long and very hazardous because of the bandits that beset the road. He killed them all, however; he left not one alive to trouble future travelers. His idea of dealing justice was simple but effective: What each had done to others, Theseus did to him. Sciron,[2] for instance, who had made those he captured kneel to wash his feet and then kicked them down into the sea, Theseus hurled over a precipice. **C** Sinir, who killed people by fastening them to two pine trees bent down to the ground and letting the trees go, died in that way himself. **D** Procrustes[3] was placed upon the iron bed which he

30

---

1. **contemptible** (KUHN TEHMP TUH BUHL): hateful; worthy of contempt; disgraceful.
2. **Sciron** (SY RAWN).
3. **Procrustes** (PROH KRUHS TEEZ).

B **LITERARY FOCUS**

In what ways does the story already fit the definition of a **myth**?

_____

_____

_____

_____

_____

_____

C **VOCABULARY**

Word Study

Use context clues to write a definition for the word *precipice*. Use a dictionary to check your answer.

_____

_____

_____

_____

D **LITERARY FOCUS**

Heroes often reflect the qualities valued by the cultures that created them. What does the character of Theseus suggest about what the ancient Greeks might have valued?

_____

_____

_____

_____

_____

Theseus **371**

C **VOCABULARY**

Selection Vocabulary

Endear means "inspire affection." Use the word in a sentence of your own.

_____

_____

_____

_____

_____

used for his victims, tying them to it and then making them the right length for it by stretching those who were too short and cutting off as much as was necessary from those who were too long. The story does not say which of the two methods was used

40 in his case, but there was not much to choose between them and in one way or the other Procrustes' career ended. **A**

It can be imagined how Greece rang with the praises of the young man who had cleared the land of these banes[4] to travelers. When he reached Athens, he was an acknowledged hero, and he was invited to a banquet by the King, who of course was unaware that Theseus was his son. In fact, he was afraid of the young man's great popularity, thinking that he might win the people over to make him king, and he invited him with the idea of poisoning him. The plan was not his, but Medea's, the heroine of

50 the Quest of the Golden Fleece, who knew through her sorcery who Theseus was. She had fled to Athens when she left Corinth in her winged car, and she had acquired great influence over Aegeus, which she did not want disturbed by the appearance of a son. But as she handed him the poisoned cup, Theseus, wishing to make himself known at once to his father, drew his sword. The King instantly recognized it and dashed the cup to the ground. Medea escaped, as she always did, and got safely away to Asia. **B**

Aegeus then proclaimed to the country that Theseus was his son and heir. The new heir apparent soon had an opportunity to

60 endear himself to the Athenians. **C**

Years before his arrival in Athens, a terrible misfortune had happened to the city. Minos, the powerful ruler of Crete, had lost his only son, Androgenes,[5] while the young man was visiting the Athenian king. King Aegeus had done what no host should do: He had sent his guest on an expedition full of peril—to kill a dangerous bull. Instead, the bull had killed the youth. Minos invaded the country, captured Athens and declared that he would raze it to the ground unless every nine years the people sent him

---

4. **banes:** causes of destruction or ruin.
5. **Androgenes** (AN DRAW JUH NEEZ).

a tribute[6] of seven maidens and seven youths. A horrible fate
70 awaited these young creatures. When they reached Crete they
were given to the Minotaur to devour.

The Minotaur was a monster, half bull, half human, the
offspring of Minos's wife Pasiphaë[7] and a wonderfully beautiful
bull. Poseidon[8] had given this bull to Minos in order that he
should sacrifice it to him, but Minos could not bear to slay it and
kept it for himself. To punish him, Poseidon had made Pasiphaë
fall madly in love with it. **D**

When the Minotaur was born, Minos did not kill him. He
had Daedalus,[9] a great architect and inventor, construct a place
80 of confinement for him from which escape was impossible.
Daedalus built the Labyrinth, famous throughout the world.
Once inside, one would go endlessly along its twisting paths

---

6. **tribute:** something paid by one nation or ruler to another as an
acknowledgment of submission.
7. **Pasiphaë.** (PUH SIHF UH EE).
8. **Poseidon:** (POH SY DUHN) god of horses and of the sea; brother of
Zeus.
9. **Daedalus.** (DEHD UHL UHS).

Summarize the "terrible
misfortune" of Athens.

_____

_____

_____

_____

_____

_____

_____

_____

Musée du Petit Palais, Avignon, France/R.G. Ojeda/
Réunion des Musees Nationaux/Art Resource, NY

A QUICK CHECK

Who is Daedalus and what is the Labyrinth?

_____
_____
_____
_____
_____

B VOCABULARY

Academic Vocabulary

How does Theseus *exhibit*, or display, his courage in this paragraph?

_____
_____
_____
_____
_____

C LITERARY ANALYSIS

What can you infer about Theseus's feelings toward Ariadne from this sentence?

_____
_____
_____
_____
_____

without ever finding the exit. To this place the young Athenians were each time taken and left to the Minotaur. There was no possible way to escape. In whatever direction they ran, they might be running straight to the monster; if they stood still, he might at any moment emerge from the maze. Such was the doom which awaited fourteen youths and maidens a few days after Theseus reached Athens. The time had come for the next

90 installment of the tribute. **A**

At once Theseus came forward and offered to be one of the victims. All loved him for his goodness and admired him for his nobility, but they had no idea that he intended to try to kill the Minotaur. He told his father, however, and promised him that if he succeeded, he would have the black sail which the ship with its cargo of misery always carried changed to a white one, so that Aegeus could know long before it came to land that his son was safe. **B**

When the young victims arrived in Crete, they were

100 paraded before the inhabitants on their way to the Labyrinth. Minos' daughter Ariadne was among the spectators, and she fell in love with Theseus at first sight as he marched past her. She sent for Daedalus and told him he must show her a way to get out of the Labyrinth, and she sent for Theseus and told him she would bring about his escape if he would promise to take her back to Athens and marry her. As may be imagined, he made no difficulty about that, and she gave him the clue she had got from Daedalus, a ball of thread which he was to fasten at one end to the inside of the door and unwind as he went on. **C** This he did

110 and, certain that he could retrace his steps whenever he chose, he walked boldly into the maze, looking for the Minotaur. He came upon him asleep and fell upon him, pinning him to the ground; and with his fists—he had no other weapon—he battered the monster to death.

> As an oak tree falls on the hillside
> Crushing all that lies beneath,
> So Theseus. He presses out the life,

The brute's savage life, and now it lies dead.

Only the head sways slowly, but the horns are useless now.

120   When Theseus lifted himself up from that terrific struggle, the ball of thread lay where he had dropped it. With it in his hands, the way out was clear. The others followed, and taking Ariadne with them they fled to the ship and over the sea toward Athens. **D**

On the way there they put in at the island of Naxos, and what happened then is differently reported. One story says that Theseus deserted Ariadne. She was asleep, and he sailed away without her, but Dionysus found her and comforted her. The other story is much more favorable to Theseus. She was

130   extremely seasick, and he set her ashore to recover while he returned to the ship to do some necessary work. A violent wind carried him out to sea and kept him there a long time. On his return he found that Ariadne had died, and he was deeply afflicted. **E**

Both stories agree that when they drew near to Athens, he forgot to hoist the white sail. Either his joy at the success of his voyage put every other thought out of his head, or his grief for Ariadne. The black sail was seen by his father, King Aegeus, from the Acropolis,[10] where for days he had watched the sea with strain-

140   ing eyes. It was to him the sign of his son's death, and he threw himself down from a rocky height into the sea and was killed. The sea into which he fell was called the Aegean ever after. **F**

So Theseus became King of Athens, a most wise and disinterested[11] king. He declared to the people that he did not wish to rule over them; he wanted a people's government where all would be equal. He resigned his royal power and organized a commonwealth, building a council hall where the citizens should gather and vote. The only office he kept for himself was that of commander in chief. Thus Athens became, of all earth's cities, the

---

10. **Acropolis** (UH KRAWP UH LIHS): fortified heights in Athens. A huge temple to Athena stands on top of the hill.
11. **disinterested**: fair; impartial. (*Disinterested* should not be confused with *uninterested*, which means "not interested.")

D **READING FOCUS**

Summarize how Theseus escapes from the Labyrinth.

_____

_____

_____

_____

_____

_____

_____

E **LITERARY ANALYSIS**

Why do you think there are two different versions of what happened on Naxos?

_____

_____

_____

_____

_____

_____

F **LITERARY FOCUS**

The Aegean Sea is a real body of water located between Greece and Turkey. What characteristic of a **myth** connects this part of the story to real life?

_____

_____

_____

_____

_____

Word Study

In this paragraph, there are several pairs of words that are in the same word family, or have the same root (for example, *governed* and *government*). Identify another pair of words in this paragraph that share the same root.

_____

_____

B LITERARY FOCUS

In a typical **myth**, the **hero** often finds qualities in himself that he didn't know that he had. What kinds of traits do you think Theseus has learned about himself by the end of the story? Explain.

_____

_____

_____

_____

_____

_____

_____

_____

_____

150 happiest and most prosperous, the only true home of liberty, the one place in the world where the people governed themselves. It was for this reason that in the great War of the Seven against Thebes,[12] when the victorious Thebans refused burial to those of the enemy who had died, the vanquished[13] turned to Theseus and Athens for help, believing that free men under such a leader would never consent to having the helpless dead wronged. They did not turn in vain. Theseus led his army against Thebes, conquered her, and forced her to allow the dead to be buried. But when he was victor, he did not return evil to the Thebans for

160 the evil they had done. He showed himself the perfect knight. He refused to let his army enter and loot the city. He had come not to harm Thebes, but to bury the Argive[14] dead, and that duty done he led his soldiers back to Athens. **A** **B**

---

12. **Thebes** (THEEBZ): chief city of Boeotia, a region in ancient Greece.
13. **vanquished:** conquered or defeated people.
14. **Argive** (AHR JYV): another word for "Greek." All of these people were Greek, but they gave allegiance to their separate, smaller kingdoms.

Applying Your Skills

Theseus

VOCABULARY DEVELOPMENT

DIRECTIONS: Circle the word or phrase that is closest in meaning to each boldfaced vocabulary word.

1. **prosperous**
   a. thoughtful
   b. devious
   c. rich

2. **consent**
   a. concur
   b. convince
   c. connect

3. **afflicted**
   a. carefree
   b. heartbroken
   c. lively

4. **acknowledged**
   a. accepted
   b. approved
   c. smart

5. **endear**
   a. convince
   b. hate
   c. make beloved

LITERARY FOCUS: MYTHS AND HEROES

DIRECTIONS: In the graphic organizer below, fill in the bottom ovals with details from "Theseus" that fulfill the definition of a **myth**.

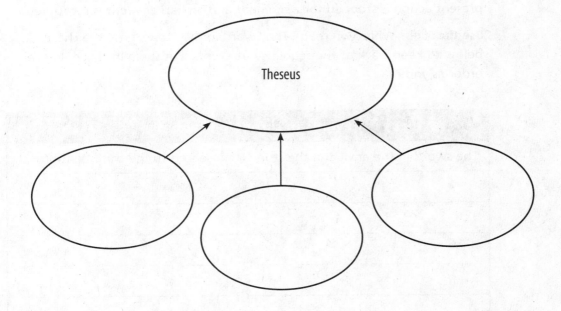

Theseus

READING FOCUS: SUMMARIZING

DIRECTIONS: On a separate sheet of paper, write a **summary** of "Theseus."

SKILLS FOCUS

Literary Skills
Analyze the components of a myth.

Reading Skills
Summarize what you read.

The Sword in the Stone

by Sir Thomas Malory

LITERARY FOCUS: ARTHURIAN LEGEND

A **legend** is a story about extraordinary events or deeds. Legends are based on real historical people or events, but often take on magical, fantastic characteristics as they are told and retold over hundreds of years.

The stories about King Arthur and his brave knights of the Round Table are known as **Arthurian legend**. King Arthur is probably based on a fifth- or sixth-century Celtic warlord who lived in Wales and defeated invaders from Germany. In the stories, King Arthur is a great warrior and the leader of his people.

READING FOCUS: UNDERSTANDING SEQUENCE OF EVENTS

The order in which things happen in a story is called the **sequence of events**. Most often, a story is told in **chronological order**. Events that happened first are told first, and so on. However, some stories have events that are told out of order. There might be a **flashback**, which is when the present action is stopped for a moment and an earlier event is recounted.

Use the Skill   While you read "The Sword in the Stone," use the chart below to keep track of the sequence of events. Put them in chronological order as you read.

Events in chronological order
The sword in the anvil and the stone is presented to the congregation.

SKILLS FOCUS

Literary Skills
Understand elements of Arthurian legend.

Reading Skills
Understand the sequence of events.

Vocabulary Development

The Sword in the Stone

SELECTION VOCABULARY

confronted (KUHN FRUHNT EHD) *v.:* faced.

> The warriors were confronted with a fierce opponent.

inscribed (IHN SKYRBD) *v.:* marked or written on a surface; engraved.

> The ring was inscribed with my initials.

tumultuous (TOO MUHL CHOO UHS) *adj.:* wild and noisy.

> The tumultuous sea turned her face green.

realm (REHLM) *n.:* kingdom.

> The king's realm stretched as far as the sea.

WORD STUDY

DIRECTIONS: In each sentence below, one word is used incorrectly. Circle the word that is used improperly and rewrite the sentence using one of the vocabulary words from above that make sense in its place.

1. The orderly meeting was marked by rowdy arguments.

_____

2. At the moment when the two boxers avoided each other, they both looked ready to kill!

_____

3. The local princess had authority over the entire world.

_____

4. Her grandmother's keepsake was encoded with the family crest.

_____

THE SWORD IN THE STONE

by Sir Thomas Malory, retold by Keith Baines

BACKGROUND

"The Sword in the Stone" tells the story of Arthur, son of Igraine and King Uther of England. Many men wanted Uther's throne, and so any heir would be seen as a dangerous rival. A wise man named Merlin took Arthur from Uther, fearing for the child's safety. Arthur was raised by Sir Ector and his wife alongside their own son, Kay. As this story begins, King Uther has just died, and a contest is being set up to decide the next king of England.

A **LANGUAGE COACH**

Look at the word *archbishop*. What is the prefix of this word? What do you think the prefix means? Use a dictionary to check your answer.

_____

_____

_____

_____

"The Sword in the Stone" from *Le Morte D'Arthur* by Sir Thomas Malory, translated by Keith Baines. Translation copyright © 1962 by Keith Baines; copyright renewed © 1990 by Francesca Evans. Reproduced by permission of **Dutton Signet, a division of Penguin Group (USA) Inc.**

The archbishop held his service in the city's greatest church (St. Paul's), and when matins[1] were done, the congregation filed out to the yard. **A** They were confronted by a marble block into which had

10 been thrust a beautiful sword. The block was four feet square, and the sword passed through a steel anvil[2] which had been struck in the stone and which projected a foot from it. The anvil had been inscribed with letters of gold:

© David Crausby/Alamy

1. **matins** (MAT UHNZ): morning prayers.
2. **anvil** (AN VUHL): iron or steel block on which metal objects are hammered into shape.

WHOSO PULLETH OUTE THIS SWERD OF THIS
STONE AND ANVYLD IS RIGHTWYS KYNGE BORNE
OF ALL BRYTAYGNE **B**

20   The congregation was awed by this miraculous sight, but
the archbishop forbade anyone to touch the sword before Mass
had been heard. After Mass, many of the nobles tried to pull the
sword out of the stone, but none was able to, so a watch of ten
knights was set over the sword, and a tournament[3] proclaimed
for New Year's Day, to provide men of noble blood with the
opportunity of proving their right to the succession.

   Sir Ector, who had been living on an estate near London,
rode to the tournament with Arthur and his own son Sir Kay,
30 who had been recently knighted. When they arrived at the tournament, Sir Kay found to his annoyance that his sword was missing from its sheath, so he begged Arthur to ride back and fetch it
from their lodging. **C**

   Arthur found the door of the lodging locked and bolted, the
landlord and his wife having left for the tournament. In order
not to disappoint his brother, he rode on to St. Paul's, determined
to get for him the sword which was lodged in the stone. The
yard was empty, the guard also having slipped off to see the
tournament, so Arthur strode up to the sword and, without
40 troubling to read the inscription, tugged it free. He then rode
straight back to Sir Kay and presented him with it. **D**

   Sir Kay recognized the sword and, taking it to Sir Ector,
said, "Father, the succession falls to me, for I have here the sword
that was lodged in the stone." But Sir Ector insisted that they
should all ride to the churchyard, and once there, bound Sir Kay
by oath[4] to tell how he had come by the sword. Sir Kay then
admitted that Arthur had given it to him. Sir Ector turned to
Arthur and said, "Was the sword not guarded?"

   "It was not," Arthur replied.

---

3. **tournament** (TUR NUH MUHNT): sport in which two knights compete on
horseback, trying to unseat each other with long pole-like weapons
called lances.
4. **oath** (OHTH): serious promise or declaration; vow.

B LITERARY ANALYSIS

Why do you think the words
on the anvil are spelled so
strangely?

_____

_____

_____

_____

C VOCABULARY

Word Study

Sheath is a noun meaning
"case or covering for the
blade of a sword." What
might the verb form of
sheath mean?

_____

_____

_____

_____

D QUICK CHECK

Why does Arthur pull the
sword out of the stone?

_____

_____

_____

_____

_____

_____

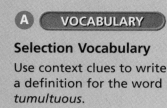

50   "Would you please thrust it into the stone again?" said Sir Ector. Arthur did so, and first Sir Ector and then Sir Kay tried to remove it, but both were unable to. Then Arthur, for the second time, pulled it out. Sir Ector and Sir Kay both knelt before him.

"Why," said Arthur, "do you both kneel before me?"

"My lord," Sir Ector replied, "there is only one man living who can draw the sword from the stone, and he is the true-born king of Britain." Sir Ector then told Arthur the story of his birth and upbringing.

60   "My dear father," said Arthur, "for so I shall always think of you—if, as you say, I am to be king, please know that any request you have to make is already granted."

Sir Ector asked that Sir Kay should be made royal seneschal,[5] and Arthur declared that while they both lived it should be so. Then the three of them visited the archbishop and told him what had taken place.

All those dukes and barons with ambitions to rule were present at the tournament on New Year's Day. But when all of them had failed, and Arthur alone had succeeded in drawing the

70   sword from the stone, they protested against one so young, and of ignoble blood, succeeding to the throne.

The secret of Arthur's birth was known to only a few of the nobles surviving from the days of King Uther. The archbishop urged them to make Arthur's cause their own; but their support proved ineffective. The tournament was repeated at Candlemas[6] and at Easter, with the same outcome as before.

Finally, at Pentecost,[7] when once more Arthur alone had been able to remove the sword, the commoners arose with a tumultuous cry and demanded that Arthur should at once be

80   made king. **A** The nobles, knowing in their hearts that the

---

5. **seneschal** (SEHN UH SHUHL): person in charge of the king's household. This was a powerful and respected position.
6. **Candlemas** (KAN DUHL MUHS): Christian festival on February 2, remembering purification of the Virgin Mary after the birth of Jesus.
7. **Pentecost** (PEHN TUH KAWST): Christian festival celebrated on the seventh Sunday after Easter, commemorating the descent of the Holy Spirit upon the Apostles.

© The Everett Collection

commoners were right, all knelt before Arthur and begged forgiveness for having delayed his succession for so long. Arthur forgave them and then, offering his sword at the high altar, was dubbed[8] first knight of the realm. The coronation took place a few days later, when Arthur swore to rule justly, and the nobles swore him their allegiance. **B** **C** **D**

---

8. **dubbed** (DUHBD): conferred knighthood on by tapping on the shoulder with a sword.

B VOCABULARY

Academic Vocabulary
Why do you think this story has been *recounted*, or told, over and over for generations?

_____

_____

_____

_____

_____

C READING FOCUS

Are all of the events in this story told in **chronological order**? If not, what events are told out of order?

_____

_____

_____

_____

_____

D LITERARY FOCUS

In what ways is "The Sword in the Stone" a **legend**?

_____

_____

_____

_____

_____

The Sword in the Stone

USE A TIME LINE

DIRECTIONS: Using a time line can help you keep track of the main events of a story. Use the time line below to put events from "The Sword in the Stone" in the correct order. Choose only the most important events. Some events may be told out of order in the story; put them in **chronological order** on the time line.

The Sword in the Stone

VOCABULARY DEVELOPMENT

DIRECTIONS: For each word pair below, write whether the words are synonyms (words with similar meanings) or antonyms (words with opposite meanings).

1. realm, empire _____

2. tumultuous, peaceful _____

3. confronted, retreated _____

4. inscribed, engraved _____

LITERARY FOCUS: ARTHURIAN LEGEND

DIRECTIONS: On a separate sheet of paper, write your own short, modern **legend**. First, think of an extraordinary deed that you are familiar with, such as an act of kindness or the breaking of a long-standing sports record. As you tell your tale, embellish, or add to, it with fantastic and magical elements.

READING FOCUS: UNDERSTANDING SEQUENCE OF EVENTS

DIRECTIONS: The following events from "The Sword in the Stone" are out of **sequence**. Put them in the correct order by writing "1" next to the event that occurs first, "2" next to the event that occurs next, and so on.

- Sir Kay tells his father that he dislodged the sword. _____
- Sir Ector, Sir Kay, and Arthur ride to the tournament. _____
- Arthur is dubbed first knight of the realm. _____
- Sir Ector asks Arthur to make Sir Kay the royal seneschal. _____
- Arthur dislodges the sword from the stone, and rides back to the tournament to give it to Sir Kay. _____
- Many nobles try, but fail, to pull the sword out of the stone. _____

SKILLS FOCUS

Literary Skills
Understand elements of Arthurian legend.

Reading Skills
Understand the sequence of events.

Birth of a Legend/Real Princess: A Portrait of Pocahontas

INFORMATIONAL TEXT FOCUS: GENERATING RESEARCH QUESTIONS

To begin researching a topic, create specific, focused **research questions**. You can use the **5W-How**? questions (Who, What, Where, When, Why, How) to help you. Then, choose the question that interests you the most.

SELECTION VOCABULARY

fidelity (FIH DEHL IH TEE) *n.:* an exact rendering.
The animals were drawn with perfect fidelity.

malevolent (MUH LEHV UH LUHNT) *adj.:* wishing evil to others.
The malevolent sea monster devoured swimmers in the lake.

gullible (GUHL IH BUHL) *adj.:* easily persuaded to believe.
Were the people gullible enough to believe in the monster?

anecdotal (AN EHK DOH TUHL) *adj.:* account that cannot be proved.
Anecdotal evidence cannot prove scientific theories.

skepticism (SKEP TIH SIH ZUHM) *n.:* a tendency to question or doubt.
Her skepticism about the huge monster was understandable.

dissuaded (DIH SWAYD IHD) *v.:* turned aside by persuasion.
Few will be dissuaded from their belief in the creature.

obscurity (UHB SKYUHR IH TEE) *n.:* state of being not well known.
As a young child, Pocahontas lived in obscurity.

pretentious (PRIH TEHN SHUHS) *adj.:* attempting to impress by pretending greater importance than is actually possessed.
The pretentious colonist wanted to marry into royalty.

deteriorating (DIH TEER EE UHR AY TIHNG) *adj.:* becoming worse.
Pocahontas's health was deteriorating when she reached the shore.

entourage (AHN TUHR AHJ) *n.:* a group of people accompanying an important person.
Because the chief was important, he traveled with an entourage.

WORD STUDY

DIRECTIONS: On a separate sheet of paper, write a paragraph that correctly uses any four of the above vocabulary words.

SKILLS FOCUS

Informational Text Skills
Generate research questions.

BIRTH OF A LEGEND

by Stephen Lyons

BACKGROUND

Loch Ness is a large lake in Scotland (*loch* means "lake" in the Scottish Gaelic language) near the city of Inverness. For years there have been people who claim to have seen a peculiar creature in Loch Ness. The creature became known as the "Loch Ness monster." The following article tells of how the mystery of the Loch Ness monster began and how it continues to fascinate.

"Many a man has been hanged on less evidence than there is for the Loch Ness Monster."

—G. K. Chesterton

When the Romans first came to northern Scotland in the first century A.D., they found the highlands occupied by fierce, tattoo-covered tribes, they called the Picts, or painted people. From the carved, standing stones still found in the region around Loch Ness, it is clear the Picts were fascinated by animals and careful to render them with great fidelity. All the
10 animals depicted on the Pictish stones are lifelike and easily recognizable—all but one. The exception is a strange beast with an elongated beak or muzzle, a head locket or spout, and flippers instead of feet. Described by some scholars as a swimming elephant, the Pictish beast is the earliest known evidence for an idea that has held sway in the Scottish Highlands for at least 1,500 years—that Loch Ness is home to a mysterious aquatic animal. **A**

In Scottish folklore, large animals have been associated with many bodies of water, from small streams to the largest lakes,
20 often labeled Loch-na-Beistie on old maps. These water-horses,

From "Birth of a Legend" by Stephen Lyons from *NOVA Online* Web site, accessed August 28, 2007 at http://www.pbs.org/wgbh/nova/lochness/legend.html. Copyright © 2000 by **WGBH Educational Foundation**. Reproduced by permission of the publisher.

A READING FOCUS

What **research questions** might you come up with if you were going to do further study on the Picts' drawings?

_____

_____

_____

_____

_____

_____

_____

_____

or water-kelpies, are said to have magical powers and malevolent intentions. According to one version of the legend, the water-horse lures small children into the water by offering them rides on its back. Once the children are aboard, their hands become stuck to the beast and they are dragged to a watery death, their livers washing ashore the following day. **A**

The earliest written reference linking such creatures to Loch Ness is in the biography of Saint Columba, the man credited with introducing Christianity to Scotland. In A.D. 565, according to this account, Columba was on his way to visit a Pictish king when he stopped along the shore of Loch Ness. Seeing a large beast about to attack a man who was swimming in the lake, Columba raised his hand, invoking the name of God and commanding the monster to "go back with all speed." The beast complied, and the swimmer was saved.

When Nicholas Witchell, a future BBC correspondent, researched the history of the legend for his 1974 book, The Loch Ness Story, he found about a dozen pre-20th-century references to large animals in Loch Ness, gradually shifting in character from these clearly mythical accounts to something more like eyewitness descriptions. **B**

But the modern legend of Loch Ness dates from 1933, when a new road was completed along the shore, offering the first clear views of the loch from the northern side. One April afternoon, a local couple was driving home along this road when they spotted "an enormous animal rolling and plunging on the surface." Their account was written up by a correspondent for the Inverness Courier, whose editor used the word "monster" to describe the animal. The Loch Ness Monster has been a media phenomenon ever since.

Public interest built gradually during the spring of 1933, then picked up sharply after a couple reported seeing one of the creatures on land, lumbering across the shore road. **C** By October, several London newspapers had sent correspondents to Scotland, and radio programs were being interrupted to bring listeners the latest news from the loch. A British circus offered a reward of £20,000 for the capture of the beast. Hundreds of Boy Scouts and outdoorsmen arrived, some venturing out in small boats, others setting up deck chairs and waiting expectantly for the monster to appear.

The excitement over the monster reached a fever pitch in December, when the London Daily Mail hired an actor, film director, and big-game hunter named Marmaduke Wetherell to track down the beast. After only a few days at the loch, Wetherell reported finding the fresh footprints of a large, four-toed animal. He estimated it to be 20 feet long. **D** With great fanfare, Wetherell made plaster casts of the footprints and, just before Christmas, sent them off to the Natural History Museum in London for analysis. While the world waited for the museum zoologists to return from holiday, legions of monster hunters descended on Loch Ness, filling the local hotels. Inverness was floodlit for the occasion, and traffic jammed the shoreline roads in both directions.

The bubble burst in early January, when museum zoologists announced that the footprints were those of a hippopotamus. They had been made with a stuffed hippo foot—the base of an umbrella stand or ashtray. It wasn't clear whether Wetherell was the perpetrator of the hoax or its gullible victim. **E** Either way, the incident tainted the image of the Loch Ness Monster and discouraged serious investigation of the phenomenon. For the next three decades, most scientists scornfully dismissed reports of strange animals in the loch. Those sightings that weren't outright hoaxes, they said, were the result of optical illusions caused by boat wakes, wind slicks, floating logs, otters, ducks, or swimming deer.

Saw Something, They Did

Nevertheless, eyewitnesses continued to come forward: with accounts of their sightings—more than 4,000 of them, according to Witchell's estimate. Most of the witnesses described a large creature with one or more humps protruding above the surface like the hull of an upturned boat. Others reported seeing a long

D **LITERARY ANALYSIS**

How might a footprint help prove the existence of the Loch Ness monster? In what ways might it not be helpful enough?

_____
_____
_____
_____
_____
_____
_____
_____
_____

E **READING FOCUS**

How might you focus a **research question** relating to Marmaduke Wetherell's findings of the footprints?

_____
_____
_____
_____

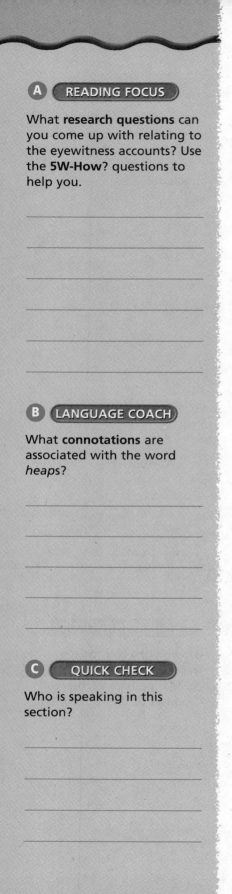

A **READING FOCUS**

What **research questions** can you come up with relating to the eyewitness accounts? Use the **5W-How?** questions to help you.

_____

_____

_____

_____

_____

B **LANGUAGE COACH**

What **connotations** are associated with the word _heaps_?

_____

_____

_____

_____

_____

C **QUICK CHECK**

Who is speaking in this section?

_____

_____

_____

_____

neck or flippers. What was most remarkable, however, was that many of the eyewitnesses were sober, level-headed people: lawyers and priests, scientists and schoolteachers, policemen and fishermen—even a Nobel Prize winner. **A**

Eyewitness Accounts

While no hard evidence for the existence of the Loch Ness Monster has yet turned up, heaps of anecdotal evidence exist. **B** Although such eyewitness accounts are of little value scientifically, they can be compelling nevertheless. Read the accounts by the following native Scots who swear they saw something in the 100 loch. These tales were collected by the producers of the NOVA film _The Beast of Loch Ness_.

"I saw it, and nothing can take that away."

Well, we're talking about an incident that happened approximately 32 years ago, almost to the very day mid-summer, June 1965. I, along with a friend, was on the south shore of Loch Ness, fishing for brown trout, looking almost directly into Urquhart Bay, when I saw something break the surface of the water. I glanced there, and I saw it, and then it wasn't there, it had disappeared. **C**

But while watching, keeping an eye, and fishing gently, I saw 110 an object surface. It was a large, black object—a whale-like object, going from infinity up, and came round onto a block end—and it submerged, to reappear a matter of seconds later. But on this occasion, the block end, which had been on my right, was now on my left, so I realized immediately that while in the process of surfacing, as it may, it had rotated. And with the predominant wind, the south-west wind, it appeared to be, I would say, at that stage drifting easily across.

So I called to my friend Willie Frazer, who incidentally had a sighting of an object on the loch almost a year ago to the very 120 day. I called him, and he come up and joined me. We realized that it was drifting towards us, and, in fact, it came to within I would say about 250, 300 yards.

In no way am I even attempting to convert anybody to the religion of the object of Loch Ness. I mean, they can believe it but it doesn't upset me if they don't believe it. Because I would question very much if I hadn't the extraordinary experience of seeing this object. If I hadn't seen it I would have without question given a lot of skepticism to what it was. But I saw it, and nothing can take that away.

130

> —Ian Cameron, a retired superintendent of the Northern Police Force, lives with his wife Jessie in Inverness, Scotland, at the head of the loch. A keen angler, he is an authority on the Atlantic salmon.

"I'm gobsmacked[1] . . . I just didn't know what it was."

Right, I'm driving along the loch side, glancing, out of the window. You can see the rock formation, I was just down on the road there, it just rises. I saw this boiling in the water. I thought, "No, it can't be anything," and I carried on a wee bit. Then I looked again, and I saw three black humps. I mean, you know, there's the chance, I've seen something in the water. But what

140

is it? **C**

So I'm gobsmacked, I'm looking out the window, I just didn't know what it was. **D** Then the people came behind me, and they obviously wanted me to move. But I didn't want to lose sight of this thing. So I just pulled over to the side, grabbed my camera, and I thought I was being very cool and very nonchalant and took two or three photos. In fact, as I say, I had taken nine or ten, without realizing, I just punched the button. It was just a pity it was a small camera.

150

NOVA: Did anybody else see anything?

WHITE: Yeah, the other two people who were there—I was just so excited I didn't get their name and address or anything—they

---

1. **gobsmacked** (GAHB SMAKT): shocked, stunned.

C READING FOCUS

What are the similarities and differences between the descriptions by Ian Cameron and Richard White? What **research questions** might you ask them if you could?

D LANGUAGE COACH

Discuss the **connotation** of the word *gobsmacked*. What are some other, less emotional, words that could be used instead?

© Vo Trung Dung/Corbis Sygma

© John Frost Newspapers

B VOCABULARY

Academic Vocabulary

Why do you think eyewitness accounts of the Loch Ness Monster keep *recurring,* or coming up again?

saw it exactly the same as me. Because the wee wifey, who would have been a lady in-her fifties, on holiday, she was Scottish, she said to me, "I've not been in the bar this morning!" And her husband said, "Ach, it's an eel! It's an eel!" And I said, "There's no eels that big!" And he said, "Ach, it's otters!" And I said, "You don't get otters swimming out like that!" A

160 I saw what I saw, and I'm not going to be dissuaded. It wasn't just an imagination. I'm a sane guy, and I've got no ax to grind. As I say I sell pet food! What use to me is the Loch Ness Monster? Unless I can invent a food called, I don't know, Monster Munchies perhaps?

—Richard White lives in the village of Muir of Ord, north of Inverness. He runs his own business selling pet food. B

REAL PRINCESS: A PORTRAIT OF POCAHONTAS

by Jessica Cohn

BACKGROUND

The story of Pocahontas, the Native American girl who encountered the English as they settled modern-day Virginia, is full of misconceptions. These false beliefs are kept alive by stories, paintings, and films, including the 1995 Disney animated feature. This article explores some of the fact and fiction around the life of Pocahontas.

Collection of the New York Historical Society, USA/Bridgeman Art Library

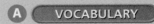

Word Study

Endorsement means "approval or support." Think of an antonym (word with the opposite meaning) for *endorsement*.

As a friend to the Jamestown[1] settlers, Pocahontas was "*the instrument to pursurve this colonie from death, famine, and utter confusion,*" wrote Captain John Smith, to Queen Anne of England, in 1616: quite an endorsement. **A** In the years that followed, Pocahontas's reputation continued to grow, as a historical figure and, even later, as the Disney-marketed, two-dimensional cartoon character bearing her name.

---

1. **Jamestown:** In Virginia, the first permanent English settlement in North America.

Based on what you have read so far, what do you think is the author's central idea about the subject?

_____

_____

_____

_____

_____

_____

_____

Why did the English think of Pocahontas as a princess? What facts argue against such a title?

_____

_____

_____

_____

_____

_____

_____

_____

_____

_____

Facts about this Native American princess have been clouded by imagination, however. Even before Jamestown was

10 settled, America was represented in European art as a welcoming Indian woman, posed in an Eden-like garden. When Pocahontas entered the scene, it was as if her name were simply attached to an existing Indian icon. **A**

Immortalized in stone monuments and eponymous[2] landmarks, Pocahontas became a shifting symbol in a stream of poetry and stories. Yet not a word written about her came from the woman herself.

Legend Has It

Pocahontas was a daughter of Powhatan, chief of the Algonquian, or Powhatan, Indians in the Tidewater area

20 of what is now Virginia. Powhatan took many wives, and Pocahontas had many siblings, so some argue that her status as a "princess" is a stretch. Yet to the colonists, who viewed royalty by European standards, she was a daughter to a chief, and therefore a princess. **B**

Her given name was Matoaka, but the pet name Pocahontas, meaning "spoiled child" or "the naughty one," according to Chief Roy Crazy Horse of the Powhatan Renape Nation, is what stuck.

---

2. **eponymous** (EH PAHN UH MUHS): named for a certain person.

In 1607, the young Pocahontas first met the English colonists, soon after they arrived on the shores of Virginia. **C** The Indian princess leapfrogged from childhood obscurity to international history when she saved the life of early settler Captain John Smith—or at least, that's how the story goes. **D**

Captain Smith's Role

According to Smith, he was captured by warriors in December 1607 and taken to Powhatan at a spot 12 miles outside Jamestown. The captain was welcomed with a feast, but was then made to stretch out on stone. Warriors stood over him with clubs, he said, as if ready to beat him. But suddenly, Pocahontas rushed to him.

He would later write that she took his "head in her arms and laid her owne upon his to save him from death." Then she pulled him upright.

In English circles, this story was interpreted as his rescue from savages. But mock executions and salvations were often dramatized in Native American ceremonies; so her display of affection could have been ritual. Interpretation of the event is complicated by the fact that the first time Smith described it in writing was in a letter to Queen Anne nearly a decade later, and he may have been trying to polish the story. Powhatan Chief Roy Crazy Horse remarks, in his essay "The Pocahontas Myth," that it "was one of three [stories] reported by the pretentious Smith that he was saved from death by a prominent woman." **E**

The next development, however, is undisputed. The fun-loving Pocahontas started to visit Jamestown regularly.

White Man's World

Sometimes the young girl carried messages from her father. Or she and other tribal members traded fur and food. Several years after meeting her, Smith described her in those times: "a child of tenne yeares old, which not only for feature, countenance, and

---

C READING FOCUS

Is the question "What was Pocahontas' relationship with the English colonists like?" a strong **research question**? Why or why not?

_____

_____

_____

_____

D VOCABULARY

Selection Vocabulary

Use context clues to write a definition for the word *obscurity*.

_____

_____

E READING FOCUS

Write what you think is the central idea in this section. Underline an example of support for the author's central idea. Then, come up with a related **research question**.

_____

_____

_____

_____

_____

B READING FOCUS

What are some possible **research questions** about the various attempts to kidnap Pocahontas? Use the **5W-How**? questions to help you think of questions.

_____

_____

_____

_____

_____

_____

proportion much exceedeth any of the rest of [Powhatan's] people but for wit and spirit the only non-pariel[3] of his countrie."

60   Settlers took note of a friendship between the girl and the captain; some read more into it. Numerous fictional accounts, such as the 2005 film *The New World*, by Terrence Malick, dramatize a romance. What's certain is that Smith was injured in fall of 1609 when gunpowder exploded, and he returned to England. By that time, the colony was expanding farther into Powhatan's territory, and relations between whites and the tribes were deteriorating.

Sometime before 1613, the princess married a warrior named Kocoum. But no "happily ever after" followed.

70   Pocahontas was targeted by Jamestown settlers in a kidnapping for ransom. **A**

Playing the Pawn

The settlers wanted to exchange the princess for English prisoners being held by Powhatan, along with firearms and food. The plot was carried forth by Captain Samuel Argall, who lured Pocahontas to a ship. The English locked her away, then made their demands.

Powhatan sent back only part of what they asked for—and told them to treat his daughter well. In April 1613, Argall returned to shore, his plan yet unfulfilled.

80   Pocahontas was moved to a settlement called Henrico, run by Sir Thomas Dale, who tried to use her for barter as well. She was sent with a band of Englishmen to strike a deal with Powhatan, but the group was attacked. In response, the English destroyed villages, killing Indians. The situation turned explosive. **B**

Pocahontas went to her father and told him she planned to marry tobacco farmer John Rolfe, a merger that would encourage goodwill. By some accounts, she declared her love for the wealthy planter. But did she?

---

3. **non-pareil:** unique or extraordinary person.

Ætatis suæ 21. A. 1616.

90   Rolfe's words about the impending union are the ones on record: "for the good of the plantation, the honor of our country, for the glory of God, for mine own salvation."

Chief Roy Crazy Horse characterizes this development as "a condition of her release." Whether it was a day of happiness or convenience—and without word from Pocahontas, we will never know—the wedding was held in April 1614, and Pocahontas became Rebecca Rolfe.

Over the Sea

In 1616, Dale took a dozen or so Native Americans to England. The princess, her husband, and their young son Thomas were
100   part of the entourage. **C** Crazy Horse called it a "propaganda campaign" for the colony.

In London, she met King James I and the royal family, and she saw Captain John Smith, whom she had believed to be dead. He claimed she was overcome with emotion as they spoke—and that she referred to him as a "father." According to Crazy Horse, she turned her back on him and in a second encounter, called him a liar. **D**

In 1617, the Rolfes boarded a return ship to Virginia, but Pocahontas fell ill at sea. When taken back to shore, in England,
110   she died, taking her heart's secrets with her, at age 21 or 22.

"All must die," she supposedly said to her husband. "'Tis enough that the child liveth." Yet Pocahontas lives on, larger than anyone's life. **E**

C **LANGUAGE COACH**

Entourage comes from the French word *entourer* ("to surround"). A related word is *tour*, which comes from the French word *tourner* ("to turn"). List two other words that contain the word *tour*.

_____

_____

D **VOCABULARY**

Academic Vocabulary

John Smith *recounted*, or gave an account of, his meeting with Pocahontas in England. Do you think his version of events is believable? Why or why not?

_____

_____

_____

_____

_____

_____

E **READING FOCUS**

What **research questions** could you generate to learn more about Pocahontas's son?

_____

_____

_____

_____

Birth of a Legend/Real Princess: A Portrait of Pocahontas

USE A CHART

DIRECTIONS: Complete the chart below by creating and answering one of each of the **5W-How?** questions for either "Birth of a Legend" or "Real Princess: A Portrait of Pocahontas." The questions you make should be helpful in summarizing the article you choose. For example, you may ask, "**When** did the events in this article take place?"

Article I chose:	
Who	
What	
Where	
When	
Why	
How	

Applying Your Skills

Birth of a Legend/Real Princess: A Portrait of Pocahontas

VOCABULARY DEVELOPMENT

DIRECTIONS: Fill in the blanks in the following sentences with the correct words from the Word Box. Some words will not be used.

Word Box

- fidelity
- malevolent
- gullible
- anecdotal
- skepticism
- dissuaded
- obscurity
- pretentious
- deteriorating
- entourage

1. The foundation of the house has been _____ since the hurricane.

2. Marc will believe anything, he's so _____!

3. Shelly didn't think the article was well-researched—most of the details were _____, and therefore unreliable.

4. What makes Narada such an excellent orchestra conductor is his _____ to the notes of the printed musical score.

5. Many of the presidents who served in the years following Abraham Lincoln have faded into _____.

6. The man's story about seeing a UFO was viewed with considerable _____ by the local press.

INFORMATIONAL TEXT FOCUS: GENERATING RESEARCH QUESTIONS

DIRECTIONS: Select either "Birth of a Legend" or "Real Princess" and write a paragraph discussing the **research questions** you think the author asked in order to write the article. Explain your ideas using support from the text.

_____

_____

_____

_____

_____

_____

_____

_____

SKILLS FOCUS

Informational Text Skills
Generate research questions.

Collection 9

VOCABULARY REVIEW

DIRECTIONS: Review and practice the selection and academic vocabulary by filling in the blanks with the correct vocabulary words from the Word Box. Some words will be not used.

Word Box

acknowledged

afflicted

anecdotal

confronted

consent

deteriorating

dissuaded

endear

entourage

exhibit

fidelity

gullible

inscribed

malevolent

obscurity

pretentious

prosperous

realm

recount

recurring

retain

skepticism

tumultuous

1. When we study and analyze a work of literature, we look for _____ themes that run through the entire piece.

2. I _____ Seamus about the money missing from the cash register, but he denied stealing it.

3. Megan got in trouble because she _____ her initials on the tree in the park.

4. The police officer asked Sarah if she could _____ the story of what she saw at the scene of the bank robbery.

5. Nearly every town and village in the king's _____ was under attack from invaders.

6. I was not _____ by the politician's arguments; I still believe the school needs more funding.

7. Mrs. Collingsworth has decided to _____ her entire personal collection of modern paintings so that everyone can see them.

8. My parents did not _____ to allowing me to go to the concert by myself.

9. The bad guy's _____ attitude was obvious from the first page of the story.

10. The new poll numbers have been released, and while the political race is close, last month's front-runner continues to _____ her lead.

Skills Review

Collection 9

LANGUAGE COACH

DIRECTIONS: Many words have **connotations**, or strong feelings that go beyond the literal meanings, attached to them. Look at the chart below. In your own words, briefly describe both the literal definition of each word and its connotations. An example is given.

Word	Definition	Connotations
fidelity	an exact rendering	extremely faithful
endear		
skepticism		
afflicted		
tumultuous		

WRITING ACTIVITY

DIRECTIONS: Pick a partner and find a short myth or legend in the library or online. Identify all of the characteristics of myths and legends that are present in the tale and make a list of them. To help you identify these characteristics, ask yourselves questions such as: Who is the hero or heroine? What is their quest? What heroic traits do they possess? What do they learn about themselves along the way? What values and beliefs are revealed about the story's culture?

Reading for Life

© Todd Davidson/Illustration Works/Corbis

Literary and Academic Vocabulary for Collection 10

illustrate (IHL UH STRAYT) *v.:* show; demonstrate.

The author used a picture to illustrate how the task should be completed.

objective (UHB JEHK TIHV) *n.:* purpose; goal.

The objective of this article is to educate people about different types of stereo systems.

insert (IHN SUHRT) *v.:* add; include; put in.

I will insert a chart in my report to show the different costs of stereo systems.

format (FAWR MAT) *n.:* design; arrangement.

Each document has a different format so people will be able to tell them apart.

product warranty (PRAH DUCT WAWR UHN TEE) *n.:* a legal document stating the manufacturer's legal responsibilities if the product fails.

According to the product warranty, the manufacturer is responsible for repairs to my new microwave for one year.

elements (EHL UH MIHNTS) *n.:* basic parts.

There are so many elements to the computer that I need help understanding how it works.

sequence (SEE KWIHNS) *n.:* the order in which things occur or are arranged.

You must follow the directions in the correct sequence, or you won't be able to put the toy together properly.

Following Technical Directions

INFORMATIONAL TEXT FOCUS: FOLLOWING TECHNICAL DIRECTIONS

The written instructions for using electronic, mechanical, and scientific products are called **technical directions**. You follow technical directions whenever you program a cell phone, set up a video game, or do an experiment in science class. At first glance, technical directions can seem hard to understand. The best way to follow technical directions is to pay attention and follow each step carefully in the correct **sequence**, or order.

SELECTION VOCABULARY

discharge (DIHS CHAHRJ) *v.:* release; let out.

> *Before opening the computer case, you should first discharge static electricity by touching something that is made of metal.*

pry (PRY) *v.:* move or separate with force.

> *Do not pry the old sound card from its slot; instead, pull it out gently.*

obstructions (UHB STRUHK SHUNZ) *n. pl.:* things that are in the way or that block something else.

> *If the sound card does not fit in the slot, check for any obstructions.*

correspond (KAWR UH SPAHND) *v.:* match; be similar.

> *Find the connector pins that correspond with each end of the audio cables.*

WORD STUDY

DIRECTIONS: The following words are related to the vocabulary words above. Based on your knowledge of the vocabulary words and the parts of speech given, write a definition for each word below.

1. corresponding, *adj.:* _____

2. obstruct, *v.:* _____

3. dischargeable, *adj.:* _____

4. pryingly, *adv.:* _____

SKILLS FOCUS

Informational Text Skills
Follow multistep instructions in technical directions.

FOLLOWING TECHNICAL DIRECTIONS

Instruction Manual: Installing a Computer Sound Card Ⓐ

1. Be sure the computer is switched off.

2. To avoid damaging your computer, touch something metal on the outside of your computer with your fingers to discharge static electricity. Ⓑ Then, unplug your computer.

3. Open the computer case.

4. Locate the slot you want on the motherboard.[1] See the user's manual for specific instructions on the location and types of slots on the computer.

5a. If the slot is empty, remove the screw that holds the metal slot cover in place, slide the cover out, and set both the screw and the cover aside for later. Ⓒ

10

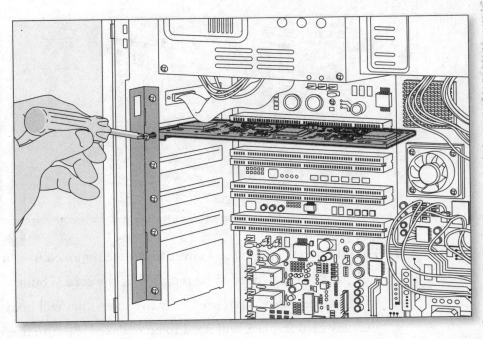

---

1. **motherboard** (MUHTH UHR BOHRD): a computer's main circuit board.

Word Study

Undue has multiple meanings. It can mean "excessive" or "not owed or currently payable." Which definition do you think is used in this sentence?

_____

_____

_____

_____

B **QUICK CHECK**

What does the illustration on this page show?

_____

_____

_____

_____

5b. If the slot currently contains the old sound card, remove the screw that holds the card in place and gently pull the card from the slot. It may need a firm yet careful tug. **CAUTION:** If rocked against the sides of the slot, the card might snap off in the slot or pry the slot from the motherboard. You will see an audio cable attached at one end to the sound card and at the other end to the CD or DVD-ROM drive. Disconnect this cable from the drive by pulling gently.

20

6. Plug the new sound card into the prepared slot by pressing down firmly until the connector is fully inserted. It should be a tight fit, but do not use undue force. **A** If you encounter resistance, take the card out, check for alignment and possible obstructions, and try again.

7. To be sure the card is in place, give it a gentle tug. It should resist and stay in place. The connector strip's metal conductors should also be just barely visible when viewed at eye level.

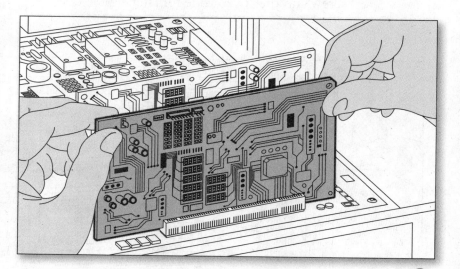

B

30

8. Find the screw and the slot cover that were removed in step 5a. Both may need to be replaced. If the card is built with an integrated[2] slot cover, only the screw that will hold the new card in place will need to be replaced. Be sure the

---

2. **integrated** (IHN TUH GRAY TIHD): combined; not separate.

slot is covered. Then, tighten the screw to hold the new sound card in place.

9. Connect the audio cable to the sound card and to the CD- or DVDROM drive. Find connector pins on the sound card and on the back of the disk drive that correspond to the plugs on each end of the audio cable. Be sure to line these pins up carefully and press gently. As in step 6, if you encounter resistance, check to see that all pins are straight and that there are no other obstructions. **C** Then, try again.

10. Close the computer case.

11. Connect the external speakers to their appropriate jacks.

12. Plug in the power cord and turn on the computer and monitor. Once the computer is up and running, insert the CD that accompanies the sound card and complete the software driver installation by following the on-screen instructions. **D**

40

50

LANGUAGE COACH

Rewrite this sentence using **synonyms** (words with similar meanings) to replace some of the more difficult words, such as *encounter*, *resistance*, and *obstructions*. Use a thesaurus if needed.

_____

_____

_____

_____

_____

_____

_____

_____

READING FOCUS

The author uses a step-by-step **sequence**. What do you think would happen if someone did not follow the proper sequence of the directions?

_____

_____

_____

_____

_____

_____

_____

Applying Your Skills

Following Technical Directions

VOCABULARY DEVELOPMENT

DIRECTIONS: Circle the letter of the antonym (word with the opposite meaning) for each vocabulary word.

1. **correspond**
   a. commute
   b. clash
   c. jibe

2. **pry**
   a. attach
   b. attempt
   c. hold

3. **discharge**
   a. find
   b. retain
   c. discard

4. **obstructions**
   a. impediments
   b. buildings
   c. openings

INFORMATIONAL TEXT FOCUS: FOLLOWING TECHNICAL DIRECTIONS

DIRECTIONS: Answer the following questions about the **technical directions** for installing a computer sound card. Write your answers in the chart.

1. What type of **sequence** does the author choose?

2. Are there graphics or different fonts to draw attention to certain parts of the document? If so, describe them.

3. What is the author's purpose? Have the sequence and graphics helped the author achieve his or her purpose?

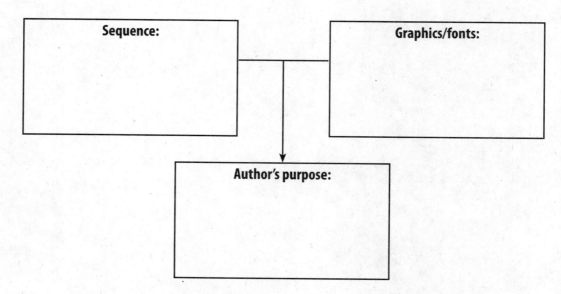

Sequence:

Graphics/fonts:

Author's purpose:

SKILLS FOCUS

Informational Text Skills
Follow multistep instructions in technical directions.

Reading Consumer Documents

INFORMATIONAL TEXT FOCUS: READING CONSUMER DOCUMENTS

When you buy a new product, papers called **consumer documents** may be included in the packaging. It is important to read the documents so you understand the product's **elements**, or basic parts, and **features**—the things that make that model different from similar models. Here are some types of consumer documents:

- **product information:** describes the product and what it does
- **service contract:** spells out the rights and obligations of the buyer, manufacturer, and seller
- **warranty:** describes what the manufacturer is obligated to do if the product fails, and tells what the consumer must do to get the product fixed
- **instruction manual:** tells how to use the product and how to solve problems that you might have with it
- **technical directions:** describes how to install and use the product

SELECTION VOCABULARY

claim (KLAYM) *n.:* demand for something due.
  You can make a claim against the company if the product breaks.

clause (KLAWZ) *n.:* single provision of a law or agreement.
  The contract contains a cancellation clause.

void (VOYD) *v.:* cancel legal force or effect.
  Use the product correctly or you will void the service contract.

discretion (DIHS KREHSH UHN) *n.:* ability to make a choice.
  The contract may be renewed at the company's discretion.

WORD STUDY

DIRECTIONS: Write "Yes" if the vocabulary word in each sentence is used correctly. Write "No" if it is used incorrectly, and rewrite the sentence so the word is used correctly.

1. Faulty brakes were the *clause* of the accident. _____

_____

2. We had an argument, so I tried to *void* her for the rest of the day. _____

_____

3. I filed a *claim* against the company because the toy was missing several parts. _____

_____

4. I know I can tell her my problems because she can keep a *discretion*. _____

_____

READING CONSUMER DOCUMENTS

Aulsound Extended Service Contract Ⓐ

> ### Read with a Purpose
> Read the following selections to learn how to understand the paperwork that comes with the purchase of some electronic equipment.

ADMINISTRATOR
Aulsound Warranty Service Corporation
P.O. Box 840001 Century City, CA 90067
SERVICE CONTRACT AGREEMENT
Digital Multitrack Recorder DMR88

TERMS AND CONDITIONS
Details of coverage. This Service Contract provides coverage of any operating parts or labor required for the product listed above, for two years from date of original purchase. There will be no cost to the Purchaser for any authorized covered repair that is performed by one of our highly skilled service associates.

Limitations. This Service Contract covers product failures occurring during normal use. It does not cover misuse or abuse of the product during delivery, installation, or setup adjustments. It does not cover damage that occurs while adjusting consumer controls, loss of data or programming support, unauthorized repair, customer-sponsored specification changes, cosmetic damage, or simple maintenance as recommended in the product owner's guide. It also does not cover repairs that are necessary because of improper installation or improper electrical connections. Consequential or incidental damages are not covered. Damage due to acts of God is not covered.

Maintenance requirement. The Purchaser must maintain the product in accordance with the requirements or recommendations set forth by the manufacturer to keep this Service Contract in force. Evidence of proper maintenance and/or service, when required by the Administrator, must be submitted to validate a claim. Ⓑ

Unauthorized-repair clause. IMPORTANT: Unauthorized repairs may void this Service Contract. The cost of these repairs will be the responsibility of the Purchaser. Ⓒ

Transfer of ownership. This Service Contract is transferable with ownership of the product. Transfer may be accomplished only if the Purchaser mails or delivers to the Administrator a twenty-five dollar [$25.00] transfer fee and registers the name and address of the new owner within fifteen [15] days of change of ownership.

Cancellation clause. This Service Contract may be canceled by the Purchaser at any time, for any reason. In event of cancellation, we will provide a pro-rated refund minus reasonable handling costs and any claims that may have been paid. Any cancellation requested by the Purchaser within thirty [30] days of the Service Contract application date will be 100 percent canceled by the Administrator.

Contract insurance. Your Service Contract is fully insured by Aulquiet Insurance Company, 80 Sampler Way, Los Angeles, CA 90017. Purchasers who do not receive payment within sixty [60] days of submitting a pre-authorized covered claim may submit the claim directly to Aulquiet Insurance Company, Contractual Liability Claims Department, at the above address.

Renewal clause. This Service Contract may be renewed at the discretion of the Administrator. The renewal premium will be based on the age of the covered product, current service costs, the covered product's repair history, and actuarial data.

Based on what you have already learned about **warranties** and **service contracts**, what **elements** are you going to be looking for as you read this document?

_____

_____

_____

_____

_____

Ⓑ **VOCABULARY**

Word Study

Validate is formed from the word *valid*, which means "having legal force." Based on that definition, what do you think *validate* means?

_____

_____

_____

_____

Ⓒ **VOCABULARY**

Selection Vocabulary

Use context clues to write a definition for *void*. Underline the clues in the text that helped you.

_____

_____

_____

_____

Troubleshooting Guide

If you encounter problems operating your Aulsound DMR88 or if the product does not work as expected, look up the problem in this table and follow the advice provided.

PROBLEM	ADVICE
The DMR88 does not turn on.	• Make sure that the power cord is plugged into an AC wall outlet. • Check the AC IN connector at the rear of DMR88. • Make sure that the DMR88 power switch is in the ON position. • If there is still no power, contact your Aulsound dealer. **D**
No sound is coming from the connected music source.	• Make sure that the MONITOR LEVEL control is raised. • Make sure that the FLIP and MONITOR SELECT switches are set correctly.
The DMR88 does not record.	• Make sure that the disc's write-protect tab is set to UNPROTECT. • Make sure that the PLAY function is not on. • Press a REC SELECT button, and make sure that the track is ready to record. • Make sure that the signal you wish to record has been selected at the recording source for the appropriate track. Use the CUE LEVEL control to determine whether the signal is being sent to the track.
Level meters do not indicate signal levels.	• Make sure that the track you wish to record has been selected. • Press the REC button, and make sure that the DMR88 is in RECORD-PAUSE mode.
Recordings play back at the wrong pitch.	• Make sure that the PITCH function is not set at VARIABLE. • Make sure that the 1.2 PLAY function is turned off. **E**

Reading Consumer Documents **1169**

D QUICK CHECK

When does the manual suggest that you contact an Aulsound dealer?

E VOCABULARY

Academic Vocabulary

What are the advantages of using the table *format*, or design, instead of a paragraph format to display the information on this page?

A QUICK CHECK

Why is the word *must* shown in all capital letters?

_____

_____

_____

_____

_____

_____

B LANGUAGE COACH

Is *guarantee* used as a verb or a noun in the second-to-last sentence?

_____

_____

C READING FOCUS

Do you think it is important to read **product information** documents when you buy a new product? Why or why not?

_____

_____

_____

_____

_____

_____

_____

_____

FCC* Information (USA)

1. **IMPORTANT NOTICE: DO NOT MODIFY THIS UNIT!**
   This unit, when installed as indicated in the instructions contained in this manual, meets FCC requirements. Modifications not expressly approved by Aulsound may void your authority, granted by the FCC, to use this product.

2. **IMPORTANT:** When connecting this product to accessories and/or another product, the high-quality shielded cables supplied with this product MUST be used. Follow all installation instructions. Failure to follow instructions could void your FCC authorization to use this product in the United States. **A**

3. **NOTE:** This product has been tested and found to comply with the requirements listed in FCC Regulations, Part 15 for Class "B" digital devices. Compliance with these requirements provides a reasonable level of assurance that your use of this product in a residential environment will not result in harmful interference with other electronic devices. This equipment generates and uses radio frequencies and, if not installed and used according to the instructions found in the user's manual, may cause interference harmful to the operation of other electronic devices. Compliance with FCC regulations does not guarantee that interference will not occur in all installations. If this product is found to be the source of interference, which can be determined by turning the unit OFF and ON, try to eliminate the problem by using one of the following measures: **B**

   - Relocate either this product or the device that is being affected by the interference.
   - Utilize other outlets that are on different branch (circuit breaker or fuse) circuits, or install AC line filter(s). In the case of radio or TV interference, relocate or reorient the antenna.
   - If the antenna lead-in is a 300-ohm ribbon lead, change the lead-in to a coaxial type cable.

If these corrective measures do not produce satisfactory results, contact the local retailer authorized to distribute this type of product. If you cannot locate the appropriate retailer, contact Aulsound Corporation of America, Electronic Service Division, 1000 Wilshire Blvd., Los Angeles, CA 90017. **C**

_____

*FCC: Federal Communications Commission, U.S. agency that regulates communication by telegraph, telephone, radio, TV, cable TV, and satellite.

Applying Your Skills

Reading Consumer Documents

DIRECTIONS: Fill in each blank with the correct vocabulary word from the Word Box.

Word Box

claim

clause

void

discretion

1. You will _____ the agreement if you break any of the rules.

2. I had to file a _____ with my insurance company after I was in a car accident.

3. According to a _____ in our lease, we cannot have pets in our apartment.

4. She left the choice of what restaurant to pick at my _____.

INFORMATIONAL TEXT FOCUS: READING CONSUMER DOCUMENTS

DIRECTIONS: On the lines below, describe the purpose of each type of **consumer document.**

1. product information: _____

_____

2. service contract: _____

_____

3. warranty: _____

_____

4. instruction manual: _____

_____

5. technical directions: _____

_____

SKILLS FOCUS

Informational Text Skills
Read consumer documents.

Collection 10

VOCABULARY REVIEW

DIRECTIONS: Write the letter of each definition in the second column next to the correct vocabulary word in the first column.

Vocabulary Words	Definitions
_____ 1. claim	**a.** match; be similar
_____ 2. clause	**b.** cancel legal force or effect
_____ 3. correspond	**c.** show; demonstrate
_____ 4. discharge	**d.** demand for something due
_____ 5. discretion	**e.** move or separate with force
_____ 6. format	**f.** purpose; goal
_____ 7. illustrate	**g.** things that are in the way or that block something else
_____ 8. insert	**h.** single provision of a law or agreement
_____ 9. objective	**i.** add; include; put in
_____ 10. obstructions	**j.** ability to make a choice
_____ 11. pry	**k.** release; let out
_____ 12. void	**l.** design; arrangement

Collection 10

LANGUAGE COACH

DIRECTIONS: A **synonym** is a word that means the same or almost the same as another word. For each word pair below, write "Yes" if the words are synonyms. Write "No" if the words are not synonyms.

1. correspond; reinstate _____

2. enormous; mammoth _____

3. barricades; obstructions _____

4. fresh; decayed _____

5. difficult; manageable _____

6. boring; exciting _____

7. graceful; elegant _____

8. discharge; liberate _____

9. furious; indifferent _____

10. delicious; appetizing _____

ORAL LANGUAGE ACTIVITY

DIRECTIONS: Choose a product that you are familiar with and know how to use. It could be a bike, a television set, a toaster, a DVD player, or something else. On a separate sheet of paper, write an **instructional manual** for this product using only your own knowledge. Do not write more than one page. Your manual should include specific, step-by-step instructions on how to use the basic **features** of the product. Suppose that the person who will read the manual has never before used the product. You will have to use clear, simple language. After you are finished writing your instructions, read them in front of the class. Then, have the class give you feedback about how clear your instructions were.

Index of Authors and Titles